FV_

 **St. Louis Community College**

Forest Park
Florissant Valley
Meramec

Instructional Resources
St. Louis, Missouri

GAYLORD

LANDSCAPE ARCHAEOLOGY

LANDSCAPE

THE UNIVERSITY OF TENNESSEE PRESS / KNOXVILLE

ARCHAEOLOGY

Reading and

Interpreting the

American Historical

Landscape

Edited by Rebecca Yamin and Karen Bescherer Metheny

Library of Congress Cataloging-in-Publication Data

Landscape archaeology : reading and interpreting the American
  historical landscape / edited by Rebecca Yamin and Karen Bescherer
  Metheny. — 1st ed.
     p. cm.
  Includes bibliographical references and index.
  ISBN 0-87049-920-3 (cloth : alk. paper)
  1. Landscape archaeology. 2. Landscape assessment. 3. Garden
archaeology. I. Yamin, Rebecca, 1942- . II. Metheny, Karen
Bescherer, 1960- .
CC75.L33 1996
930.1—dc20   95-32484
                                                  CIP

For our children

Contents

Preface: Reading the Historical Landscape   xiii
Rebecca Yamin and Karen Bescherer Metheny

Acknowledgments   xxi

Introduction: Close Attention to Place—Landscape Studies
    by Historical Archaeologists   xxiii
Anne Elizabeth Yentsch

PART I LANDSCAPE BIOGRAPHIES

1   Why Gardens?   3
    Mary C. Beaudry

2   Method in Landscape Archaeology: Research Strategies
      in a Historic New Jersey Garden   6
    Karen Bescherer Metheny, Judson Kratzer, Anne Elizabeth Yentsch,
      and Conrad M. Goodwin

3   The Greenhouse Effect: Gender-Related Traditions
      in Eighteenth-Century Gardening   32
    Carmen A. Weber

4   Giant in the Earth: George Washington, Landscape Designer   52
    Dennis J. Pogue

5   The Archaeology of Rachel's Garden   70
    Larry McKee

6   Father Rapp's Garden at Economy: Harmony Society Culture
       in Microcosm   91
    *Lu Ann De Cunzo, Therese O'Malley, Michael J. Lewis,
       George E. Thomas, and Christa Wilmanns-Wells*

PART II VERNACULAR AND SACRED SPACE

7   Social Relations and the Cultural Landscape   121
    J. Edward Hood

8   "One of the Best Farms in Essex County": The Changing
       Domestic Landscape of a Tenant Who Became an Owner   147
    Sara F. Mascia

9   Farmers and Gentlemen Farmers: The Nineteenth-Century
       Suburban Landscape   175
    Rebecca Yamin and Sarah T. Bridges

10 Charleston Townhouses: Archaeology, Architecture, and the
       Urban Landscape, 1750–1850   193
    Martha A. Zierden and Bernard L. Herman

11 The Construction of Sanctity: Landscape and Ritual in a
       Religious Community   228
    Elizabeth Kryder-Reid

12 "The Transient Nature of All Things Sublunary": Romanticism,
       History, and Ruins in Nineteenth-Century Southern Maryland 249
    Julia A. King

    Selected References   273

    Contributors   279

    Index   285

Illustrations

FIGURES

0.1	The Vergelegen Estate in South Africa	xxxi
0.2	The Changing Face of Rachel's Garden	xxxiv
2.1	A View of Morven, Princeton, New Jersey	7
2.2	Detail of a 1781 Military Map of Princeton	9
2.3	Association of Trees at Morven with Specific Generations of the Stockton Family	11
2.4	1881 Plan of Morven Depicting the Horse Chestnut Walk	12
2.5	Archaeological Excavations of the Horse Chestnut Walk	12
2.6	Exploratory Trenches Revealing Garden Features and Yard Surfaces	14
2.7	Eighteenth-Century Stone Steps at Morven	15
2.8	Areal Excavation along the Front of the West Wing of Morven	18
2.9	An Ornamental Eighteenth-Century Garden Feature	21
2.10	Areal Excavation of Gravel Walk along the Eastern Axis of the Garden	24
2.11	Trenches and Excavation Units in the Western Half of the Garden	24
2.12	Reconstructed Plan of the Eighteenth-Century Garden at Morven	27
2.13	Evidence of an Eighteenth-Century Planting Bed	28
3.1	Mount Clare, South Facade and Garden	35
3.2	Plan of the Mount Vernon Greenhouse	37
3.3	Relationship between the Lloyd-Tilghman-Goldsborough Women	38

3.4	Plan of the Mount Clare Orangery	40
3.5	Wye House Orangery Facade	41
3.6	Plan of the Wye House Orangery	41
3.7	Margaret Tilghman Carroll	44
3.8	Fairhill Facade and Gardens	46
3.9	Bush Hill	47
3.10	Intermarriage among the Logan, Pemberton, and Norris Families	48
4.1	Hypothesized Evolution of the Mount Vernon Mansion	54
4.2	Changes to the Layout of Mount Vernon	55
4.3	Plan of Mount Vernon by Samuel Vaughan	58
4.4	Drawing of the 1784 Greenhouse and Slave Quarter Wings	59
4.5	Bird's-Eye View of Mount Vernon by H. Whateley	61
4.6	Site Plan of the "Vineyard Inclosure"	61
4.7	View of Posthole/Mold and Drainage Ditch Associated with the "Fruit Garden" at Mount Vernon	62
4.8	Artifacts from Mount Vernon	63
5.1	Plan View of the Hermitage Garden	71
5.2	Aerial View of the Hermitage Garden and Mansion	72
5.3	Bricks from the Hermitage	73
5.4	Plan for a Large Kitchen Garden	76
5.5	Brick-Filled Postholes Related to an Early Garden Fence at the Hermitage	80
5.6	The Jackson Tomb in the Hermitage Garden	82
5.7	Excavation Unit in the Northeast Corner of the Hermitage Garden	83
5.8	Profile Drawing of the Brick Footing for the Garden Fence	85
5.9	A Party in the Backyard of the Hermitage Mansion	85
6.1	Plan of the Town of Economy and Land of the Harmony Society	93
6.2	Plan of George Rapp's House and Garden in Economy	94
6.3	George Rapp's Garden, Northeast View	95
6.4	George Rapp's Garden, East-Southeast View	95
6.5	Detail of George Rapp's Garden at Economy	102
6.6	Turris Antonia	107
6.7	Architectural Study of the Pavilion for George Rapp's Garden	108
7.1	Example of an Open Field Region Township	126
7.2	Map of Branscombe	127
7.3	Map of Southern New England	135
7.4	A Nucleated Village in the Middle Connecticut River Valley	135
8.1	Portion of USGS Newburyport East Quadrangle Map Showing Site Location	157
8.2	View of the Spencer-Pierce-Little House from the Southeast	158
8.3	"Plan of the 'Homestead' of Boardman's Farm"	161
8.4	Edward Henry Little (1819–1877)	162
8.5	Plan of the Domestic Compound at the Spencer-Pierce-Little Farm	166
8.6	View of the Tree-Lined Driveway at the Farm	167

8.7 View from the West of the Spencer-Pierce-Little House and
        Tenant House   168

8.8 View from the Southwest of the Spencer-Pierce-Little House and
        Tenant House   169

9.1 The Hopper House, 1989   176

9.2 "Residence of Henry A. Hopper, Esq."   178

9.3 The Hopper Property as Shown in Bromley's Atlas of Bergen
        County, 1913   181

9.4 "Map of Thirty Miles around New York City"   183

9.5 "The Thrifty Farmstead"   184

9.6 "The Gentleman Farmer's Seat"   184

9.7 Detail of the Hopper House   187

10.1 Map of Peninsular Charleston Showing Sites Excavated   195

10.2 Site Map of the Miles Brewton House   197

10.3 The Heyward-Washington House   198

10.4 Gabriel Manigault House and Lot, East Bay Street   199

10.5 The Earliest Surviving Copy of the Grand Modell   201

10.6 Plan of Lots and Buildings on King Street   205

10.7 Thomas Bradford House and Lot, Church Street   206

10.8 Front View of the Miles Brewton House   208

10.9 Posthole/Postmold beneath the Brick Wall between the Garden and Workyard
        at the Miles Brewton House   209

10.10 Lot Plans for Ansonborough, Meeting, and Hasell Streets   210

10.11 Queen Street, James McDowall Property   211

10.12 Stratigraphy of the Miles Brewton Courtyard   212

10.13 Meeting Street Tenements Adjacent to Court House Square   214

10.14 John Duncan's House and Lot   215

10.15 Samuel Prioleau's Estate, Church Street   216

10.16 Matthew Webb's King Street Property   217

11.1 St. Mary's Parish Church and Rectory   229

11.2 Redemptorist Fathers in the Garden with St. Mary's Church in the Background 233

11.3 1897 Map of the St. Mary's Site   235

11.4 Ca. 1892 Photograph Showing the Redemptorists' Transformation of the
        Carroll Garden   237

11.5 Ca. 1876 View of the Redemptorist Rectory   239

11.6 View of the "Old Carroll House" from the East   242

11.7 Map of the St. Mary's Site   246

12.1 "Ruins of the Church in Prince William's Parish, Sketch No. 3"   252

12.2 "Ruins at Jamestown"   253

12.3 Location of the Southern Maryland Region   254

12.4 Reconstructed St. Mary's City Statehouse of 1676   258

12.5 Subdivision of Mattapany Farm, 1873   259

12.6 Carved Table Stone Found at the Probable Site of the Christopher
        Rousby Grave   261

12.7   Surviving Early-Nineteenth-Century Susquehanna Dwelling   261
12.8   1824 U.S. Army Engineer's Map Showing Buildings at Susquehanna   262
12.9   Archaeological Plan of the 1798 Carroll Dwelling   264
12.10 Distribution of Wrought Nails at Susquehanna   265
12.11 1848 U.S. Coast and Geodetic Survey Map Showing Susquehanna   266
12.12 Distribution of Nineteenth-Century Refuse at Susquehanna   266
12.13 Relationship of the Ruin to Rooms at Susquehanna   267

TABLES

2.1   Measurements and Approximate Ages of Trees at Morven   11
8.1   The Agricultural Ladder   149
9.1   Cash Value of Saddle River Farms   180
9.2   Ceramic Index Calculations for the Kitchen Midden at
        Henry A. Hopper's Farm   189
9.3   Ceramic Index Calculations for the Cellar Fill at Henry A.
        Hopper's Farm   189

Preface: Reading the Historical Landscape

Rebecca Yamin and Karen Bescherer Metheny

> Our human landscape is our unwitting autobiography, reflecting our tastes, our values, our aspirations, and even our fears, in tangible, visible form. . . . the cultural record we have "written" in the landscape is liable to be more truthful than most autobiographies because we are less self-conscious about how we describe ourselves.
>
> *(Peirce E. Lewis 1979:12)*

In the introduction to *The Interpretation of Ordinary Landscapes,* D. W. Meinig suggests that "if we want to understand ourselves, we would do well to take a searching look at our landscapes" (1979:2). This volume includes many searching looks at the landscape, not just to understand ourselves, but to understand the context for other people's lives in other times (Lowenthal 1985), to unravel the landscapes they created, and to explain the meanings embedded in them. The purpose of this volume is to provide an overview of recent work in landscape archaeology that focuses on reading the historical landscape as if it were a book, finding the plots and subplots that have been written on the land by both the conscious and unconscious acts of the people who lived there.

Each of the twelve chapters describes and interprets archaeological data in the process of analyzing the symbolic significance of a historical landscape. For many years, archaeologists avoided studying what a distinguished colleague calls "contingent and mental phenomena" (Trigger 1991) because they were not directly observable, could not be measured, counted, or neatly stored on a laboratory shelf. But no archaeologist digs a hole without asking the meaning of what he or she finds, what it says about the people who left a record of their actions—and thoughts—in the ground (Tilley 1991). For archaeologists working in a post-processualist framework, including all of the authors represented here, the interesting questions have to do with meaning. Using a manner of reasoning (hermeneutics) that moves back and forth between past and present, between different categories of data—archaeological evidence, oral history, written sources, ethnographic data, anthropological theory, human experience—until the part and the whole begin to make sense, the post-processualist constructs a story about people in the past. This book is made up of many such stories as they relate to historical landscapes—stories about gardens conceived by elite men and women and honoring elite women, about the garden of a religious leader, about houselots tilled by farmers and transformed by forces beyond their farmyards, about the layers of landscape change in a southern city and the layers of change within a gentleman's estate that became home to a religious order, about ruins left standing in the rural landscape. Ian Hodder (1991:8) has noted that "there have been very few post-processualist studies that have said 'I will put theory in second place, treat it simply as baggage, and set off to tell a story.'"[1] Hopefully, this volume will begin to fill that gap.

Hodder (1991:13) also has called on archaeologists working in a post-processual framework to react against charges of methodological naiveté, to be more specific about the methods they use in place of standard empiricist methods. It is necessary to describe how narratives are constructed and why not every construction is as good as every other. The contributions included here also address this issue, albeit indirectly. Following Anne Yentsch's introduction and a short essay by Mary Beaudry, the volume begins with an explicitly methodological chapter about field and analytical techniques and conceptual devices developed for dissecting the multilayered landscape at Morven in Princeton, New Jersey, methods that made the meaning of that landscape more accessible. While no other chapter deals specifically with field techniques, all demonstrate how different categories of data—from drawings and maps to personal letters to the attitudes of oral informants—are woven together to create a coherent explanation for a historical landscape and how coherence itself is used to measure the adequacy of the explanation.

Many of the contributions draw on data and specialists outside the discipline of anthropology. Palynologists and ethnobotanists identify and date historic-period plants and trees; pedologists analyze the chemical components of historic-period soils; garden historians explain parterres and changing fashions in flowers and plants. The blending of data from the sciences and humanities enriches the interpretation of past landscapes and demonstrates the power of a synthesis between the positivist methods of science and the more contextual historical particularism of the post-processual approach (Trigger 1991). Although project staffing may be multidisciplinary, the analysis is fundamentally anthropological. It is for this reason that, while recognizing the significant contributions of these other specialists to the various studies discussed here, none of the chapters in this volume describes their work in detail. *The Archaeology of Garden and Field,* edited by Naomi F. Miller and Kathryn L. Gleason (1994), covers from a global perspective many of the more technical aspects of these specialists' contributions to prehistoric and historic-period landscape analysis. *Earth Patterns,* edited by William M. Kelso and Rachel Most (1990), also contains a section on "Landscape Science."

The focus of this volume is the interpretation of historical landscapes. The contributions are about people and places and, most important, the interaction between humans and the landscape. Because the landscape is the stage for human action, it both reflects past activities and encodes the cultural landscape in which people's views of the world are formed. The trick is to disentangle the various strata that represent physical changes to the land or changing land-use practices in order to analyze the changing symbolic meanings of the landscape over time. The challenge of this kind of stratigraphic analysis is one of the things that makes landscape archaeology so interesting. Not only must we recognize buried layers of earth that belong to different time periods—the essential task of stratigraphic excavation—but we must match those layers of earth with survivals in the present: the pattern of tree plantings, the position of structures, the course of pathways. As demonstrated by many of the chapters in this book, the interplay of past and present is a fundamental—perhaps the fundamental—problem in landscape archaeology, both in the reading and interpretation of past cultural landscapes.

Archaeologists also must sort through past and present interpretations of landscape that often are built upon fragments of mythic history or contemporary ideologies (Yentsch 1988; McKee, this volume) while maintaining a critical awareness of today's cultural biases, including their own (Shanks and Tilley 1987), as they interpret and reinterpret the evidence of past landscapes. As demonstrated by many of the chapters here, methodology becomes inseparable from interpretation. The use of converging lines of evidence drawn from a variety of related fields strengthens the process of archaeological inference (Wylie 1993).

Our concern for context and interpretation is shared by other students of the landscape, and landscape archaeologists would benefit from a close reading of their work. Cultural geography, in particular, shares a number of common goals and interests, including a close relationship with anthropology. While traditional cultural geography focused largely on the visible, material landscape and the study of form and space, contemporary cultural geographers draw from many theoretical approaches—many of which we would consider to be part of a post-processual framework, including structuralism, Marxism, phenomenology, and hermeneutics—to explore issues of symbolism and meaning, human perception and the experience of landscape, and the interaction of individuals, culture, and society with the landscape (e.g., Agnew and Duncan 1989; Cosgrove 1984; Cosgrove and Daniels 1988; Harvey 1973, 1985; Ley 1977; Meinig 1979; Tuan 1977, 1979). Convergence of our two fields centers on interpretation, more so than methodology, and arises from a common grounding in anthropological and social theory and a mutual dissatisfaction with positivist frameworks of analysis (Hodder 1987; Norton 1989). The concern for situating landscape formation and change in a cultural and social context distinguishes contemporary cultural geography from earlier research just as it sets landscape archaeology apart from earlier treatments of landscape by historical archaeologists.

Landscape archaeologists have much to gain from cultural geography in several specific areas. Cultural geographers have studied a number of landscape forms, from cemeteries to town plans and house types to visual representations of landscape (e.g., Jackson 1984; Jordan 1982; Stilgoe 1982; Wood 1992), that are familiar to historical archaeologists, but from a slightly different perspective. The mapping of cultural traits, for instance (e.g., Jackson 1978;

Meinig 1965; Wacker 1968, 1975), something historical archaeologists generally do not do, provides us with a basis for regional comparisons that we otherwise would not have. The use of spatial models and regional analyses by cultural geographers reminds us of the value of using multiple scales of analysis and of the need for comparative research to look beyond the bounds of individual gardens and landscapes (see Zierden and Herman, this volume). The work of J. B. Jackson (1984), Meinig (1979), and others serves to remind us, as well, of the need to expand our focus to include not just those sites that are well documented and well known to us (those most often the subject of preservation efforts) or those that are highly visible (the sites of elites), but also the ordinary and the everyday landscape. As Yentsch points out in her introductory essay to this volume, early archaeological studies of the landscape in North America were focused on elite landscapes, a factor related both to funding sources and the early association of garden archaeology with the preservation movement in the United States. The expansion of our scope to include other landscapes, demonstrated by the chapters in the second half of this volume, is a reflection of the growth of the field, but there is a continuing need for published studies that explore issues of gender, ethnicity, class, and economic history as they relate to landscape formation, alteration, and meaning (e.g., Praetzellis and Praetzellis 1989; Wall 1994, chapter 3). We also need to incorporate within our analytical and interpretive framework the question of human agency—who actually built and maintained the gardens and landscapes in our studies, not just who conceptualized their appearance and controlled the capital and labor used to shape the land (cf. Weber 1992).

We hope this volume will be of use to cultural geographers as well. Archaeological data have not been a traditional source of information on historical landscapes for cultural geographers, yet landscape archaeology recovers physical evidence that is available nowhere else—morphological and environmental data that are essential to the reconstruction and interpretation of historical landscapes. Because the archaeological record preserves evidence of everyday landscape use, as well as the intentional and unintentional effects of its use and alteration, it constitutes a source that is more objective, more comprehensive, and less biased than written sources. Landscape is "autobiographical" (Lewis 1979), as we noted at the beginning of this discussion.

Ed Hood's introduction to the second half of this volume and a number of other recent studies suggest that the line between landscape archaeology and cultural geography is beginning to blur (for a detailed discussion, see Wagstaff 1987; see also Bender 1993). Examples of the successful integration of archaeological, anthropological, and geographical approaches to data recovery and the interpretation of historical landscapes include the study of Burgundian landscapes by Crumley and Marquardt (1987) and the ongoing work in Montserrat by Pulsipher (1994). Current interpretations of the landscape also reflect a common theoretical thread. The concept of multiple, stratified layers of meaning within the landscape drives many recent studies by anthropologists, cultural and social geographers, and historical archaeologists alike. Anthropologist Margaret Rodman (1992), for instance, has combined the concepts of multivocality and discourse analysis in anthropology with the concept of place used by cultural geographers such as Tuan (1977, 1991) and Entrikin (1989) in a recent discussion on landscape. Rodman uses the term "multilocality" to express the idea that "place"—the meaning of a landscape—is socially constructed at many levels by many individuals and groups: "a single physical landscape can be multilocal in the sense that it shapes and expresses polysemic meanings of place for different users. Multilocality conveys the idea that a single place may be experienced quite differently [by different people]" (1992:647).

Within historical archaeology, Martin Hall (1991, 1992a, 1992b, 1994) and his colleagues (Brink 1992; Markell 1992; Winer 1995) use a discursive framework to uncover multiple meanings embedded in colonial and contemporary South African landscapes, revealing a dialogue of power, domination, and resistance. Their work also examines economic, social, class, and gender relations that are signified within the landscape. In North America, archaeologists and historians also have begun to consider the layers of meaning within the historical landscape, not only for the wealthy and the social elite but also for the middle class, the working classes, and the poor, for slaves and free persons, for men and women, in rural and urban settings (e.g., Beaudry 1993; Hall 1992b; Mrozowski 1987, 1991; Mrozowski and Beaudry 1990; Praetzellis and Praetzellis 1992; Upton 1990, 1992; Weber 1992; see also Yentsch, this volume). Taken together, the above-mentioned works and the essays in this volume suggest that the current direction of landscape studies lies in interpretive, contextual, multidisciplinary research.

Landscape archaeology is a relatively new subspecialty within historical archaeology. The authors included in this volume are at the cutting edge of this discipline. Their work sets an example for future studies and points to deficiencies in the field that must still be addressed. The chapters are organized into two groups, the first restricted to analyses that focus on individual gardens and the second to studies that find meaning in the larger landscape. A short introduction to the first section, entitled "Why Gardens?" by Mary Beaudry, places the analysis of gardens into the broader context of late-twentieth-century environmental concerns, while the introduction to the second section, "Social Relations and the Cultural Landscape" by J. Edward Hood, illustrates the power of landscape analyses that extend beyond the bounds of individual gardens. Whether looking at a single garden or a sweeping landscape, the authors share a commitment to holding a dialogue with the past, with extracting those tastes, values, aspirations, and fears that are the "unwitting autobiography" of the people who molded the land.

NOTE

1. A noteworthy exception to this is the story of a Wahpeton Dakota woman, told by Janet Spector (1993) through the discovery of a delicate bone-handled awl.

REFERENCES

Agnew, John A., and James S. Duncan, editors
1989   *The Power of Place.* Unwin Hyman, Winchester, Massachusetts.
Beaudry, Mary C.
1993   Public Aesthetics Versus Personal Experience: Worker Health and Well-Being in 19th-Century Lowell, Massachusetts. *Historical Archaeology* 27(3):90–105.
Bender, Barbara, editor
1993   *Landscape: Politics and Perspectives.* Berg Publishers, Providence, Rhode Island.
Brink, Yvonne
1992   Places of Discourse and Dialogue: A Study in the Material Culture of the Cape During the Rule of the Dutch East India Company, 1652–1795. Ph.D. diss., Department of Archaeology, University of Cape Town.

Cosgrove, Denis E.

1984   *Social Formation and Symbolic Landscape.* Barnes & Noble Books, Totowa, New Jersey.

Cosgrove, Denis, and Stephen Daniels, editors

1988   *The Iconography of Landscape: Essays on the Symbolic Representation, Design and Use of Past Environments.* Cambridge University Press, Cambridge.

Crumley, Carole L., and William H. Marquardt, editors

1987   *Regional Dynamics: Burgundian Landscapes in Historical Perspective.* Academic Press, San Diego.

Entrikin, J. Nicholas

1989   Place, Region and Modernity. In *The Power of Place,* edited by John A. Agnew and James S. Duncan, pp. 30–43. Unwin Hyman, Winchester, Massachusetts.

Hall, Martin

1991   High and Low in the Townscapes of Dutch South America and South Africa: The Dialectics of Material Culture. *Social Dynamics* 17(2):41–75.

1992a   People in a Changing Urban Landscape: Excavating Cape Town. Inaugural Lecture, University of Cape Town. New Series No. 169:1–27.

1992b   Small Things and the Mobile, Conflictual Fusion of Power, Fear, and Desire. In *The Art and Mystery of Historical Archaeology: Essays in Honor of James Deetz,* edited by Anne Elizabeth Yentsch and Mary C. Beaudry, pp. 373–99. CRC Press, Boca Raton, Florida.

1994   The Secret Lives of Houses and Women, Gables and Gardens in the Eighteenth Century Cape. Seminar paper, University of California-Berkeley and University of Chicago, January 1994.

Harvey, David W.

1973   *Social Justice and the City.* The Johns Hopkins University Press, Baltimore, Maryland.

1985   *Consciousness and the Urban Experience.* The Johns Hopkins University Press, Baltimore, Maryland.

Hodder, Ian

1987   Converging Traditions: The Search for Symbolic Meanings in Archaeology and Geography. In *Landscape and Culture: Geographical and Archaeological Perspectives,* edited by J. M. Wagstaff, pp. 134–45. Basil Blackwell, New York.

1991   Interpretive Archaeology and Its Role. *American Antiquity* 56(1):7–18.

Jackson, John Brinckerhoff

1984   *Discovering the Vernacular Landscape.* Yale University Press, New Haven.

Jackson, Richard H.

1978   Religion and Landscape in the Mormon Cultural Region. In *Dimensions of Human Geography: Essays on Some Familiar and Neglected Themes,* edited by Karl W. Butzer, pp. 100–127. Department of Geography Research Paper 186. University of Chicago, Chicago, Illinois.

Jordan, Terry G.

1982   *Texas Graveyards: A Cultural Legacy.* University of Texas Press, Austin.

Kelso, William M., and Rachel Most, editors

1990   *Earth Patterns: Essays in Landscape Archaeology.* University Press of Virginia, Charlottesville.

Lewis, Peirce E.

1979   Axioms for Reading the Landscape: Some Guides to the American Scene. In *The Interpretation of Ordinary Landscapes: Geographical Essays,* edited by D. W. Meinig, pp. 11–32. Oxford University Press, New York.

Ley, David

1977   Social Geography and the Taken-for-Granted World. *Transactions, Institute of British Geographers* 2(4):498–512.

Lowenthal, David

1985   *The Past Is a Foreign Country.* Cambridge University Press, Cambridge.

Markell, Ann B.

1992   Walls of Isolation: The Garden Fortress of Governor Willem Adraiaan van der Stel. Paper presented at the annual meeting of the Society for Historical Archaeology, Richmond, Virginia.

Meinig, D. W.

1965   The Mormon Culture Region: Strategies and Patterns in the Geography of the American West, 1847–1964. *Annals of the Association of American Geographers* 55(2):191–220.

Meinig, D. W., editor

1979   *The Interpretation of Ordinary Landscapes: Geographical Essays.* Oxford University Press, New York.

Miller, Naomi F., and Kathryn L. Gleason, editors

1994   *The Archaeology of Garden and Field.* University of Pennsylvania Press, Philadelphia.

Mrozowski, Stephen A.

1987   Exploring New England's Evolving Urban Landscape. In Living in Cities: Current Research in Urban Archaeology, edited by Edward Staski. *Special Publication Series* No. 5:1–9. Society for Historical Archaeology.

1991   Landscapes of Inequality. In *The Archaeology of Inequality,* edited by Randall H. McGuire and Robert Paynter, pp. 79–101. Basil Blackwell, Cambridge, Massachusetts.

Mrozowski, Stephen A., and Mary C. Beaudry

1990   Archaeology and the Landscape of Corporate Ideology. In *Earth Patterns: Essays in Landscape Archaeology,* edited by William M. Kelso and Rachel Most, pp. 189–208. University Press of Virginia, Charlottesville.

Norton, William

1989   *Explorations in the Understanding of Landscape: A Cultural Geography.* Contributions in Sociology No. 77. Greenwood Press, Westport, Connecticut.

Praetzellis, Adrian, and Mary Praetzellis

1989   "Utility and Beauty Should Be One": The Landscape of Jack London's Ranch of Good Intentions. *Historical Archaeology* 23(1):33–44.

1992   Faces and Facades: Victorian Ideology in Early Sacramento. In *The Art and Mystery of Historical Archaeology: Essays in Honor of James Deetz,* edited by Anne Elizabeth Yentsch and Mary C. Beaudry, pp. 75–99. CRC Press, Boca Raton, Florida.

Pulsipher, Lydia Mihelic

1994   The Landscapes and Ideational Roles of Caribbean Slave Gardens. In *The Archaeology of Garden and Field,* edited by Naomi F. Miller and Kathryn L. Gleason, pp. 202–21. University of Pennsylvania Press, Philadelphia.

Rodman, Margaret C.

1992   Empowering Place: Multilocality and Multivocality. *American Anthropologist* 94(3):640–56.

Shanks, Michael, and Christopher Tilley

1987   *Social Theory and Archaeology.* University of New Mexico Press, Albuquerque.

Spector, Janet D.

1993   *What This Awl Means: Feminist Archaeology at a Wahpeton Dakota Village.* Minnesota Historical Society Press, St. Paul.

Stilgoe, John R.

1982   *Common Landscape of America, 1580 to 1845.* Yale University Press, New Haven.

Tilley, Christopher

1991   *Material Culture and Text: The Art of Ambiguity.* Routledge, New York.

Trigger, Bruce G.

1991   Distinguished Lecture in Archeology: Constraint and Freedom—A New Synthesis for Archeological Explanation. *American Anthropologist* 93(3):551–69.

Tuan, Yi-Fu

1977   *Space and Place: The Perspective of Experience.* University of Minnesota Press, Minneapolis.

1979   Thought and Landscape: The Eye and the Mind's Eye. In *The Interpretation of Ordinary Landscapes: Geographical Essays,* edited by D. W. Meinig, pp. 89–102. Oxford University Press, New York.

1991   Language and the Making of Place: A Narrative-Descriptive Approach. *Annals of the Association of American Geographers* 81(4):684–96.

Upton, Dell

1990   Imagining the Early Virginia Landscape. In *Earth Patterns: Essays in Landscape Archaeology,* edited by William M. Kelso and Rachel Most, pp. 71–86. University Press of Virginia, Charlottesville.

1992   The City as Material Culture. In *The Art and Mystery of Historical Archaeology: Essays in Honor of James Deetz,* edited by Anne Elizabeth Yentsch and Mary C. Beaudry, pp. 51–74. CRC Press, Boca Raton, Florida.

Wacker, Peter O.

1968   *The Musconetcong Valley: A Historical Geography.* Rutgers University Press, New Brunswick, New Jersey.

1975   *Land and People: A Cultural Geography of Pre-Industrial New Jersey, Origins and Settlement Patterns.* Rutgers University Press, New Brunswick, New Jersey.

Wagstaff, J. M., editor

1987   *Landscape and Culture: Geographical and Archaeological Perspectives.* Basil Blackwell, New York.

Wall, Diana diZerega

1994   *The Archaeology of Gender: Separating the Spheres in Urban America.* Plenum Press, New York.

Weber, Carmen A.

1992   A Reassessment of Gender and Landscape: The Archaeology of Women and Men in the Garden. Paper presented at the annual meeting of the Society for Historical Archaeology, Kingston, Jamaica.

Winer, Margot

1995   The Painted, Poetic Landscape: Reading Power in Nineteenth-Century Textual and Visual Representations of the Eastern Cape Frontier. In *The Written and the Wrought: Complementary Sources in Historical Anthropology, Essays in Honor of James Deetz,* edited by Mary Ellin D'Agostino, Elizabeth Prine, Eleanor Casella, and Margot Winer, pp. 74–109. Kroeber Anthropological Society Papers No. 79.

Wood, Denis, with John Fels

1992   *The Power of Maps.* The Guilford Press, New York.

Wylie, Alison

1993   Invented Lands/Discovered Pasts: The Westward Expansion of Myth and History. *Historical Archaeology* 27(4):1–19.

Yentsch, Anne

1988   Legends, Houses, Families, and Myths: Relationships Between Material Culture and American Ideology. In *Documentary Archaeology in the New World,* edited by Mary C. Beaudry, pp. 5–19. Cambridge University Press, Cambridge.

Acknowledgments

It has taken a long time to bring this book to completion. Conceived as a collection of case studies representing the innovative scholarship of young landscape archaeologists, many of whom had not yet finished their academic training, it has grown into a more ambitious work. With time and the impressive efforts of all the contributing authors, the case studies have become scholarly papers and the short introductory pieces have become essays in their own right. The trouble with doing a book in an evolving field is just that. It changes, and, in this case, the changes have a great deal to do with the ongoing work of the authors represented here. While our original précis for the book emphasized the newness of the field and the freshness of the perspectives offered in these papers, the finished product is a tribute to the maturation of scholarship relating to historical landscapes.

We wish to thank all of these authors for their hard work and incredible patience. The symposia out of which this volume grew were first presented at the annual meetings of the Council for Northeast Historical Archaeology (CNEHA), the Eastern States Archaeological Federation (ESAF), and the Society for Historical Archaeology (SHA) in 1989 and 1990; the editorial process has been virtually ongoing since then. We also wish to express our appreciation to Mary Beaudry, John Worrell, and James Deetz, who acted as discussants for the various sessions, and to Carmen Weber, who helped organize and co-chaired the SHA symposium with Karen Bescherer Metheny and served as a discussant for both that symposium as well as the earlier CNEHA session.

Anne Yentsch, under whose direction we both worked on the Morven Landscape Archaeology Project in Princeton, New Jersey, in great part inspired this volume. She suggested the original symposia, which were organized by Karen Bescherer Metheny, and invited Rebecca Yamin to serve as senior editor of the publication. But, more important, she taught us both to think about the landscape in a hermeneutic way, to keep searching the data for internal consistency, and to insist on an interpretation of the past that makes coherent sense. Her introduction to the volume, "Close Attention to Place," is testimony to her deep understanding of the potential and power of landscape studies. We are indebted to Anne for her influence on our professional development and her leadership in the field of landscape archaeology.

The acquisitions editor at the University of Tennessee Press, Meredith Morris-Babb, and our reviewers, Joseph Wood, Carroll Van West, and Charles Faulkner, provided invaluable guidance in terms of the organization of the volume. They also drew our attention to what this volume is not, which led us to more clearly define what it is. We are particularly grateful to Van West for seeing logic in the forest where we had only seen trees.

Introduction: Close Attention to Place— Landscape Studies by Historical Archaeologists

Anne Elizabeth Yentsch

> Through the close study of a place, its people and character . . . we come closer to our own reality. It is difficult to impose a story and a plot on a place. But truly knowing a place provides the link between details and meaning.
>
> *(Louise Erdrich 1985)*

Landscape is one of the newer emphases in historical archaeology. It is still an untapped resource, an area of study that dovetails nicely with many relevant issues in today's world—from the concerns of city planners, environmentalists, and ecologists to those of people who simply love beauty in their gardens. It merges the aesthetic with the scientific; it provides, as gardens did in days gone by, a meeting place where minds can contemplate choice things, discourse with company, or meditate alone.

In her introduction ("Why Gardens?") to part I of this volume, Mary Beaudry gives additional reasons why archaeologists have turned to gardens with renewed vigor, cutting through modern lawns to find fence lines, buried paths, and the soils from eighteenth-century planting beds. She sees it as a natural extension of a deepening interest in historic houses, adding sophistication and depth to the preservation movement. That it is; funding from preservation-related sources provided the financial backbone for a majority of the case studies here and in the earlier *Earth Patterns: Essays in Landscape Archaeology* (Kelso and Most 1990). The preservation linkage can also be discerned in the lack of studies herein that touch on the landscape of minorities, of working-class people, and of ordinary farmers (for an exception, see Hood, this volume; this study exemplifies the type of landscape research done by Robert Paynter and his students at the University of Massachusetts; also see Mrozowski 1987). It is not that historical archaeologists do not wish to study these folk, simply that funding sources are usually attached to other types of preservation projects. This constraint means that we understand far more about the meaning of certain types of landscapes than others.

Does such work, as Beaudry suggests, create an arena where historical archaeologists can adapt and modify the battery of techniques used to rediscover the prehistoric landscape?[1] It could, it should, but the promise remains tantalizingly out of touch—in sight, but not in reach. Miller's bibliography (Miller 1989a; Miller and Good 1988) indicates that a small start has been made, but bridging articles are still the exception. Because of the small number of projects that make archaeobotanical evidence central, the association of meaning aligned with the dominant element—flora—in most landscapes is not firmly drawn at any site studied by historical archaeologists to date. Nor are the techniques of archaeobotany (e.g., Miller and Gleason 1994) fully employed or successfully integrated into the interpretation of historical landscapes.

There is no doubt but that historical archaeologists study the landscape differently in many respects from their colleagues in classical archaeology or prehistory. This is not solely due to the way archaeobotanical evidence is used. Some differences arise because of field methods; others are created by the existence of written texts. Often, different goals derive from the requests of archaeological "consumers" for precise information on ornamental plants and trees, on gardens designed for pleasure, or on extraordinary horticultural practice. We are asked less frequently to find out what humans, of this group or that group, ate or to see how human social action, broadly speaking, impacted the regional landscape. Requests to historical archaeologists may be phrased in specific terms: How did George Washington plant his orchard? Tell us so that we can implement an accurate restoration. In these cases, historical archaeologists are expected to supply answers with exceedingly fine-lined chronologies (i.e., 1760–75 or 1785–99). The influence of this dimension of the discipline can be seen vividly in many of the studies in this volume.

Since our ancestors in historical time periods devoted much time and attention to writing about plants, productive crops, even prices and yields, historical archaeologists also begin with evidence that other archaeologists work to discover. Further, we excavate deposits in which it is possible for living seeds of modern and historical origins—or recent and old seeds—to merge; this can be seen, or read between the lines, in Naomi F. Miller's tables (1989b) with their designations of very fragile, fragile, somewhat fragile, somewhat sturdy, and woody remains. Despite this obstacle, historical archaeologists are now inserting archaeobotanical questions into their research designs (Kelso 1991, 1993a, 1993b; Kelso et al. 1989; Mrozowski 1987; Praetzellis and Praetzellis 1992). Yet, the tentative use of information on plants in studies of symbolic meaning embedded in historical landscapes indicates this type of research is still in a formative stage.

While the studies in this volume look at meaning in the landscape, they are based on a limited set of data. It is well to be aware that a false dichotomy exists between the archaeological and architectural study of form on the land—the static aspect of landscape symbolism—and the ingredients that made the landscape dynamic, ever-changing, and mutable. Sophisticated, in-depth analysis is presently reserved for aspects of the landscape that appear reliable (if not permanent), and, except in a few cases (e.g., Kelso 1991, 1993a, 1993b; Kelso and Beaudry 1990; Miller 1989b), research has focused on those aspects that do not require botanical evidence to support interpretation of landscape's symbolic role in culture. This issue is raised here because the symbolism attached to plants is many layered and deeply woven throughout diverse domains of everyday life in agricultural communities such as those discussed in this volume.

Why have the symbolic meanings associated with plants been bypassed by historical archaeologists in much of their work? It is tempting to think that because the plants themselves are ephemeral, their meaning is seen as elusive. However, the best answer is perhaps that the study of landscape's symbolism is a relatively new endeavor, one viewed skeptically by those who seek absolutes. Because architectural elements of landscape design were more fixed, archaeological consumers are more comfortable with results predicated upon them. Yet landscapes were multivocal and carried meaning, within American society, at each different social level. The historical landscape served different constituencies simultaneously in a way that ceramic pots did not. What a Chinese immigrant saw in the western mountain ranges as he designed gardens on a grand scale (Fee 1993) was different from what his Irish counterpart saw in the very same region; African Americans in the East, in turn, perceived and used their land in a different fashion from that seen by slave masters who lived side by side with their slaves but in far greater luxury (Upton 1985, 1990). Yet, in all cases, perceptions of the land and the meanings it held were integrated within their cultural identities.

If we recognize that studies of the historical landscape are also used to build and reaffirm modern self-images and cultural identities—a process that is presently paralleled in landscape design and garden history and highly visible in a recent outflow of garden books[2]—how then do we proceed to look at meaning and to separate its past from its present, its varied nuances from its core? Taken as a whole, the chapters in this book suggest that we must first pay close attention to method, for in studies of meaning embedded in the land, theory hovers close to the ground and is intricately related to methodology.

METHODS THAT PLACE PEOPLE ON THE LAND

This volume illustrates how historical archaeologists use scientific techniques, tried-and-true field techniques, and incorporate historical evidence into research designs. It illustrates how good historical archaeology is focused upon people. It shows that the theoretical distance seen in earlier landscape archaeology studies of great gardens with their concentration on dominant individuals (i.e., the work by Ivor Noël Hume, William Kelso, and Mark Leone) presented but one view of the past—one in which cultural "others" were masked, whether housewife or slave. Carmen Weber (chapter 3) reintroduces women into the landscape in her discussion of the gardening interests and activities of Margaret Tilghman Carroll, daughter of one of the scions of Maryland's Eastern Shore and bride of Charles Carroll the Barrister. Mistress Carroll provided advice, through her brother-in-law, Tench Tilghman, to George Washington— sound advice that helped create the Mount Vernon landscape described by Pogue (chapter 4; see especially figure 4.4, which shows Mount Vernon's greenhouse). Weber's method draws on feminist theories and feminist concepts; because it does so, it enables her to discern that horticulture was a highly valued activity among women as well as among men.[3]

Conversely, J. Edward Hood's essay on land use in post-medieval England and his comparison of its colonial variations at Deerfield, Massachusetts (chapter 7), is an excellent example of the way that Marxist scholars attend to the subject of agricultural history and land use. Sara Mascia uses a similar process (chapter 8), but orients her work to the problem of discerning how individuals worked themselves up the agricultural ladder, leaving traces of upward social mobility encoded in the land. Both archaeologists, although using differing theoretical perspectives, start with documents. Mascia provides a thoughtful discussion of the varieties of historical information and comparative artifacts that can be used to "explode" the archaeological evidence. Hood stresses the active role of the cultural landscape in enculturation, its use in the production and the constitution of human society. While we take it as a given that land acquisition is one means to accumulate wealth, Hood's analysis of how the "natural" landscape serves to reproduce class-based systems of social inequality while also serving as an arena for resistance is insightful. It illustrates the way that meaning and function intertwine and highlights how alternative theoretical approaches reveal new dimensions of familiar entities.

Yamin and Bridges (chapter 9) also choose an alternative strategy, one occasionally used by historical archaeologists, for their investigation of a New Jersey farm owned by Henry Hopper. The ties between landscape archaeology and mythic history (Leach 1990), described eloquently here, are apparent throughout the volume and are one of its implicit themes. The relation between land and myth impacts archaeology in a myriad of ways. It creates a situation in which careful sorting through multiple layers of meaning is required to contextually place and assess the significance of a historical landscape (e.g., Upton 1985, 1990, 1992). Take the way the Hopper house was known in local circles: "one of the town's last farmsteads, a fragment and a symbol of a bygone way of life." Because of the importance of its prior owner, one of Bergen County's leading citizens, Yamin and Bridges expected to find "a rich local history and oral tradition" associated with the Hoppers; instead, they found that the third generation of Crouchers to grow up in the house saw it as their family's symbolic space.

Rather than perceiving its former owner as illustrious, the Crouchers attributed a slightly impoverished, "even slightly disreputable" hue to him, but this was not the impression given in a 1920s county history that asserted the importance of the Hopper house and its place among the county's ancestral homes. The inconsistency Yamin and Bridges found is one historical archaeologists often encounter. Raymond Firth has called these anomalies "disjunctions": "a gap between the overt superficial statement of action and its underlying meaning. On the surface a person is saying or doing something which our observations or inferences tell us should not be simply taken at face value—it stands for something else, of greater significance to him" (Firth 1975:26). Using these disjunctions to orient the analytical phases of the Hopper house project produced a resolution that gave the interpretation of the landscape particular insight. Use of a contextual stance required Yamin and Bridges to juxtapose the site, its artifacts, its family, and land-use history against the reality of a planned community across the street from the Hopper home. They show that historical archaeology is richer when it calls upon many sources and when it pays close attention to situatedness or the interplay between mythical history and the more objective reality.

Situatedness is a term used by hermeneutic scholars to denote the experiential relationships that exist between a person and his or her social/physical space. A place in space can be as small as a hidden circle of grass beneath a willow tree or it can be expanded to truly large areas like regions or more inclusive communities such as the social and physical spaces encompassed within small towns and cities. It can be discussed in systemic terms with change on the land tied to changes in the family life cycle or to differences in gender. Archaeologists often think of this as activity area research, which is at heart a spatial study and another method used by historical archaeologists.

LANDSCAPE AS EXPRESSIVE SPACE

Zierden and Herman (chapter 10) outline a series of transformational processes in which Charlestonians participated at the community level, processes that affected the organization of space in the town: conversion, accommodation, intensification, enclosure, infill, backlot development, intrasite and intersite variation, centralized control, regulation. They also see the townscape as designed and contrived, something that was pushed and pulled into shape in this Carolina port. Reading the interconnected patterns among stratigraphic profiles and chronologies, in the faunal and botanical samples, among the artifacts and the architectural features, they give site occupants a peripheral location in the study, but do not divorce individuals from it. One sees this in small ways. For example, Zierden and Herman assert that the city's topography and native environment did not, or were not, allowed to impede the vision of its city fathers. "Streams and tidal ditches were topographical nuisances to be filled," and were soon overcome, they write.

An underlying concern with the expressive qualities of landscape aesthetics is at the heart of symbols and meaning studies in landscape archaeology; it consists of a careful search for the symbolic messages encoded in the appearance of a dirt path, a wooden fence, a brick wall topped with broken glass, straight streets, curving lanes, and tidal ditches. Variations in the small details of daily life often derive from the nuances of material symbolic expressions even as they do from change in practicalities or transformations of social relationships. These nuances only appear with careful fieldwork. Yet many times they signal the existence of new orders and new ways of doing things in the family, in the town, and on the land.

As historical archaeologists we first began to see their tracks in a series of excavations done in the 1960s and 1970s when the William Paca Garden, Carter's Grove, and Kingsmill were first excavated. While traces of the landscaped grounds at the Governor's Palace had been recovered thirty years before (Martin 1991; Noël Hume 1974), architectural archaeologists were responsible for their excavation; buildings were their goals, and meaning for them resided in high style architecture (Hosmer 1985). The stellar sites and applied excavation strategies of the 1970s (Kelso 1984a, 1984b) opened up landscape archaeology and awakened interest among a new generation, who by the mid-1980s began to draw upon anthropological history to look at a wider variety of evidence (e.g., Beaudry 1986; Ernstein 1989; Harrington 1989) while joining forces with vernacular architects and art historians (e.g., Kryder-Reid and Ruggles 1994; Leone 1984; Paynter, Reinke, and Garrison 1987; Yentsch et al. 1987). They also sought the knowledge of practical scholars and landscape designers such as Rudy and Joy Favretti (1990, 1991), Peter Martin (1991), Elizabeth McLean (1984), and Barbara Paca (Paca-Steele and Wright 1987). In some cases, the research was done with an eye for the native's point of view and to discern culture's order in space. A session at Monticello (Kelso and Most 1990), focused primarily on colonial landscapes, laid it out for colleagues to see. The meaning of landscape was targeted, primarily through studies of houses and their yards, and an evolution in ornamental land use began to appear that could be associated with changes in the symbolism associated with eighteenth-century mansions and their carefully laid-out grounds.

ORDER IN THE COLONIAL LANDSCAPE

These first planned American landscapes, or pleasure gardens, enclosed space to make it protected, thus maintaining a connection with the working gardens of earlier colonists. It is no accident that the gardens slowly appeared beside the homes of wealthier families starting in the 1650s, because for most of the people most of the time, there was little leisure and far too much to do to support the additional gardening activities needed to sustain an ornamental landscape. As the frontier moved westward and the settlements near the coast became more familiar, civilized spaces, protective enclosures became less essential. By this time, too, building on the visual illusions created by the landscape of Versailles and its Italian precedents (Wölfflin [1888] 1966), men in England had begun to design gardens that carried ornamental landscapes close to the house. Locating a pleasure garden immediately in front of or behind a mansion allowed the landscape to, in Deetz's words (1990), contextualize a dwelling, to provide a setting that joined the man-made and the natural in a different way. It made mansions much more effective status symbols because it enabled them to transcend the human need for shelter and to incorporate other messages about social position within their fabric in new ways.

There is less resemblance between elite gardens of the seventeenth and the eighteenth centuries than one might imagine; differences between the ornamental gardens of the wealthy and those that ordinary colonists tended also continued to exist. However, elite gardens provided opportunities for men to be like their peers and yet to be distinct. What Vincent Scully saw in an analysis of Italian town architecture—"individuality tempered by context" (1991:206)—was present in the New World too. The options available were not infinite; differences in architecture and material provided the primary embellishments.[4] However, both adaptability and variability were possible, and with these, the cultural cues encoded in a garden became elements in the material discourses of colonial communities, especially among the rich.

In the early eighteenth century a few colonists began to draw their garden locations into direct association with family homes by placing the formal garden either in front of or behind the mansion. By the 1720s, a few gentlemen had incorporated the concept of a terraced, outward-looking vista into symmetrical garden designs in Williamsburg, at the Governor's Palace (Martin 1991); in Annapolis, at the Calvert governors' home (Yentsch 1994); and on the Virginia frontier, at Germanna (Martin 1991; Sanford 1990). Soon other men began to bring their gardens in line, filling and cutting away the soil from New England to the Carolinas. Horticultural competition had sprung full blown onto American soil even as it did at other distant outposts of civilization (e.g., South Africa, West Africa, the Caribbean) (Brink 1992; Hall 1991). And if a planter did not have extraordinary means at his disposal, he could adapt a series of illusory devices to create a larger or smaller, closer or more distant, image of earthly delight.[5]

By mid-century, the passion for formal, ornamental gardens was in full swing; it throve at town and country estates such as the William Paca and Charles Carroll gardens in Annapolis (Kryder-Reid 1991, 1994; Leone 1988); the Benjamin Chew and William Peter gardens outside Philadelphia (Yentsch 1992a; Yentsch and Kratzer 1991); the William Middleton gardens outside Charleston, South Carolina (Trinkley, Adams, and Hacker 1992); and Drayton Hall (Wheaton 1989). Not the least of these were Richard and Annis Stockton's gardens in Princeton, New Jersey (Yentsch et al. 1987; Metheny et al., this volume), where, drawing upon the work of Paca-Steele and Wright (1987) in Annapolis, we began to realize that true gardening has a dual orientation—plant content and architectural form—played out within parameters that are culturally set. These parameters include a culturally relative deep structure of underlying symbolic forms. Crack the code, see how it is organized, and a garden's or working farm's parts can be seen as expectable, hence predictable (Yentsch 1990). An archaeologist can begin to imagine an older landscape as its contemporary occupants saw it. One can see readily that, looking inward, a terraced garden gave added grandeur to a city mansion while its private view out across the land was an element that enabled a wealthy man to flaunt a vista. At first archaeologists saw garden features as design lines visible in plan view, but as we gained analytical sophistication, we began to see the smaller pieces of designs as symmetrically located devices placed to draw the eye and, later, as experiential settings (Kryder-Reid 1994).

Morven archaeologists began to apply such concepts to understand its sequence of built landscapes (chapter 2, this volume). Perhaps the biggest breakthrough came when we knew enough about the garden to apply Barbara Paca's model to the excavation strategy and realized that if Richard and Annis Stockton were using a Renaissance system of logic, given that they had a walk here, a house of X dimensions there, and a terrace with steps at point P, they would also have added design elements at various other places, at points A, B, C, or D (see figure 2.12). Yet it is not easy to transfer in the abstract a set of cognitive measures from one era to another, for most archaeologists have been enculturated to perceive objects and space in feet and inches. No one looks intuitively at an eighteenth-century garden and sees its terrain in terms of rods or perches, triangles, octagons, or panopticons. It is one thing in archaeology to think that you have recognized, after the fact, a symbolic system in action. This is a common occurrence. It is another to be able to take the symbols, delineate their systemic relationships in time past, and reapply them in today's world. The re-use of such a cognitive process is what enables an archaeologist both to test its parameters and to discover more about the beliefs that formed it. Metheny et al. write of this as an interactive approach.

As archaeologists learn more about the ideas by which men (and some women) designed gardens and built landscapes in earlier times, they may be able to shorten the usual archaeological testing procedure, get closer to the heart of things with fewer five-foot squares, and produce more informative results. This will make it more feasible for preservationists who apply the findings to garden planning in order to incorporate the benefits of archaeology into long-range goals. This is the applied side of archaeology. It is inseparable, however, from the study of meaning because it channels the ways that studies of meaning can proceed. Historical archaeologists can also learn more about the people of past time, including the ways they used the land as an element in their recursive social organization and in political and religious institutions, by analyzing landscapes and the simultaneous or successive layers of meaning each may possess—in other words, by looking at the symbolic content of the landscape and giving credence to multivocality.

GARDENS AS POLITICAL STATEMENTS

Martin Hall (1992:377–78) suggests that we conceive of gardens as places of object-centered discourse and then attend to their comparisons by looking at the way each makes a "statement." Hall uses the concept of "statement" as defined by Foucault: "Instead of being something said once and for all . . . the statement, as it emerges in its materiality, appears with a status, enters various networks and various fields of use, is subjected to transferences or modifications, is integrated into operations and strategies in which its identity is maintained or effaced" (Foucault 1972:105, quoted in Hall 1992:377). Hall emphasizes the connection with artifacts: "A statement is a relation with a domain of objects, whether those objects be spoken words, written texts, or material artifacts" (1992:377).

This is a critical, useful concept to keep in mind when reading the chapters in this volume. These essays, as a whole, illustrate various facets of meaning and relate them to different aspects of culture: from legitimating authority to expressing religious ideology, from maintaining culture heroes and memories of remarkable events to transforming the land and considering the way class relations shape the landscape of a region. They analyze conscious changes in the land and some that went unnoticed. The chapters start, aptly enough, with the formal gardens and landscapes of political leaders (or their spouses; see Carmen Weber's chapter on Margaret Carroll). In chapter 4, for example, Pogue describes his search for the material record of George Washington's changes on the land. But to recognize why the gardens of national leaders are significant, one must also realize that gardens and landscapes can serve as political metaphors.

The political symbolism of colonial gardens was first discussed in archaeological circles by Leone (1984), who asserted that Maryland gardens were a premeditated means to assert authority in a period of growing dissension and social upheaval. Kryder-Reid (1994:136) glosses Leone's position as follows: "[Leone] proposed that, through the rationalization of space (by manipulating geometry and laws of optics) and through precedent (the display of knowledge of the past), Paca was attempting to naturalize the existing social hierarchy and his position in it. By embedding that which was not natural (his wealth and social position) in that which appeared natural (the garden and the principles it represented), Paca was creating not just an attractive landscape, but an ideology."

As she explains, by utilizing a landscape myth—an "objectified, idealized vision of nature" (1994:136)—that masked the profit-making process on which Paca's wealth was based, his exploitation of human labor appeared natural, hence legitimate. Kryder-Reid cogently argues the process whereby ornamental gardens misrepresented the reality of class relations that characterized Annapolis, and she links horticultural practice and garden design to eighteenth-century views of luxury, including a hierarchical view of those who had the "right" to possess luxuriant landscapes (Kryder-Reid 1991, 1994).

That formal gardens were luxurious creations—domains of earthly delight—is not at issue. Contemporary texts indicate that eighteenth-century folk took pleasure in the sensuous qualities gardens embodied: silken petals, verdant turf, perfumed, wholesome air, contrasts between sunshine and shadow, even shimmering, whispering ponds where goldfish lurked. That these pleasures were embedded in nature is also not at issue. Neither is the question of whether or not the wealthy believed they had the right to possess a luxuriant landscape whereas those of the lower classes did not. What is critical is the extent to which gardens were convincing metaphors that effectively enhanced social solidarity among the various social sectors of the community. Did they mask the reality of class relations? Or were they effective symbols of status and power precisely because people did know how much skill, effort, control, and slave labor went into their maintenance? Much rests on these questions, so critical to understanding resistance and social interaction among all members of society.

The most clear-cut evidence that ordinary people understood the symbolism of ornamental landscapes comes from the seventeenth-century South African estate of Vergelegen, excavated by Ann Markell. Markell (1992, 1995) recounts the protest of Dutch settlers against the governor and how they sought his removal. As their resistance came to a successful end, the settlers exhibited their new power in a particularly forceful way. They trampled, tore at, and destroyed both the mansion and its ornate garden (figure 0.1). One could say they ripped the symbols of their enemy's power from the face of the land. As desecrated land, the symbolic message of house *and* garden was reversed. Yet the governor's removal also reveals that the rebels knew full well the garden's symbolic representation of power and status. It was never masked. The point to be made is that gardens were part of eighteenth-century discourse, symbolically charged, and, like any symbol, gardens were capable of yielding multiple or changing meaning, capable of discovery or unmasking. Colonial landscapes, including formal gardens, were mutable, and because some held special roles in myth and history—and even today require special care-takers—they have multifaceted meaning that a purely functional or technological analysis cannot reveal.

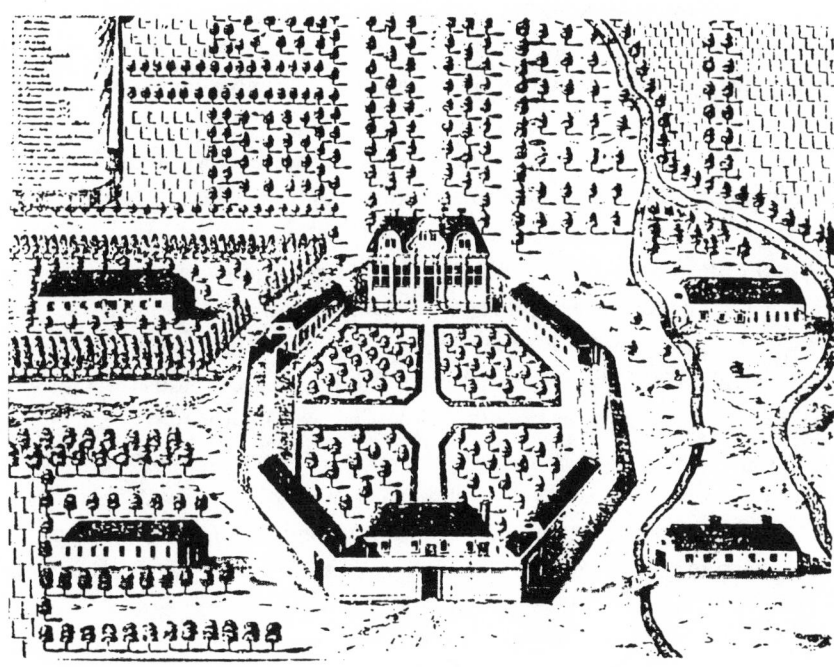

Figure 0.1. The Vergelegen estate in South Africa (Brink 1992). Reprinted with the permission of Yvonne Brink.

The eighteenth century was an era when gardens were conflated with mansions, with family, with individual wealth, status, and reputation. They became the measure of colonial gentlemen with social and political aspirations worldwide. Hence not only did a gentleman have to have a garden, but elitist history dictates that archaeologists today have to find it if they work on a site whose owner was heroic. There are serious questions that attend these studies; the excavation of an eighteenth-century landscape requires going through and/or stripping away later ones. It is costly to do so because of the record-keeping involved. Gardens below plow zones are not found on every site; in many they reside below complex stratigraphic layers associated with the landscaped grounds of subsequent families (e.g., Morven, Cliveden, Belmont; see Yentsch and Kratzer 1994, or chapter 2, this volume; see also De Cunzo et al., chapter 6, this volume).

Dennis Pogue and his predecessors have had to tackle this problem too. Pogue's study of Mount Vernon (chapter 4) is an excellent example of the trials, tribulations, and success such work encounters. He enables us to see the activities at Mount Vernon that created first one stylish landscape (ca. 1760) and then another (ca. 1785) when the former passed from grace. George Washington formed the latter from more naturalistic elements; he separated the dependencies and work areas, isolating them from constant view; he added groves of trees and a serpentine drive. Washington destroyed the old order—what some considered the permanence of geometry—and imposed the new with its variety and irregularity. This made the land responsive to the times in its formal areas and informal spaces—near the house, but down the slope and in field and orchard too.

Pogue discusses these layers of meaning in the Mount Vernon landscape in a matter-of-fact way, concentrating on its patterning and leaving its symbolism in the background. Washington's plantation landscape made a vivid impression on Andrew Jackson in 1815. In his discussion of Rachel's Garden at Jackson's Hermitage (chapter 5), Larry McKee makes meaning focal by considering the intentions of the Jackson family and situating them in their political sphere before assessing how they saw their land and what they did to its garden space.

McKee's chapter illustrates the process whereby landscapes become highly charged with symbolic meaning. His emphasis on intention and perception—the ideational aspects of culture—derives from the work of James Deetz (1990:1), who writes of landscape as the connective tissue binding houses to communities. The cultural landscape not only brings harmonious order to a natural pattern that otherwise appears chaotic and disorderly to individuals within any given culture; it also positions people in the society and in such a way that others can read the clues and discern social roles, hierarchical positions, or symbolic associations. By making changes, large and small, people can create garden areas for reverie and contemplation—as Jackson sought to do—or ones that also serve as power statements emphasizing wealth and social distinctions (e.g., Leone et al. 1989). During a lifetime of successful, upward mobility in social, economic, or political spheres, the landscape surrounding a home is often changed to accommodate the aspirations and intentions of its linked household.

Andrew Jackson's household was complex and extended—an attribute associated with many elite and formal "power gardens"—from the time he first obtained the Hermitage lands. Yet Jackson did not choose his "unpretentious plot" because of topographic features that could embellish a formal surround for a status-marking mansion. McKee believes the present garden was originally designed as a very large kitchen garden to provide produce for the growing household; its simplicity gave it a visual affinity with the yards of other prosperous farmers' homes. It was perceived as Rachel's Garden from its first decade onward, but when Andrew Jackson placed his wife's grave in it, the garden assumed sacred symbolism as a memorial. This association grew as other members of the family, including Andrew Jackson, were buried within.

This is a set of circumstances that could arise at any plantation or farm; it makes one realize that the small, shady family burial plots seen throughout the South sitting in fields close to old farmhouses were once vitally as well as visually connected to the houses from which they are now estranged. But what happened at many farms and plantations—in direct opposition to what took place at Rachel's Garden—was a disintegration of the prior landscape, a contraction of their symbolic ceremonial space into ever narrower confines as trees died, weedy plants intruded onto garden paths, and men turned to machine-driven agriculture. The process was accretionary; gradually, the practical or natural tugged away at the order of the former landscape. Gradually, the division between the living and the dead became more abrupt as the intervening garden space—the connective tissue—condensed. Few landowners could afford restoration or revitalization; fewer still considered it an option when the land changed hands. Rachel's Garden could as easily have shrunk to just the burial plot had her husband not been a politically important man and a national hero.

In Rachel's Garden, although the garden fell into disrepair for a time, the state of affairs was different from those that governed many others. However, the process whereby society recreated the landscape was accretionary *across* the land. By small steps, the connective ties between family plots, their garden space, and family eroded at many country homes. By small steps, though always with the stated objective of maintaining an "unchanging" landscape, the Ladies' Hermitage Association altered Rachel's Garden. While the symbolic meaning of the family plots decreased as the sacred space grew smaller, that of Rachel's Garden was maintained and its significance enhanced.

The changes wrought were stylistic and almost imperceptible in the overall scheme of things: small enlargements, consistent fencing, fewer practical fruit and vegetable plants, more rigidly edged paths (figure 0.2). Over a span of one hundred years, the garden was gradually formalized and changed to the point where neither Andrew Jackson nor his wife might have recognized it as theirs. Today, it is a rich, dense garden because it possesses so many layers of meaning. While the staff at the Hermitage seeks to restore it to an earlier time and to reinsert some of the ordinary people who never became national heroes into its confines, McKee strives to reconstruct the different phases in its past—to write a narrative of its symbolic history based on old paths and former fences. The chapter illustrates that symbolic meaning must be read by pairing the prouder elements of the landscape with elements as humble as broken bricks. This is, in part, because "the small mirrors the large" in cosmography or world view (Tuan 1977:100).

Figure 0.2. The changing face of Rachel's Garden at the Hermitage, where a more recent, neatly laid path of brick lies above the older one. Photograph by Larry McKee. Courtesy of the Ladies' Hermitage Association.

GARDENS THAT ENCAPSULATE WORLD VIEWS

Even as Rachel Jackson was planting her garden to obtain food for her family, George Rapp was designing a two-acre garden to explicitly express a radical social philosophy (De Cunzo et al., chapter 6). It reincarnated elements of Rapp's German homeland and established a mythic space for worship inside the town of Economy. The garden, as De Cunzo et al. note, was extraordinary. It drew on classical and medieval spatial concepts of a universe divided into four quarters (Tuan 1977:95–96). Each quarter differed; one was a vineyard, another an orchard. Rapp placed the ornamental flower garden outside his back door, and beyond the central pond and fountain he established a wilderness section. Careful research at the site enabled archaeologists to supplement surviving descriptions of the garden, historical plant lists, and limited pictorial evidence with very precise information on the location, configuration, and plan of specific garden features and plants, information that is essential in restoration.

But the more provocative aspect of the work done by De Cunzo and her colleagues is their analysis of the garden as a material metaphor of the utopian world view that framed community life. They show how the garden, as a worldly, earthly paradise, expressed the spiritual aspects of Harmonist society and discuss the way in which it exhibited the otherworldliness so integral in grand cosmic schemes. Biblical imagery provided inspiration for the design of water features, for the vineyard, and for the choice of trees and plants. Rapp also drew on a second source: traditional styles in secular German gardens. One could say that the sacred and the secular, the past and the future, were merged within the garden's confines, and that its visionary associations were well recognized by members of the Harmonist congregation, who gathered to sing, to celebrate, and to worship within Rapp's garden.[6] Because the garden was resonant with meaning, it renewed and gave potency to George Rapp's vision.

By showing how archaeological research integrates with a broad-based interdisciplinary approach, De Cunzo et al. lay the framework for further study at Old Economy Village and at other utopian communities. Kryder-Reid also lays a framework for future landscape scholars (chapter 11). Yet what she considers is an interrupted, autocratic pastoral vision, its transformation into a working religious landscape, and its subsequent evolution. This is a complex process. That the Annapolis landscape would be transformed when the Redemptorist Fathers purchased the Carroll estate and turned its lands from city villa to religious retreat was inevitable. Kryder-Reid alludes to this when she writes that "the study of landscape strikes at the core of how we make sense of the world." Join this to Emerson's belief that "we are symbols and inhabit symbols" (Emerson [1844] 1934:155), and the inevitability of change becomes apparent. The Redemptorists' vision of the world, imbued with Catholicism and based on vows of poverty, chastity, and obedience, was antithetical to that of the estate's prior owners. To have lived on the luxuriant estate and given their labor to the land's sustenance with the goal of creating an unchanging landscape—as the Ladies' Hermitage Association and the Mount Vernon Ladies' Association sought—would have turned the grounds into a memorial to the Carroll family rather than one dedicated to God.

Kryder-Reid suggests that it was the rituals embedded within the day-to-day communality of Redemptorist life that permitted the congregation to rework its physical surroundings gradually, if not inadvertently, without creating cognitive dissonance. The Redemptorists mediated the changes in social space in such a way that change could be wrought gradually. House walls were removed; arbors, vineyards, and an immense wine cellar were added; barns, outbuildings, religious statuary, and productive field crops pierced the land in unexpected places—wherever a need was perceived. Gone was the display; in its stead was a working farm. Eventually the terraced parterres were planted with graves. The Redemptorists simply viewed the land differently and made sense of it in other ways than those that characterized the world view of the prior owners. These religious men remade the land as they lived upon it, distanced from the secular world by their vows, their communal lifestyle, and the high walls of the old Carroll garden.

Yet as they lived upon the estate, the town of Annapolis changed, and with its growth, the Catholic inhabitants' need for the resources of their Church grew. In response, the

Redemptorists became more involved with the outside community. This too left an imprint on the physical configuration of their estate, introducing a worldliness by the twentieth century that the older, private order had eschewed in prior years. Kryder-Reid shows how a consequent beautification of the grounds and improvements around the house reflected the evolving focus of the Redemptorists.

Her point throughout is simply that the relation between societies and their space is recursive, endowed with the same ability that ritual symbolic action possesses: the ability to act upon and construct the social identities of individuals and, in so doing, to expand and reshape the cultural self or alter a person's perceptions of the way the world is built. In other words, landscape is a potent, energizing material force in the creation of cultural identity, and it is the archaeologist's task to delineate the ways in which it acts upon a culture even as people seek to shape it for themselves in individual ways. This theme is present to varying degrees in each of the chapters in this volume; it is given a different twist in Julia King's study of Maryland ruins (chapter 12).

LIVING WITH RUINS

King's chapter is a companion to another article on rural landscapes in southern Maryland (King 1994) that looks at land use and the ways in which the land reflected the organization of rural society. It is an apt illustration of Peter Schmidt's observation that landscape is "a series of images in which history is held" (quoted in Yentsch 1988:5). King's chapter suggests a series of questions akin to those that appeared when I studied the mythology associated with old houses (Yentsch 1988). To my mind, it is a more thought-provoking topic, for the questions it raises are truly fascinating, touching on gender responsibilities in the society and family obligations throughout successive generations. If houses are family histories writ small, then rural landscapes and the maintenance of ruins within them are family history writ large. When state institutions or religious buildings enter the scene, ruins then become mythical expressions of local and regional histories.

This occurs because ruins are mnemonic: they call to mind past events and individuals long gone. They collapse the generations between ancestors or the original settlers of a town and reinsert these old folk into the ethnographic present. Thus, as King shows, eighteenth-century men perceived ruins as sacred entities that evoked melancholy pleasures and that bridged time. Homes and lands gained stature through the association.

King has located three landscape ruins within southern Maryland, yet she has not gone searching for them. This situation suggests that far more exist and that they are taken-for-granted entities that have escaped archaeological notice because of the values accorded ruins in today's world. There is, in Firth's words, a disjunction. Why have ruins not been studied more by historical archaeologists? Does the scientific search for objective reality make it hard to grapple with the complexity of mythic history? A small sortie reveals that there were tabby ruins in Georgia believed to be the remnants of Spanish missions until archaeologists revised history by attributing a nineteenth-century origin to tabby as a construction material and by showing the fragile wattle-and-daub material that the Spanish really used (Thomas 1988:7–10). Yet tabby was used in the early eighteenth century too. So what is myth, what is reality, and why does oral lore cling so closely to crumbling walls?

There are ruins in the Caribbean. St. Pierre was deliberately left as a memorial to the dead after a volcano destroyed the whole town. Others are merely abandoned forts and plantations; some, like the citadel in Haiti, are immense (Brown n.d.). If we want to stay in the continental United States, there are inadvertent ruins in the landscapes of many towns and villages to consider too. There are ruins such as field systems, left by productive toil and labor (Hood, this volume), and commercial ones such as Savannah's Round House, inhabited by ghostly trains. Each and every one bespeaks the past and each can be read to discover more.

Looking at the modern world reveals the great variety of meanings attached to the land and the pan-human responses these draw. If this volume has a single, unifying theme, it is that we inhabit social spaces where people walked before and that they left their mark upon the land in reverent and sacrilegious ways. The land is scarred by violence, by carelessness, by greed, and catastrophe, but it also exhibits touches of love, stewardship, and whimsy, and it documents family life. It is a common ground where the interests of scholars and everyday people meet and merge. Not all care to study class relationships, religious belief systems, or social structure. Some simply want to read the land to see what went before, for among the pleasures of life they include these: that gardens are spaces of earthly delight and that landscapes reconnect time.

These essays indicate that one way of making historical archaeology relevant to a wider audience than one could otherwise hope to reach—a way to set aside the narrow special interests the field now endorses—is to expand and extend the work begun here. With their focus on meaning, the chapters that follow are indicative of the insight, the scholarly rigor, and the varieties of interpretive techniques that are being brought to bear upon landscape archaeology by a new generation trained in the 1980s. They clearly show two things: Landscape studies stretch the mind and bring us closer to an integrated anthropological history than we have been before. By paying close attention to place, they also disclose aspects of social interaction as varied as the gardens people create.

NOTES

1. For example, Crumley and Marquardt 1987; Dimbleby 1985; Ford 1979; Holloway and Bryant 1987; Pearsall 1989; Piperno 1988.
2. Each month sees another major publishing firm launch a garden history book. A careful perusal of bookstore shelves indicates one can buy books on the history of gardens in Rome or Venice (e.g., Coffin 1991); on French, English, Chinese, and Japanese garden designs (e.g., Adams 1979); on gardens built by princes (Woodbridge 1986); and the styles preferred by African Americans (Westmacott 1992), elite colonists in Virginia (Martin 1991), and modern American men (Verey 1990). There are evocative books on desert gardens (Bowers 1993), on native plants of North America, on gardens of the Renaissance (Lazzaro 1990); compendiums of photographs, accompanied by lyrical texts, that discuss what ladies in the Gilded Age attempted in the garden (Griswold and Weller 1991); and books on how to recreate the ambience of the past (Favretti and Favretti 1990, 1991; Verey 1989).
3. There is an unclear understanding of how active women were in horticultural pursuits. A small number of colonial women were well known for their gardening expertise; they corresponded with eminent botanists, experimented with plants, and/or maintained elaborate gardens. A larger number planted herbs and vegetables to feed their families. Among the poor, some women sold their garden produce at local markets; these included slaves in North America and the Caribbean (Pulsipher 1994; Yentsch 1994).

Men viewed these activities in a variety of ways; many took the position expressed by Henry Laurens, a Charlestonian, who wrote of his wife in 1763: "That lady has a wonderful inclination and some taste for Gardening, but I am forced to check her Ardor a little now and then as I am not quite weary of her company nor satisfied with her services. If I was not to interpose I believe she wou'd soon become the Sexton's property for Gardening in this moist uncertain Climate is often injurious and sometimes destructive to our good Women" (Rogers 1984:149).

Suzanne Spencer-Wood (1995) has also done thought-provoking work on the impact of women and the domestic reform movement on aspects of nineteenth-century city landscapes such as parks and playgrounds.

4. The species of flowering plants grown in early formal gardens were restricted by climate and season (Strong 1989).

5. See, for example, the use of point perspective employed by George Mason at Gunston Hall, so insightfully analyzed by Epperson (1993).

6. A similar use of garden space is evident at Koreshan State Historic Park in Estero, Florida, where a leader of a late-nineteenth-century utopian community also designed a garden to reflect his cosmic scheme. Performances, parades, music, and song brought its members through the garden grounds. Photographs of group and family members inside its space are testimony of its significance to them while the vistas contained therein denote hierarchy within the garden as well (Yentsch 1992b).

REFERENCES

Adams, William Howard
1979   *The French Garden, 1500–1800.* George Braziller, New York.

Beaudry, Mary C.
1986   The Archaeology of Historical Land Use in Massachusetts. *Historical Archaeology* 20(2):38–46.

Bowers, Janice Emily
1993   *A Full Life in a Small Place and Other Essays from a Desert Garden.* University of Arizona Press, Tucson.

Brink, Yvonne
1992   Places of Discourse and Dialogue: A Study in the Material Culture of the Cape During the Rule of the Dutch East India Company, 1652–1795. Ph.D. diss., Department of Archaeology, University of Cape Town.

Brown, Sarah
n.d.   American Tourists in the Caribbean, 1830–1934. Work in progress.

Coffin, David R.
1991   *Gardens and Gardening in Papal Rome.* Princeton University Press, Princeton.

Crumley, Carole L., and William H. Marquardt, editors
1987   *Regional Dynamics: Burgundian Landscapes in Historical Perspective.* Academic Press, San Diego.

Deetz, James
1990   Prologue: Landscapes as Cultural Statements. In *Earth Patterns: Essays in Landscape Archaeology,* edited by William M. Kelso and Rachel Most, pp. 1–4. University Press of Virginia, Charlottesville.

Dimbleby, Geoffrey W.
1985   *The Palynology of Archaeological Sites.* Academic Press, New York.

Emerson, Ralph Waldo
1934   The Poet. 1844. In *The Essays of Ralph Waldo Emerson,* edited by Edward F. O'Day. Heritage Press, New York.

Epperson, Terrence W.
1993   Panoptic Plantations: The Garden Sights of Thomas Jefferson and George Mason. Unpublished ms. in possession of the author.

Erdrich, Louise
1985   Where I Ought To Be: A Writer's Sense of Place. *New York Times Book Review,* 28 July 1985:24.

Ernstein, Julie H.

1989   Eliciting Cultural Diversity from Eighteenth-Century Painted Landscapes of Tidewater Maryland. Paper presented at the annual meeting of the Eastern States Archaeological Federation, East Windsor, Connecticut.

Favretti, Rudy, and Joy Favretti

1990   *For Every House a Garden: A Guide to Reproducing Period Gardens.* University Press of New England, Hanover, New Hampshire.

1991   *Landscapes and Gardens for Historic Buildings: A Handbook for Reproducing and Creating Authentic Landscape Settings.* Second edition, revised. American Association for State and Local History, Nashville, Tennessee.

Fee, Jeffrey M.

1993   Idaho's Chinese Mountain Gardens. In *Hidden Heritage: Historical Archaeology of the Overseas Chinese,* edited by Priscilla Wegars, pp. 65–96. Baywood Publishing Company, Amityville, New York.

Firth, Raymond

1975   *Symbols: Public and Private.* Cornell University Press, Ithaca, New York.

Ford, Richard I.

1979   Paleoethnobotany in American Archaeology. In *Advances in Archaeological Method and Theory,* vol. 2, edited by Michael B. Schiffer, pp. 285–336. Academic Press, New York.

Foucault, Michel

1972   *The Archaeology of Knowledge.* Tavistock, London.

Griswold, Mac, and Eleanor Weller

1991   *The Golden Age of American Gardens: Proud Owners, Private Estates, 1890–1940.* H. N. Abrahms, New York.

Hall, Martin

1991   High and Low in the Townscapes of Dutch South America and South Africa: The Dialectics of Material Culture. *Social Dynamics* 17(2):41–75.

1992   Small Things and the Mobile, Conflictual Fusion of Power, Fear, and Desire. In *The Art and Mystery of Historical Archaeology: Essays in Honor of James Deetz,* edited by Anne Elizabeth Yentsch and Mary C. Beaudry, pp. 373–99. CRC Press, Boca Raton, Florida.

Harrington, Faith

1989   The Emergent Elite in Early 18th Century Portsmouth Society: The Archaeology of the Joseph Sherburne Houselot. *Historical Archaeology* 23(1):2–18.

Holloway, Richard G., and Vaughn M. Bryant Jr.

1987   New Directions of Palynology in Ethnobiology. *Journal of Ethnobiology* 6:47–65.

Hosmer, Charles B., Jr.

1985   The Colonial Revival in the Public Eye: Williamsburg and Early Garden Restoration. In *The Colonial Revival in America,* edited by Alan Axelrod, pp. 52–70. W. W. Norton and Company, New York.

Kelso, Gerald K.

1991   Interdisciplinary Research in Historic Landscape Management. *CRM Supplement* 14(6):1–11.

1993a Pollen-Record Formation Processes, Interdisciplinary Archaeology, and Land Use by Mill Workers and Managers: The Boott Mills Corporation, Lowell, Massachusetts, 1836–1942. *Historical Archaeology* 27(1):70–94.

1993b The Kirk Street Agents' House, Lowell, Massachusetts: Interdisciplinary Analysis of the Historic Landscape. *Landscape Journal* 12(2):143–55.

Kelso, Gerald K., and Mary C. Beaudry

1990   Pollen Analysis and Urban Land Use: The Environs of Scottow's Dock in 17th-, 18th-, and Early 19th-Century Boston. *Historical Archaeology* 24(1):61–81.

Kelso, Gerald K., William F. Fisher, Karl J. Reinhard, and Stephen A. Mrozowski

1989   Contextual Archaeology at the Boott Mill Boardinghouse Backlots. In Interdisciplinary Investigations of the Boott Mills, Lowell, Massachusetts. Vol. 3: The Boarding House System as a Way of Life, edited by Mary C. Beaudry and Stephen A. Mrozowski, pp. 231–78. Cultural Resource Management Study No. 21. Division of Cultural Resources, North Atlantic Regional Office, National Park Service, Boston.

Kelso, William M.

1984a *Kingsmill Plantations, 1619–1800: Archaeology of Country Life in Colonial Virginia.* Academic Press, New York.

1984b Landscape Archaeology: A Key to Virginia's Cultivated Past. In *British and American Gardens in the Eighteenth Century,* edited by Robert P. Maccubbin and Peter Martin, pp. 159–69. The Colonial Williamsburg Foundation, Williamsburg, Virginia.

Kelso, William M., and Rachel Most, editors

1990 *Earth Patterns: Essays in Landscape Archaeology.* University Press of Virginia, Charlottesville.

King, Julia A.

1994 Rural Landscape in the Mid-Nineteenth-Century Chesapeake. In *Historical Archaeology of the Chesapeake,* edited by Paul A. Shackel and Barbara J. Little, pp. 283–99. Smithsonian Institution Press, Washington, D.C.

Kryder-Reid, Elizabeth

1991 Landscape and Luxury: The Garden of Charles Carroll of Carrollton. Paper presented at the annual meeting of the Society for Historical Archaeology, Richmond, Virginia.

1994 "As Is the Gardener, So Is the Garden": The Archaeology of Landscape as Myth. In *Historical Archaeology of the Chesapeake,* edited by Paul A. Shackel and Barbara J. Little, pp. 131–48. Smithsonian Institution Press, Washington, D.C.

Kryder-Reid, Elizabeth, and D. Fairchild Ruggles, editors

1994 Site and Sight in the Garden. *Journal of Garden History* 14(1).

Lazzaro, Claudia

1990 *The Italian Renaissance Garden.* Yale University Press, New Haven.

Leach, Edmund

1990 Aryan Invasions Over Four Millennia. In *Culture Through Time: Anthropological Approaches,* edited by Emiko Ohnuki-Tierney, pp. 227–45. Stanford University Press, Stanford.

Leone, Mark P.

1984 Interpreting Ideology in Historical Archaeology: Using the Rules of Perspective in the William Paca Garden in Annapolis, Maryland. In *Ideology, Power and Prehistory,* edited by Daniel Miller and Christopher Tilley, pp. 25–36. Cambridge University Press, Cambridge.

1988 The Relationship Between Archaeological Data and the Documentary Record: 18th Century Gardens in Annapolis, Maryland. *Historical Archaeology* 22(1):29–35.

Leone, Mark P., Elizabeth Kryder-Reid, Julie H. Ernstein, and Paul A. Shackel

1989 Power Gardens of Annapolis. *Archaeology* 42(2):35–39, 74–75.

Markell, Ann

1992 Walls of Isolation: The Garden Fortress of Governor Willem Adraiaan van der Stel. Seminar paper for "Critical Views of the Material World." Centre for African Studies, University of Cape Town.

1995 The Historical Archaeology of Vergelegen, an Early Farmstead at the Cape of Good Hope. *Historical Archaeology* 29(2):10–34.

Martin, Peter

1991 *The Pleasure Gardens of Virginia: From Jamestown to Jefferson.* Princeton University Press, Princeton.

McLean, Elizabeth

1984 Town and Country Gardens in Eighteenth-Century Philadelphia. In *British and American Gardens in the Eighteenth Century,* edited by Robert P. Maccubbin and Peter Martin, pp. 136–47. The Colonial Williamsburg Foundation, Williamsburg, Virginia.

Miller, Naomi F.

1989a Bibliography of Archaeobotany at Historic Sites: Addendum. Report on file at University Museum, Museum Applied Science Center for Archaeology, University of Pennsylvania, Philadelphia.

1989b What Mean These Seeds: A Comparative Approach to Archaeological Seed Analysis. *Historical Archaeology* 23(2):50–59.

Miller, Naomi F., and Kathryn L. Gleason, editors

1994 *The Archaeology of Garden and Field.* University of Pennsylvania Press, Philadelphia.

Miller, Naomi F., and Irene Good
1988   Bibliography of Archaeobotany at Historic Sites. Report on file at University Museum, Museum Applied Science Center for Archaeology, University of Pennsylvania, Philadelphia.

Mrozowski, Stephen A.
1987   The Ethnoarchaeology of Urban Gardening. Ph.D. diss., Department of Anthropology, Brown University. University Microfilms, Ann Arbor.

Noël Hume, Audrey
1974   Archaeology and the Colonial Gardener. *Colonial Williamsburg Archaeological Series* No. 7. The Colonial Williamsburg Foundation, Williamsburg, Virginia.

Paca-Steele, Barbara, and St. Clair Wright
1987   The Mathematics of an Eighteenth-Century Wilderness Garden. *Journal of Garden History* 6(4):299–320.

Paynter, Robert, Rita Reinke, and J. Ritchie Garrison
1987   Vernacular Landscapes in Western Massachusetts. Paper presented at the annual meeting of the Society for Historical Archaeology, Savannah, Georgia.

Pearsall, Deborah M.
1989   *Paleoethnobotany: A Handbook of Procedures.* Academic Press, San Diego.

Piperno, Dolores R.
1988   *Phytolith Analysis: An Archaeological and Geological Perspective.* Academic Press, San Diego.

Praetzellis, Mary, and Adrian Praetzellis, editors
1992   Tar Flat, Rincon Hill, and the Shore of Mission Bay: Archaeological Research Design and Treatment Plan for SF-480 Terminal Separation Rebuild, vol. 2. Report prepared for California Department of Transportation. Cultural Resource Facility, Anthropological Studies Center, Sonoma State University, Rohnert Park, California.

Pulsipher, Lydia Mihelic
1994   The Landscapes and Ideational Roles of Caribbean Slave Gardens. In *The Archaeology of Garden and Field,* edited by Naomi F. Miller and Kathryn L. Gleason, pp. 202–21. University of Pennsylvania Press, Philadelphia.

Rogers, George C., Jr.
1984   Gardens and Landscapes in Eighteenth-Century South Carolina. In *British and American Gardens in the Eighteenth Century,* edited by Robert P. Maccubbin and Peter Martin, pp. 148–58. The Colonial Williamsburg Foundation, Williamsburg, Virginia.

Sanford, Douglas W.
1990   The Gardens at Germanna, Virginia. In *Earth Patterns: Essays in Landscape Archaeology,* edited by William M. Kelso and Rachel Most, pp. 43–57. University Press of Virginia, Charlottesville.

Scully, Vincent
1991   *Architecture: The Natural and the Manmade.* St. Martin's Press, New York.

Spencer-Wood, Suzanne W.
1995   Turn of the Century Women's Organizations, the Design of Urban Landscapes, and the Origin of the American Playground Movement. Paper presented at the annual meeting of the Society for Historical Archaeology, Washington, D.C.

Strong, Roy
1989   *Creating Formal Gardens.* Conran Octopus Ltd., London.

Thomas, David Hurst
1988   *St. Catherine's: An Island in Time.* Georgia History and Culture Series. Georgia Humanities Council.

Trinkley, Michael, Natalie Adams, and Debi Hacker
1992   Landscape and Garden Archaeology at Crowfield Plantation: A Preliminary Examination. Research Series No. 32. Chicora Foundation, Inc., Columbia, South Carolina.

Tuan, Yi-Fu
1977   *Space and Place: The Perspective of Experience.* University of Minnesota Press, Minneapolis.

Upton, Dell

1985   White and Black Landscapes in Eighteenth-Century Virginia. *Places* 2(2):59–72.

1990   Imagining the Early Virginia Landscape. In *Earth Patterns: Essays in Landscape Archaeology,* edited by William M. Kelso and Rachel Most, pp. 71–86. University Press of Virginia, Charlottesville.

1992   The City as Material Culture. In *The Art and Mystery of Historical Archaeology: Essays in Honor of James Deetz,* edited by Anne Elizabeth Yentsch and Mary C. Beaudry, pp. 51–74. CRC Press, Boca Raton, Florida.

Verey, Rosemary

1989   *Classic Garden Design: How to Adapt and Recreate Garden Features of the Past.* Random House, New York.

1990   *The American Man's Garden.* Bullfinch Press. Little, Brown and Company, Boston.

Westmacott, Richard

1992   *African-American Gardens and Yards in the Rural South.* University of Tennessee Press, Knoxville.

Wheaton, Thomas

1989   Drayton Hall: Archaeological Testing of the Orangery. New South Associates Technical Report No. 11, Stone Mountain, Georgia.

Wölfflin, Heinrich

1966   *Renaissance and Baroque.* 1888. Translated by Kathrin Simon, with an introduction by Peter Murray. Cornell University Press, Ithaca, New York.

Woodbridge, Kenneth

1986   *Princely Gardens: The Origins and Development of the French Formal Style.* Rizzoli, New York.

Yentsch, Anne

1988   Legends, Houses, Families, and Myths: Relationships Between Material Culture and American Ideology. In *Documentary Archaeology in the New World,* edited by Mary C. Beaudry, pp. 5–19. Cambridge University Press, Cambridge.

1990   Historic Morven: The Archaeological Reappearance of an 18th Century Princeton Garden. *Expedition* 32(2):14–23.

1992a   A Landscape Research Plan for the National Trust Property of Cliveden on Germantown Avenue in the Germantown Suburb of Philadelphia, Pennsylvania. Report submitted to Martin Jay Rosenblum, R.A., and Associates, Philadelphia, Pennsylvania. On file at Cliveden, Germantown Avenue, Germantown, Pennsylvania.

1992b   Historical Archaeology and a Holistic Interpretation Plan for the Koreshan State Historic Park, Lee County, Florida. Report submitted to Janus Research/Piper Archaeology, St. Petersburg, Florida. On file at Koreshan State Historic Park, Estero, Florida.

1994   *A Chesapeake Family and Their Slaves: A Study in Historical Archaeology.* Cambridge University Press, Cambridge.

Yentsch, Anne E., and Judson M. Kratzer

1991   An Archaeological Strategy for the Recovery of the 18th-Century Gardens at Belmont in Fairmount Park, Philadelphia. Prepared for Martin Jay Rosenblum, R.A., and Associates, Philadelphia, Pennsylvania.

1994   Techniques for Excavating and Analyzing Buried Eighteenth-Century Garden Landscapes. In *The Archaeology of Garden and Field,* edited by Naomi F. Miller and Kathryn L. Gleason, pp. 168–201. University of Pennsylvania Press, Philadelphia.

Yentsch, Anne, Naomi F. Miller, Barbara Paca, and Dolores Piperno

1987   Archaeologically Defining the Earlier Garden Landscapes at Morven: Preliminary Results. *Northeast Historical Archaeology* 16:1–29.

PART I

LANDSCAPE BIOGRAPHIES

1

Why Gardens?

Mary C. Beaudry

As America moves toward the close of the twentieth century, its citizens face the threat of a nation increasingly urbanized, suburbanized, built up, condoed, and paved over. Hence there is little to wonder at in the recent surge of interest in landscape preservation and landscape archaeology. Preservationists are concerned both with protecting green spaces against the incursions of what seems an inexorable onslaught of ill-conceived development (for example, through the insistence on carving the countryside into subdivisions of half-acre tracts rather than consideration of cluster housing in development planning) and with recovering and reconstituting past landscapes. Earlier landscapes evoke a shared sense of place and of national identity by recalling America as it was before the "pavement revolution" and by reminding us that our ancestors gained control over what was to them a wilderness. Our national mythology lauds forebears who tamed nature (cf. Yentsch 1988) and who brought the land under cultivation; our ancestors' legacy to us certainly includes buildings, artifacts, inventions, a form of government, traditions, and beliefs, but it also includes the land and the way in which our predecessors shaped it. Landscape as cultural artifact—the cultural landscape—is a vital link with the past as well as an important subject of study for a variety of disciplines that fall loosely under the rubric of American studies. Gardens, especially formal pleasure gardens, are a form of past cultural landscape that has increasingly come under the microscopic scrutiny of archaeological investigation.

There are several reasons for the vigorous interest in garden excavations. First and foremost is a recognition that saving historical houses is not enough. Early incarnations of the preservation movement naturally focused on the domiciles of famous Americans or on homes and other structures of particular architectural merit or age, but the success of the movement gradually lessened the urgency of preserving the buildings in and of themselves. In the past decades, preservationists have slowly turned their attention to attempting to recapture and recreate past settings in their entirety—witness the growth in popularity of so-called living history museums such as Plimoth Plantation, Old Sturbridge Village, and so forth. Such interpretive efforts bring with them a need for accuracy in reconstruction that extends beyond houses and their furnishings. Historic houses may often be flanked by outbuildings and enclosed by walls or fences, but in all cases they are situated in a culturally ordered landscape of yard and garden, field and forest.

Initial efforts at reconstructing historical landscapes and gardens (for example, Colonial Williamsburg in the 1930s and 1940s) were based solely on documentary research. The results may have been aesthetically pleasing, but often they were intellectually unsatisfactory, for historical records tend to be spotty, incomplete, vague, and subject to multiple interpretations. Until recently, much the same could be said of archaeological attempts to reconstruct landscape on anything other than a regional scale. Scientific and technological innovations of the late twentieth century have changed all this, though; nowadays, the battery of techniques available to archaeologists aiming to recover data on past landscapes is impressive indeed. Palynology, phytolith and soils analysis, ethnobotany, tree coring, geophysical prospecting and remote sensing of various sorts, and even the study of root casts have been added to the traditional techniques of meticulous excavation, recording, stratigraphic interpretation, and artifact analysis, making landscape archaeology a highly sophisticated and accurate method of learning about past landscapes and gardens. The truth is that archaeology is the *only* means at hand for recovering precise information about the earlier configuration and content of landscapes and former gardens; our need to recover the human "feel" of past landscapes has indeed been tempered by our twentieth-century need for accuracy and faith in science.

More and more, researchers are interested in how people in the past made the landscape—intentionally or otherwise—and in how people made active use of the landscape at both conscious and unconscious levels. What's more, landscape archaeology is increasingly a rubric for the study not just of gardens and formal landscapes but of land use over time through a broad, intensive use of sources in a multidisciplinary and fully ethnographic enterprise. The empiricism requisite for landscape studies is not rooted in the positivism of the New Archaeology of the 1960s and 1970s; rather, it follows a trend Colin Renfrew has referred to as "cognitive processual" (Renfrew 1989). Such an approach blends concern for scientific method and the search for generalizations about the past with attention to the singular, the everyday, and even the idiosyncratic uses of and attitudes toward past landscapes.

Archaeology is more interpretation than discovery, however (cf. Binford 1988:19–20), and historical archaeologists bring to their interpretation of past landscapes and gardens many points of view; the field of landscape archaeology is thus rich and varied. While most agree that delineating the form of earlier landscapes, especially of gardens (the majority of attention to date has been on eighteenth-century formal gardens; see for example Kelso 1984; Leone 1984, 1987, 1988; Yentsch et al. 1987) is critical, archaeologists' differing focuses of analysis—on the botanical, symbolic, or ideological content of a garden—are reflective of the manifold functions the cultural landscape had in the past. Gardens were places of beauty and repose, and people made gardens as much for pleasure as for sustenance and perhaps profit. Once a garden existed, however, it took on a symbolic role that may or may not have been what its owner intended; the same is true in a broader sense of the human-altered landscape.

Archaeologists are working with other scholars to elucidate the past meaning as well as past form of historical landscapes and gardens, but at the same time they are playing a part in creating a new symbolic import for historical gardens. More and more, reconstruction of historical gardens mediates between our reliance on technology and our suspicion and distrust of it; garden archaeology combines the precision of science with recovery of a past we need to know as orderly, peaceful, and full of the natural beauty we associate with a preindustrial age. Landscape archaeology, blending science and humanism, contributes to our self-image as a nation carved from the wilderness while constructing for us a past ideally suited for the late twentieth century.

REFERENCES

Binford, Lewis R.
1988   *In Pursuit of the Past: Decoding the Archaeological Record.* Thames and Hudson, London.
Kelso, William M.
1984   Landscape Archaeology: A Key to Virginia's Cultivated Past. In *British and American Gardens in the Eighteenth Century,* edited by Robert P. Maccubbin and Peter Martin, pp. 159–69. The Colonial Williamsburg Foundation, Williamsburg, Virginia.
Leone, Mark P.
1984   Interpreting Ideology in Historical Archaeology: Using the Rules of Perspective in the William Paca Garden in Annapolis, Maryland. In *Ideology, Power and Prehistory,* edited by Daniel Miller and Christopher Tilley, pp. 25–36. Cambridge University Press, Cambridge.
1987   Rule by Ostentation: The Relationship Between Space and Sight in Eighteenth-Century American Landscape Architecture in the Chesapeake Region of Maryland. In *Method and Theory for Activity Area Research: An Ethnoarchaeological Approach,* edited by Susan Kent, pp. 604–33. Columbia University Press, New York.
1988   The Relationship Between Archaeological Data and the Documentary Record: 18th Century Gardens in Annapolis, Maryland. *Historical Archaeology* 22(1):29–35.
Renfrew, Colin
1989   "Problems in Establishing an Archaeology of the Mind." Lecture presented for the Context and Human Society Series, Boston University, 30 March 1989.
Yentsch, Anne E.
1988   Legends, Houses, Families, and Myths: Relationships Between Material Culture and American Ideology. In *Documentary Archaeology in the New World,* edited by Mary C. Beaudry, pp. 5–19. Cambridge University Press, Cambridge.
Yentsch, Anne E., Naomi F. Miller, Barbara Paca, and Dolores Piperno
1987   Archaeologically Defining the Earlier Garden Landscapes at Morven: Preliminary Results. *Northeast Historical Archaeology* 16:1–29.

2

Method in Landscape Archaeology: Research Strategies in a Historic New Jersey Garden

Karen Bescherer Metheny, Judson Kratzer, Anne Elizabeth Yentsch, and Conrad M. Goodwin

Although the landscape has always been a domain of archaeological research, landscape archaeology is only a nascent subfield within North American historical archaeology; its methods and strategies are still in a developmental phase. A potentially valuable case study, then, is the landscape archaeology project at Morven in Princeton, New Jersey, where a wide range of methodological and research strategies was tested and employed over three field seasons. Archaeologists used this assemblage of analytical tools and field techniques to identify and distinguish between the often complex and sometimes poorly visible stratigraphic remains of seven garden surfaces. Initial research strategies were often modified, occasionally discarded, and still others adapted as knowledge of the site and its earlier landscapes increased. Key elements of the research program included the use of a contextual framework of analysis, the development of an emic grid, and the application of an interactive, interdisciplinary approach to the study of the Morven landscape. This chapter evaluates the effectiveness of these strategies within the context of the Morven project and for the practice of landscape archaeology generally.

Morven was the eighteenth-century estate of Richard Stockton, a signer of the Declaration of Independence. The original dwelling, built in the 1750s, was gradually transformed over time into the larger, Georgian-style mansion that visitors see today (figure 2.1). It is the association with a Signer that gives this historic New Jersey home much of its symbolic importance. However, Morven was home to several generations of Stocktons, many of whom achieved a level of national, state, and local importance. In addition, the house served as New Jersey's gubernatorial residence from 1953 to 1981. Thus, Morven's significance extends

Figure 2.1. A view of Morven, Princeton, New Jersey. Photograph by Joseph Crilley. New Jersey State Museum.

well beyond the eighteenth century and the local Princeton community. In recognition of this, Morven was designated a National Historic Landmark in 1971 and is listed on both the National and New Jersey Registers of Historic Places.

This historic property was the subject of intensive documentary, architectural, and archaeological research between 1987 and 1989 in preparation for its conversion to a museum of cultural history (Albee 1990; Greiff 1989a, 1989b; Miller and Yentsch 1988; Miller et al. 1990; Yentsch 1990; Yentsch, Bescherer, and Miller 1989; Yentsch, Kratzer, and Bescherer 1990; Yentsch et al. 1987).[1] A primary goal of the archaeological investigation was the recovery of physical evidence from the eighteenth-century landscape and the extensive ornamental gardens that once surrounded the home of Richard and Annis Stockton (ca. 1760–89). However, subsequent households also left their imprints on the Morven landscape. The above-ground features of the eighteenth-century gardens, heavily damaged during the American Revolution, were altered beyond recognition by later generations of Stocktons; further modifications were made by twentieth-century tenants and, after 1953, by the State of New Jersey. In all, seven households manipulated the land surface and plantings within the present five-acre plot; this area constitutes the core of the original three-hundred-acre estate and is the only portion that has remained intact over the years. The character of the property reflects this gradual transformation: some original elements of house and yard have been retained to the present day while others have been obscured or hidden, thus blending past with present.

Learning to read the Morven landscape presented several problems. Key methodological questions arose almost immediately. The formulation of an effective research strategy was a primary concern: what were the most effective means of recovering the various types of physical evidence from the earlier garden? A second concern, one that was of critical importance during the second and third field seasons, was how to distinguish between the different garden surfaces, often shallow deposits with low artifact densities and poor visibility. Foremost, perhaps, was the problem of how to cope with the scale of the landscape. An analysis of the built environment must consider the broader relationships and associations within the landscape, including those that may extend beyond the immediate environs of the garden: walkways lead somewhere, fences enclose specific areas, and terraces create visual illusions, elevate land surfaces, and divide sections of the garden. The scope of our research had to encompass large areas to properly address the cultural landscape at Morven. Not only was it necessary to incorporate within a framework of study those garden features within the existing five-acre plot, but also we needed to visualize, if possible, those areas of the original eighteenth-century estate that are no longer part of the present property in order to understand the overall relationships embedded within the eighteenth-century landscape.

THE GARDEN OF RECORD

Documentary evidence for the eighteenth-century garden at Morven is sparse and is generally inconclusive as to both its form and content (Greiff 1989a; 1989b). The poetry and writings of Annis Boudinot Stockton, Morven's first mistress, contain many references to the garden landscape and, as such, constitute the primary source of information on the early garden. The passages are often suggestive, offering glimpses of planting beds, trees, and garden features, so that one begins to sense how the property was shaped by its owners. Letters from abroad, written ca. 1766–67, describe Richard Stockton's efforts to collect bulbs and cuttings for Annis's "sweet little flower-garden." For her shell grotto, planned as a museum for ancient relics, he also collected several souvenirs, including "a piece of Roman brick which [he] knocked off the top of Dover Castle, . . . a piece [of wood] from the king's coronation chair," and other curiosities (Greiff 1989b:27–29). Yet, for all their interest, these passages lack the concrete details that might usefully guide archaeological testing.

The same letters make tantalizing reference to Twickenham, the estate of Alexander Pope. Stockton wrote of his intention to visit there in the company of a draftsman whom he would hire to record the design of the garden landscape. This reference has frequently been cited as evidence that Twickenham served as the model for Morven's first garden and is the basis for a family tradition that has been successfully perpetuated through the years (Bill 1954; Bill et al. 1978; Kornwolf 1984; Lockwood 1931; Maccubbin and Martin 1984).

Much of Morven's early history is based on myth and family tradition, and it is difficult at times to separate fact from fiction. Indeed, throughout this project we were confronted with the conflicting evidence of the written record, oral tradition, and below-ground remains. In this instance, there was no actual evidence that Stockton made the journey to Twickenham, and, in any case, by that time Pope's famous garden no longer existed. According to landscape historian Peter Martin, Pope's garden was "altered . . . beyond recognition" within a year of his death in 1744, some twenty years before Stockton's trip abroad (Martin 1984:61). It is also known that the gardens at Morven were well established before Stockton made the trip to England. Despite a long-standing tradition, then, the facts did not support the use of Pope's Twickenham as a model for investigating the Morven landscape.

A second document did provide some insight into the configuration of the early garden. A French military map of Princeton, drawn during the Revolutionary War, shows the Morven landscape in some detail (figure 2.2). The 1781 Berthier map depicts the block of the main house, centrally placed within the lot, surrounded by what appear to be walkways, roads, and other less recognizable landscape features. The most interesting and intriguing features of the map, from our perspective, were the enclosed areas shown to the north of the house (below the structure, figure 2.2). Four major divisions have been drawn: two squares and two ells. These features may represent parterres and strongly suggest that the configuration of the garden was based on the dimensions of the house. Other lines on the map suggest that the garden was terraced, a common practice in other formal gardens of the period. While it has been argued that such maps are quite accurate in detail, the actual size of the Berthier map made its use in planning an archaeological investigation problematic: the drawing of the Stockton residence and gardens is less than half an inch in size.

While the written record provided few substantive details on the configuration and content of the eighteenth-century garden, certain documents suggested that the garden's

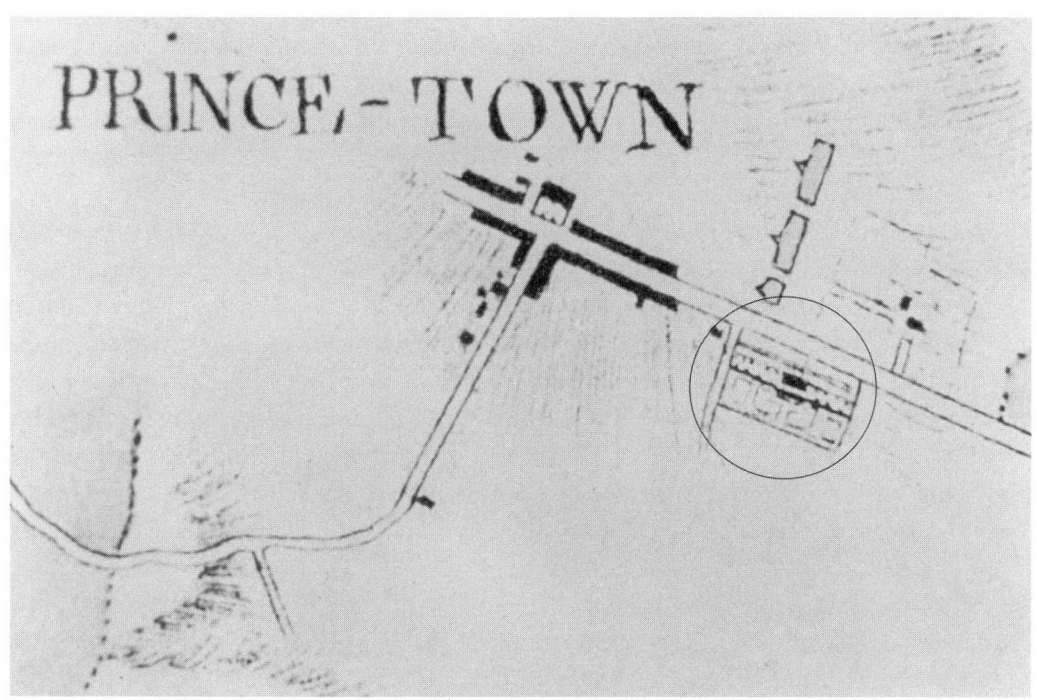

Figure 2.2. Detail of a 1781 military map of Princeton, drawn by Louis-Alexandre Berthier, showing the Stockton estate at Morven. Note the two square- and ell-shaped areas below the house (north) that may represent parterres, as well as a series of lines that suggest the garden at Morven was terraced. Courtesy of Princeton University Libraries. Photograph by Tony Masso for the New Jersey State Museum.

below-ground visibility might have been impaired, damaged, or even destroyed over the years. Contemporary sources indicated that the Stockton property suffered greatly under British occupation during the Revolutionary War. In 1783, Charles Thomson, then secretary to the Continental Congress, wrote, "There have been gardens & walks but they are all a waste & only traces of them left" (Sheridan and Murrin 1985:17). The garden's continued use and alteration through subsequent generations also suggested that it might be difficult archaeologically to trace the remains of the early garden.

CREATING A FRAMEWORK
FOR ARCHAEOLOGICAL TESTING

Beginning in the summer of 1987, a variety of exploratory methods was used to test the potential for the study and recovery of the eighteenth-century garden landscape and to provide a point from which to begin more intensive investigations. A modern vegetation survey, a geophysical survey, and limited subsurface testing were components of this initial phase.

The vegetation survey and tree-coring program within the present garden were part of a multifaceted archaeobotanical study at Morven. Vegetation surveys have been implemented in other landscape archaeology projects (e.g., De Cunzo et al., this volume; Weber et al. 1990) and may be useful in establishing relationships between past and present landscape features and in predicting the location of non-extant garden features. The results of the Morven study are discussed in detail elsewhere (Miller and Yentsch 1988). Not only did the survey provide a context for the uncharred seed assemblages extracted during flotation (Miller 1989:51), but the identification and aging of trees was also helpful in understanding the physical and symbolic changes in the Morven landscape over time (see also Yentsch et al. 1987). One particular example illustrates how this type of survey, when combined with documentary and oral histories, may be useful in locating earlier garden features.

A characteristic of the present Morven landscape is the association of certain trees with historical events and past households. The trees appear to be old, giving some credibility to family traditions. However, once the trees were cored and assigned to specific generations of the Stockton family, it was clear that many of the "old" trees attributed to Richard Stockton's period were actually planted in the late nineteenth to early twentieth century (table 2.1, figure 2.3). Nonetheless, one horse chestnut tree was dated to ca. two hundred years in age (Lockwood 1988:48). The early date and the alignment of the tree with the front porch of the house suggested a possible association with the Horse Chestnut Walk, an eighteenth-century landscape feature known from Stockton family tradition and nineteenth-century maps of the property (figure 2.4). Excavation units placed off the east wing of the house in 1988 revealed two walks along the same alignment (figure 2.5): the fragile remains of a fieldstone path[2] constructed in the third quarter of the eighteenth century, and, above it, a solidly constructed mid-nineteenth-century walk surfaced with white gravel and mica. Archaeology thus confirmed a relationship between a living tree and a historical landscape feature. Not only did the excavation verify the existence of the "Horse Chestnut Walk" of family lore, but it also showed the changing appearance of the walk through time.

Table 2.1
Measurements and Approximate Ages of Trees at Morven[a]

Tree Sample	Species	Dia.	Cir.	Growth Rings Counted	Core Length	Average Years /Inch	Radius	Age[b]
1	*Picea ablies* (Norway Spruce)	30"	8.0'	56	9.50"	5.90	14.5	85
2	*Liriodendron tulipifera* (Tulip Tree)	24"		45	9.50"	4.74	11.0	52
3	*Platanus acerifolia* (Sycamore)	26"		26	4.00"	6.50	11.5	75
4	*Tsuga canadensis* (Hemlock)	15"	4.3'	46	5.00"	9.20	7.0	64
5	*Robinia pseudoacacia* (Black Locust)	20"		Would not core; no estimate possible				
6	*Magnolia* (Magnolia)	20"	6.4'	62	4.25"	14.59		89
7	*Aesculus* (Horse Chestnut)	30"	8.7'	Unable to render an estimate				
8	*Pinus strobus* (White Pine)	30"	8.1'	61	9.00"	6.70	14.0	94
9	*Pinus strobus* (White Pine)	21"	6.1'	53	7.75"	6.80	9.5	65
10	*Platanus acerifolia* (Sycamore)	37"	10.4'	71	10.00"	7.10	[c]	124
11	*Quercus palustris* (Pin Oak)	28"	8.0'	60	10.00"	6.00	13.5	81
12	*Liriodendron tulipifera* (Tulip Tree)	54"	15.2'	40	8.00"	5.00	26.0	130
13	*Catalpa speciosa* (Catalpa)	36"		48	8.25"	5.80	17.0	98
14	*Acer saccharum* (Sugar Maple)	30"	9.9'	63	9.25"	6.80	14.0	95
15	*Aesculus* (Horse Chestnut)	33"		121	9.25"	13.08	15.5	202
16	*Liriodendron tulipifera* (Tulip Tree)	32"		65	8.75"	7.43	15.0	111
17	*Aesculus* (Horse Chestnut)	29"		68	5.00"	13.60	13.5	183
18	*Paulownia tomentosa* (Paulownia)	34"		24	2.75"	8.73	16.0	139
19	*Juglans regia* (English Walnut)	27"		69	9.50"	7.26	12.5	91
20	*Morus rubra* (Mulberry)	31"		62		7.75	14.5	112
21	*Picea abies* (Norway Spruce)	30"		Poor core—same as other Norways				
22	*Liriodendron tulipifera* (Tulip Tree)	30"	8.7'	51	8.70"	5.80	14.5	84
23	*Platanus acerifolia* (Sycamore)	28"	7.2'	50	9.70"	5.15	13.0	67
24	*Liriodendron tulipifera* (Tulip Tree)	29"	8.3'	22	7.30"	3.00	14.0	42
25	*Picea abies* (Norway Spruce)	29"		41	5.90"	6.00	14.0	84
26	*Tsuga canadensis* (Hemlock)	17"		26	3.70"	7.00	8.0	56

[a]Measurements of 26 trees and their approximate ages, obtained through coring (Lockwood 1988), indicate that many of the "old" trees thought to date back to the eighteenth century actually span a 150-year period; indeed, some trees are little more than 50 years old.

[b]Approximate age. Since most of these species tend to have wider rings when they are young, the age estimates may possibly be as much as ten to fifty years too high. The range of error increases with the age of the tree (Lockwood 1988:48).

[c]Core too difficult to read.

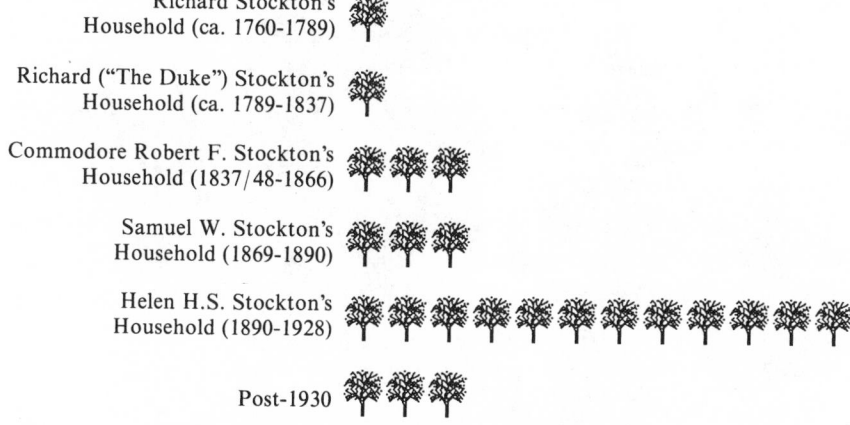

Richard Stockton's Household (ca. 1760-1789)

Richard ("The Duke") Stockton's Household (ca. 1789-1837)

Commodore Robert F. Stockton's Household (1837/48-1866)

Samuel W. Stockton's Household (1869-1890)

Helen H.S. Stockton's Household (1890-1928)

Post-1930

Figure 2.3. Twenty-three trees on the Morven property may be assigned to specific generations or households of the Stockton family using the dates obtained through coring. Courtesy of Expedition magazine.

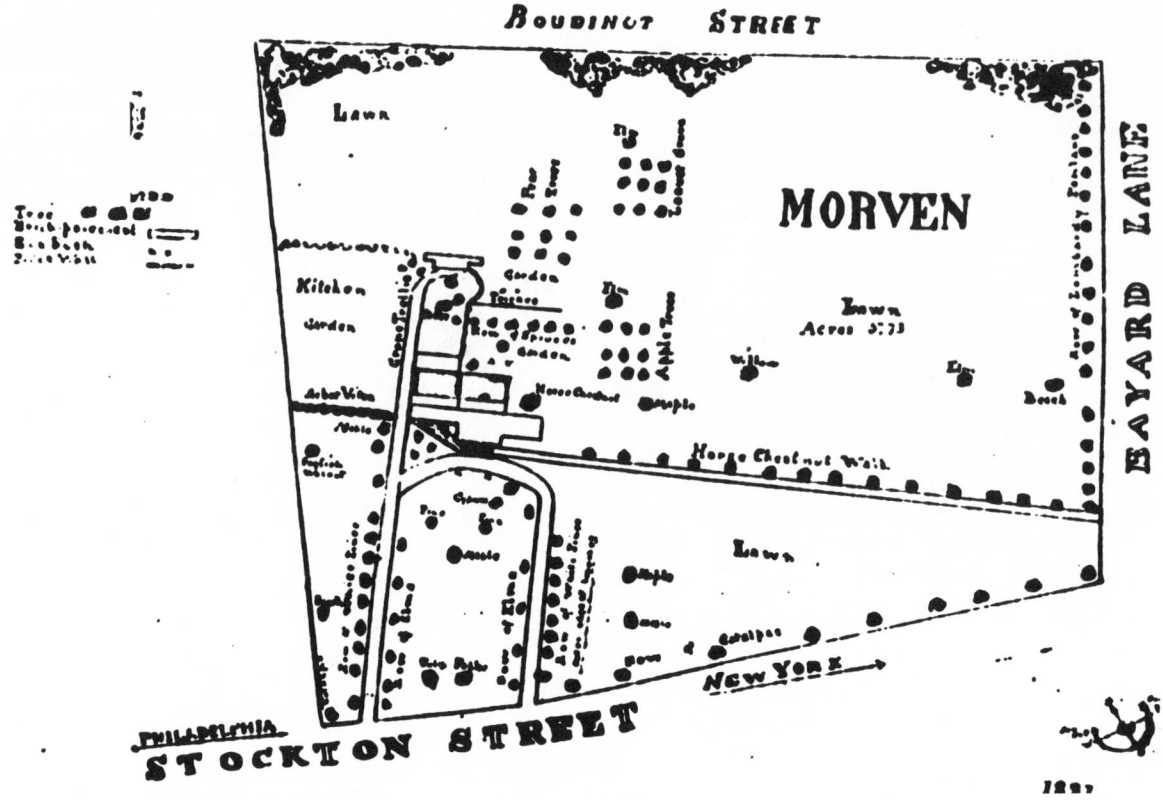

Figure 2.4. 1881 plan of Morven depicting the Horse Chestnut Walk. This representation of the garden, drawn by Helen Hamilton Shields Stockton, seems to blend elements from the pre-1881 garden with features from the later Colonial Revival garden (ca. 1891 and after). For this reason, the map's accuracy has been questioned; many believe that its basis lies in family tradition and myths about the past, not in fact. Nonetheless, the map does contain some historical landscape features, including the Horse Chestnut Walk, the existence of which was documented archaeologically in 1988. Courtesy of the Garden Club of America.

Figure 2.5. Archaeological excavations of the Horse Chestnut Walk, showing the remains of two walkways along the same alignment. The upper walk consisted of white gravel with mica inclusions; the sub-base of this walk (upper left), made of recycled cut sandstone, contained mid-nineteenth-century artifacts in its matrix. The lower walk (right), made of local fieldstone, was laid out in the third quarter of the eighteenth century. New Jersey State Museum.

Other nondestructive methods were used to explore the site's below-ground resources during this phase, specifically ground-penetrating radar and a magnetometer survey, preceded by a soil resistivity study (Bevan 1987). The results of the remote-sensing survey, which detected eight anomalies in the yard and scatters of cultural debris beneath the parking lot, were used to guide the placement of the first test units in 1987. Of the six anomalies targeted for further investigation, three were found to be modern while the origins of two others were not fully revealed until the second and third field seasons. The sixth anomaly, however, corresponded to a major eighteenth-century landscape feature, the corner of a stone terrace. This discovery in 1987 provided an initial framework for reconstructing the garden layout and guided the placement of additional excavation units.

The low number of recorded anomalies and the subsequent discovery of several large features that went undetected during the survey (including the foundation of a late-eighteenth-century or early-nineteenth-century outbuilding, 24-by-24 feet in size, with a cellar depth in excess of nine feet) illustrate the difficulties that are often encountered in remote sensing.[3] Although the resistivity study indicated average conditions for radar survey, Bevan encountered heavy electrical interference during the survey, probably from the communications antenna located at the adjacent municipal building (Bevan 1987:1–3). The clutter of modern utility lines and other buried metal objects in the project area also may have caused irregular electromagnetic readings (1987:5).

Nonetheless, the application of remote sensing techniques at Morven led to several important discoveries, including the terrace steps. The detection of this major eighteenth-century garden feature during the first season was critical to formulating archaeological research strategies in 1988 and 1989. The survey also led to the discovery in later seasons of two other buried eighteenth-century garden features. The presence of multiple features in those areas, including a large mulberry tree and a buried oil tank, made it difficult to identify the actual source of the echoes recorded in 1987, but the anomalies were found to coincide with the northwest corner of the eighteenth-century terrace and its associated features, and the remains of two garden walkways—an eighteenth-century fieldstone walk overlaid by a nineteenth-century gravel walk—along the eastern axis of the garden.

TESTING THE ARCHAEOLOGICAL RECORD

Four distinct archaeological testing strategies were implemented in 1987. Test units were placed in the vicinity of anomalies detected during the geophysical survey. Mechanically dug trenches were used to generate continuous soil profiles across the property and to reveal artificial alterations to the landscape through terracing or filling. Standard five-foot-square test units were used to sample the archaeological deposits in two ways: first, units were sited in relation to extant architectural or landscape features on both sides of the house; second, test units were placed systematically across the north yard to expose earlier yard surfaces.

Mechanical trenching produced immediate results, providing clues to the original configuration of the eighteenth-century garden that were useful in planning further excavation and research strategies. Six gradall trenches of variable length, two to three feet in depth (dug to subsoil), and five to six feet in width, were excavated during the summer of 1987 (figure 2.6). The trenches were dug to within 100 feet of the house on either side to avoid utility lines and to prevent damage to archaeological features clustered near the house.

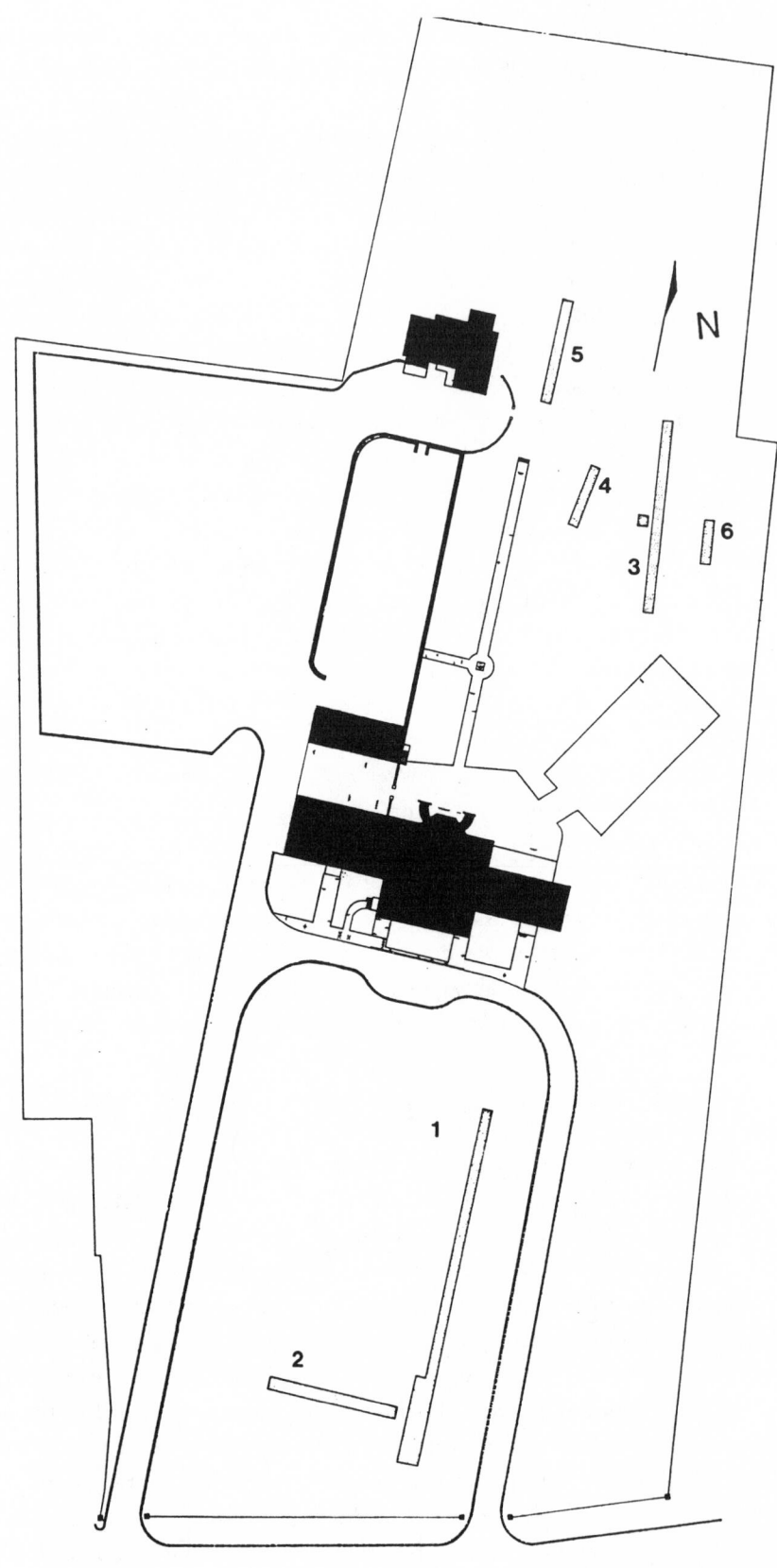

Figure 2.6. Exploratory trenches were used in 1987 to reveal buried garden features and earlier yard surfaces. After a drawing by Paula Dardaris for the New Jersey State Museum.

Two trenches, one oriented on a north-south axis, 170 feet in length, and one oriented east-west, 65 feet in length, were placed in the front yard. No garden features, buried yard surfaces, or fill episodes were located in these trenches, suggesting that the south yard had been regraded some time in the past. In the north or backyard of the house, however, a third trench, 93.5 feet in length, revealed tree holes, planting beds, and potential buried surfaces. At the site of an anomaly recorded during the remote sensing survey, approximately 180 feet from the northeast corner of the house and two to three feet below modern grade, the edge of a stone feature was exposed in the west wall of the trench. Hand-excavated units abutting the trench were used to expose the feature, a set of fieldstone steps from a buried eighteenth-century garden terrace (figure 2.7). The absence of the feature in the east wall of the trench suggested that the terrace ended here. To trace its configuration, two trenches, 17 feet and 21 feet in length, were excavated mechanically to the east and west of the main trench. The terrace fall was detected in the soil profile of the west trench, indicating its continuation across the yard. Its absence in the eastern trench, together with the additional evidence of a north-south walkway at the top of the stairs, clearly marked this location as the northeast corner of the buried garden terrace. This information was used to develop a conjectural plan of the eighteenth-century garden and its relationship to the house from which testing and excavation could proceed.

Figure 2.7. Eighteenth-century stone steps, remnants of a buried garden terrace at Morven, were initially located via mechanical trenching and then fully exposed in hand-excavated units. Photograph by Tony Masso. New Jersey State Museum.

Carefully controlled trenching proved to be the most revealing and successful exploratory strategy used at Morven. The results of other testing strategies were more problematic. As discussed above, although the remote sensing survey located a major eighteenth-century landscape feature northeast of the house, excavation units placed in the location of other recorded anomalies were less productive while other substantial garden features went undetected altogether. Hand-dug test units also produced mixed results. Test units next to the house and outbuildings revealed a complex mixture of architectural, household, and landscape features and deposits that, given their limited horizontal exposure, could not be clearly understood or related to a broader conceptualization of the eighteenth-century garden landscape. Sampling in the north yard was more successful in this respect. Eleven five-foot-square units were systematically excavated across the yard for a distance of sixty feet. This strategy was used to delineate the boundaries of a specific landscape feature discovered following the removal of a 1950s-era brick patio. The feature was tentatively identified in 1987 as an eighteenth-century fieldstone walk along the eastern axis of the garden. However, because the remaining fieldstone was often thinly dispersed, scattered, or disarticulated, it was not entirely clear (until the 1988–89 field seasons when block excavation methods were used) that this was a walk or indeed that it was a single feature, nor was its relationship to a later nineteenth-century walk along the same axis fully recognized. In each archaeological situation, the lack of contiguous excavation units hindered the recognition of interrelated features and deposits within the earlier garden landscape.

In spite of these difficulties, the exploratory phase at Morven was successful for two reasons. First and most important, the potential for the recovery of intact eighteenth-century deposits was confirmed in dramatic fashion. This was amply demonstrated not only in terms of the preservation of archaeological features and earlier garden surfaces, but also in terms of archaeobotanical remains. Second, on the basis of information recovered using these exploratory strategies, particularly trenching, it was possible to construct a hypothetical plan of the eighteenth-century garden that could be tested during the next season and used to guide future excavations.

This program also demonstrated both the effectiveness of certain techniques for exploring and sampling the landscape and the limitations of these same techniques, without some refinement in methodology, for recovering and understanding the remains of earlier landscapes. The application of systematic sampling (whether mechanical or hand-excavated) is useful in a project such as this, particularly when tracing a particular landscape feature, such as a garden walk or terrace fall, but it is most effective as a tool for tracing the configuration of a buried garden surface when used with a conceptual framework as a basis for testing. Without a more precise understanding of its dimensions, the earlier garden at Morven could not be effectively sampled within the limited time frame (and budget) of the project.

Other limitations were evident. The sampling strategies used in 1987 did not provide adequate exposure of landscape features, which often encompass large areas in their construction, daily use, and visual perspective, nor did they reveal the relationships between garden features across broad expanses. Both elements are critical to the analysis and synthesis of data; without them, the landscape remains largely enigmatic, a collection of isolated soils and buried features. The testing program revealed the stratigraphic complexity of the ar-chaeological landscape at Morven, one that was continuously modified over a 230-year pe-riod, often leaving only the faintest traces of earlier features and garden surfaces. At the same time, the testing program emphasized the weakness of a methodology that lacked some means to link these features and soils across the garden. Given the size of the project area and the complexity of the archaeological record, we needed to revise our earlier strategies and devise other more effective, cost-efficient, and time-efficient methods to investigate the property. Several methodological changes were made with these goals in mind.

METHODOLOGY IN THE GARDEN

The process of developing a landscape archaeology program at Morven was an interactive one. Through trial, error, and success, a specialized recovery plan was devised. As our knowl-edge of the garden layout developed, these strategies could be used to greater advantage. In turn, as techniques were refined, the visibility of the earlier garden increased. The inter-change of data and methodology thus enhanced our ability to reconstruct the eighteenth-century landscape at Morven. Frequent communication with other historical archaeologists and with a number of project consultants (landscape architects, garden historians, architec-tural historians, paleoethnobotanists) contributed to this interactive process.

In the second season of fieldwork, areal excavation replaced dispersed test units. We felt that this particular approach would give the greatest visibility to each garden sequence, en-compassing areas large enough to properly address both the scale of garden features and the meaning of the cultural landscape as shaped by each household. Block excavations directly adjacent to the house would provide chronological information for the architectural histori-ans, while the horizontal exposure of archaeological deposits abutting the house would re-veal the articulation between house and garden. Within the garden itself, areal excavation would expose the interrelationships between various garden elements and landscape surfaces.

This strategy was first applied in front of the west wing at Morven. This portion of the building, which may incorporate the remains of the first house within its structure, has func-tioned as a service or kitchen wing since the mid-eighteenth century. The use of horizontal excavation facilitated the recognition of three distinct archaeological landscapes across the front of the wing (figure 2.8). The eighteenth-century living surface (1754–89) included a red shale border adjacent to the house, planting holes, and a series of postholes interpreted as the remnants of a piazza along the front of the building. The second generation of the Stock-ton family (1789–1837) installed a cobblestone apron above the earlier, decorative border. Large quantities of bone and late-eighteenth- to early-nineteenth-century ceramics were recovered from a midden that gradually built up over the cobble surface, suggesting a dra-matic shift in land use from a decorative landscape to a kitchen-related work area. A sand sub-base for a brick patio was installed in the mid-nineteenth century by the third genera-tion (1837–66), marking a return to a more formal, landscaped facade. The installation of the patio resulted in the partial destruction of the cobblestone apron. The modern landscape includes boxwood plants and brick walks installed during the governors' era; many of these plantings and walks were removed at the start of excavation.

Figure 2.8. Areal excavation along the front of the west wing of Morven revealed three distinct archaeological landscapes: the mid-eighteenth-century living surface, with a decorative red shale border, planting holes, and postholes from a piazza (lower right); a late-eighteenth to early-nineteenth-century cobblestone work area (upper left); and the sand sub-base for a mid-nineteenth-century brick paving (middle). New Jersey State Museum.

Areal excavation seemed ideally suited for interpreting the complex stratigraphic sequences near the house. Before the success of this methodological approach could be measured in the garden, however, we needed to learn how to read the landscape. The focus and visibility of archaeological deposits are often poor in landscape archaeology. Garden surfaces and planting beds generally contain few artifacts (but see Bescherer et al. 1990, Brown and Samford 1990, and Edwards 1986 for discussions of how eighteenth-century gardeners used household refuse, including bone, glass, and ceramic vessels, to improve drainage within specific types of planting beds), while a fill layer, if brought from off-site, may confuse the reading of the soil because its matrix may contain artifacts that are unrelated to the site. At Morven, alterations to the landscape were accomplished primarily by filling, rather than by removal of soils,[4] or through gradual soil accumulation, thereby creating a complex stratigraphic sequence and obscuring or confusing the visibility of each garden sequence. A major concern, then, was how to recognize and define the various garden sequences across the site.

Working out from the house, we began to visualize each garden sequence as a series of horizontal planes that extended across the site and were in some way articulated with each other. Large-scale excavation facilitated the recognition of stratigraphic sequences and the relationships between landscape features along horizontal planes. By perceiving the landscape as a series of related horizons, it was possible to link soil profiles, garden features, and their

related plantings across broad expanses in culturally meaningful ways. In the eighteenth century, each horizontal plane might contain parterres, planting beds, and walkways along the
major axes of the garden, while steps along a terrace fall might link one horizontal plane to
the next. Since the use of terracing and the creation of vistas often depended on the manipulation of space and perspective, topographic information and the elevations of garden features also had to be incorporated into a reconstruction of the eighteenth-century landscape.

To sharpen the focus of the eighteenth-century garden at Morven, the depth readings
of excavated garden features and deposits were translated daily into above-sea-level measurements. Depth ranges were established for each garden sequence using dated or identified
deposits. In this way, it was possible to relate non-artifact-bearing tree stains and planting
holes to a particular landscape sequence. This strategy was very useful for comparing archaeological features separated by a great distance, for correcting the often deceptive appearance of the site's topography, for "seeing through" visual obstructions such as a building or
garden wall, and for comparing measurements taken from different datum points.

This technique is particularly useful for understanding relationships in a terraced garden. For example, a meaningful comparison between two sets of excavation units along the
conjectured terrace line in the north yard initially was hindered by the distance between the
units (100 feet) and by the presence of two garden features, a grove of trees and a high brick wall,
that obstructed the view. The excavation area to the northeast contained the terrace fall located in 1987; this included the fall line, the set of fieldstone steps, and evidence for a walkway
along the upper edge of the terrace. To the northwest (in the vicinity of an anomaly detected
in the 1987 geophysical survey), two large stone slabs were exposed approximately 1.8 feet
above an unidentified fieldstone feature. A series of fill layers separated these two features.

A comparison of above-sea-level readings for both excavation areas suggested that the
stone slabs found to the northwest (213.46 feet ASL) were on the same horizontal plane as
the top of the terrace steps and the upper terrace (213.48 feet ASL) in the northeast corner
of the garden, while the elevation of the unidentified fieldstone feature (211.67 feet ASL)
was comparable to the bottom of the terrace steps and the base of the terrace fall (211.78 feet
ASL). This suggested that one or both of the features to the northwest were elements of the
eighteenth-century terraced garden. Because of the potential association, this area of the
garden was targeted for further excavations in 1989. The unidentified fieldstone feature was
shown to be an oval pad of unknown function (its full dimensions were not ascertainable
because the feature was partially buried by the stone slabs and fill). While no datable materials were recovered, the ASL reading and the local fieldstone used in its construction identified this feature as part of the eighteenth-century garden.[5] The stone slabs, though located
on the same plane as the upper terrace, covered a portion of the lower eighteenth-century
oval and were therefore attributed to nineteenth-century landscaping undertaken after the
terrace was buried.

Other conceptual devices may help to increase the focus or visibility of earlier landscapes.
For instance, while landscape sequences are usually artifact-poor in the traditional sense, they
do contain features such as walkways, planting beds, and decorative elements. It is possible to
recognize patterning with respect to design, configuration, and composition among these
types of features, just as with more familiar artifact types. The eighteenth-century garden

walks or pavements at Morven were characteristically constructed of a reddish-purple shale, dry-laid fieldstone, or white limestone. Later walkways, installed during the mid-nineteenth century, were composed of white gravel with crushed mica inclusions. Once we were able to discern a pattern, these distinctive materials and forms were useful in tracing the various garden sequences across the yard.

The reddish-purple gravel border, for example, was encountered in several units off the front (south) of the west wing at Morven during the 1988 field season. Made of Brunswick shale, which is indigenous to the area, this border or apron was clearly artificial in origin and could be dated from ca. 1760 on the basis of artifacts recovered immediately above the deposit (molded white salt-glazed stoneware plate rims; white salt-glazed stoneware with scratch blue decoration) and from the absence of later materials in the deposit below. Once the shale was recognized as a diagnostic feature of the eighteenth-century garden landscape, it was possible to trace its use across the site through horizontal excavation and, by association, identify other features within the eighteenth-century garden that were constructed of the same material. The red shale was consistently found in units adjacent to the house, providing evidence of its use as a border around much of the perimeter of the eighteenth-century structure. Excavation units in the north yard also demonstrated its use as a walkway surfacing material in various parts of the eighteenth-century garden.

Archaeologists tend to think of small objects as diagnostic artifacts and good chronological time markers, but in landscape archaeology large-scale entities, such as garden features, serve this purpose as well. The recognition of landscaping materials as diagnostic artifacts is an important step in interpreting the landscape. The use of crushed red shale has been documented at several other gardens in the mid-Atlantic region. William Penn referred to the desirability of such a gravel in a letter dating from 1686, in which he expressed an interest in obtaining it for the gardens at Pennsbury Manor along the Delaware River: "there is a rare gravil at Philadelphia y^t is red & binds, twere well if ye walks about ye house were graveld" (letter to James Harrison, 17 November 1686). Comparable treatments with red shale or a reddish sand were recorded archaeologically at two other sites in Pennsylvania (Bescherer, Kratzer, and Goodwin 1990; Bescherer et al. 1990). These deposits date from the early to mid-nineteenth century, suggesting that this treatment may have been part of an emerging landscape tradition in the mid-Atlantic region.

Clearly, garden features are themselves culture-bearing artifacts and part of a past material culture. A unique eighteenth-century garden feature discovered at Morven in 1989 (figure 2.9) seems to be entirely ornamental in purpose. It appears to be a spiral made of fieldstone, possibly in the shape of a nautilus shell or perhaps a rose. The unevenness of its surface precludes its interpretation as a foundation or base for anything larger than an urn or small statue. It remains to be seen how this decorative element fits into the eighteenth-century garden and how best to interpret it, but certainly this artifact held a cultural (and possibly symbolic) significance within its eighteenth-century context.

Because the act of shaping the landscape is culturally meaningful, other soil layers may be useful in interpreting the physical landscape. The identification of the original topsoil or humus layer at the site was useful in reconstructing cultural sequences at Morven. The presence of this dark organic layer served as a marker, while its absence generally pointed to the

Figure 2.9. An ornamental garden feature, constructed of local fieldstone in the shape of a spiral or perhaps a shell, embellished the eighteenth-century landscape at Morven. New Jersey State Museum.

artificial alteration of the yard surface. In undisturbed sequences along the front of the house, the original humic layer consistently appeared below eighteenth-century deposits at 216 feet ASL. However, this soil was absent from certain units off the east wing. The lack of an organic topsoil layer between the earliest identified eighteenth-century deposit and what appeared to be sterile subsoil pointed to the need for further excavation in these units. The clayey soil was subsequently identified as a secondary deposit originating from the eighteenth-century east wing cellar excavation. The original topsoil, or humus, layer was found beneath it.

It has long been recognized, too, that fill is an artifact and that its layers carry cultural significance (e.g., Deetz 1977:15). Rubertone has observed that fill deposits are, in fact, useful cultural artifacts that create, destroy, or protect landscape surfaces (1989:51–52; see also Yentsch 1992). It is this deliberate action, the alteration of the landscape, that is of interest to archaeologists. The study of nineteenth-century fill layers at Morven allowed us to document the effects of such an action and to interpret an important transition within the garden and within the Stockton household.

A deep fill layer above the eighteenth-century stone terrace in the north yard dated to the tenure of Commodore Robert Field Stockton (1837–66). A single diagnostic artifact, a transfer-printed Staffordshire plate dating from 1810 to 1815, was recovered at the interface of the fill and the lower terrace; the fill itself contained mid-nineteenth-century materials.

This filling episode effectively hid the earlier, outdated ornamental garden and leveled the garden surface. There is ample archaeological evidence that both the north and south yards were relandscaped at this time. Long white gravel walks were installed above the earlier eighteenth-century fieldstone walks in the north yard. A brick wall, which still stands, was erected to divide the formerly open landscape into public and private space (Yamin 1988). In the south yard, the Horse Chestnut Walk was resurfaced; fragments of whiteware and ironstone were found within the recycled cut stone sub-base. A small artificial mound or hillock was created in the yard just south of the central entryway.

The changes within the garden at Morven are consistent with some rather dramatic changes to the house proper. Architectural analysis indicates that the commodore enlarged, modernized, and transformed the interior and exterior of the structure during a major period of renovation (Albee 1990). The documentary evidence suggests that Commodore Stockton was an innovator, entrepreneur, and self-made man who relied on his own abilities and talents, and not those of his ancestors (Greiff 1989a). The changes to the house and landscape add to this interpretation. The fill deposits, in particular, which buried (and protected) the eighteenth-century terraced garden, take on a new level of meaning and cultural significance when viewed in this context (for a detailed discussion, see Yamin 1989).

THE CONTEXT OF AN
EIGHTEENTH-CENTURY GARDEN

An essential element of our methodological approach to recovering the eighteenth-century garden at Morven was an awareness of the cultural context in which it was created. The characteristic bilateral symmetry of the Georgian period was an obvious starting point for predicting the location of landscape features (see Yentsch et al. 1987 for a full discussion). Barbara Paca and St. Clair Wright, consultants to the project, have convincingly demonstrated the use of geometric principles in eighteenth-century garden design and the link between houses and the plans of these gardens; the latter often were proportionally based on the dimensions of the house (Paca-Steele and Wright 1987). The central axis of the house and its overall dimensions were seen as key elements guiding the plan of the eighteenth-century garden at Morven. Because of these potential relationships, it is helpful to link the excavation grid to the structure. At Morven, the southeast corner of the building was selected as site datum and zero/zero point on the grid.

After the exploratory phase, a hypothetical plan of the garden was created based on our knowledge of eighteenth-century landscaping practices and on specific archaeological and architectural data, including the easternmost boundary of the garden as defined by the eastern axial walk, the northeast corner of the terrace as defined by the stone steps, the northern edge of the upper terrace, and the central axis of the house. We assumed that divisions within the garden and the placement of walks and terraces would be guided by their geometric relationships to the house and that major garden features would be symmetrically placed to either side of the central axis. The distances between the central axis and identified archaeological features were used to predict the location of other features, including the garden's western axis, within the five-foot square grid system. Our first attempts to actually locate these features were not without problems, however.

We had assumed that an excavation grid tied to the house would follow most closely the divisions, major axes, and significant features of a garden that had been laid out in relation to the dimensions of the house. While our essential premise was correct, the accuracy of our predictive framework was affected by our own biases, the result of viewing the landscape with a modern eye. First, the grid was based on a traditional archaeological system of measurement (feet and inches), not an eighteenth-century one. Second, the original dimensions of the house were not precisely known at this time; therefore, calculations based on the central axis of the present structure had the potential to introduce a degree of error into the model for testing the garden.

By late summer of 1988, however, architectural analysis and archaeological data began to shed light on these problems. While the central block of the eighteenth-century structure was built to the same dimensions as the present one, the wings have changed considerably over time. When the original dimensions were ascertained, it was evident that in the eighteenth century the east wing was several feet shorter than its western counterpart; thus, the house plan was balanced but not truly symmetrical.[6] The midpoint of the eighteenth-century structure (based on the length of the central block and two wings) lay several feet west of its position today.

When the predictive framework was adjusted in light of this information, the distance between the eastern garden walk and the original central axis of the house was found to be approximately 82.5 feet, or the equivalent of five perches. The perch, an eighteenth-century surveyor's measurement, is equal to 16.5 feet and is part of Gunter's chain of 66 feet (Paca-Steele and Wright 1987:305); Richard Stockton would have used this measurement to construct the house at Morven and would have duplicated the measurement in a garden plan based on the dimensions of the house. Given the distance between the central and eastern axes (82.5 feet or five perches), the width of the eighteenth-century garden would have been 165 feet, or ten perches. When put to the test, this new grid successfully predicted the location of the central and western axial walks and the terrace steps at the end of each walk. Our predictive model, then, was an effective tool for locating and interpreting the earlier landscape only when it was truly emic in perspective.

READING THE LANDSCAPE

The use of an emic grid brought many archaeological features into focus and provided a meaningful perpsective for understanding and interpreting the eighteenth-century landscape. Once the configuration of the eighteenth-century garden was established, it was possible to apply a variety of research strategies to greater advantage over a very large area of the site. The grid, together with a cumulative knowledge of eighteenth-century features and soils, allowed us to predict the location of garden features and the nature of deposits before excavation began. Other aids, such as a split-spoon (half-inch soil corer), a post-hole digger, and probes, allowed us to preview the deposits in any given area. Once located, features were exposed and traced through the garden at strategic intervals using areal excavation (figure 2.10), systematic sampling with hand-dug units, or mechanical trenching (figure 2.11).

The various techniques and analytical tools discussed in this chapter greatly enhanced our ability to read the soils and to recognize features and planting sufaces from the eighteenth-century garden. Of these, three or four seem especially relevant to the practice of landscape archaeology.

Figure 2.10. *Areal excavation of a mid-nineteenth-century gravel walk along the eastern axis of the garden at Morven. The earlier eighteenth-century walk, which lies beneath it, is also exposed in several units. New Jersey Sate Museum.*

Figure 2.11. *In the western half of the garden, trenches and excavation units were placed at strategic intervals to locate and trace the eighteenth-century axial walk and terrace steps. Photograph by Clem Fiori. New Jersey State Museum.*

The careful and selective use of mechanical trenching was particularly useful in this study and, in combination with other techniques discussed here, was critical to the success of the landscape archaeology program in all its phases: as an exploratory tool, as a means of generating long, continuous stratigraphic profiles across the yard and examining soil development in areas of deep fill, and also as a means of tracing landscape features over large areas. In short, it is an effective and practical tool for managing the sheer size of the built landscape. Trenching is a legitimate approach to landscape studies, and if executed carefully and within a specific research framework, trenches can provide significant quantities of data on earlier landscapes with minimal damage or impact to archaeological resources. Deposits and features from all periods are recorded in stratigraphic profile, thus evidence from each garden sequence is preserved. At Morven, trenching was used selectively in areas of the garden with fill layers or soils with low artifact densities: upper layers of soil were removed mechanically; deposits directly above the eighteenth-century garden surface were then excavated by hand. Despite the stratigraphic complexity of the archaeological landscape, this project demonstrates that it is possible to use mechanical trenching effectively, without damage to archaeological resources, as a way to grapple with the problem of scale in landscape studies.

Cultural deposits within the landscape are often elusive, soils thinly laid, the remains of garden features tenuous and insubstantial. Fill layers, used to create new living surfaces or to hide old ones, may be difficult to distinguish from other soils based on color and composition. The recognition of these soils is essential to the analytical process in landscape archaeology. Broad exposure is often the only way to identify and examine such remains. At Morven, we found areal excavation to be the best method for tracing garden soils and features over large areas, for constructing complete stratigraphic profiles that are necessary for interpreting the sequence of landscape development, and for revealing the interrelationships between features. In combination with above-sea-level measurements, horizontal exposure allowed us to make meaningful distinctions between the different garden horizons across the site.

Since we also hoped to learn about the content, as well as the configuration, of the eighteenth-century garden, an archaeobotanical study was an essential aspect of the Morven program. As part of its interdisciplinary approach to recovering earlier landscapes, the Morven research team included a paleoethnobotanist, a pollen specialist, and a phytolitharian. The results of these analyses are discussed in detail elsewhere (Kelso 1988; Lockwood 1988; Miller 1988, 1989; Miller and Yentsch 1988; Miller et al. 1990; Piperno 1988). It is sufficient to note here that the potential for such studies is high. Phytolith analysis, in particular, may hold the greatest potential for landscape studies, although the success of this type of analysis ultimately depends on the completion of a comparative collection for species identification. Miller (1989) has also shown the value of a modern vegetation survey as a prelude to landscape archaeology. Archaeobotanical analyses should be an integral component of every landscape study. The identification of plant species provides compelling evidence of how plants were used over time, evidence that is essential to an understanding of past cultural landscapes.

A final observation concerns the need for methodological flexibility and for the constant evaluation of the effectiveness of those methods. The recovery of an archaeological landscape is an interactive process. Strategies and tools for data recovery and analysis must be adjusted in light of the information that is recovered. We found at Morven that, as a first stage in analysis, quick artifact inventories for the major features and soil strata were useful in this respect. These inventories provided a *terminus post quem* and a qualitative, though not quantitative, sense of the artifactual content for each deposit examined. Although preliminary, these initial interpretations were based on a reading of the soils and an understanding of their actual artifact content. Because generally few artifacts are found in the archaeological landscape, its interpretation is less dependent on a quantitative analysis of artifacts and more on the reading of soils. (Obviously this is less true for areas with a high density of artifacts, particularly areas near the house; these areas require a detailed artifactual analysis to understand spatial patterning and land use.) The advantage of this tool in landscape studies is obvious in that the immediate interpretation of soils and features in the field, rather than in the laboratory, allows us to evaluate the success of our methodology while we are still in the field. It puts the archaeologist in a position to judge the relative success or weakness of a particular technique or strategy, to make adjustments, and to control the direction of the excavation from the field. Our investigative framework at Morven was most successful in locating features and distinguishing between historical landscapes when these excavation and sampling strategies and analytical tools were used interactively. This combination allowed us to trace the eighteenth-century garden landscape across much of the property during the two intensive seasons of fieldwork that followed the testing phase.

The reconstructed eighteenth-century landscape that has emerged from this study, while incomplete, centers on a terraced ornamental garden with at least four tiers. In addition to the upper terrace that was investigated in detail, there is evidence of a small, shallow terrace immediately adjacent to the house, the terrace at the base of the steps excavated in 1987, and a fourth terrace lying to the north of the present property line. The presence of the fourth terrace is suggested by an analysis of topographic maps and a walk-over survey of the adjacent property. The natural slope of the land and the view toward the distant Sourland Mountains undoubtedly enhanced the effect of descending terraces, while the vista from the house and terraced garden would have encompassed these hills as well as the woodlands, streams, and grass lawns described in poetic verse by Annis Stockton.

The upper terrace of the ornamental garden was defined by three major axial walks, three sets of terrace steps, and a series of crosswalks along the edge of the upper terrace and at the base of the shallow terrace fall near the house (figure 2.12). Our exploration of the garden's interior, via mechanical trenching, provided several types of data that are intriguing because they suggest that traces of the garden's interior plantings still exist and that it may be possible to reconstruct the actual plan of parterres and formal beds in the eighteenth-century garden at Morven. One trench revealed evidence of two such features: a border bed adjacent to the central garden walk and an interior planting bed with dozens of individual planting stains still preserved in the soil (figure 2.13). A second trench contained evidence of fence lines and a series of linear planting beds containing fragments of several eighteenth-century flowerpots.

Converging lines of evidence suggest a carefully planned ornamental garden that made advantageous use of its position on a hilltop to create a series of terraces and to expand the visual range of the garden landscape beyond the confines of the formal garden. Within the garden proper, the symmetry of its features and design and the beauty of its plantings undoubtedly inspired Annis Boudinot Stockton to write that "the amusement and the pleasure of a garden to me is the most rational, delightful and pure of any thing this world can indulge us with" (Greiff 1989b:30).

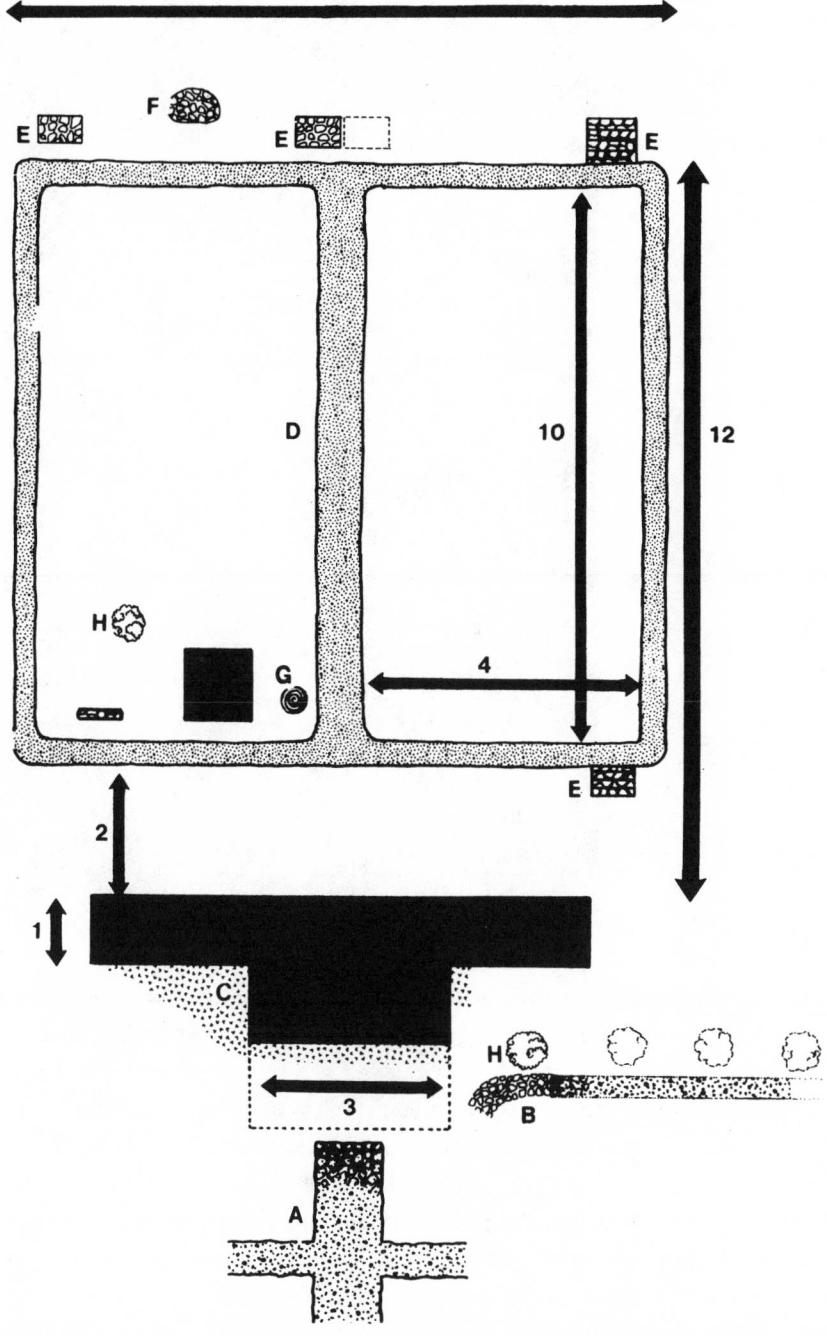

Figure 2.12. Reconstructed plan of the eighteenth-century garden at Morven. The house and an icehouse (in black) are shown as they would have appeared in the eighteenth century. Excavated garden features include: A) a fieldstone forecourt; B) an eighteenth-century version of the Horse Chestnut Walk; C) a red shale apron; D) garden walks within the upper terrace; E) terrace steps; F) an unidentified oval fieldstone feature; and G) a spiral-shaped fieldstone feature. The locations of two trees (H) that stood in the eighteenth century are also shown. The arrows indicate the dimensions of house and garden in perches. Drawing by Julie Hunter Abbazia, based on a field drawing by Judson Kratzer.

Figure 2.13. Evidence of an eighteenth-century planting bed. Dozens of individual planting holes are still visible in the archae-ological landscape. The planting bed lies adjacent to the border bed for the central axial walk. New Jersey State Museum.

As historical archaeologists begin to formulate research strategies for landscape archaeology pro-grams, a comparison of findings and project methodology becomes essential. It is important that we continue to evaluate and refine our field techniques and our analytical frameworks as we learn to read the landscape in its various guises. The process of reading the landscape is an interac-tive one, requiring an interchange of ideas and approaches as well as methodological flexibility.

In three years of work at Morven, several methods of excavation and data recovery were tried in order to define the eighteenth-century ornamental garden. Some methods were found to be ineffective or insufficient for the needs of a landscape study; others, after experi-mentation, were adjusted to meet the needs of the project. This study demonstrates the value of nondestructive exploratory techniques in landscape archaeology; however, a mixture of exploratory strategies, including deep trenching and remote sensing, was necessary just to begin to trace the remains of the eighteenth-century garden. Archaeologically, we used sev-eral techniques to improve the visibility or focus of the earlier garden surface. The combina-tion of areal excavation, mechanical trenching, and several analytical tools, such as the conversion of transit readings to above-sea-level measurements and the use of an emic grid, was highly effective in reconstructing Richard and Annis Stockton's eighteenth-century garden.

What is surprising is how much the remnants of earlier landscapes endure, how recur-rent filling episodes protect as well as obscure. The extent of preservation at Morven is remarkable, not only for the eighteenth-century landscape but for later gardens as well. Perhaps the most significant conclusion to be drawn from the Morven project is that archaeological landscapes, like the more traditional subjects of archaeological inquiry, can be reconstructed and interpreted in culturally meaningful ways. The landscape appears in many contexts, so a methodological flexibility is crucial. Landscape archaeology is a field in which the lines between disciplines and between archaeologists break down. The value of an interdisciplinary approach is evident. But at its most basic level, this type of study forces us to sharpen our ability to read the soil. It is our skill in the field and our ability to extract and interpret the data of past landscapes that ultimately will determine the success of our endeavor.

NOTES

1. This interdisciplinary research program was conducted under the auspices of the New Jersey Department of State and the Division of Cultural History, New Jersey State Museum.
2. Here the term "fieldstone" refers to flat, shale-like rocks that are indigenous to this region. Local fieldstone was used in the construction of the foundation at Morven as well as for various garden features and walkways.
3. The use of remote sensing for the detection of buried garden features and landscape surfaces may have some particular problems that are inherent in the types of features we hope to detect, for example, factors related to composition, hardness, breadth, or thickness. For further discussion, see Yentsch and Kratzer 1994.
4. An exception to this is the eighteenth-century terrace. The soil profile of the upper terrace fall showed evidence of deliberate soil removal from its base, undoubtedly to enhance the effect of terracing. The absence of pollen from this locus, where such remains might be expected due to the rapid burial of the terrace in the nineteenth century, suggests that the original organic topsoil was removed sometime before the terrace was buried and most probably during its construction (Kelso 1988:58, 61).
5. This is supported by evidence for another feature that appears to have a symmetrical relationship with the oval pad; this second feature was found on the opposite side of the central walk at a comparable distance (33 feet) from the central axis.
6. While there is some question as to when the east wing was first constructed, archaeological and architectural evidence suggest that a wing was present by the 1760s. The relationship between the garden and the central axis of the eighteenth-century house, calculated using the measurements of the original east wing, supports this interpretation.

REFERENCES

Albee, Peggy
1990   Historic Structure Report for Morven. Ms. on file, New Jersey State Museum, Trenton.
Bescherer, Karen, Conrad M. Goodwin, Judson Kratzer, and Anne Yentsch
1990   The Gardens at Grumblethorpe, Germantown, Pennsylvania. Morven Research Group in Landscape Archaeology, Landscape Archaeology Report No. 2. Report on file, Philadelphia Society for the Preservation of Landmarks, Philadelphia and New Jersey State Museum, Trenton.
Bescherer, Karen, Judson Kratzer, and Conrad M. Goodwin
1990   The Highlands Garden Project, Fort Washington, Pennsylvania: 1989 Archaeological Explorations. Morven Research Group in Landscape Archaeology, Landscape Archaeology Report No. 3. Report on file, Highlands Historical Society, Fort Washington and New Jersey State Museum, Trenton.
Bevan, Bruce
1987   A Geophysical Survey at Morven. Ms. on file, New Jersey State Museum, Trenton.

Bill, Alfred Hoyt, with Walter E. Edge

1954   *A House Called Morven.* Princeton University Press, Princeton.

Bill, A. H., W. E. Edge, C. M. Greiff, and B. F. Schwartz

1978   *A House Called Morven: Its Role in American History.* Revised edition. Princeton University Press, Princeton.

Brown, Marley R., III, and Patricia M. Samford

1990   Recent Evidence of Eighteenth-Century Gardening in Williamsburg, Virginia. In *Earth Patterns: Essays in Landscape Archaeology,* edited by William M. Kelso and Rachel Most, pp. 103–21. University Press of Virginia, Charlottesville.

Deetz, James

1977   *In Small Things Forgotten: The Archaeology of Early American Life.* Anchor Press, Doubleday, Garden City, New York.

Edwards, Andrew

1986   Bottles and Bones and *Asparagus? Colonial Williamsburg* 8(4):40–42.

Greiff, Constance M.

1989a   Morven: A Documentary History. Vol. I and II. Heritage Studies Inc., Hopewell, New Jersey. Report on file, New Jersey State Museum, Trenton.

1989b   Morven: A Documentary History. Appendices. Heritage Studies Inc., Hopewell, New Jersey. Report on file, New Jersey State Museum, Trenton.

Kelso, Gerald K.

1988   Exploratory Pollen Analysis at Morven, Princeton, New Jersey. In Morven Interim Report No. 2: Archaeobotanical Results from the 1987 Excavation at Morven, Princeton, New Jersey, edited by Naomi F. Miller and Anne Yentsch, pp. 56–63. New Jersey State Museum, Trenton.

Kornwolf, James D.

1984   The Picturesque in the American Garden and Landscape Before 1800. In *British and American Gardens in the Eighteenth Century,* edited by Robert P. Maccubbin and Peter Martin, pp. 93–106. The Colonial Williamsburg Foundation, Williamsburg, Virginia.

Lockwood, Alice G. B.

1931   *Gardens of Colony and State.* Charles Scribner's Sons, New York.

Lockwood, Laurence R.

1988   Estimates of Tree Ages at Morven. In Morven Interim Report No. 2: Archaeobotanical Results from the 1987 Excavation at Morven, Princeton, New Jersey, edited by Naomi F. Miller and Anne Yentsch, pp. 46–49. New Jersey State Museum, Trenton.

Maccubbin, Robert P., and Peter Martin, editors

1984   *British and American Gardens in the Eighteenth Century.* The Colonial Williamsburg Foundation, Williamsburg, Virginia.

Martin, Peter

1984   *"Pursuing Innocent Pleasures": The Gardening World of Alexander Pope.* Archon Books, Hamden, Connecticut.

Miller, Naomi F.

1988   Vegetation Survey and Macroremains, 1987. In Morven Interim Report No. 2: Archaeobotanical Results from the 1987 Excavation at Morven, Princeton, New Jersey, edited by Naomi F. Miller and Anne Yentsch, pp. 27–45. New Jersey State Museum, Trenton.

1989   What Mean These Seeds: A Comparative Approach to Archaeological Seed Analysis. *Historical Archaeology* 23(2):50–59.

Miller, Naomi F., and Anne Yentsch, editors

1988   Morven Interim Report No. 2: Archaeobotanical Results from the 1987 Excavation at Morven, Princeton, New Jersey. New Jersey State Museum, Trenton.

Miller, Naomi F., Anne Yentsch, Dolores Piperno, and Barbara Paca

1990   Two Centuries of Landscape Change at Morven, Princeton, New Jersey. In *Earth Patterns: Essays in Landscape Archaeology,* edited by William M. Kelso and Rachel Most, pp. 257–75. University Press of Virginia, Charlottesville.

Paca-Steele, Barbara, and St. Clair Wright
1987   The Mathematics of an Eighteenth-Century Wilderness Garden. *Journal of Garden History*
6(4):299–320.

Penn, William
1686   Letter to James Harrison, 17 Nov. 1686. Microfilm reel 5, frame 600, Pennsbury Manor,
Morrisville, Pennsylvania. Original on file, Historical Society of Pennsylvania, Philadelphia,
Pennsylvania.

Piperno, Dolores
1988   Phytoliths at Morven. In Morven Interim Report No. 2: Archaeobotanical Results from the
1987 Excavation at Morven, Princeton, New Jersey, edited by Naomi F. Miller and Anne
Yentsch, pp. 50–55. New Jersey State Museum, Trenton.

Rubertone, Patricia
1989   Landscape as Artifact: Comments on "The Archaeological Use of Landscape Treatment in Social, Economic and Ideological Analysis." *Historical Archaeology* 23(1):50–54.

Sheridan, Eugene R., and John M. Murrin, editors
1985   *Congress at Princeton. Being the Letters of Charles Thomson to Hannah Thomson June–October 1783.*
Princeton University Press, Princeton.

Weber, Carmen A., Elizabeth Anderson Comer, Louise E. Akerson, and Gary Norman
1990   Mount Clare: An Interdisciplinary Approach to the Restoration of a Georgian Landscape. In
Earth Patterns: Essays in Landscape Archaeology, edited by William M. Kelso and Rachel Most,
pp. 135–52. University Press of Virginia, Charlottesville.

Yamin, Rebecca
1988   To Restore or Not to Restore: Morven's Interpretive Question. Paper presented at the annual
meeting of the Council for Northeast Historical Archaeology, Quebec, Canada.
1989   The Public and Private Mr. Stockton: Morven's Commodore. *New Jersey Folklore Society Review* 10(2–3):3–16.

Yentsch, Anne
1990   Historic Morven: The Archaeological Reappearance of an 18th Century Princeton Garden.
Expedition 32(2):14–23.
1992   Working with Fill in San Francisco. In Tar Flat, Rincon Hill, and the Shore of Mission Bay:
Archaeological Research Design and Treatment Plan for SF-480 Terminal Separation Rebuild,
vol. 2, edited by Mary Praetzellis and Adrian Praetzellis, pp. 4/103-4/120. Report prepared
for California Department of Transportation. Cultural Resources Facility, Anthropological
Studies Center, Sonoma State University, Rohnert Park, California.

Yentsch, Anne E., and Judson M. Kratzer
1994   Techniques for Excavating and Analyzing Buried Eighteenth-Century Garden Landscapes. In
The Archaeology of Garden and Field, edited by Naomi F. Miller and Kathryn L. Gleason, pp.
168–201. University of Pennsylvania Press, Philadelphia.

Yentsch, Anne, Judson Kratzer, and Karen Bescherer
1990   Management Summary of the 1989 Field Season at a National Historic Landmark: Morven in
Princeton, New Jersey. Ms. on file, New Jersey State Museum, Trenton.

Yentsch, Anne E., Naomi F. Miller, Barbara Paca, and Dolores Piperno
1987   Archaeologically Defining the Earlier Garden Landscapes at Morven: Preliminary Results.
Northeast Historical Archaeology 16:1–29.

Yentsch, Anne, Karen Bescherer, and Naomi F. Miller, editors
1989   Morven Interim Report No. 1: Results of the 1987 Archaeological Reconnaissance at
Morven, Princeton, New Jersey. Ms. on file, New Jersey State Museum, Trenton.

3

The Greenhouse Effect: Gender-Related Traditions in Eighteenth-Century Gardening

Carmen A. Weber

Since the seventeenth and eighteenth centuries, the role of women in American gardening has changed significantly. Women are a guiding force in twentieth-century garden restorations and garden clubs and have, in several instances, initiated the examination of past gardens (see Hosmer 1981:908 regarding the garden at Stratford Hall; also note the restoration of the William Paca garden, spearheaded by Mrs. St. Clair Wright). However, the role of women in eighteenth-century gardening, particularly garden design, is more obscure. Women "in the garden" are largely invisible, overshadowed in the historical record by the horticultural pursuits and accomplishments of men.

How do we delineate the influence of women in eighteenth-century gardening? Is the historical record biased? Do historical documents written by men merely define the male conception of control over nature and, by extension, as the historian Carole Fabricant (1979) suggests, over women? Or did women also attempt to control nature and, correspondingly, their own lives? Can this behavior be observed in the historical or archaeological record?

To provide at least partial answers to these broad questions, this study considers the role of women in garden design and operation in the eighteenth century. I focus on a single element within the eighteenth-century mid-Atlantic garden landscape, the greenhouse, to investigate the issue of gender-related traditions in eighteenth-century gardening. The examination of primary records such as personal diaries, correspondence, and other documents is the starting point for this study. Much of this research centers on Mount Clare, Maryland, where the gardening activities of Margaret Carroll are recorded in the accounts and correspondence of men of the period. The diary of Philadelphia resident Deborah Logan describes the gardening interests of both women and men. Her recollections of period gardens in Philadelphia provide comparative data for the study. Other examples are drawn from the Chesapeake and Philadelphia regions.

However, the isolated descriptions found in individual documents do not produce clear evidence of the extent to which women were involved in garden design in the eighteenth century. These documents instead record the individual interests of certain women (and men) in gardening and landscape design. The problem, then, is to find other sources—archaeological, architectural, artifactual—that might reveal the otherwise invisible role of women in the eighteenth-century garden, as well as to find new ways to look at the documentary record.

While the evidence is indirect, this study shows that the involvement of women in garden design is clearly visible when questions regarding gender are asked of the available data. The research presented here illustrates both the various types of data available for exploring gender questions as well as the potential for such a study. Most important, this investigation demonstrates that by using an ethnographic approach to the study of material culture, it is possible to learn a great deal about the role of women from historical documents and the archaeological and architectural records.

THE ROLE OF WOMEN IN THE GARDEN

The involvement of women in the day-to-day management of kitchen gardens for daily sustenance was clearly acknowledged a century earlier, as for example in Vicar William Lawson's *The Country Housewife's Garden* ([1617] 1983). The image of women as providers of the bounty of Mother Nature was not accepted by all men, however. Johannes Volckamer described the effect of women on that prized possession, an orange tree, in 1714: "Once, in winter, I noticed a woman of my gardener's household seated upon a beautiful orange tree in full bloom. The next day, the tree started drying up from the top downwards, and so rapid was the progress of the disease that in the course of a few days it had infected every single branch, causing all the leaves to wilt and die" (quoted in Yentsch 1990:182). Clearly, in this instance the writer directly related the tree's demise to its contact with a woman.

Despite Volckamer's pronouncement, women did successfully cultivate and grow rare and exotic plants. Queen Henrietta Maria of England owned a greenhouse with a stove in the seventeenth century. This botanical venture, which required a substantial structure, servants, and a skilled gardener, produced orange and lemon trees and other exotics estimated at a value of £546 (Yentsch 1990:179). Stephen Switzer, in his 1715 *Noblemen, Gentlemen, & Gardener's Recreation,* noted that among the many interests of Queen Mary, she enjoyed "measuring, directing or ordering her Buildings; but in Gard'ning, especially Exoticks, she was particularly skilled" (quoted in Green 1967:72). Queen Mary was responsible for the design and installation of the Fountain Garden at Hampton Court and the evergreen gardens of box and yew at Kensington, built in the Dutch fashion favored by her husband, William of Orange. In the early eighteenth century, her sister, Queen Anne, modified the gardens at Kensington, adding an orangery designed by Christopher Wren. Queen Caroline, wife of George II, created a landscape garden at Richmond, her summer residence between the years 1718 to 1737. Her construction of Merlin's Cave in 1735 was an attempt to legitimize the claim of the Hanover royal family to the English throne by demonstrating a relationship to former English kings (Colton 1976). This symbolism was turned against the queen by her political opponents through political satire, aptly demonstrating the versatility of symbolic associations and the ways in which various members of society can redefine their meanings.

These examples describing the involvement of noble Englishwomen in garden design demonstrate that while the situation and degree of control varied in each case, women definitely influenced garden design in seventeenth- and eighteenth-century England. Queen Caroline's garden at Richmond demonstrates that ideological statements were made through the medium of garden design not only by men in the eighteenth century (e.g., Leone 1984; Leone et al. 1989), but also by women.

MRS. CARROLL'S GREENHOUSE

Margaret Tilghman Carroll was raised on the Eastern Shore of Maryland (Trostel 1980). In 1763, at the age of twenty-one, she married forty-year-old Charles Carroll, the Barrister. Six years earlier, he had begun construction on his plantation, Mount Clare, outside of Baltimore. In 1760, Carroll ordered various materials for the house from his London merchant. He also requested a thermometer, possibly for his greenhouse, and Phillip Miller's *Gardener's Dictionary* (Trostel 1980). His 1759 copy of the *Dictionary* was the seventh edition of this popular reference book and contained information on the construction of greenhouses and the stoves used to heat them. This purchase is significant for two reasons: first, the order coincided with the completion of construction on the main house and suggests that Charles Carroll was now turning to other interests, quite possibly the construction of the greenhouse at Mount Clare; second, Carroll would have had access to the latest information on greenhouse technology through his purchase of the *Dictionary*.

Miller recommended that the length of the greenhouse "be proportional to [the] number of Plants they contain or [the] Fancy of the Owner. [The] Depth should never be greater than their Height in the Clear, which in small or middling Houses, may be sixteen or eighteen feet, but for Large ones, from twenty through twenty-four feet is a good Proportion, for if long & too narrow it will have a bad Appearance both within & without, nor will it contain so many Plants . . ." (see entry for "Greenhouse," Miller 1759). He also recommended the construction of rooms at the back of the structure, to be used as a tool house, and a room upstairs, to be accessed by a separate entrance.

In addition, Miller's *Dictionary* described a stove or heating system, consisting of flues ten inches wide and two feet deep, running under the floor and connected to a rear funnel or chimney. This system was operated from a fire box at one end, accessible from the toolhouse in the rear of the greenhouse. Miller stated that a flue system under the floor was an old method of heating greenhouses and one that required skillful management to avoid problems with overheating. He also discussed a newer flue system, which he illustrated in the text, that would run up the wall in the rear of the building. Finally, Miller advocated wings on the greenhouse, constructed with sloping glass roofs and divided by glass doors. He felt these types of wings were necessary to accommodate many varieties of exotics, each of which required different amounts of heat.

The first direct reference to a heated greenhouse, or orangery, at the Carrolls' Mount Clare plantation is from a 1770 diary entry, written by a visitor to the estate. Mrs. Mary Ambler wrote of "a Green House with a good many Orange & Lemon Trees just ready to bear . . ." (Trostel 1980:47–48). She also described a "Pinery," then under construction. A 1775 Peale landscape painting of Mount Clare depicts the greenhouse as a building with attenuated windows (figure 3.1).

No direct evidence for the construction date of the Mount Clare greenhouse exists; however, from indirect evidence, we can infer that it was built no earlier than 1760, when the Barrister completed work on the main house and when he ordered the thermometer, and no later than 1770, when Mrs. Ambler described a greenhouse already in operation. It remains a matter of speculation, however, whether the greenhouse was constructed before the Barrister's marriage to Margaret Tilghman in 1763.

THE HISTORICAL RECORD

The orangery is significant not only because of its importance in the Mount Clare landscape and in the Chesapeake region as a sign of elite status, but also because of Margaret Carroll's interest in it. Glimpses of Margaret Carroll's general interest in the Mount Clare gardens surface in the Barrister's correspondence with his London merchant. In 1767 Carroll wrote, "My wife takes much Pleasure in Gardening and sends you a list of Peaches . . ." (quoted in Trostel 1980:57). This particular interest is also evident in surviving copies of Mrs. Carroll's recipes, including one for peach cordial. In 1768, the Barrister asked his merchant to "Procure . . . a

Figure 3.1. Mount Clare, south facade and garden. Painting by Charles Willson Peale, 1775. Courtesy of The National Society of Colonial Dames of America (NSCDA) in the State of Maryland, Mount Clare Museum House, Carroll Park, Baltimore, Maryland.

Bearing Lemon Tree or two in Boxes with Earth that have been Inoculated from Good fruit as the Trees Raised from the seed are Generally worthless" (quoted in Trostel 1980:58).

Mrs. Carroll's gardening activities are also well documented after the death of Charles Carroll in 1783. In 1784, George Washington wrote to Margaret Carroll's brother-in-law, Tench Tilghman, requesting information on the orangery at Mount Clare. His letter stated: "I shall essay the finishing of my green house this fall, but find that neither myself, nor any person about me is so well skilled in the internal construction as to proceed without a probability at least of running into errors . . . the information I wish to obtain is, the [details] of Mrs. Carroll's Green-house. . . ." (quoted in Trostel 1980:77). Tilghman's reply described various technical recommendations, made by Mrs. Carroll, on structural dimensions, the number of flues and their location, the type of roof, windows, doors, etc., all based upon her personal experience and expertise as a gardener and perhaps as a designer. "She has always found the flues mark'd in the plan sufficient for her House . . . ," he noted, and "It is the Custom in many Green Houses to set the Boxes upon Benches—But *Mrs. Carroll* says they do better upon the Floor . . ." [emphasis added]. Tilghman concluded, "I hope your Excellency will understand this imperfect description of a matter which I do not know much about myself" (quoted in Trostel 1980:77).

Mrs. Carroll's involvement with President Washington culminated in the shipment of trees from her greenhouse to the Mount Vernon greenhouse. As the Mount Vernon greenhouse burned down in 1835, knowledge of its configuration comes from a plan drawn by George Washington (figure 3.2; see also an 1803 drawing of the greenhouse from a fire insurance policy in figure 4.4). The present reconstruction is based on this plan. The core of the building, forming almost a square, is similar to the Mount Clare orangery in several respects, including the division of rooms and the use of corner chimneys. Unfortunately, the plan does not illustrate the placement of the flues for the heating system. According to Washington's diary entries, a range of exotics, including some purchased from Philadelphia nurseryman John Bartram, were maintained in his greenhouse (Williams 1923:195).

ARCHAEOLOGICAL AND ARCHITECTURAL EVIDENCE FROM MOUNT CLARE

While the correspondence of elite males indirectly reveals Margaret Carroll's expertise and experience as a gardener, the architectural and archaeological records at Mount Clare directly reveal her interest in the landscape there and her influence in the changes made to the plantation after the death of her husband. Upon Charles Carroll's death, Margaret Carroll received a life interest in either the Carrolls' Annapolis house or Mount Clare, one-half the income from the Barrister's sizable estate, and the income from her own inheritance. She chose to live at Mount Clare, which had become a permanent residence for the Carrolls during the Revolutionary period. The next year, Margaret Carroll purchased seventy-two yards of striped muslin and forty-nine yards of shalloon from her brother-in-law, Tench Tilghman, presumably to change the curtains and chair covers at Mount Clare. Other changes made to Mount Clare during Mrs. Carroll's widowhood included the installation of two fine mantels in the former office wing of the house; the office was changed to a drawing room at

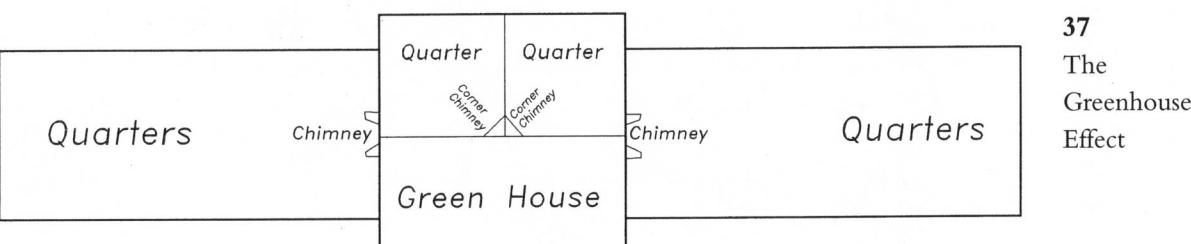

Figure 3.2. Plan of the Mount Vernon greenhouse, based on a plan drawn by George Washington. Drawing by Joel Paulson.

this time. In the parlor and dining room, the mantels were redone in the federal style (Trostel 1980:75–76, 80). These changes seem to reflect an increase in the number of guests entertained at Mount Clare by Margaret Carroll.

Excavations in the kitchen wing were conducted in 1986 by the Baltimore Center for Urban Archaeology under the direction of Gary Norman and the author. The excavations revealed changes to the configuration of the wing and its attachment to the house, alterations that most likely were made during the same period as Mrs. Carroll's other changes at Mount Clare. The excavations uncovered the stone foundation of a hyphen that at one time connected the kitchen to the main house. Archaeological evidence for an addition to the east side of the kitchen was obscured by later activities. Inside the kitchen, two ash pits with associated supports, apparently built for cooking stoves, were found, as well as two fireplaces (Norman 1987). The stoves may have been added to help with the extra cooking required for additional guests. These renovations clearly indicate Margaret Carroll's intention to shape the house and landscape at Mount Clare as she desired.

Greenhouses, or orangeries, existed at other plantations and townhouses in the eighteenth-century Chesapeake region. While the orangery as a symbol for the elite has been previously discussed (Yentsch 1990), the documentary record for orangeries of the Chesapeake Tidewater region suggests that it was a symbol of particular importance to women. An examination of kinship ties in the Chesapeake is enlightening in this regard. Margaret Tilghman Carroll, from the Eastern Shore of Maryland, was related to the Lloyd family, owners of Wye House and the Wye House orangery. Mrs. Carroll was a great-granddaughter of Henrietta Maria Neale, a seventeenth-century occupant of the Wye House property who was reputed to be the godchild of Queen Henrietta Maria of England—the same queen who built an orangery in England in the seventeenth century. One of Margaret Carroll's bequests in her 1817 will was a ring containing a miniature of Charles I, Queen Henrietta Maria's husband, which she had inherited from her mother, who had in turn received it from Henrietta Maria Neale. This ring was inherited by Mrs. Carroll's niece, Elizabeth Tench Goldsborough, along with the remainder of Mrs. Carroll's jewelry (Trostel 1980:88). It is important to note in the context of this study that successive generations of Tilghman women inherited this heirloom; it was through the Tilghman family that Elizabeth Goldsborough was related to Margaret Carroll (figure 3.3). This suggests a tightly bound network of kin and the strength of tradition among Chesapeake women.

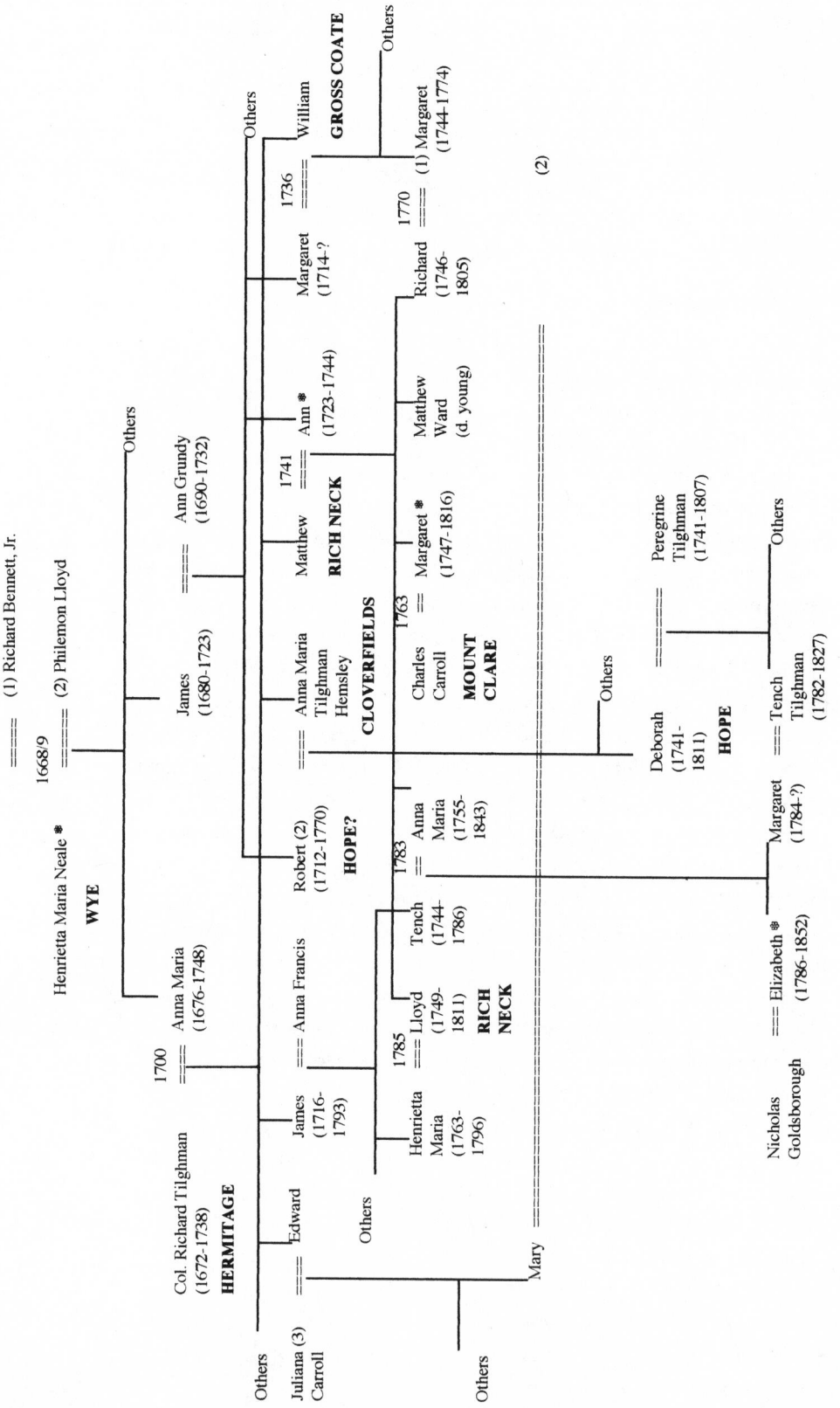

Figure 3.3. Relationship between the Lloyd-Tilghman-Goldsborough women.

❋ Owners of Ring with Minature of Charles I

The data also suggest the possibility that the orangery was one of the links between these women and that ideas and interests were exchanged through this network. A comparison of greenhouse plans and construction techniques for the orangeries associated with these women is useful. An archaeological excavation at the site of the Mount Clare orangery was conducted in 1984 by Dr. Charles Cheek with students from a University of Maryland field school. The excavation exposed the fire box, some of the flues in the front of the greenhouse, a central wall with a chimney for the flues, and a portion of a back room. There was no evidence of flues in the rear wall. The back room contained a chimney and floor flues. Figure 3.4 illustrates the flue and chimney placement in a plan drawing of the excavation. The construction date of the flues could not be determined (Charles Cheek 1988, personal communication).

The eighteenth-century orangery at Wye House, home of Mrs. Carroll's female relatives, still stands (figure 3.5). The building style of the orangery reflects the Georgian style popular in the Chesapeake, but has taller windows, extending almost to the ground. These windows take full advantage of the sunlight and also allow the trees in their tubs to be moved outdoors more easily in good weather. While architectural historians generally agree that there were two periods of construction for the orangery at Wye House, the exact dates remain unclear (Forman 1967; Weeks 1984). From their analyses it appears that the first period of construction, possibly occurring in the 1750s, consisted of the central portion of the building. It included a rear or back room with a fireplace. The wall between the front and rear rooms contained a flue system. The original fire box for this flue seems to underlie the present east wing. During the second period of construction, generally dated to the 1780's, wings were added, along with a rear room behind the east wing. The wings were heated by a fuel system under the floor, with a fireplace opening to the rear room, as recommended by Miller (figure 3.6). The Wye House orangery also possessed an upstairs room, accessible from the exterior of the building by a set of rear stairs, again as advocated by Miller. However, contrary to Miller's advice, the wings did not contain sloping glass roofs and, therefore, they essentially represent a reproduction of the original form with flues placed under the floor. As historians have noted, without excavation and a structural examination beneath the floors and behind the walls, it is not possible to state with certainty which configuration or which elements, such as the flues, date to which construction period (Forman 1967; Weeks 1984).

While the construction dates of different elements cannot be clarified without further archaeological study, a comparison of the excavated Mount Clare orangery and the extant Wye House orangery suggests that certain similarities exist between them. The exteriors of these two structures are Georgian in appearance, with attenuated windows (see figures 3.1 and 3.5). Although the exterior design of greenhouses was not discussed extensively in Miller's *Gardener's Dictionary,* the accompanying illustration resembles a simple Georgian building. The exterior of the Wye House orangery has definite architectural ties to Georgian residences of the Chesapeake region, particularly in the execution of the wings, which do not resemble the glass conservatory wings advocated and portrayed by Miller.

The use of flues under the floor may date from the first construction period of each orangery. While referred to as an old system by Miller, Margaret Carroll at least seemed to prefer this flue arrangement. In addition, both flues appear to have been constructed with brick walls. Without archaeological excavation of the Wye orangery, the placement of the flues in the floor remains uncertain; however, the Wye orangery does contain one flue along

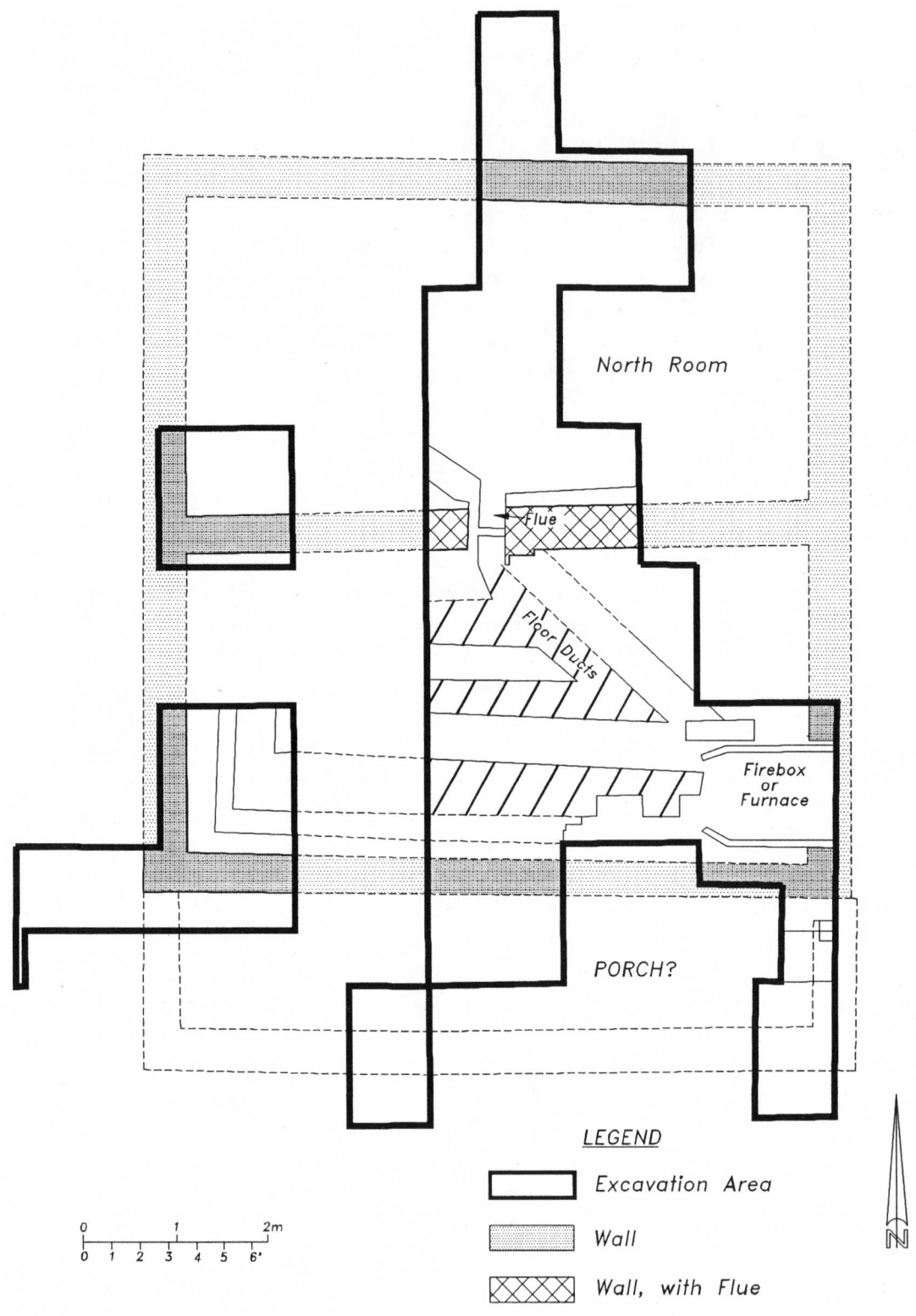

North Room

Flue

Floor Ducts

Firebox
or
Furnace

PORCH?

LEGEND

Excavation Area

Wall

Wall, with Flue

0   1   2m
0 1 2 3 4 5 6'

N

Figure 3.4. Plan of the Mount Clare orangery, based on 1984 archaeological excavations. Courtesy of the Baltimore Center for Urban Archaeology.

Figure 3.5. Wye House orangery facade.

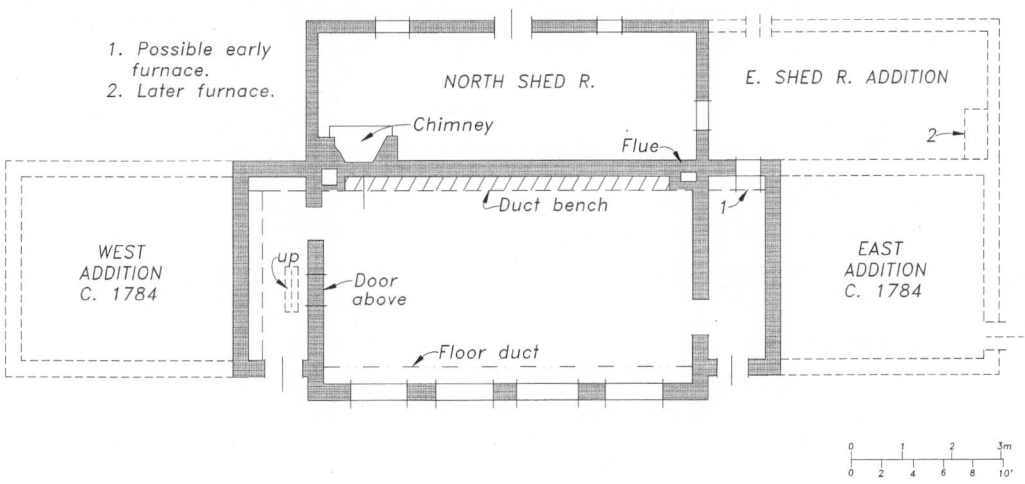

Figure 3.6. Plan of the Wye House orangery, based on a HABS drawing (Forman 1967). Drawn by Joel Paulson.

the south wall, as did the Mount Clare orangery. Another structural similarity is the placement of the fire box in the east wing of each building, although the location of this feature was never specified by Miller. Both buildings also contained rooms on the rear or north side, as recommended by Miller; however, the function of the chimneys in these rooms and the function of the flues beneath the floor in this particular room at Mount Clare remain unclear. Again, without archaeological evidence it is not known if the rear, or north, room at Wye possesses flues beneath the floor. Finally, the central section of the Wye orangery almost forms a square, the shape of the Mount Clare orangery.

It is difficult to attribute the construction of specific elements of the Mount Clare orangery to Margaret Carroll. The same is true in terms of attributing aspects of the Wye House orangery to her influence, since other women who married into the Lloyd family may have ordered renovations to the Wye House orangery. For example, Edward Lloyd married Elizabeth Tayloe of Mount Airy, Virginia, in 1767. Mount Airy also had an orangery, elements of which may have influenced the 1780s renovations at Wye House (Forman 1967:73). These lines of inquiry require further research; however, a combination of archaeology, historical research, and architectural analysis of all these sites could clarify these relationships.

The association of these women with orangeries is significant nonetheless. The evidence, though indirect, supports the suggestion that Chesapeake women adopted and continued a tradition of building orangeries, or heated greenhouses, as part of the formal garden. This tradition is defined by a continuation in the conservative nature of the technical construction of orangeries in the Chesapeake region and by the refinement of their use for a specific purpose, such as growing orange and lemon trees. For example, while Miller recommended the use of plant stands in the greenhouse, Margaret Carroll conveyed to George Washington, through Tench Tilghman, the information that trees grew just as well standing directly on the floor. This probably relates to the continued use of floor ducts, an older approach to greenhouse cultivation advocated by Margaret Carroll. She also recommended large windows to give air to the trees, as well as a large door to avoid damage when moving the trees. It should be emphasized that *she* gave advice on construction of the orangery. Washington contacted Tilghman originally because, as he stated in his letter, neither he nor others at Mount Vernon knew how to proceed with construction. Finally, Tilghman apologized to Washington for his lack of knowledge on the subject.

A GENDER-RELATED TRADITION

The apparent continuum of an orangery tradition descends as a gender-related tradition from Queen Henrietta Maria to the interrelated Lloyd, Tilghman, and Goldsborough families in the Chesapeake region. The identification of individual women belonging to the kinship group is a complex process. Male genealogists have traced the men in the family, particularly those with similar names, through their political careers. However, one male architectural historian has stated that "after a brief study of the county's family trees, [one] may never want to hear the words 'Henrietta Maria' again" (Weeks 1984:29). Another male genealogist, a family descendant in fact, has said:

> Henrietta Maria Lloyd is perhaps better known to Marylanders of today than any of
> the men of the Lloyd family, no matter how important their service to the country
> may have been. She probably vies with Mistress Margaret Brent for the distinction of
> being the most famous woman of early Maryland. . . . The descendants of Henrietta
> Maria Lloyd appear to be exceptionally numerous, a thing explained by the fact that
> anyone descended from her knows it, no matter how ignorant he or she may be of the
> rest of their ancestors, and claims that descent with intense pride. This pride cannot be
> explained by the usual reasons for there is no record that this woman accomplished
> anything unusual for one of her time and position. (Tilghman 1953:93)

Tilghman attributed the fame of this woman to her feminine virtues. I would speculate that the female descendants of Henrietta Maria Lloyd helped convey family legend and may have participated in it through the symbolism of their orangeries.

Oranges and lemons played a role in the prestigious social entertainments of these women. When Mrs. Carroll entertained Mrs. Washington in 1789, among the "considerable preparation" described by Robert Lewis were "fruits &c. which had been plucked from the trees in a green House lying on the tables in great abundance" (quoted in Trostel 1980:78). The social importance of these valuable fruits was displayed in other forms as well. In a 1775 portrait of Margaret Carroll by Charles Willson Peale, Mrs. Carroll was shown holding a spray of orange leaves (figure 3.7). Interestingly, she later had the portrait changed; the revision is recorded by Peale in his day book for June 1788 (Trostel 1980). X-ray analysis of the painting revealed that the style of her hair was changed from that of a tightly pulled-back pompadour to a style that was fuller at the sides. In addition, the circular window in the pediment of the house was changed to reflect the lunette-shaped window installed by Margaret Carroll. Finally, the spray of orange leaves in her right hand was altered—the oranges were painted out (Trostel 1980:52). The first two alterations, actual physical changes made to property and person by Margaret Carroll after the Barrister's death, reflect her new status as a widow. The third alteration is no less symbolic of her status. I would suggest that Margaret Carroll had the oranges painted out of her portrait because by the 1780s the leaves alone had status value for "people who counted" in her society. The earlier appearance of a single orange, reputedly from the Wye House orangery, in the 1755 portrait by John Hesselius of Deborah Lloyd (Weeks 1984:64), a cousin of Margaret Carroll, both illustrates the use of the symbol and supports the argument of change in the symbol itself through time.

Chesapeake society was important to Margaret Carroll. The decline in social activities in Annapolis after the Revolution probably influenced her decision to live at Mount Clare after 1783 (Trostel 1980:57). The remodeling of Mount Clare by Mrs. Carroll during her widowhood created more elaborate spaces for entertaining on a large scale. Surviving her husband by thirty-four years, she chose not to remarry. Lesbock (1984) has demonstrated that wealthy widows often preferred to remain unmarried, thus retaining control of their wealth. Through widowhood, Margaret Carroll retained control over the house and gardens at Mount Clare. This fact may be the unstated symbolism of the alterations to her portrait. Her changes to the estate during this period demonstrate her control of the property and her considerable wealth. Her interests in the orangery demonstrate her attempts to control nature. In sum, Margaret Carroll's actions demonstrate a control over her own life.

EIGHTEENTH-CENTURY
PHILADELPHIA GREENHOUSES

The examination of another widow and her greenhouse adds a new dimension to this study. Deborah Norris Logan lived outside Philadelphia at her country estate, Stenton, for eighteen years after the death of her husband, Dr. George Logan. Archaeological excavations at Stenton, conducted by Barbara Liggett between 1968 and 1970, revealed the configuration of a greenhouse added by Deborah Logan between 1811 and 1815 (Liggett 1973). Diaries,

Figure 3.7. Margaret Tilghman Carroll, 1742–1817. Portrait by Charles Willson Peale, 1770–71; altered by Peale in 1778. Courtesy of The National Society of Colonial Dames of America (NSCDA) in the State of Maryland, Mount Clare Museum House, Carroll Park, Baltimore, Maryland.

begun by Deborah Logan when she was fifty-three and kept between the years 1815 and 1839, confirm the existence of the greenhouse. The analysis of a brick feature identified as the greenhouse or plant room floor in the Liggett report indicates that the floor existed prior to the date given in the diary for the floor's reconstruction (Liggett 1973:17–18). This may have been the location of an earlier greenhouse at Stenton, constructed by Deborah Logan's father-in-law.

Deborah Logan began her diaries in a conscious attempt to preserve a past she saw fading away in the early nineteenth century. She quoted Dr. Johnson in the opening passage of her diary: "One generation of Ignorance effaces the whole series of unwritten History. Books are faithful repositories, which may be a while neglected or forgotten; but when they are opened again will again impart their instruction: Memory once interrupted is not to be recalled" (Book No. 1, 1815). Among the pages of her diaries she recalled the lives of important figures of the not-so-distant Revolutionary period and the eighteenth century in the Philadelphia region, especially those of her husband, Dr. George Logan, and his family.

Through her journal, Deborah Logan also created a vision of the gardens of the Philadelphia region in the eighteenth century. Though her memory was occasionally at odds with the descriptions of others, Mrs. Logan's entries nonetheless provide insight into this aspect of Philadelphia society. In 1832, she noted:

> There is a Report of the Committee of the Horticultural Society in the "Register" for last week in which is displayed a great ignorance of the former taste for Gardening amongst us when it states, that Mr. Pepper's Green house, originally built by the late Dr. Barbon, was the first Green house built in Pennsylvania; this is not So.—The Greenhouse at Sprigetsbury, built by Margaret Freame daughter of William Penn, was the first;—the one attached to the House of my Father [Charles Norris] . . . was the next; and to this was added a hot-house, with its bark-bed and roof of Glass, where upwards of 50 Pine-apples were raised of a Season, besides many rare plants. . . .
>
> My father [in-law] Logan, had also a Green house in town, as well as a good one here [at Stenton], for he was an excellent Horticulturalist, and had many rare and beautiful Plants; indeed the large and fine Orange and lemon trees which now ornament Pratts Greenhouse at Lemon Hill were originally of his raising. . . . Israel Pemberton likewise had a Green House for his wife's Amusement, and there was one at Fair-hill [home of Isaac Norris Jr.]. . . . (Book No. 13, 13 February 1832)

The diary records the involvement of women in gardening and in the operation of greenhouses in at least two instances, stating also that a woman constructed the first greenhouse in the Philadelphia region,[1] but Mrs. Logan also described the participation of men in the cultivation of greenhouse exotics.

Other than the evidence uncovered at Stenton, dated from Deborah Logan's lifetime, research reveals few details on these greenhouses. Philadelphia's urban sprawl has overtaken the once remote sites of Sprigettsbury, the Pemberton estates of Evergreen and "The Plantation," and the Isaac Norris estate of Fairhill. Since these greenhouses no longer stand, an architectural analysis of their technical attributes cannot be undertaken. Additionally, these sites appear to have little archaeological potential; urbanization has apparently obliterated all evidence of the eighteenth-century landscape.

Some visual evidence of these early gardens remains, however. A drawing of Fairhill depicts a structure that could be the greenhouse (figure 3.8). Similarly, a 1793 drawing of Bush Hill, an estate owned by the bachelor governor, James Hamilton, portrays a greenhouse (figure 3.9). A Philadelphia map of 1796 shows outbuildings around Sprigettsbury, Bush Hill, and the Pemberton estate, any of which could represent a greenhouse (Hills 1796). Based on these visual representations, the Fairhill greenhouse externally resembles that at Mount Clare, while the length of the Bush Hill greenhouse is reminiscent of the Wye House orangery.

Although primary as well as secondary sources were consulted during this research (e.g., Eberlein and Hubbard 1939; Faris 1932; McLean 1983; Westcott 1895), no descriptions of these structures could be located. The only other evidence for a greenhouse at Bush Hill is a reference in a 1927 revised edition of John F. Watson's 1844 *Annals of Philadelphia*. Watson made reference to greenhouses on the properties of Charles Norris (townhouse located at Third and Chestnut Streets), Israel Pemberton (this could refer to Evergreen or "The Plantation"), William Logan (Stenton), James Hamilton (Bush Hill), and Isaac Norris (Fairhill), among others, but he did not provide descriptions of any of the structures (Watson [1844] 1927:400).

The historical evidence for eighteenth-century greenhouses in the Philadelphia region, while incomplete, does not indicate any specific gender-related tradition. Both men and women enjoyed greenhouse exotics in eighteenth-century Philadelphia. However, the symbolic status role of the greenhouse, identified by Yentsch (1990) for the elite of Maryland, clearly existed. At least three references to the greenhouse at the Proprietary estate of Sprigettsbury were located. The earliest reference comes from the diary of John Smith, a Quaker merchant, in the winter of 1745: "In the afternoon, the weather being agreeable,

Figure 3.8. Fairhill facade and gardens. Pen-and-ink drawing. The greenhouse is to the left of the main house. Courtesy of the Winterthur Library: Joseph Downs Collection of Manuscripts and Printed Ephemera.

Figure 3.9. Bush Hill. Engraving from the New York Magazine, 1793. The greenhouse is the second building to the right of the main house. Reprinted in Gardens of Colony and State (Lockwood 1931). Courtesy of the Garden Club of America.

John Armitt and I rode to Charles Jenkin's ferry on Schuykill. We ran and walked a mile or two on the ice. On our way thither we stopped to view the proprietor's green-house, which at this season is an agreeable sight; the oranges, lemons and citrons were, some green, some ripe, some in blossom" (quoted in Myers 1904:71). Ten years later, Daniel Fisher, a recent arrival to Philadelphia from Virginia, praised the greenhouse and its plants, which had been placed in the gardens for the summer season; these consisted of "a good many orange, lemon, and citron trees, in great perfection, loaded with abundance of fruit, and some of each sort seemingly ripe" (quoted in Jenkins 1899:134). Deborah Logan also mentioned the greenhouse in her description of Sprigettsbury: "And the Greenhouse, under the supervision of old Virgil the Gardener, produced a flowering Aloe which almost half the town went to see & that produced a comfortable Revenue to the old man . . ." (Book No. 10, 10 October 1836). Not only did the Penn family pay a gardener to maintain the grounds during their lengthy absence from Pennsylvania,[2] but Philadelphians also apparently paid for the privilege of enjoying the Proprietary garden.

The owners of the greenhouses identified in eighteenth-century Philadelphia formed the core of the Quaker elite in the city. The Logan, Pemberton, and Norris families maintained their status through a complex web of intermarriage (figure 3.10). John Smith, who later was to marry Hannah Logan, visited the estates of the Pembertons and George Emlen while planning a garden for his plantation at Point-no-Point (Myers 1904:93). John Smith's diary also graphically illustrates this social web in the 1740s and 1750s. The threads of their lives were woven together through religious meetings, teas, and suppers, as well as through business dealings

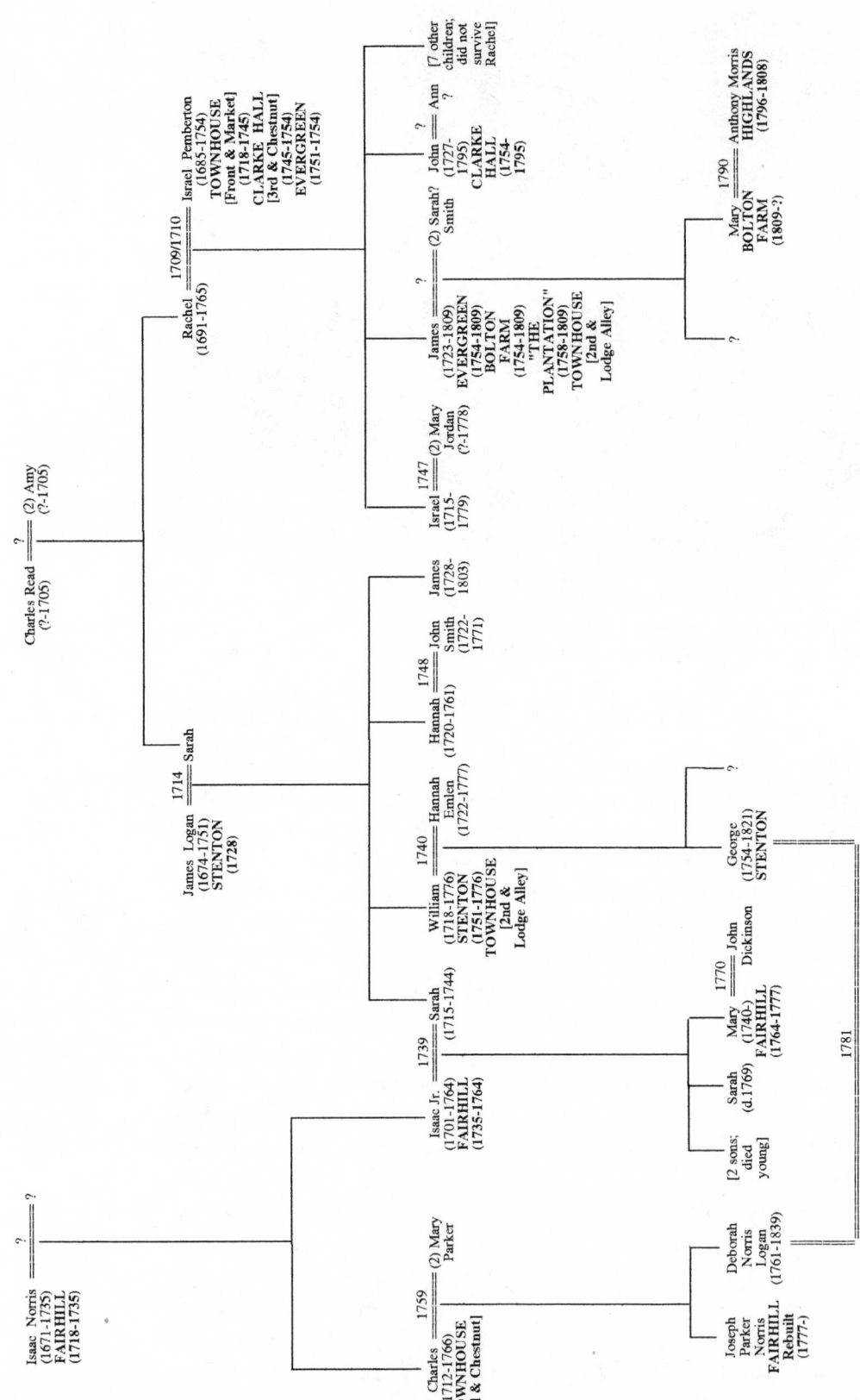

Figure 3.10. Intermarriage among the Logan, Pemberton, and Norris families.

among the men, most of whom identified their occupation as "merchant" (Tolles 1948). To this web of interrelationships we may also add a shared interest in and an exchange of ideas concerning the operation of greenhouses and the cultivation of exotics. While the religious unity of the Quaker elite became splintered later in the eighteenth century over issues raised by the Revolution, their social and business relationships continued into the nineteenth century.

GENDER IN THE GARDEN

The difference in the use of the greenhouse as a status symbol between the Chesapeake Tidewater and Philadelphia regions may illustrate differences in gender roles between the two areas. The functioning of the greenhouse as a symbol for women in the Chesapeake developed in the late eighteenth century. There, the symbolism of the greenhouse became embodied in the orange. Women were associated with oranges in paintings and at social functions; in the nineteenth century, the word "orangery" replaced "heated greenhouse" in the region. In Philadelphia, no references are made to orangeries; in fact, in 1760 the famous botanist, John Bartram, wrote to fellow horticulturist Peter Collinson in England, "I am going to build a greenhouse . . .—to put some pretty flowering winter shrubs, and plants for winter diversion:—not to be crowded with orange trees, or those natural to the Torrid Zone, but such as will do, being protected from frost" (quoted in Faris 1932:63). The stove or hypocaust system for heating greenhouses in the Chesapeake Tidewater may not have existed at all in Philadelphia in the eighteenth century. Collinson responded to Bartram by advising him to "contrive and make a stove in it [the greenhouse], to give heat in severe weather" (quoted in Faris 1932:64). Unfortunately, the lack of any physical or descriptive evidence of eighteenth-century greenhouses does not allow for a full analysis of their technical construction.

In Philadelphia, men and women apparently participated equally in the pursuit of gardening. Both sexes refer to various gardening activities and visits to gardens in the eighteenth century. In the early nineteenth century, both Deborah Logan and John Bartram (Faris 1932:39) added similarly styled greenhouses directly to the backs of their houses. Numerous estates of the late eighteenth and early nineteenth century, such as the Woodlands, Lemon Hill, and the Highlands, had greenhouses, presumably built by men (Mark Bower 1990, personal communication). Men founded the Pennsylvania Horticultural Society in 1827, which to this day annually sponsors the Philadelphia Flower Show (Janet Evans 1990, personal communication). Equal participation of men and women in gardening may reflect the equality women held in Quaker society in religious pursuits and education (Bronner 1982:44). Quaker women may not have felt compelled to create a tradition of feminine prowess to pass on to succeeding generations, at least in the sphere of eighteenth-century gardening.

The research discussed here illustrates an approach utilizing historical research along with archaeological and architectural investigations to examine the material culture of the eighteenth century. This study of one specific example of material culture, the greenhouse, begins to define the role of women as well as of men in the eighteenth-century gardening world of the Chesapeake and Philadelphia regions, although additional research is needed to fully delineate the roles of men and women in garden design and construction. While not all the questions posed above have been answered, the results of this study suggest that gender roles as well as other traditions and relationships of the past can be identified "in the garden."

1. As evidence of Margaret Freame's role in constructing the greenhouse at Sprigettsbury, Deborah Logan cited a letter she found while editing the correspondence between James Logan and the Penns (Book No. 10, 10 October 1829); a search of this correspondence at the Historical Society of Pennsylvania for the date given by Deborah Logan did not reveal this letter. In addition, Margaret Freame's letters to her brother John Penn in England, written between 1734 and 1741, do not mention a greenhouse. See Penn Papers, Private Correspondence, vol. 1, pp. 162, 219, 231; vol. 2, pp. 7, 17, 57–58, 75, 115, 125, 135, 149, 153, 163, 173, 181, 189–93; Historical Society of Pennsylvania, Philadelphia.

2. Other letters and diaries indicate a professional gardener, James Alexander, also maintained the grounds for the Penns (McLean 1983:139; Myers 1904:265).

REFERENCES

Bronner, Edwin B.

1982   Village into Town, 1701–1746. In *Philadelphia: A 300–Year History,* edited by Russell F. Weigley, pp. 33–67. W. W. Norton and Company, New York.

Colton, Judith

1976   Merlin's Cave and Queen Caroline: Garden Art as Political Propaganda. *Eighteenth-Century Studies* X:1–20.

Eberlein, Harold D., and Cortland Van Dyke Hubbard

1939   *Portrait of a Colonial City.* J. B. Lippincott Company, Philadelphia.

Fabricant, Carole

1979   Binding and Dressing Nature's Loose Tresses: The Ideology of Augustan Landscape Design. *Studies in Eighteenth-Century Culture* VIII: 109–35.

Faris, John T.

1932   *Old Gardens in and About Philadelphia and Those Who Made Them.* Bobbs-Merrill Company, Indianapolis, Indiana.

Forman, Henry Chandlee

1967   *Old Buildings, Gardens and Furniture in Tidewater Maryland.* Tidewater Publishers, Cambridge, Maryland.

Green, David

1967   *Sarah Duchess of Marlborough.* Charles Scribner's Sons, New York.

Hills, John

1796   *Plan of the City of Philadelphia and Its Environs.* John Hills, Philadelphia.

Historical Society of Pennsylvania

1734–37   Penn Papers. Private Correspondence, vol. 1–2. Manuscript Collection, Historical Society of Pennsylvania, Philadelphia.

Hosmer, Charles B., Jr.

1981   *Preservation Comes of Age: From Williamsburg to the National Trust, 1926–1949.* University Press of Virginia, Charlottesville.

Jenkins, Howard M.

1899   *The Family of William Penn, Founder of Pennsylvania Ancestry, and Descendants.* Privately printed, Philadelphia.

Lawson, William

1983   *The Country Housewife's Garden.* 1617. Reprint. Breslich & Foss, London.

Leone, Mark P.

1984   Interpreting Ideology in Historical Archaeology: Using the Rules of Perspective in the William Paca Garden in Annapolis, Maryland. In *Ideology, Power and Prehistory,* edited by Daniel Miller and Christopher Tilley, pp. 25–36. Cambridge University Press, Cambridge.

Leone, Mark P., Elizabeth Kryder-Reid, Julie H. Ernstein, and Paul A. Shackel
1989   Power Gardens of Annapolis. *Archaeology* 42(2):35–39, 74–75.

Lesbock, Suzanne
1984   *The Free Women of Petersburg: Status and Culture in a Southern Town.* W. W. Norton and Company, New York.

Liggett, Barbara
1973   Summary Report on Archaeology at Stenton. Submitted to the Colonial Dames of America in the Commonwealth of Pennsylvania.

Lockwood, Alice G. B.
1931   *Gardens of Colony and State.* Charles Scribner's Sons, New York.

Logan, Deborah Norris
1815–39 Deborah Logan Diaries, 1815–1839, Book Nos. 1–17. Historical Society of Pennsylvania, Manuscript Collection, Philadelphia.

McLean, Elizabeth
1983   Town and Country Gardens in Eighteenth Century Philadelphia. *Eighteenth-Century Life* VIII(2):136–47.

Miller, Phillip
1759   *The Gardener's Dictionary.* Seventh edition. John Rivington, London.

Myers, Albert Cook, editor
1904   *Hannah Logan's Courtship.* Ferris and Leach Publishers, Philadelphia.

Norman, J. Gary
1987   Restoration Archaeology Report: Archaeological Investigations of the Kitchen Wing, Mount Clare Mansion, Baltimore, Maryland (18BC10K). Ms. on file, Baltimore Center for Urban Archaeology.

Tilghman, J. Donnell
1953   Wye House. *Maryland Historical Magazine* XLVIII(2):89–108.

Tolles, Frederick B.
1948   *Meeting House and Counting House: The Quaker Merchants of Colonial Philadelphia.* University of North Carolina Press, Chapel Hill.

Trostel, Michael
1980   *Mount Clare: Being an Account of the Seat built by Charles Carroll, Barrister, upon his Lands at Patapsco.* National Society of Colonial Dames of America in the State of Maryland, Baltimore.

Watson, John F.
1927   *Annals of Philadelphia, and Pennsylvania, in the Olden Time.* 1844. Revised edition. Edited by Willis P. Hazard. Leary, Stuart and Company, Philadelphia.

Weeks, Christopher
1984   *Where Land and Water Intertwine: An Architectural History of Talbot County, Maryland.* The Johns Hopkins University Press, Baltimore.

Westcott, Thompson
1895   *The Historic Mansions and Buildings of Philadelphia.* Walter H. Barr, Philadelphia.

Williams, Lila L.
1923   Mount Vernon. In *Historic Gardens of Virginia,* edited by Edith Tunis Sale, pp. 189–97. The William Byrd Press Inc., Richmond, Virginia.

Yentsch, Anne
1990   The Calvert Orangery in Annapolis, Maryland: A Horticultural Symbol of Power and Prestige in an Early Eighteenth-Century Community. In *Earth Patterns: Essays in Landscape Archaeology,* edited by William M. Kelso and Rachel Most, pp. 169–87. University Press of Virginia, Charlottesville.

4

Giant in the Earth: George Washington, Landscape Designer

Dennis J. Pogue

George Washington was the proprietor of Mount Vernon for forty-five years. During this period he fought in two wars, served two terms as president of the United States, and held numerous other public offices. He also transformed the modest holding established by his father, Augustine, into a sprawling, 7,600-acre plantation with four outlying farms. The center of the plantation was his home at the "Mansion House Farm." In addition to expanding his property and reorganizing both the agricultural and crafts operations at the plantation, Washington enlarged the house and rearranged the homelot. This transformation into a late Georgian "mansion," with a variety of supporting outbuildings and a pleasure ground with extensive gardens and ambitiously planned ornamental landscape features, reflects the emergence of new fashions in English architectural and landscape design, as received and interpreted by George Washington. A wealth of documentary and graphic evidence, combined with archaeological data derived from excavations undertaken since the 1930s, provides an unusually rich record of these changes. That they are documented so fully at this site provides a unique opportunity to trace the evolution of the implementation in America of the new English aesthetic.

The story of George Washington's transformation of his home at Mount Vernon reflects the personal expression of the tastes and desires of one man and how they changed over time. His choices also reflect, and their implementation was made possible by, his prominent social and economic position as a member of Virginia's landed gentry. As was typical for this time, Washington acted as his own architect and nurseryman, depending on a number of

English publications and the advice of his peers to guide his attempts to emulate current fashions. This study of Mount Vernon, then, provides insight into the mentalité of Virginia's elite during a half century of remarkable changes in American culture and society.

Recently completed excavations have revealed the size and general layout of an area, designated by George Washington as the "Vineyard Inclosure," that included a "fruit garden" and extensive nursery beds. These important elements of the Mount Vernon landscape reflect Washington's goal of improving the plantation's self-sufficiency, as well as his long-term interests in horticultural experimentation. This project will be described in some detail as an example of the implementation of recently developed methods in landscape archaeology. Those data are then considered within the context of the broader changes in landscape design at Mount Vernon, focusing in particular on the supportive role of the "Vineyard Inclosure" in carrying out Washington's new plan.

THE GEOMETRIC DESIGN

Washington's first attempts to reshape his home followed his return from the French and Indian War. To solidify his position among Virginia's planter elite, Washington sought to expand his inherited holdings in slaves and in land. Those resources were devoted to the cultivation of tobacco as a cash crop. His marriage in 1759 to a wealthy widow, Martha Dandridge Custis, provided him with the financial means to carry out that program. By 1799 Mount Vernon had more than tripled in size, with 320 slaves distributed among the five farms (Wall 1980). Washington's unqualified adoption of the tobacco system is further evidenced by his entrance into the trans-Atlantic consignment trade, with the attendant credit-based marketing of his crop through London merchants (Ragsdale 1989).

As George Washington enlarged his plantation and entered the tobacco trade, he also expanded and rearranged the domestic seat. Additions were made to the house built by his father (ca. 1735) and acquired in 1754 from the estate of his elder half brother, Lawrence (figure 4.1) (Wall 1945). Four outbuildings—a kitchen, dairy, washhouse, and storehouse—flanked the house along the landward approach. These structures were placed in pairs on line with, and at angles to, the dwelling and were connected by walls to the west facade at the north and south corners. The locations of the four outbuildings and other structural remains were discovered through archaeological excavations conducted by Morley J. Williams and Charles Cecil Wall in the 1930s (Pogue 1988).

In 1760 two additional structures that may have been privies were erected on the mansion's east front. They and the four earlier outbuildings were linked to the house by means of "running Walls for Pallisades" (figure 4.2) (Jackson and Twohig 1976:258, 268). At the same time, the two matching rectangular gardens that flanked the driveway were enclosed with brick walls, although a portion of the wall for the north garden does not seem to have been completed until ca. 1775. The drive passed down a relatively narrow alley bounded by the garden walls and terminated at a circle on the west front of the house, so that the house and the four outbuildings formed a trapezoidal forecourt oriented toward the circle (Pogue 1988). Washington's modifications, as a whole, represent a well-conceived plan to regularize the diverse elements of Mount Vernon's earlier landscape.

Phase I

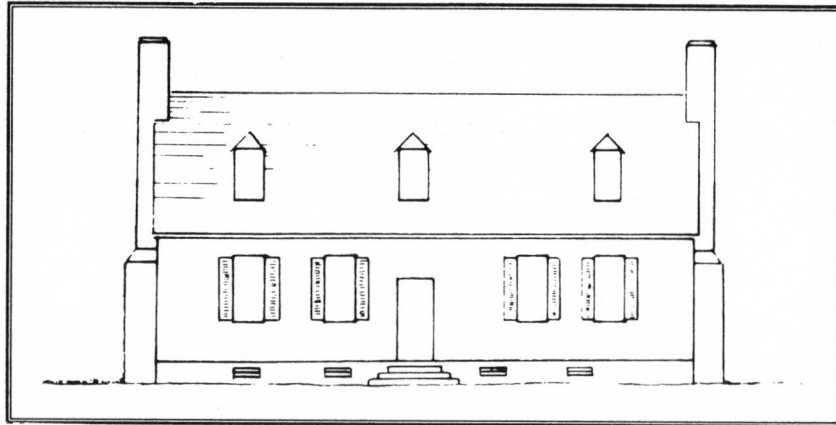

Phase II

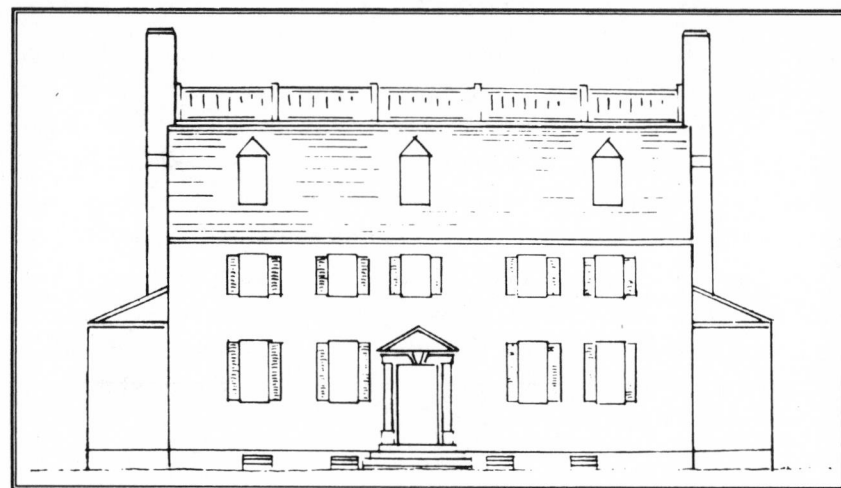

Phase III

Figure 4.1. Hypothesized evolution of the Mount Vernon mansion, west front. Courtesy of the Mount Vernon Ladies' Association.

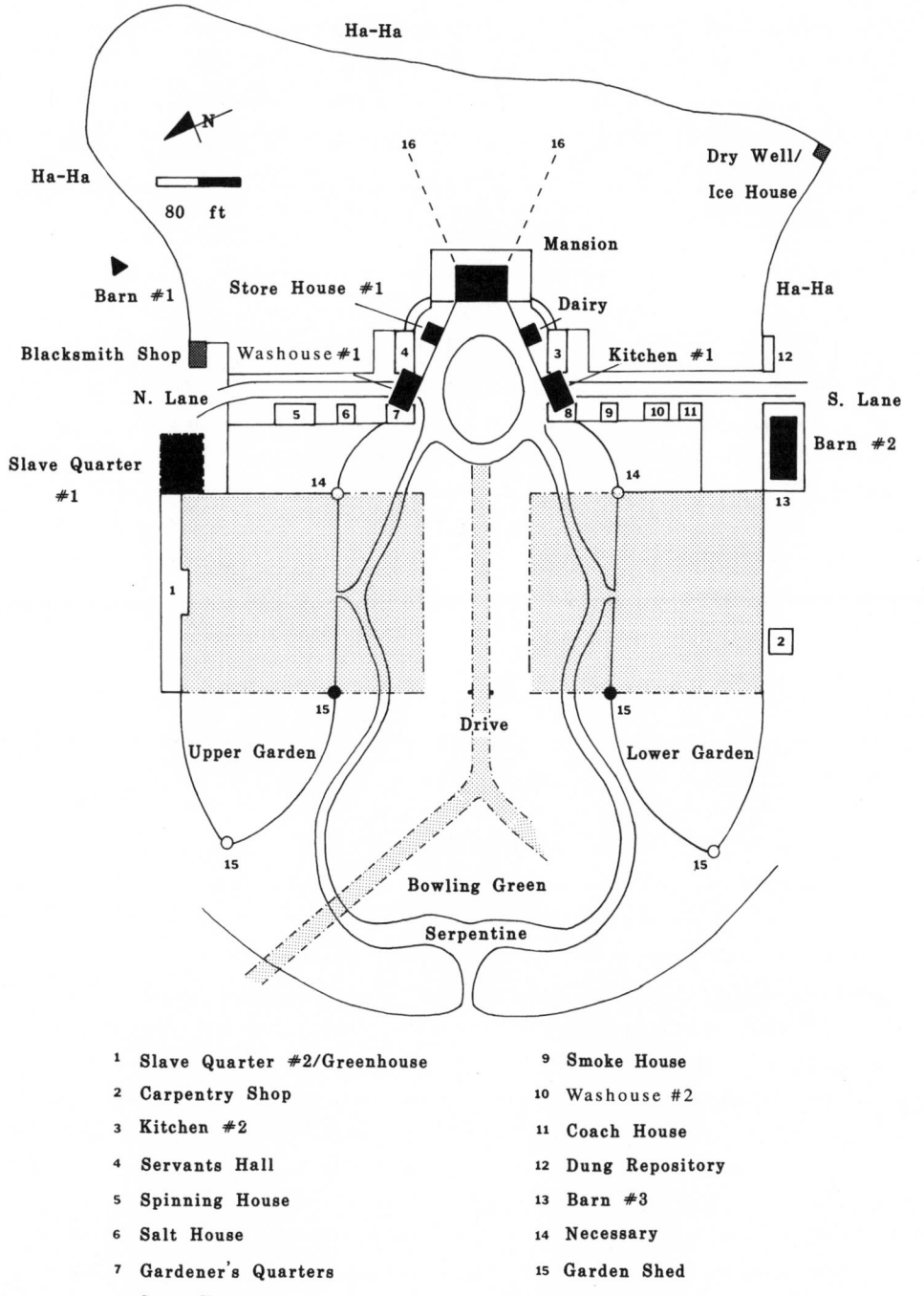

Ha-Ha

Ha-Ha

80 ft

Barn #1

Blacksmith Shop

Washouse #1

N. Lane

Slave Quarter
#1

Store House #1

Mansion

Dairy

Kitchen #1

Dry Well/
Ice House

Ha-Ha

Barn #2

Upper Garden

Drive

Lower Garden

Bowling Green

Serpentine

1	Slave Quarter #2/Greenhouse	9	Smoke House
2	Carpentry Shop	10	Washouse #2
3	Kitchen #2	11	Coach House
4	Servants Hall	12	Dung Repository
5	Spinning House	13	Barn #3
6	Salt House	14	Necessary
7	Gardener's Quarters	15	Garden Shed
8	Store House #2	16	Necessary ?

Figure 4.2. Changes to the layout of Mount Vernon over Washington's lifetime. Elements of the earlier geometric plan (before ca. 1775) include the smaller mansion house and various outbuildings (darkened and labeled) and gardens and a central drive (stippled). Structures and features of the later, more naturalistic landscape are labeled 1–15. Areas marked 16 indicate the sites of two additional outbuildings: one known foundation (to the south) that may have been a privy erected as part of the early plan and used until 1796; and the probable location (to the north) of a second privy that may have been built at the same time. The blacksmith shop and the dry well/ice house (shaded and stippled) were standing during both periods. The ha-has date to the later plan.

The configuration of the new homelot strongly resembles that of Belvoir, the home of the Fairfax family, located less than four miles downriver from Mount Vernon. Belvoir was built between 1736 and 1741. Washington visited the plantation on numerous occasions, as a youth and as an adult, until the house and several outbuildings were destroyed by fire in 1783 (Shott 1978:5–11). Archaeological investigations at Belvoir, conducted in the 1970s, revealed the layout of the house and its associated dependencies. Three major brick outbuildings flanked the house at angles on the landward side, with two on the north and the third on the south. Brick walls connected the two nearer structures to the main house. The walls extended beyond the house to the east and finally terminated at the corners of two smaller brick foundations that may have been privies (Shott 1978:54, 189–90).

Both the Belvoir and Mount Vernon landscapes recall the geometric, formal style that had been the fashion in America for several decades. An elaborate formal garden was installed by the late seventeenth century at the College of William and Mary in Williamsburg (Kornwolf 1984:95), and archaeological evidence for an even earlier formal garden, installed ca. 1680, has been revealed at Bacon's Castle in Surry County (Luccketti 1990). Formal gardens were, by definition, artificial in appearance and were characterized by a rigidly symmetrical layout, incorporating such elements as terraces, parterres, and linear plantings (Kornwolf 1984:94–97).

THE NATURALISTIC DESIGN

Just prior to the outbreak of the American Revolution, George Washington embarked upon a second phase of alterations to his home and to the surrounding landscape. Once again the house was enlarged, the four outbuildings attached to the west facade were demolished and replaced, and the gardens and grounds were reorganized. The result was a nearly complete transformation that incorporated current concepts of naturalistic design within the constraints of the initial layout. The "picturesque" or "naturalistic" aesthetic was substituted for the previous formal style. The new landscape was less symmetrical in layout, with plantings and other elements that appeared natural and curvilinear shapes for walkways, driveways, and planting beds. In addition, the new plan clearly indicates a concern to preserve and to incorporate the natural vistas.

To enlarge the house, Washington added wings to both gables and raised the roof to two and one-half stories. The facade was made fashionable through the addition of numerous architectural details. Colonnades linked the house with two new, symmetrically placed dependencies. Washington also added a pediment above the main door facing the circle, a columned two-story piazza running the length of the east front, a cupola, and a "Palladian" window, which he installed in the newly added large dining room (Wall 1945, 1980). These architectural features were generally successful in masking the flaws inherent in almost doubling in size what had been an unpretentious farmhouse of modest proportions.

The earlier constricted, geometric plan of the gardens and grounds was also replaced with a more open, naturalistic scheme. The new outbuildings were set farther back from the dwelling, with the two dependencies linked to the corners of the house by open colonnades and the others arranged in two flanking lines running parallel with the long axis of the dwelling. Those structures were set in two groups, north and south, and fronted on a lane that intersected with the entrance circle. The rectangular garden enclosures were reconfigured into narrower, but longer, elliptical shapes that better fit the new, open design. The driveway was removed, allowing for the placement of a bowling green bounded by a serpentine walk and naturally planted "wildernesses" between the gardens. Numerous meandering ha-has, or walls that served as physical barriers but not as visual impediments, were also erected in the 1780s (de Forrest 1982; Pogue 1988).

The newly created landscape is a hybrid, clearly showing the combination of an English Renaissance tradition united with the emerging picturesque aesthetic. The flanking colonnades are extremely unusual in that they are open on both sides, allowing the panoramic view of the Potomac to be visible from the forecourt. The open piazza running the length of the east front is equally notable for this period and may be an innovation introduced to America by George Washington (Charles Brownell 1990, personal communication). It provided a convenient domestic space that was ideally situated to take advantage of the natural vista. Both of these features reflect Washington's apparent desire to accentuate the natural advantages of the site in accordance with picturesque design.

The view of the mansion looking east down the main axis of the bowling green highlights the bilateral symmetry and, together with the visually elevated facade, produces a classical Georgian effect. The linkage of the flanking outbuildings to the house by colonnades serves to make the structure appear larger than it is. The trapezoidal shape of the bowling green, with the long axes converging toward the house, is a common Georgian device that also serves to heighten the prominence of the structure when viewed from a distance (Leone 1988a, 1988b; Weber et al. 1990). The new "naturally" planted "wildernesses" and the serpentine-shaped walkways flanking the bowling green, along with the open colonnades, introduce the more modern perspective. In addition, the river approach included a deer park and "hanging wood" on the bank below the dwelling. These served to set off the structure, framed by a "natural" belt of trees and shrubs, on its imposing prominence overlooking the Potomac River. This virtually complete makeover was documented by Samuel Vaughan, who drew a plan of Mount Vernon during a visit to the plantation in 1787 (figure 4.3).

The noted English architect Benjamin Henry Latrobe, who visited Mount Vernon in 1796, described the layout of the estate and recorded his opinions of it in his journal. Latrobe's review was mixed, to say the least. He criticized the arrangement of the entranceway, which took the visitor on a circuitous route through the south group of service buildings before arriving at the circle, and summarized the entire plan as "extremely formal." He was particularly displeased by finding that most formal of all English landscape features, "a parterre, chipped and trimmed with infinite care into the forms of a richly flourished Fleur de Lis: The expiring groans I hope of our Grandfather's pedantry." Even so, Latrobe appreciated the picturesque elements and concluded that "Nature has lavished magnificence" on the site, "nor has Art interfered but to exhibit her to advantage" (Carter 1977[1]:165). Most visitors were less critical than Latrobe. For example, a Polish traveler named Julian Niemcewicz, after visiting Mount Vernon in 1798, commented that: "The whole plantation, the garden, and the rest prove well that a man born with natural taste may guess a beauty without having ever seen its model" (Niemcewicz 1965:98).

Niemcewicz's comment raises the interesting question of how George Washington was exposed to principles of English landscape design. Though relatively poorly educated and little traveled abroad, Washington was well read. His library contained numerous gardening references, including several well-known examples, such as Mawe and Abercrombie's *The*

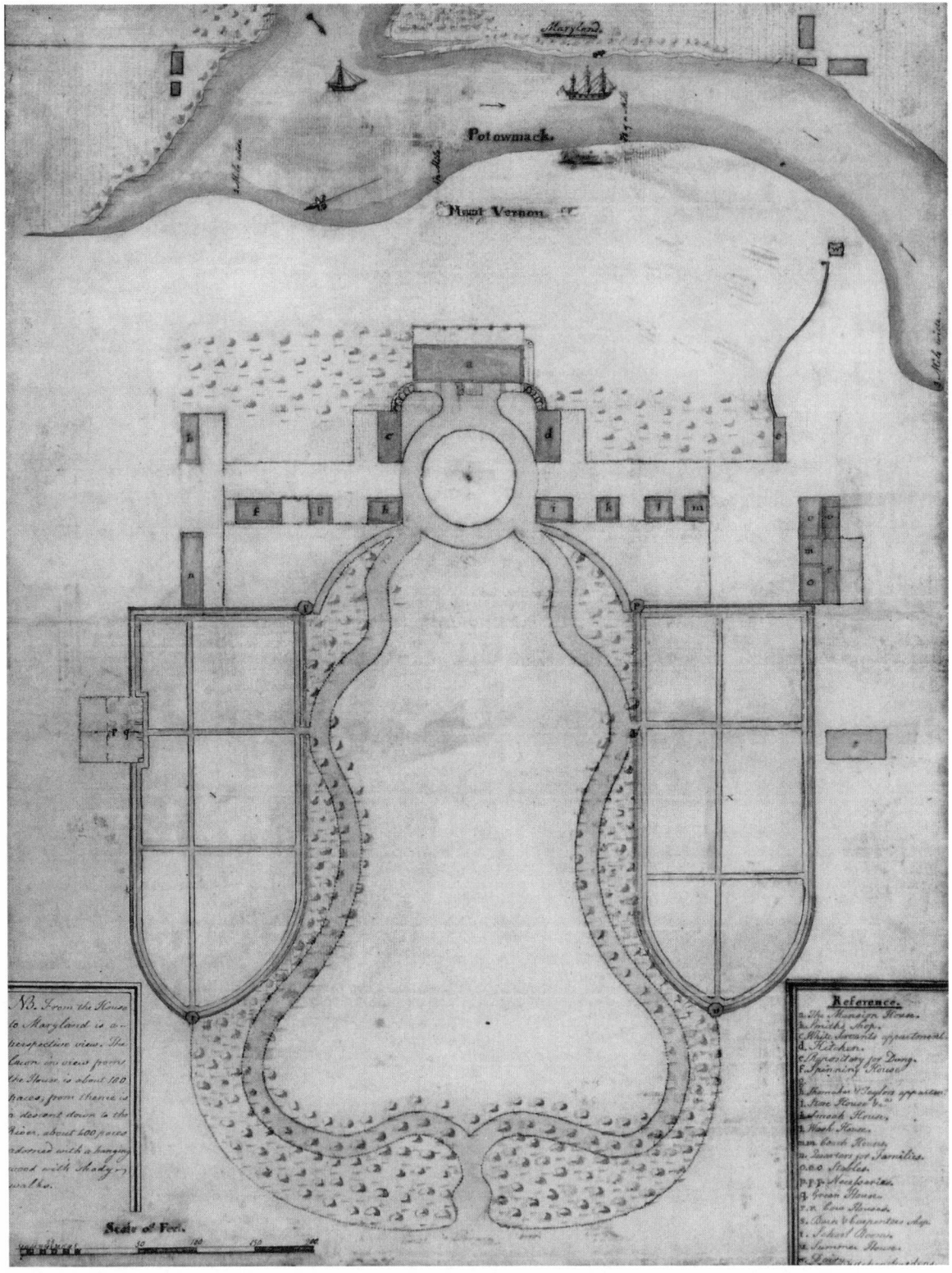

Figure 4.3. Plan of Mount Vernon (1787) by Samuel Vaughan, showing a naturalistic landscape design. Courtesy of the Mount Vernon Ladies' Association.

Universal Gardener and Botanist (1778), Miller's *Abridgement of the Gardener's Dictionary* (1763), and Langley's *New Principles of Gardening* (1728). Langley was a particularly strong advocate of the naturally picturesque style. The designs of several of the architectural details, particularly the Palladian window, chimney pieces, and doorways, were drawn from various builders' pattern books (Reiff 1986:277). Finally, Washington received advice from friends, acquaintances, and workmen on many occasions and visited several gardens during his travels in the mid-Atlantic region (Leighton 1976:247–70). With the rarity of professional architects and landscape designers in America, this seems to have been a common practice among members of the colonial gentry (Macomber 1969).

A substantial brick greenhouse situated adjacent to the upper garden was constructed in 1784 (figure 4.4). This structure greatly increased Washington's capacities for growing and experimenting with exotic plants, as well as for ornamental gardening in general. Washington's design of this structure was influenced by the advice of Tench Tilghman, his former military aid, who in turn enlisted the help of his sister-in-law, Margaret Tilghman Carroll of Baltimore. Mrs. Carroll was extremely knowledgeable on the subject and was able to offer advice on a wide range of issues (Leighton 1976:264; Macomber 1953; see also Weber, chapter 3, this volume). The investment in specialized gardening structures like the greenhouse, in combination with a concern for managing the natural surroundings, has been interpreted as a particularly conspicuous claim to high social status among the gentry elite. By manipulating the natural world—establishing and maintaining intricate and fashionable gardens and other landscape features—the owner announced his position of high status. This claim was strengthened by the possession of such a specialized structure as a greenhouse (Yentsch 1990).

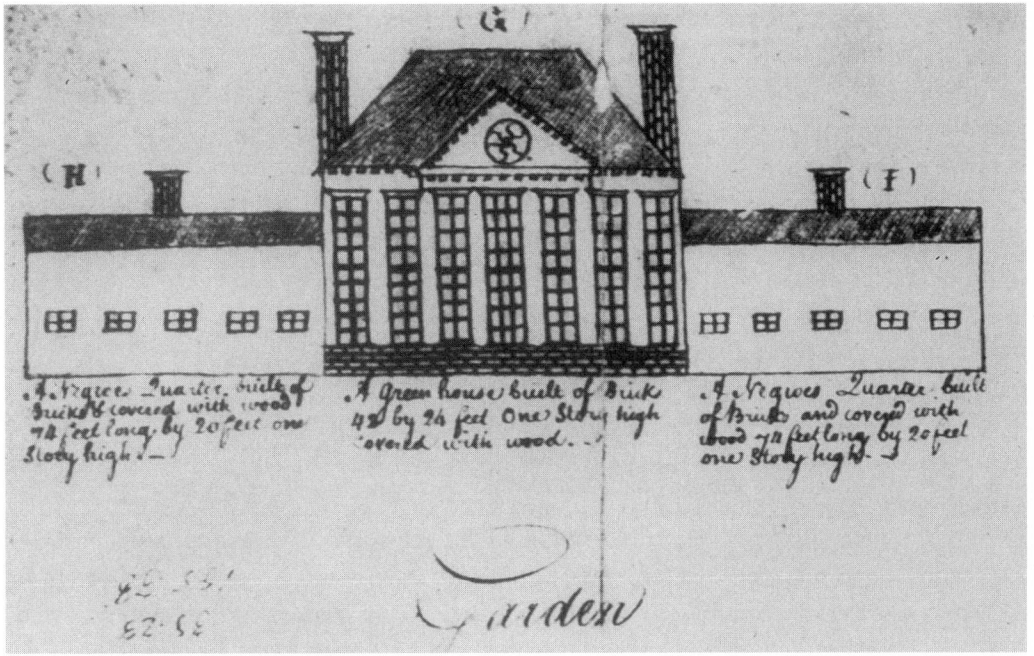

Figure 4.4. Drawing of the 1784 greenhouse (center) and slave quarter wings (added in 1793) from a fire insurance policy issued in 1803. Virginia State Library and Archives.

George Washington's efforts to replace the earlier geometric grounds with the new picturesque layout are a remarkable indication of the changing fashion in landscape design during this period (cf. Kornwolf 1984). Although the placement of the gardens and out-buildings was still symmetrical and Latrobe's comment on the existence of a parterre indicates that elements of old-style formalism remained, the combination of the undulating shapes of the ha-has, the bowling green, and other features clearly reflects the new picturesque fashion. That Washington was able to produce this much more open design while operating within the constraints of the existing plan is a considerable accomplishment.

"VINEYARD INCLOSURE" EXCAVATION

Extensive archaeological investigations were conducted in an area indicated by documentary records as the site of George Washington's "Vineyard Inclosure." An experimental vineyard had been established there in the 1770s. Beds for nurturing the multitude of seedlings required to implement the new picturesque design, along with a "fruit garden," were laid out in the mid-1780s. Those later developments clearly were related to the overall landscape changes carried out at that time and complemented the recently built greenhouse. The area continued to serve as nursery, fruit garden, and botanical garden throughout George Washington's lifetime (de Forrest 1982). While the written record pertaining to this area is voluminous, it unfortunately does not provide such crucial data as the size of the enclosure, the layout of the fruit garden, and the distances between the trees there. The archaeological excavation was carried out in an attempt to provide this spatial evidence.

Today the area is used primarily as a meadow and is enclosed by a post-and-rail fence that was erected several decades ago. The eighteenth-century "Inclosure" is recorded as having been surrounded by a similar type of fence, as was a grove of trees shown there on several mid-nineteenth-century plans and bird's-eye views (figure 4.5). This suggests that the fruit garden continued to exist in some form well into the next century. As fruit trees and fences both have limited life spans, it is likely that the trees were periodically replaced and the rail fence was rebuilt. Therefore, any fence lines and tree holes revealed archaeologically require careful analysis to differentiate between those associated with the eighteenth-century "Inclosure" and subsequent versions.

As the remains of the vineyard/fruit garden/nursery were hypothesized to be numerous but also spatially dispersed, a strategy of stripping the overlying plowed soil in twenty-one units of various sizes was adopted. In this way, large sections of the targeted area could be examined intensively in hopes of identifying postholes for fence lines, tree root molds, planting holes, and any other archaeological remains. In addition, one 5-by-10-foot unit and two 5-by-5-foot units placed at the edges of the meadow in relatively undisturbed contexts were excavated stratigraphically (figure 4.6).

The general lack of intact strata, combined with a paucity of diagnostic artifacts recovered from the features selected for excavation, makes dating of features difficult. Except for the three test units located outside the existing fenced area, which were excavated by hand and revealed intact stratigraphic deposits, all areas examined have been plowed. Most of the features are situated below plow zone and intruding subsoil, providing little opportunity to establish relative chronology. In effect, the site plan that has been generated is a true two-

Figure 4.5. Bird's-eye view of Mount Vernon (1859) by H. Whateley, showing the "Vineyard Inclosure" located between the new tomb and the stable. Lithograph courtesy of Mount Vernon Ladies' Association.

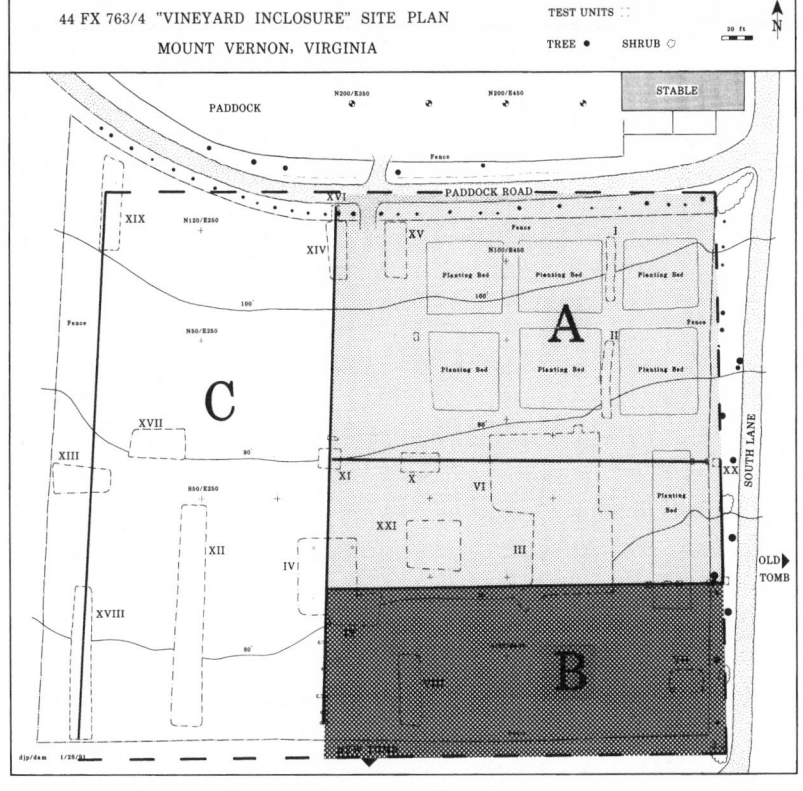

Figure 4.6. Site plan of the "Vineyard Inclosure," with the hypothesized boundaries (fences and ditches) indicated. The area devoted to the fruit garden is shaded and marked A and B; the area marked B is the section of the garden that was cut off by a fence in the 1790s and presumably converted to planting beds. The area originally devoted to planting beds is marked C.

dimensional representation. As a result, interpretation of the functions and dates of those features largely has been based on tracing and inferring spatial relationships, combined with the little stratigraphic data available from the hand–excavated units.

Numerous archaeological features were revealed that together indicate a pattern suggestive of the boundaries for the fruit garden. These seem to be related to other postholes, which are interpreted as additional fence lines that bounded a larger rectangular area, slightly

Figure 4.7. View of test unit at the "Vineyard Inclosure," facing west, with posthole/mold and drainage ditch associated with the "fruit garden" revealed below the plow zone and numerous fill layers.

less than three acres in size (360 by 400 feet), suggestive of the "Vineyard Inclosure." Several generations of fences that surrounded the area—eighteenth, nineteenth, and twentieth century in date—are indicated. Three ditches, measuring between two feet and three and a half feet in width, also appear to be associated with the fruit garden. Their placement suggests that they served for drainage as well as for boundaries (figure 4.7). No evidence for the vineyard or for the nursery planting beds was found.

Contemporary gardening authorities commonly recommended the siting of orchards and fruit gardens on gently sloping terrain oriented to the south (cf. Weber et al. 1990:139). The area examined possesses a full southern exposure, but the topography is relatively steep, falling thirty-five feet between the paddock road on the north and the new tomb on the south. The destructive impact of water runoff seems likely to have posed a considerable danger to young plants, possibly necessitating the placement of the ditches.

According to George Washington's writings, he frequently called for the construction of "live fences" at the plantation that seemingly consisted of closely planted hedges in conjunction with a ditch and bank. In 1792 he referred to "a live fence" as forming at least "one side of the fence to the Vineyard Inclosure" (Fitzpatrick 1939:229). In addition, in that same year, he ordered that "[t]he old ditch and bank which splits this inclosure in two is to be levelled" (Fitzpatrick 1939:179). The ditch that runs north and south and is thought to have formed the western boundary of the fruit garden may be associated with a live fence, or may be the "old ditch" referred to, or both.

Excavation of a ten-foot section of that ditch yielded the majority of the very few artifacts from unplowed contexts generated by the project. Sixty-four fragments of green wine bottle glass were found, most of which mend to form a bottle with a diagnostically late-eighteenth-century profile. In addition, a fragment of an unusual hand-molded brick or tile with two concave edges was found in the same stratum (figure 4.8). Several virtually identical examples have been found at Mount Vernon over the years as the result of various construction and restoration projects. Unfortunately, none derives from undisturbed or precisely recorded contexts. Two other types of molded bricks of the kind that most likely were used to cap the water table portion of a foundation have also been found on the estate, with several of these recovered in general association with the kitchen on the circle that was torn down in 1775 (Pogue 1988). As no existing structures, garden walls, or other landscape features exhibit either style of molded brick, it is possible that all those bricks are remnants of non-extant eighteenth-century outbuildings.

Figure 4.8. Artifacts from Mount Vernon. Clockwise from upper left: mended portion of a late-eighteenth-century green glass bottle and a molded brick or tile, both excavated from the ditch that may have formed the west boundary for the fruit garden; molded brick found in the south grove near the kitchen and hypothesized to have been part of a decorative water table for one of the earlier outbuildings. Photograph by Paul Kennedy.

In addition to the fence lines and ditches, numerous features marking the locations of tree roots were revealed. Many of these are of a size consistent with fruit trees, but this type of evidence is far from diagnostic. In the eighteenth century, orchards and fruit gardens were laid out systematically with a standard interval between the rows of trees and between trees within rows (Kelso 1984; Leighton 1976; Weber et al. 1990). Therefore, it was anticipated that the root molds from the fruit trees laid out in 1786 would form a regular pattern and would be oriented squarely with the enclosure.

Only two of the molds seem to have that potential. They form a line parallel with the east-west boundaries and are thirty feet apart, an interval that could fit with the 1786 planting. In addition, these molds were situated within larger, subcircular features that may be the remains of planting holes. The planting of fruit trees in large holes where nutrients were placed to foster growth was recommended by numerous authorities in the colonial period (Langley 1728; Miller 1771). The failure to locate additional planting holes suggests that, if they existed, they have been destroyed by plowing and erosion.

The area interpreted as the fruit garden is rectangular (approximately 360 by 260 feet), slightly less than two acres in size (figure 4.6). The 1786 description of the garden plan calls for four quadrants, with up to nine rows of trees planted in each (Jackson and Twohig 1978:286). A pattern of trees spaced thirty feet apart within rows and with twenty feet between rows could have fit within the enclosure indicated. This is a slightly tighter interval between rows than was normally recommended for orchards (usually between twenty-five and forty feet) by gardening authorities of the period (cf. Leighton 1976). George Washington himself recommended a forty-foot interval between trees and between rows when he advertised his farms for rent in 1793 (Fitzpatrick 1940a:444–45). That document specifies that additional fruit trees could be planted between those rows, however, which could have reduced the interval between rows to twenty feet. An interval of approximately thirty feet between rows and between trees in rows was found at the eighteenth-century orchard at Mount Clare (Weber et al. 1990:140), and an interval of twenty-five feet between trees and forty feet between rows was revealed for a late-eighteenth- to early-nineteenth-century orchard at Monticello (Kelso 1984:166).

Washington always referred to the area he planted with fruit trees as a "fruit garden," instead of as an orchard (cf. Jackson and Twohig 1978:286). According to gardeners' dictionaries of the period, fruit gardens exhibited subtle differences from orchards; common references to planting trees in fruit gardens along walls and in espaliers suggest their placement in a tighter, confined space. One result seems to have been a closer spacing of the trees. According to Mawe and Abercrombie (1803:98), while "Standard fruit trees should generally be allowed thirty or forty feet distance," in a garden the minimum distance was "from twenty to thirty feet." However, the 1771 edition of Miller's *The Gardener's Calendar,* a later edition of a volume owned by Washington, stipulates a thirty-foot spacing for trees placed in standard rows in fruit gardens, an interval no different from that recommended for orchards (Miller 1771:65). If the planting interval in the "Vineyard Inclosure" was thirty feet between trees and twenty feet between rows, as the archaeological data suggest, that seems consistent with the spacing recommended for a fruit garden.

The 360-by-260-foot fruit garden laid out in 1786 appears to have been reduced by a third to 240 by 260 feet in the 1790s. Excavations revealed a row of posts, set at a ten-foot interval, running between the garden's east and west boundaries, apparently marking a post-and-rail fence. If this interpretation is correct, Washington's decision to truncate the garden may have been based upon the need for additional planting beds, or possibly by the difficulty in growing fruit trees in the lower portion of the enclosure, or both.

Samples of soils extracted from several of the postholes/molds and from the two possible planting holes were analyzed in hopes of identifying plant remains—seeds, pollen, and opal phytoliths. As pollen is wind-blown and seeds commonly are transported by natural agents, they may be found at great distances from their original locations. Recovery of seeds and pollen grains may allow identification of the types of trees growing in the general vicinity, however (Miller et al. 1990). Phytoliths, literally "plant stones," are mineral particles produced within living plants as a result of normal physiological processes. These are released into the ground when the plant decays and therefore may identify plant species that were in that spot (Piperno 1988:142–47). The results of the analyses were disappointing. Unfortunately, the state of preservation for pollen was found to be poor, with very few pollen grains identified. No seeds or phytoliths were recovered. The absence of phytoliths may constitute useful negative evidence, however, as fruit trees do not produce phytoliths (Piperno 1988:19–40).

In addition to the fence line and the ditches that seem to be associated with the fruit garden, numerous other postholes and other features were revealed that suggest the boundaries for the entire "Vineyard Inclosure." Although incomplete, this evidence suggests a rectangular area bounded on the north by the paddock road, on the east by the south lane, on the south by the new tomb, and on the west by a later service lane. The area is divided into two unequal halves by the north-south ditch, with the fruit garden originally cultivated in the larger, eastern portion (figure 4.6). The documentary evidence indicates that planting beds for a wide variety of hedging material, vegetables, trees, and grasses were located in the areas not devoted to the fruit garden. No archaeological evidence was found for the beds, and it seems likely that those shallow features have been completely disturbed by plowing and erosion.

LANDSCAPE IDEOLOGY

Numerous scholars have pointed out that by the early eighteenth century, members of the Virginia planter gentry were willing and able to mark their social prominence by adopting a patrician culture of conspicuous display. Manipulation of landscape and adherence to changing fashions in architecture and other domains of material culture became important means of symbolizing gentry status (Hudgins 1990; Isaac 1982; Kelso 1984, 1990; Sanford 1990). George Washington's long-term development of Mount Vernon's landscape clearly reflects this ideology. In addition, the changes he made were consciously patterned after currently fashionable ideas in English architectural and landscape design. This dependence on English design prototypes, in turn, reflects a trend toward the "re-Anglicization" of American culture. Finally, the changes may be viewed as a means of reifying both Washington's gentry status and the authority of his class during a period of social upheaval.

Isaac (1982) has portrayed the decades just before the American Revolution as a period of dramatic social change. At mid-century, Virginia society was dominated by the planter class, whose status was closely linked with the Church of England. The disestablishment of the Anglican Church as a result of a series of popular religious evangelical movements in the

1740s threatened the authority of the landed elite. The downturn in the tobacco market, a demographic shift brought about by a changing economy and westward expansion, and the events leading to the Revolution and break with England all combined with the religious upheaval to redefine the roles of the various components of Virginia society. To varying degrees, all of these developments fostered the erosion of the authority of Virginia's planter elite.

Among scholars who contend that, in the years just prior to the Revolution, American culture had come to be more like that of Britain than ever before, Deetz (1977), Greene (1988), and Isaac (1982) have produced particularly detailed studies. Their arguments for this "re-Anglicization" are supported by changes in architectural design, foodways, burial practices, and a variety of other forms of material culture.

Leone (1988a, 1988b) uses the interpretation of a broad crisis in gentry authority, combined with the trend toward re-Anglicization, to guide his study of eighteenth-century Annapolis. Support for this hypothesis is provided by patterns in architectural and landscape design and in material culture. The Annapolis gentry is viewed as responding to the crisis by building a series of formal gardens "to convince people that a rational social order based on nature was possible and that those with such access to its laws were its natural leaders" (Leone 1988a:250).

It is noteworthy that George Washington implemented his second round of alterations to Mount Vernon beginning in the years just prior to the Revolution. There is no indication that George Washington's patriotism and extended public service were the results of any conscious realization of their potential for reducing the erosion of the authority of his class. The initiation of landscape modifications in the context of broader social and cultural changes suggests that the changes may signify an attempt to reify his personal authority, however. Washington's conscious imitation of contemporary English fashions also supports the suggestion that at the highest levels of society, at least, American culture was achieving a closer approximation of its English counterpart.

The initial expansion and reorganization of Mount Vernon was the natural consequence of George Washington's intention to emulate the leading men of his colony and engage in the region's traditional agricultural pursuit—production of tobacco for export to England as a cash crop. The decline of tobacco as a profitable export crop forced Washington to diversify his operation and to make his plantation more self-sufficient. An even more ambitious round of building and landscaping resulted in the creation of an estate incorporating current English fashions. Construction of the greenhouse and the establishment of the nursery in the "Vineyard Inclosure" in the 1780s indicate the extent of Washington's commitment to carry out the new design and, along with the fruit garden laid out in 1786, demonstrate his intense interest in matters horticultural.

No original documents have been found detailing Washington's design plans, but abundant circumstantial evidence indicates the various influences on his thinking. It is likely that his vision of Mount Vernon evolved over time, resulting in a remarkable combination of old and new, adapting the new ideas to the specific natural environment and to the constraints imposed by earlier construction.

George Washington also found great pleasure in pursuing his lifelong preoccupation with landscaping and reorganizing his Mount Vernon home. This is amply recorded in his writings. In a letter written at the time of his final retirement from public service in 1797, he succinctly drew a telling contrast between his dutiful public activities and those domestic pursuits that were closer to his heart: "I am once more seated under my own Vine and fig-tree, and hope to spend the remainder of my days . . . in peaceful retirement, making political pursuits yield to the more rational amusement of cultivating the Earth" (Fitzpatrick 1940b:432).

The fashionable facade he created would perform its intended role as symbol of the position of its owner and of the success of the plantation it epitomized for nearly three decades. With Martha Washington's death in 1802, three years after the passing of her husband, the plantation was broken up among several heirs. Declining productivity was the norm over the succeeding half century, and the mansion and associated grounds were in such poor condition by 1853 that Anne Pamela Cunningham was compelled to form the Mount Vernon Ladies' Association with the mandate of rescuing and preserving this first American landmark (Wall 1980). The result has been to preserve, albeit buried, the record of five decades of landscape design that reflects a period of major changes to American society.

REFERENCES

Carter, Edward C., editor
1977   *The Virginia Journals of Benjamin Henry Latrobe, 1795–1798.* Two volumes. Yale University Press, New Haven.

Deetz, James
1977   *In Small Things Forgotten: The Archaeology of Early American Life.* Anchor Press, Doubleday, Garden City, New York.

de Forrest, Elizabeth K.
1982   *The Gardens and Grounds at Mount Vernon.* Mount Vernon Ladies' Association, Mount Vernon, Virginia.

Fitzpatrick, John C., editor
1939   *The Writings of George Washington from the Original Manuscript Sources,* vol. 32. United States Government Printing Office, Washington, D.C.
1940a   *The Writings of George Washington from the Original Manuscript Sources,* vol. 34. United States Government Printing Office, Washington, D.C.
1940b   *The Writings of George Washington from the Original Manuscript Sources,* vol. 35. United States Government Printing Office, Washington, D.C.

Greene, Jack P.
1988   *Pursuits of Happiness: The Social Development of Early Modern British Colonies and the Formation of American Culture.* University of North Carolina Press, Chapel Hill.

Hudgins, Carter L.
1990   Robert "King" Carter and the Landscape of Tidewater Virginia in the Eighteenth Century. In *Earth Patterns: Essays in Landscape Archaeology,* edited by William M. Kelso and Rachel Most, pp. 59–70. University Press of Virginia, Charlottesville.

Isaac, Rhys
1982   *The Transformation of Virginia, 1740–1790.* Institute of Early American History and Culture, University of North Carolina Press, Chapel Hill.

Jackson, Donald, and Dorothy Twohig, editors
1976   *The Diaries of George Washington,* vol. 1. University Press of Virginia, Charlottesville.
1978   *The Diaries of George Washington,* vol. 3. University Press of Virginia, Charlottesville.

Kelso, William M.
1984   Landscape Archaeology: A Key to Virginia's Cultivated Past. In *British and American Gardens in the Eighteenth Century,* edited by Robert P. Maccubbin and Peter Martin, pp. 159–69. The Colonial Williamsburg Foundation, Williamsburg, Virginia.

1990   Landscape Archaeology at Thomas Jefferson's Monticello. In *Earth Patterns: Essays in Landscape Archaeology,* edited by William M. Kelso and Rachel Most, pp. 7–22. University Press of Virginia, Charlottesville.

Kornwolf, James D.

1984   The Picturesque in the American Garden and Landscape Before 1800. In *British and American Gardens in the Eighteenth Century,* edited by Robert P. Maccubbin and Peter Martin, pp. 93–106. The Colonial Williamsburg Foundation, Williamsburg, Virginia.

Langley, Batty

1728   *New Principles of Gardening.* London.

Leighton, Ann

1976   *American Gardens in the Eighteenth Century.* Houghton Mifflin, Boston.

Leone, Mark P.

1988a   The Georgian Order as the Order of Merchant Capitalism in Annapolis, Maryland. In *The Recovery of Meaning: Historical Archaeology in the Eastern United States,* edited by Mark P. Leone and Parker B. Potter Jr., pp. 235–61. Smithsonian Institution Press, Washington, D.C.

1988b   The Relationship Between Archaeological Data and the Documentary Record: 18th Century Gardens in Annapolis, Maryland. *Historical Archaeology* 22(1):29–35.

Luccketti, Nicholas

1990   Archaeological Excavations at Bacon's Castle, Surry County, Virginia. In *Earth Patterns: Essays in Landscape Archaeology,* edited by William M. Kelso and Rachel Most, pp. 23–42. University Press of Virginia, Charlottesville.

Macomber, Walter M.

1953   The Rebuilding of the Greenhouse-Quarters. Mount Vernon Ladies' Association, *Annual Report* 1952:19–26.

1969   Mount Vernon's "Architect." *Historical Society of Fairfax County, Virginia* 10:1–10.

Mawe, Thomas, and John Abercrombie

1778   *The Universal Gardener and Botanist.* London.

1803   *Gardener's Calendar and General Dictionary.* London.

Miller, Naomi F., Anne Yentsch, Dolores Piperno, and Barbara Paca

1990   Two Centuries of Landscape Change at Morven, Princeton, New Jersey. In *Earth Patterns: Essays in Landscape Archaeology,* edited by William M. Kelso and Rachel Most, pp. 257–76. University Press of Virginia, Charlottesville.

Miller, Philip

1763   *Abridgement of the Gardener's Dictionary.* London.

1771   *The Gardener's Calendar.* London.

Niemcewicz, Julian

1965   *Under Their Vine and Fig Tree: Travels in America in 1797–1799, 1805,* edited by M. Budka. Grassman Publishing, Elizabeth, New Jersey.

Piperno, Dolores R.

1988   *Phytolith Analysis: An Archaeological and Geological Perspective.* Academic Press, San Diego.

Pogue, Dennis J.

1988   Archaeology at George Washington's Mount Vernon: 1931–1987. Mount Vernon Ladies' Association Archaeology Department, File Report No. 1.

Ragsdale, Bruce A.

1989   George Washington, the British Tobacco Trade, and Economic Opportunity in Prerevolutionary Virginia. *The Virginia Magazine of History and Biography* 97(2):133–62.

Reiff, Daniel D.

1986   *Small Georgian Houses in England and Virginia: Origins and Development Through the 1750s.* Associated University Presses, London.

Sanford, Douglas W.

1990   The Gardens at Germanna, Virginia. In *Earth Patterns: Essays in Landscape Archaeology,* edited by William M. Kelso and Rachel Most, pp. 43–57. University Press of Virginia, Charlottesville.

Shott, George C.
1978   U.S. Army Engineer Museum Archaeological Investigations of Belvoir Historic Site, Fort Belvoir, Virginia. U.S. Army Engineer Center and Fort Belvoir, Fort Belvoir, Virginia.

Wall, Charles C.
1945   Notes on the Early History of Mount Vernon. *William and Mary Quarterly* (Third Series) II:173–90.
1980   *George Washington: Citizen-Soldier.* University Press of Virginia, Charlottesville.

Weber, Carmen A., Elizabeth Anderson Comer, Louise E. Akerson, and Gary Norman
1990   Mount Clare: An Interdisciplinary Approach to the Restoration of a Georgian Landscape. In *Earth Patterns: Essays in Landscape Archaeology,* edited by William M. Kelso and Rachel Most, pp. 135–52. University Press of Virginia, Charlottesville.

Yentsch, Anne
1990   The Calvert Orangery in Annapolis, Maryland: A Horticultural Symbol of Power and Prestige in an Early Eighteenth-Century Community. In *Earth Patterns: Essays in Landscape Archaeology,* edited by William M. Kelso and Rachel Most, pp. 169–87. University Press of Virginia, Charlottesville.

5

The Archaeology of Rachel's Garden

Larry McKee

... the place that touches the heart most is the garden.

(Julia Rider 1914)

Why do archaeologists study gardens? Often it is because we are paid to do it by preservation organizations eager to employ our techniques and skills in gathering evidence useful in restoring relict gardens. Archaeologists usually are not content just to provide a catalog of finds and a set of plans showing the location of former garden features. Data analysis is as important as data recovery in these projects, and we strive to reconstruct meaning, as well as to provide raw information, through our work. Toward this end, the archaeological study of historical landscapes and gardens puts great emphasis on understanding the significance of landscape to those who once inhabited the places we study. The hope is that there will be enough clues left in the ground and from other sources to relay people's intentions in constructing their physical surroundings as they did as well as their perception of the results of their efforts.

This chapter discusses the archaeological study of the formal garden at the Hermitage, the home of Andrew Jackson, located near Nashville, Tennessee. Research on what is now known as Rachel's Garden (a twentieth-century appellation, referring to Jackson's wife) was conducted as an initial phase in restoring the plot to its 1840s-era appearance, the chosen "ethnographic present" of the site's public interpretation. The garden has undergone frequent cycles of restoration during its last hundred years of care at the hands of the Ladies'

Hermitage Association (LHA). Because of this attention, the garden remains a lively and flourishing place, but at the outset of archaeological study it was unclear to what degree the LHA's work had altered the garden's original form. Excavation was thus geared specifically toward finding out how the fence lines, internal layout, pathways, and plantings had changed since the garden's creation in the early 1820s.

This chapter establishes the "heredity" of current garden attributes. It also considers questions about the garden's meaning—the reasons it was planted in the first place, the role it played in the plantation landscape as a whole, the reasons for changes made to it during its use by the Jackson family, and the way it has been used in the public interpretation of the site. Work on these questions is not just a matter of academic theorizing. The goal in trying to reconstruct the evolution of the garden's social context—the changing motivations and perceptions surrounding it—is to provide some foundation and guidance for decisions about how best to recreate the details of the garden's physical appearance. It also will add to the restored garden some of its original social and emotional meaning, admittedly a difficult task. If successful, visitors may then move beyond viewing the garden as just quaintly old-fashioned and toward seeing it, and feeling it, as the Jackson family intended.

THE CURRENT GARDEN

The garden at the Hermitage lies immediately adjacent to the east side of the mansion (figures 5.1 and 5.2). It is laid out as a square measuring approximately 260 feet on a side, completely bounded by a white picket fence with a low brick footer wall. The fence has a single public gate, in line with the mansion's side door, and two service gates. Paths around the garden's interior perimeter and crossing its center divide the garden into four more or less equal quadrants. The paths are edged with bricks and bounded by planting beds six to eight feet wide.

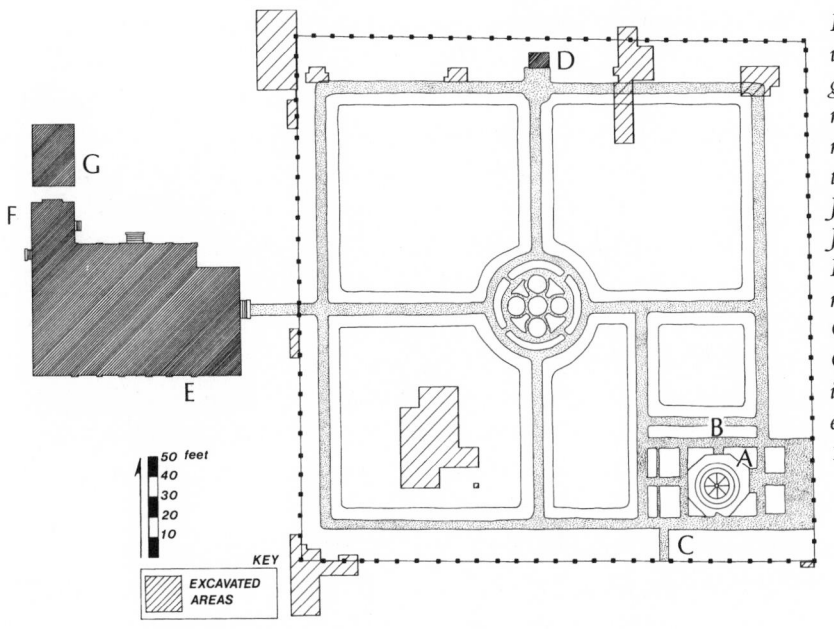

Figure 5.1. Plan view of the Hermitage garden, showing its relationship to the mansion. A) Jackson tomb; B) Alfred Jackson's grave; C) Jackson family graves; D) brick privy; E) mansion; F) kitchen; G) smokehouse. Crosshatching indicates areas excavated during 1988 and 1989.

Figure 5.2. Aerial view, taken in 1974, of the Hermitage garden and mansion, looking west-southwest. Courtesy of the Ladies' Hermitage Association.

The large open central areas of three of the quadrants are planted as lawns. The tomb of Andrew and Rachel Jackson is situated in the fourth quadrant, the garden's southeastern section. On one side of the tomb is a small plot containing the remains of family descendants. On the other side is the solitary grave of "Uncle" Alfred Jackson, a Hermitage slave and later a caretaker of the property. His epitaph reads "Faithful Servant of Andrew Jackson." The rest of the tomb quadrant is divided into a number of small brick-edged plots. Large trees keep the tomb area appropriately shaded.

The center of the garden is occupied by a set of small circular and curvilinear beds arranged in a neat geometric pattern. These are edged with an unusual type of brick, longer than standard building bricks and with a beveled "neck" at one end (figure 5.3). These bricks are used to edge some segments of the garden paths as well.

The only structure in the garden other than the tomb is a small brick privy or "necessary" at midpoint along the north fence line. By undocumented tradition this is an original garden feature, modified to become a women's bathroom during the early decades of this

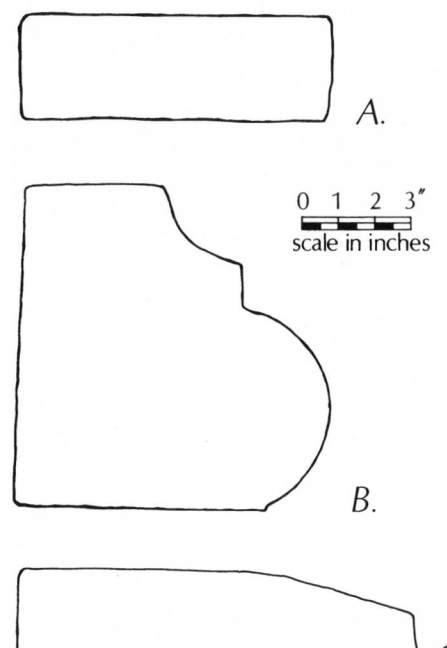

Figure 5.3. Bricks from the Hermitage. A) standard-size building brick used in original construction; B) "pillar" brick, used in construction of the bases of the mansion's pillars; C) "neck" brick used in the garden.

0 1 2 3″
scale in inches

A.

B.

C.

century. The building is no longer used, although site visitors can look into its open door and see, usually with some amusement, its three-seat arrangement.

Findings made during archaeological research in 1988 and 1989 support the interpretation that many of the current garden features—the pathways, the complex central bed, the fence lines, and the brick privy—are surviving remnants of a major (but again undocumented) reorganization of the garden that took place in 1835 and 1836. This coincided with the reconstruction and redesign of the mansion after a fire gutted the structure in October of 1834.

During the excavation it also became clear that certain seemingly small details of the garden had been embellished and formalized since that time, making the garden into something of a cleaned-up version of what the Jacksons would have known. Until some time during the second and third decade of this century, the garden had several different styles of perimeter fencing, rather than its current single style of tall, thin white pickets with a continuous brick footing. At some point in the late nineteenth century the garden perimeter was expanded approximately twenty feet along the north and east sides. Excavation also revealed that in an earlier period the pathways were edged with mostly broken and misfired bricks laid horizontally and rather casually, in sharp contrast to the current vertically-set soldier coursing along the path borders.

The formal and tidy nature of the current garden can be linked to the efforts of the Ladies' Hermitage Association, the century-old preservation organization that administers the property, to crystallize the Jackson family's personal and emotional involvement with the plot. Next to the mansion, the garden has always been the most important tool used in maintaining the memory of Andrew and Rachel Jackson. The three hundred thousand people a year who walk its paths are told that everything in the garden is as it was in the time the Jackson family lived on the property. Guidebook entries and signs also convey the message that Rachel and Andrew Jackson had an especially deep love for the garden and that it served as a place of retreat from the toil of their busy and troublesome public lives. One surprising find during documentary research for this project was that the role of the garden in shaping public opinion and emotions did not originate with the Ladies' Hermitage Association, but can be traced back to the Jacksons' own time.

THE ORIGINS OF THE HERMITAGE GARDEN

Andrew Jackson bought the Hermitage in 1804 (see Remini 1988:51 and throughout for details on Jackson's life at the Hermitage). For the next fifteen years, he and his sometimes large extended household lived in a set of log cabins set up as a compound near one of the two major springs on the property. Two of these cabins are still preserved in a drastically worked-over state in an area of the property known as the first Hermitage (see Smith 1976). In 1815, at the Battle of New Orleans, Jackson commanded the United States forces that defeated the British, a victory that catapulted him into national prominence. Jackson and his circle of aggressive friends and advisors began to build on this attention as he moved toward participation in national politics. By 1819 Jackson's fame and reputation had grown too large for the cabins that made up his first home at the Hermitage, and he began construction of a new, large, and more fitting brick house. As part of the initial siting of the mansion, an adjacent one-acre plot was set aside for development as a garden.

What were the motivations for planting the garden in the first place? There is no documentation or surviving oral tradition about any garden associated with the log dwellings at the first Hermitage. The inclusion of a garden in the initial plans for the new residence at the Hermitage suggests that such a landscape feature was deeply embedded in the way the Jacksons envisioned their new home. Although no professional architect was employed to design the new house, Jackson imported a gardener from Philadelphia to lay out the garden. The man hired, William Frost, was described in a letter of introduction as "a regular bred English gardener" (J. Jackson 1819). This description seems to be a key element in the man's letter of introduction to Andrew Jackson, but it is unclear whether it refers to his particular *style* of gardening or to his nationality. Frost is known to have worked at the Hermitage until at least September of 1820, the date of his last salary entry in Jackson's account records (A. Jackson 1820:10). An intensive search for further record of Frost's life and work has thus far proven fruitless.

Jackson's plans for his new home may have been directly influenced by a visit to Mount Vernon in 1815. Washington's garden had quite an impact on Jackson and his entourage. This description comes from a memorandum that, although written in the hand of a close Jackson aide, Major John Reid, was signed by Jackson himself:

> A neat little flower garden, laid out and trimed [*sic*] with the utmost exactness,
> ornamented with green and hot houses in which flourish the most beautiful of the
> Tropical plants affords a happy relief to the solemn impressions produced by a view of
> the antique structure it adjoins, and leads you insensibly into the most delightful
> reverie, in which you reveiw [*sic*] in imagination the manner in which the greatest and
> the best of men after the most busy and eventful life, retired into privacy and amused
> the evening of his days. . . . All the splendor of the most elegant architecture and the
> most fanciful decorations can produce no such impressions. (Bassett 1927:219–20)

Mount Vernon's combination of architecture and horticulture was in no way unusual, and it is likely that Jackson visited many other such estates during this period. The fashion of the time certainly dictated that anyone building a grand home, especially in a rural setting, would also undertake some formal estate landscaping. But several other elements played a role in Jackson's intentions and motivations in planting the garden.

Why was it fashionable to plant elaborate gardens, and why did the Jacksons participate in this architectural trend in the particular way they did? Dell Upton has written about how the Virginia rural landscape could be "manipulated by the informed" to reflect the power, wealth, and intellect of the colonial slaveholding elite (Upton 1990:84–85). A recent review of eighteenth-century gardening in Williamsburg notes that much of even the more mundane horticultural activities of the day—particularly the adaptation of English plants and methods to the American climate and soils—were carried out by "a small group of well-educated elite" (Brown and Samford 1990:103–4). Architectural and historical research carried out in and around Annapolis, Maryland, during the 1980s provides perhaps the best analysis of the connections between plants, landscaping, wealth, and power (e.g., Leone 1984, 1987; Yentsch 1990). The argument boils down to the idea that people use their physical setting to make a "more or less explicit statement of their position in the world" (Deetz 1990:3). In particular, the early American aristocracy used the landscape as one method of legitimizing and solidifying its power and control over society through an exhibition of its parallel control over nature. The best image and example of this in colonial America is the orangery, a type of greenhouse in which tropical and tender plants (especially citrus trees) could flourish and be forced to produce fruit and flowers out of season (Yentsch 1990:180; see also Weber, chapter 3, this volume).

The first version of the Hermitage mansion, constructed between 1819 and 1821, was definitely not designed to match the glories of Mount Vernon or any other late-colonial-period estate. The adjacent garden was also an unpretentious plot, hardly intended to convey ideas about its owner's control of nature. The Hermitage garden is not the site of any large-scale terracing or grade alteration as seen in many other grand plantation landscapes, although the natural slope across its expanse could have easily supported such features. Its basic foursquare layout strongly supports its interpretation as a typical English kitchen garden, albeit on a large scale (cf. Kelley 1984). Figure 5.4 shows a recommended design for such a large-scale kitchen garden as published in a book by a well-known nineteenth-century horticulturist, John C. Loudon. Its central element is strikingly similar, even in size, to the Hermitage garden. Excavation findings indicate the layout was embellished over time, but never fundamentally changed. It would seem that the Jacksons wanted their garden to function primarily to produce food for the mansion household and only secondarily as an ornamental pleasure garden meant to convey messages about power and control.

The horticultural form chosen by the Jacksons does have indirect parallels with one well-known colonial garden, at Bacon's Castle, in Surry County, Virginia. Archaeological work at the site revealed the impressive 362-by-192-foot remains of a garden first laid out in the 1680s. At the time, this area was still part of the "rugged and violent seventeenth-century Virginia frontier," and, as the site's investigator observed, gardens were still mainly "essentials, rather than extras" (Luccketti 1990:23, 39). The designer of the garden at Bacon's Castle altered "a traditional English plan to suit his needs in a new environment by installing a seventeenth-century pleasure garden stripped of the bulk of its ornamental features in order to produce

Figure 5.4. Plan for a
large kitchen garden,
from Loudon 1850 (first
published in 1818).

1. Slips, with standard apples, pears, cherries, filberts, &c., at the sides. 2. Ponds. 3. Culinary department, bordered with dwarf apple trees or gooseberry bushes, &c. 4. Forcing department. 5. Vineries, fig-house, and for forcing strawberries, &c. 6. Water-basin, or pump. 7. Pine-stove. 8. Peach-houses. 9. Pits. 10. Back-shed. 11. Frame-ground. 12. Cucumber ridge, early carrots, or potatoes under hoops, &c. 13. Melon or cucumber ranges. 14. Mush-room-sheds, tool-house; sheds for wintering vegetables, &c. 15. Gardener's house. 16. Fruit and onion room, with lodging-room for under-gardener, and seed-room over. 17. Department for compost, mixing and turning dung, &c.

food for the table" (Luccketti 1990:39). In frontier Virginia, gardens, along with architecture and other elements of material culture, were used by the emerging elite "as visible means to distinguish themselves from lesser planters"; the ability of these planters to support such status display was "representative of the incipient maturity of Virginia" (Luccketti 1990:39, 41).

The parallels between late-seventeenth-century Virginia Tidewater and early-nineteenth-century Middle Tennessee are at least superficially obvious. The Jackson family's move from the log cabins of the first Hermitage to their new tall brick house is a manifest sign of the region's own incipient maturity. The initial version of the garden at the Hermitage would have been much more elaborate than typical farmstead vegetable plots in the region, as reflected by its size, its formal layout, its paths edged with beds planted with ornamental species, and its fence separating it from both human and animal intruders. Despite these features, it was still a stripped-down version of grander landscaping seen along the mid-Atlantic coast.

The garden's relative simplicity may have been linked not just to necessity or economy, but also perhaps to a conscious desire to minimize the visual impact—the "statement"—of the estate's landscape. In the 1820s, Middle Tennesseans still clung to the vestiges of a frontier, "back country" outlook, which rejected the excesses of the wealthy in other parts of the southern United States. Rachel Jackson had arrived in the area as part of the first group of white settlers, and Andrew Jackson, orphaned at a young age, came to Nashville as a young lawyer with plenty of ambition but little in the way of financial resources. Jackson never referred to the Hermitage as a plantation, and, like his neighbors, specifically labeled himself a farmer rather than a planter, despite the fact that Jackson's land and slave holdings, like more than one hundred other operations in the county, fell well within the limits of any definition of what constituted a plantation (see Ash 1988; Bailey 1982, 1983; Goodstein 1989; Owsley 1965; Smith 1985; and Walker 1943 for discussion of these points).

Visitors to the Hermitage commented frequently on the unpretentious nature of the estate. A. Levasseur, who accompanied Lafayette during his visit to the Hermitage in 1825, observed that "the first thing that struck me on arriving at the General's was the simplicity of his house. . . . I asked myself if this could really be the dwelling of the most popular man in the United States" (Levasseur 1829:340). The original garden, and the unadorned Georgian I-house that went with it, signified two entwined messages about Andrew Jackson and his family. It both marked their membership in the first rank of the elite, while at the same time avoiding an ostentatious display that would have set them apart from this community.

RACHEL JACKSON'S GARDEN

The garden began to accrue new meaning quickly in the decade after its establishment as it became directly linked with Rachel Jackson, a connection sealed by her death in December of 1828 and by her subsequent entombment in the garden's southeast corner. Rachel Jackson's strong association with the garden signals an important shift in the United States at this time in the cultural perception of home life, gardens, and gardening. Colonial and early national period gardens are remembered as the domain of elite men, "brothers of the spade," who had the time and talent to experiment with plants and create dazzling landscapes as well as to revolutionize society. (Some elite women of the eighteenth century are certainly also remembered as active gardeners; see Bescherer, Kratzer, and Yentsch 1990, and Weber, chapter 3, this volume.) Women became more directly and openly associated with gardening as a result of emerging nineteenth-century ideas about the division of labor and the "separate spheres" of each gender. Southern plantation households had some distinct manifestations of these ideas. Gardens and gardening activities served not only as a respite from routine but also as an important element in one of the main tasks of the plantation mistress: overseeing the provisioning of the household's table (Clinton 1982:23; Fox-Genovese 1988:78–79, 118).

The Hermitage garden is remembered as Rachel Jackson's domain not just because of her actions, but also because of her culture's willingness to acknowledge (and perhaps require) her role in cultivating it.

In 1827, a visitor to the Hermitage recorded these impressions about the garden, and about Rachel Jackson's involvement with it: "After I was rested, she proposed walking into the garden, which is very large and quite her hobby. I never saw any one more enthusiastically fond of flowers. She culled for me the only rose which was in bloom and made up a pretty nosegay; after an agreeable stroll we returned to the drawing room. . . . Mrs. Jackson would not permit me to go without a bouquet, which she arranged very tastily . . ." (Conner 1827). Rachel died one year later, in 1828, just weeks before she and her husband were scheduled to leave for Washington to begin his first presidential term.

THE HERMITAGE GARDEN AS A MEMORIAL

Rachel's death served as a tragic climax to the bitter 1828 presidential campaign, in which her reputation and character were prime targets of mudslinging (see Remini 1988:157–71). With her burial, the garden assumed a new role in the plantation landscape, and it is at this point that Andrew Jackson began to take a documented interest in the garden. His letters from the White House back to family members in Tennessee make it clear that Jackson saw the garden in a new light, as a way to memorialize his wife. Less than a year after Rachel's death, he wrote about his concern for its appearance. In a letter to his son, he asked for a report on the appearance of her tomb: "still you have not informed me of its situation, and whether the weeping willows that we planted around it, are growing, or whether the flowers reared by her industrious, and beloved hands, have been set around the grave as I had requested" (A. Jackson [1829] 1929). In 1830, in a letter to one of Rachel's nephews, he made explicit his attitude toward the garden: "[t]hat garden is now to me a consecrated plot, & I wish it carefully attended to, particularly the square around the sacred tomb" (A. Jackson 1830).

In 1831 Jackson contracted with builder David Morrison to have a small but impressive stone-pillared and copper-domed tomb erected over his wife's grave in the garden, reserving a spot beside her for himself. Its construction stretched out through most of the following year. Jackson, then in Washington, wrote several letters to his son at the Hermitage to express his anxious concern that the project be done swiftly and with great care. Morrison wrote to Jackson about his plans, expressing his confidence "that it may fully meet publick expectation," a telling comment (Morrison 1831).

Rachel's lengthy epitaph, carved into the slab covering her grave at the time of the tomb's construction in 1831, memorializes her personal attributes:

> Her face was fair, her person pleasing, her temper amiable, her heart kind. She delighted in relieving the wants of her fellow creatures and cultivated that divine pleasure by the most liberal and unpretending methods. To the poor she was a benefactor; to the rich an example; to the wretched a comforter; to the prosperous an ornament. Her piety went hand in hand with her benevolence, and she thanked her Creator for being permitted to do good. A being so gentle and so virtuous slander might wound but could not dishonor; even death, when he tore her from the arms of her husband, could but transport her to the bosom of her God.

For over 150 years this has served as the main text specifically intended to shape visitors' opinions about Rachel Jackson, with the surrounding garden supplying a powerful supplement and background to the message. Rachel's epitaph stands in sharp contrast to her husband's, on a slab just a few feet away, which by his decree listed only his name (using his military, rather than political, title) and birth and death dates.

During Jackson's years in Washington he wrote several times to his son, Andrew Jackson Jr., about his concern over the garden and tomb area. In April of 1833 Jackson had received a report from a friend that the garden was not "attended to as [it] should be." The letter went on to note that the friend had instructed Dick, a slave assigned to house and yard duties, to "put the garden in order forthwith, and keep it so, that the walks, border, and squares must all be *cleaned* and *kept so*" (Lewis [1833] 1931; emphasis as in original).

In 1835, apparently having received better reports in subsequent communications, Jackson wrote to his son that "I am delighted to hear that the garden has regained its former appearance, that it always possessed whilst your dear mother was living, and that just attention is now paid to her monument. This is truly pleasing to me, and is precisely as it ought to be" (A. Jackson [1835] 1931a). In the most poignant family reminiscence, probably thoroughly tainted by nostalgia, Jackson's granddaughter, "Little Rachel," described Jackson's daily visits to the garden and tomb in the last years of his life: "No one ever went to the tomb with him. Every evening, just about the time the sun would be nearly down, he went to the tomb, but he always went alone. I always went to the gate, and saw him in, but I realized he was going to the tomb. He would stay there a half hour, I suppose, then return. He did this as long as he was able to walk" (Caldwell 1949:104). It is significant that the overwhelming emphasis in the family correspondence and remembrances concerning the garden is on the rights, duties, activities, and expectations of the people involved with it, rather than on its horticultural attributes.

In October of 1834 a fire gutted the Hermitage mansion. The structure emerged from almost two years of reconstruction as a grand example of Greek Revival architecture. The house had also undergone extensive expansion and redecoration in 1831, and thus was completely transformed from the relatively plain two-story dwelling first built in the early 1820s. This steady architectural evolution was no doubt spurred by the desire to keep the appearance of the house in synchronization with its owner's own evolution in prestige and power, as well as being a reflection of changing architectural fashion (for more extensive discussion of the mansion's architectural changes, see McKee, Hood, and Macpherson 1991; Remini 1984:184–90; and Trescott 1981).

Archaeological work in the Hermitage garden showed that it too underwent extensive alteration from 1834 to 1836, although no mention of these changes is made in documentary sources on the site. The fence along the mansion side of the garden was shifted slightly away from the structure and was probably changed to its present form—tall, thin pickets set close together, painted white, and footed with a low brick wall. The footing constructed in 1836 did not extend all the way around the garden, as it does currently, and the fence around the other three sides was probably built in a different, less ornamental style. In the course of the post-fire changes, the garden's complex center bed was either added or at least redefined by the use of the long beveled "neck" bricks illustrated in figure 5.3.

The archaeological association of fragments of the neck bricks with fragments of the 1836 mansion's pillar base bricks allowed the garden changes to be dated to the post-fire period. Examples of the two styles of brick were found together in the backfill of the postholes associated with the earlier garden fence line, abandoned at the time the brick-footed fence was installed (figure 5.5). Fragments of the pillar bricks were also recovered from the builder's trench associated with the brick footer beneath the garden fence. Test excavations of one of at least three brick kiln sites on Hermitage property also yielded a neck brick fragment (Smith et al. 1977:87). Archaeomagnetic dating provided a firing date of 1835 for the kiln (DuBois 1978). A neck brick was also found incorporated into the foundation of the brick privy or "necessary" located in the garden (Smith 1982:27), allowing its otherwise undocumented construction to be dated to the post-fire period as well.

Figure 5.5. Top exposure of brick-filled postholes related to an early garden fence line along the west side of the Hermitage garden. The fill from these holes included examples of both pillar and neck bricks. The drain tile dates to the 1930s. View is looking toward the south.

It is important to note that the changes of 1834 to 1836 did not alter the garden's basic foursquare plan. Archaeological work in other areas of the garden (especially across several sections of pathways and in the centers of the lawn quadrants) did not reveal any major restructuring or abandoned original features. The new fence line, center bed, and privy were apparently meant to embellish and ornament the foursquare plan, making it a little grander in keeping with the new look of the house.

The privy seems an unusual garden feature by current standards. Jackson had seen such facilities at Thomas Jefferson's country retreat, Poplar Forest, and at Mount Vernon some twenty years before. As archaeologist Samuel D. Smith pointed out in his discussion of the necessary's excavation, "the facility probably served more as a status symbol or garden embellishment than as something essential to the normal or traditional style of life" (Smith 1982:28).

Andrew Jackson, in residence at the White House throughout the period of the post-fire reconstruction, had turned over most of the decision-making power about the house's redesign to his son. His only comment, although indirect, about the changes to the garden suggests that he still saw it as a practical, contributing part of the plantation, as well as a memorial to his wife. In a letter concerning preparations for his return home at the end of his second presidential term, he made one thing clear to his son: "I cannot be without a good vegetable garden . . ." (A. Jackson [1837] 1931b).

Little documentation exists about the garden during Jackson's quiet retirement at the Hermitage preceding his death in 1845. Correspondence among family members in the early 1850s records something of a renaissance in the garden's upkeep and appearance at this time, coinciding, significantly, with the last period of prosperity that the family experienced. One letter, from Andrew Jackson III to his sister Rachel, records the changes: "Papa has been buying a great many flowers and trees. The flowers are sayed [*sic*] to be very rare and beautiful by the man who sold them. . . . The garden has got a nice fence around it now which makes it look a great deal better . . ." (A. Jackson III 1850). In 1852 Rachel received a letter from her mother, Sarah York Jackson, which records the fact that the garden continued to be planted with both food-producing and ornamental species. "We have also had a very cold weather here . . . all our early flowers are destroyed, also all the first plantings of vegetables. . . . We have now about fifty varieties of roses . . ." (S. Jackson 1852).

THE GARDEN'S DECLINE AND RESTORATION

In 1856 the state of Tennessee purchased five hundred acres of the Hermitage, including the mansion and garden, from Andrew Jackson Jr. The purchase was made mostly as a way to provide some financial relief to the debt-ridden family, and the state never quite decided what to do with the property. Members of the Jackson family continued to live in the mansion until the early 1890s (see Horn 1950:39–43). During this period, the garden continued to play an important role in the way visitors perceived the site, especially in defining the property's steady decline. One Jackson biographer, James Parton, wrote in his journal about his distress over the condition of the garden and tomb in 1859: "House locked and empty. Went into garden, close behind. 1 1/2 acre. Beds bordered with upright bricks, all of which were loose and many gone—some lying about beds. Paths were pebbled, but not well. A large, mean, ill-kept garden. . . . [Tomb] much dilapidated & very shabby. Mrs. J's slab well under the foot. Gaps in pavement as though the foundation had sunk. Roof leaky, in [?] plaster ceiling pealing & discolored. Scandalous, 5 dollars a year would have kept it in perfect order" (Parton 1859:39–41).

During the Civil War, a detachment of Union soldiers was assigned to guard the property soon after the Federal occupation of Nashville in 1862. According to undocumented tradition, the horses of the troops were corralled in the garden, with subsequent ill-effects on the paths and plantings. No archaeological evidence of such large-scale depredation was found, and this is very likely an example of the "black legends" told by southerners about the atrocities and general bad manners of invading Union forces.

Photographs of the postwar period show the tomb and surrounding area in drab disarray, contributing visual evidence to the written accounts of the site's decline during the period (figure 5.6). The garden's survival in any state at all can be attributed almost completely to the fact that it served as the Jackson family burial ground. Archaeological investigation did uncover several episodes of fence line shifts and repair datable to this period. The continued effort to keep the garden boundaries intact during a period when only minimal efforts were being made to maintain the house suggests a strong acknowledgment of the continued importance of not just the tomb, but the entire garden. Excavation in the garden's northeast corner exposed nearly two feet of slope-wash fill covering an earlier version of the perimeter path, providing vivid evidence of the quick processes of decay taking place within the garden during the second half of the nineteenth century (figure 5.7).

Figure 5.6. The Jackson tomb in the Hermitage garden, ca. 1875. Courtesy of the Ladies' Hermitage Association.

Figure 5.7. Excavation unit in the Hermitage garden's northeast corner, showing the depth of fill over buried bricks bordering an early version of the path. View is toward the west.

THE LHA'S GARDEN:
REVITALIZATION AND REINTERPRETATION

In 1889 a private organization, the Ladies' Hermitage Association, was formed to administer the Hermitage property in partnership with the state of Tennessee, which retained ownership of the site. The group's charter defined its function: "to beautify, preserve, and adorn" the Hermitage "throughout all coming years in a manner most befitting the memory of that great man and commensurate with the gratitude of his countrymen" (Dorris 1915:35). Some of the group's earliest and most intense restoration efforts were expended on the garden, with the work explicitly intended to restore its paths, plantings, and fence lines to what the Jackson family would have known. The garden was also seen as a minor source of revenue, with flowers and plants sold from it to finance site-preservation activities.

There is no detailed record of what state the garden was in when the LHA took on its restoration or what major changes were wrought during the early years of the group's tenure at the site. However, excavation uncovered extensive evidence of the association's garden projects. The brick footing, originally laid only on the mansion side of the garden with a short return toward the east at the southwestern corner, was added to at least twice (figure 5.8). By the 1930s the footer extended around the entire 1,040-foot perimeter of the garden. At some point in the late nineteenth century the fence line was also pushed out at least twenty feet along both the north and east sides of the garden. Excavation has found traces of the original north fence line, but much of the evidence for it has been erased by subsequent planting activities. The work uncovered more definite remains of early connecting fence lines extending west across the mansion's backyard from the garden's northwest corner area. A photograph taken in the first decade of this century (figure 5.9) shows three different styles of fencing near the garden's northwest corner, probably an artifact of the successive phases of garden boundary extension. As part of the Work Projects Administration's involvement at the Hermitage during the 1930s all four sides of the garden fence were rebuilt in a single style, based on the tall white picket fence that may have been the design first used in 1836 along the mansion side of the garden.

Changes in the position of the garden's northern boundary gradually enclosed the entire privy within the garden. Originally, the structure's southern entrance side was probably even with the fence. When it was first built, those using the privy could only enter it from inside the garden, while the task of cleaning it out took place outside the garden.

The LHA renovated the privy in the early 1900s for use as a women's bathroom, with the adjacent area serving as a work and plant-propagation space. Excavation 35 feet east of the privy in the summer of 1989 found the backfilled remains of a rectangular pit, 6.0 feet by 8.5 feet by 2.8 feet deep. The surface at the bottom of the pit was covered with broken and whole flowerpots, buckets, window glass, and bottles dating from the 1910s, providing evidence of the feature's use as a deep cold frame during the early twentieth century. An absence of antebellum-period artifacts from the pit precludes its interpretation as a facility dating from the early period of the garden's use. No other such features dating from the Jackson family period were found during archaeological investigation. Consistent amounts of window glass recovered from the excavation of other garden areas suggest the use of less elaborate cold frames in the garden during its original period of use.

The most extreme change wrought by the LHA involves a key element in any garden, the plants that grow in it. Except for a few herbs, the garden currently has no non-ornamental plants. The emphasis on flowering species, reflecting the policy and practice of the LHA since its inception, has had the effect of completely erasing any sign of the plot's important original function in producing fresh fruits and vegetables for the mansion household. The current absence of food-producing plants in the garden is related to the lack of documentation of the specific vegetables grown by the Jacksons and the limited labor available to tend such plants. Archaeological explorations of the lawn quadrants, by tradition the site of the vegetable beds, turned up no remnants of such features in these thoroughly disturbed areas.

The Ladies' Hermitage Association's revitalization of the garden has been a continuous process. There have been phases of intense activity alternating with periods of benign neglect. The changes that have occurred during these cycles have been accompanied by continued explicit statements of the group's guiding philosophy: that the garden would remain unchanged from the way the Jacksons originally planned and maintained it. The LHA's goal of keeping the garden authentic led to a major confrontation in the early 1920s between competing factions within the organization. One group performed some extensive cleanup in the garden in that year, removing a number of old trees and shrubs. This sparked a huge controversy, and ultimately the governor of Tennessee became involved in the dispute. The regent of the LHA at the time reacted to the report that she had ordered the removal of a tree by writing "no person will have the audacity to face me with so false an accusation" (Lindsley et al. 1921:8). Much of this conflict centered on disputes about which elements of the garden

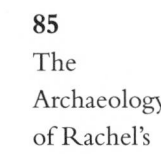

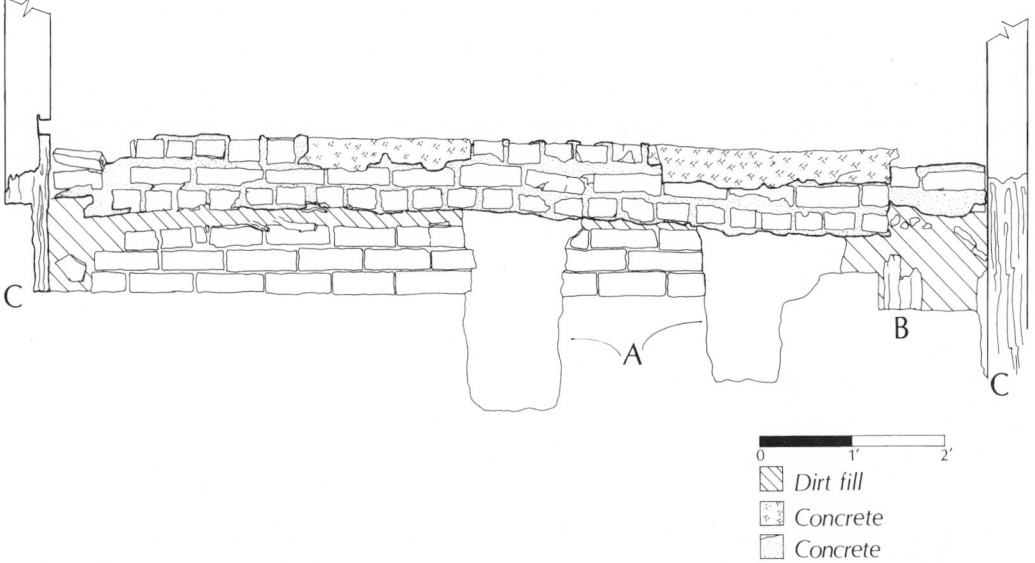

◼ Dirt fill
▦ Concrete
▢ Concrete

Figure 5.8. Profile drawing of the brick footing for the garden fence near its southwest corner. Lower three mud-mortared courses of brick date to the 1830s, upper courses to the twentieth century. A) late-nineteenth-century postholes punched through original footing; B) remnant of ca. 1930s wooden fence post; C) current fence posts.

Figure 5.9. A party in the backyard of the Hermitage mansion during the first decade of the twentieth century. Note the different styles of fencing along the west side of the garden near its northwest corner. Courtesy of the Ladies' Hermitage Association.

were original, or at least true to the spirit of the garden as the Jackson family knew it, and which were the product of the LHA administration's use of the Hermitage "as a medium of its own particular esthetic taste" (Lindsley et al. 1921:3). No doubt the 1920s battle over the Hermitage garden was a sign of some deeper, long-standing rivalries within the LHA. The fact that the garden served as the arena for a particularly vehement manifestation of these antagonisms again suggests the emotional power centered on this part of the Hermitage landscape.

In their work to preserve the Hermitage, the LHA has followed a policy that can be described as physical hagiography. The particular bent of the hundred years of garden restoration efforts has increased the garden's formality and "tidiness," through the standardization of fencing and pathway borders, and has downplayed the garden's critical role in provisioning the mansion household, through an emphasis on ornamental species. Visitors to the site are expected to absorb some of Jackson's essence and gain some insight into his life by tromping through his mansion and garden and experiencing it "as it was in his lifetime" (Lindsley et al. 1921:15). Not surprisingly, as the primary custodian of Jackson's memory, the LHA has carefully managed the man's image as reflected by his home estate. The organization has long sought to avoid mention of the many controversial elements of Jackson's career, which is in keeping with long-standing trends at most public historical sites. In its current form, the Hermitage is clearly intended to present a softened, essentially positive view of a complex man. The garden and the rest of the site are meant to be seen as the quiet rural retreat of a wealthy family, with few visible reminders of the means that supported such splendor. Slavery is the most obvious element currently lacking much presence in the interpretation of the site, but such quotidian details of plantation life as vegetable gardens are absent as well.

FURTHER RESTORATIONS, FURTHER MEANINGS

Is this reading too much into the garden? Has there ever really been any conscious manipulation of the landscape by the site's preservation stewards to make the garden more than just a refuge for quaint plants from the good old days? Gardens are commonly perceived as soft, neutral elements of the landscape, especially when contrasted with the more stirring, active role expected of buildings. This may work toward disarming the viewer's perceptual screens and filters, thus delivering a garden's intended message more effectively. At the Hermitage, such textual analysis may be beside the point. During most of its history, the LHA has been very explicit about using the garden to promote its particular vision of how it wants Rachel and Andrew Jackson to be remembered. This horticultural statement making follows the example set by Andrew Jackson himself, in his use of the garden to first mark his place in the local elite and, after his wife's death, as a memorial to her and ultimately to himself.

Plans are being formulated at this time for another round of garden-restoration activities at the Hermitage. Findings from the first two seasons of archaeological research on the garden (McKee 1991) are being used to fill in some of the details of how the garden has evolved. As reported throughout this discussion, the garden has changed physically only in minor ways, but with accompanying major shifts in meaning. The Hermitage garden will probably take

on a much less tidy look in the future, with the anachronistic lawns now covering the central
quadrant areas replaced with vegetable beds, the fences shifted to a less decorative, more
"functional" style, and the brick border along the pathway given a more haphazard appearance.

The current phase of garden restoration will be in keeping with current trends in the
preservation movement, which have declared the more everyday and "human" side of the
past, warts and all, to be the qualities to be esteemed and emphasized (see Chappell 1989 and
Wallace 1986 for discussions of this point). The resulting garden will no doubt be described
as accurate, representing what the Jacksons themselves would have known. The problem with
this is that neither documents nor archaeology will ever provide enough fine-grained evidence
to refurbish the garden to a truly accurate state. The restoration will require some "curatorial
calls," based on best-approximation guesses that are supposed to be objective. As with all
interpretation, these will inevitably be guided by the conscious and unconscious agendas and
points of view of those, including the archaeologists, with a say in the restoration process.

Through time, the Ladies' Hermitage Association's deeply emotional ties to Jackson
and its essentially defensive posture in regard to his memory have loosened. This shift in
outlook, coupled with the professionalization of the site's management, has led to a new
interpretive program focusing on the physical context and realities of life at this Middle Tennessee cotton plantation. Despite this, there is no question that the garden that emerges from
the current restoration efforts will continue to deliver strong statements to site visitors about
the personalities of Andrew Jackson and his family. It will be interesting to see how the analysts of future generations evaluate the deeper meaning of the garden's altered form and how
this message will be further transformed in future cycles of restoration.

ACKNOWLEDGMENTS

The Ladies' Hermitage Association has provided the main funding for the ongoing archaeological and documentary research on the Hermitage garden. Additional funding for the 1989
season came from the Garden Club of Nashville and from the Safeco Insurance Company's
Community Involvement Program. I have received enormous support throughout the project
from George Anderjack, executive director of the Hermitage; Keith DeMoss, current regent
of the LHA; Annie Laurie Berry and Fletch Coke, past regents of the organization; and from
Sharon Macpherson, Mark Provost, and Susan Stahl, staff members at the Hermitage.

Lucinda A. Brockway, of Kennebunk, Maine, who is currently serving as the lead consultant on the Hermitage garden restoration project, has been very gracious in sharing with
me her knowledge about nineteenth-century landscape design. She should be particularly
credited and thanked for bringing the work of John C. Loudon to my attention.

Kevin E. Smith worked as the assistant field director on the project in 1988 and was
joined in the position by Steven D. Ruple in the 1989 season. Smith also co-authored an
earlier, very different version of this paper which we presented at the 1990 annual meeting of
the Society for Historical Archaeology in Tucson, Arizona.

All excavation photographs in this chapter were taken by the author. The historical photos
are from the Hermitage research files. The drawn figures were prepared by Hannah K. McKee.

Ash, Stephen V.
1988   *Middle Tennessee Society Transformed, 1860–1870.* Louisiana State University Press, Baton Rouge.

Bailey, Fred A.
1982   The Poor, Plain Folk, and Planters: A Social Analysis of Middle Tennessee Respondents to the Civil War Veteran's Questionnaires. *The West Tennessee Historical Society Papers* XXXVI:5–24.
1983   Tennessee's Antebellum Society from the Bottom Up. *Southern Studies* XXII:260–73.

Bassett, John Spencer
1927   *Correspondence of Andrew Jackson,* vol. 2. Carnegie Institution of Washington, Washington, D.C.

Bescherer, Karen, Judson M. Kratzer, and Anne Yentsch
1990   Reflections of Changing World Views: Garden Evolution in the Mid-Atlantic Region. Paper presented at the annual meeting of the Society for Historical Archaeology, Tucson, Arizona.

Brown, Marley R., III, and Patricia M. Samford
1990   Recent Evidence of Eighteenth-Century Gardening in Williamsburg, Virginia. In *Earth Patterns: Essays in Landscape Archaeology,* edited by William M. Kelso and Rachel Most, pp. 103–21. University Press of Virginia, Charlottesville.

Caldwell, Mary French
1949   *Andrew Jackson's Hermitage.* The Ladies' Hermitage Association, Nashville.

Chappell, Edward A.
1989   Social Responsibility and the American History Museum. *Winterthur Portfolio* 24(4):247–65.

Clinton, Catherine
1982   *The Plantation Mistress.* Pantheon Books, New York.

Conner, Juliana
1827   Diary entry, 3–4 Sept. 1827. Manuscript Collection, Tennessee State Library and Archives.

Deetz, James
1990   Prologue: Landscapes as Cultural Statements. In *Earth Patterns: Essays in Landscape Archaeology,* edited by William M. Kelso and Rachel Most, pp. 1–4. University Press of Virginia, Charlottesville.

Dorris, Mary C.
1915   *Preservation of the Hermitage, 1889–1915.* Privately published by the author.

DuBois, Robert L.
1978   Letter to Samuel D. Smith, 1 May 1978. Hermitage Research Files, Hermitage, Tennessee.

Fox-Genovese, Elizabeth
1988   *Within the Plantation Household: Black and White Women of the Old South.* University of North Carolina Press, Chapel Hill.

Goodstein, Anita Shafer
1989   *Nashville 1780–1860: From Frontier to City.* University of Florida Press, Gainesville.

Horn, Stanley F.
1950   *The Hermitage: Home of Old Hickory.* The Ladies' Hermitage Association, Nashville.

Jackson, Andrew
1820   Farm Journal, entry dated 1 Sept. 1820. Hermitage Research Files, Hermitage, Tennessee.
1830   Letter to Samuel J. Hays, 19 Apr. 1830. Special Collections, University of Arkansas.
1929   Letter to Andrew Jackson Jr., 20 Aug. 1829. In *Correspondence of Andrew Jackson,* vol. 4, edited by John Spencer Bassett, pp. 62–63. Carnegie Institution of Washington, Washington, D.C.
1931a Letter to Andrew Jackson Jr., 1 May 1835. In *Correspondence of Andrew Jackson,* vol. 5, edited by John Spencer Bassett, pp. 342–43. Carnegie Institution of Washington, Washington, D.C.
1931b Letter to Andrew Jackson Donelson, 11 Jan. 1837. In *Correspondence of Andrew Jackson,* vol. 5, edited by John Spencer Bassett, pp. 449–50. Carnegie Institution of Washington, Washington, D.C.

Jackson, Andrew, III
1850   Letter to Rachel Jackson Lawrence. Hermitage Research Files, Hermitage, Tennessee.

Jackson, John
1819   Letter to Andrew Jackson, 30 Apr. 1819. Hermitage Research Files, Hermitage, Tennessee.
Jackson, Sarah Y.
1852   Letter to Rachel Jackson Lawrence, 10 Apr. 1852. Hermitage Research Files, Hermitage, Tennessee.
Kelley, Mary Palmer
1984   The Early English Kitchen Garden, Medieval Period to 1800 A.D. Garden History Associates, Columbia, South Carolina.
Leone, Mark P.
1984   Interpreting Ideology in Historical Archaeology: Using the Rules of Perspective in the William Paca Garden in Annapolis, Maryland. In *Ideology, Power and Prehistory,* edited by Daniel Miller and Christopher Tilley, pp. 25–36. Cambridge University Press, Cambridge.
1987   Rule by Ostentation: The Relationship Between Space and Sight in Eighteenth-Century American Landscape Architecture in the Chesapeake Region of Maryland. In *Method and Theory for Activity Area Research: An Ethnoarchaeological Approach,* edited by Susan Kent, pp. 604–33. Columbia University Press, New York.
Levasseur, A.
1829   *Lafayette in America in 1824 and 1825.* White, Gallagher and White, New York.
Lewis, Major William B.
1931   Letter to Andrew Jackson, 21 Apr. 1833. In *Correspondence of Andrew Jackson,* vol. 5, edited by John Spencer Bassett, pp. 61–65. Carnegie Institution of Washington, Washington, D.C.
Lindsley, Louise G., Mary C. Dorris, Maggie L. Hicks, Mrs. Harry Evans, and Mrs. R. A. Henry
1921   The Situation at the Hermitage. Privately published pamphlet. Hermitage Research Files, Hermitage, Tennessee.
Loudon, John C.
1850   *The Villa Gardener.* Second edition. Orr, London.
Luccketti, Nicholas
1990   Archaeological Excavations at Bacon's Castle, Surry County, Virginia. In *Earth Patterns: Essays in Landscape Archaeology,* edited by William M. Kelso and Rachel Most, pp. 23–42. University Press of Virginia, Charlottesville.
McKee, Larry
1991   Archaeological Research on Rachel's Garden at The Hermitage, 1988–89. Hermitage Research Files, Hermitage, Tennessee.
McKee, Larry, Victor P. Hood, and Sharon Macpherson
1991   Reinterpreting the Construction History of the Service Area of the Hermitage Mansion. In *Text-Aided Archaeology,* edited by Barbara J. Little, pp. 161–76. CRC Press, Boca Raton, Florida.
Morrison, David
1831   Letter to Andrew Jackson, 6 Dec. 1831. Hermitage Research Files, Hermitage, Tennessee.
Owsley, Frank Lawrence
1965   *Plain Folk of the Old South.* Quadrangle Books, Chicago.
Parton, James
1859   Untitled manuscript describing visit to Nashville and the Hermitage. Hermitage Research Files, Hermitage, Tennessee.
Remini, Robert V.
1984   *Andrew Jackson and the Course of American Democracy, 1833–1845.* Harper and Row, New York.
1988   *The Life of Andrew Jackson.* Harper and Row, New York.
Rider, Julia O.
1914   A Visit to the Hermitage, September 1914. Hermitage Research Files, Hermitage, Tennessee.
Smith, Samuel D.
1982   Archaeological Salvage and Recording of the Hermitage Garden "Necessary." Hermitage Research Files, Hermitage, Tennessee.

Smith, Samuel D., editor

1976   An Archaeological and Historical Assessment of the First Hermitage. Division of Archaeology, Tennessee Department of Conservation Research Series No. 2.

1985   Woodlawn Mansion, Nashville, Tennessee: History, Architecture, and Archaeology. Division of Archaeology, Tennessee Department of Conservation.

Smith, Samuel D., Fred W. Brigance, Emanuel Breitburg, Stephen D. Cox, and Michael Martin

1977   Results of the 1976 Season of the Hermitage Archaeology Project. Hermitage Research Files, Hermitage, Tennessee.

Trescott, Jerry

1981   Architectural Analysis of the Hermitage Mansion. Hermitage Research Files, Hermitage, Tennessee.

Upton, Dell

1990   Imagining the Early Virginia Landscape. In *Earth Patterns: Essays in Landscape Archaeology,* edited by William M. Kelso and Rachel Most, pp. 71–86. University Press of Virginia, Charlottesville.

Walker, Arda

1943   Andrew Jackson: Planter. *East Tennessee Historical Society Publications* 15:19–34.

Wallace, Michael

1986   Visiting the Past: History Museums in the United States. In *Presenting the Past: Essays on History and the Public,* edited by Susan Porter Benson, Stephen Brier, and Roy Rosenzweig, pp. 137–61. Temple University Press, Philadelphia.

Yentsch, Anne

1990   The Calvert Orangery in Annapolis, Maryland: A Horticultural Symbol of Power and Prestige in an Early Eighteenth-Century Community. In *Earth Patterns: Essays in Landscape Archaeology,* edited by William M. Kelso and Rachel Most, pp. 169–87. University Press of Virginia, Charlottesville.

6

Father Rapp's Garden at Economy: Harmony Society Culture in Microcosm

Lu Ann De Cunzo, Therese O'Malley,
Michael J. Lewis, George E. Thomas,
and Christa Wilmanns-Wells

> I am letting the earth be brought into my garden for two hills, one for a vineyard
> and the other for a pile of stones in the midst of a small forest, the other two
> quarters are reserved for fruit bearing trees and flower beds, and the middle point
> is measured off for a fountain and lake.
>
> *(George Rapp 1824)*

In the years after 1824, George Rapp, the Harmony Society's founder and spiritual leader, created the garden described above in the two-acre block behind his house in Economy, Pennsylvania (translated and quoted in Arndt 1982:301). As restored in the 1960s, the garden today in many ways forms the centerpiece of Old Economy Village. Owned and administered by the Pennsylvania Historical and Museum Commission, Old Economy Village is mandated as a museum charged with interpreting the history, life, and thought of the Harmony Society.

THE HARMONY SOCIETY

Spiritual life in southern Germany simmered and occasionally erupted in the seventeenth and eighteenth centuries into conflicts among the state church authorities, esoteric philosophers, sectarian revivalists, and religious enthusiasts of many persuasions. Into this milieu of religious diversity and ferment, George Rapp was born in 1757 in Iptingen, Wurttemberg. The son of a farmer (Arndt 1965:15, 17), Rapp was trained as a weaver. Like others of his time, he too became dissatisfied with the established church and its strict hierarchy, which provided little opportunity for an uneducated weaver to study theology formally and to ultimately achieve the social, intellectual, "gentlemanly" status of *Pastor* (Kantzenbach 1984:12).

Rapp's dissent, wrought in the mystic, pietist tradition of the region, was expressed in his first confession of faith to the church authorities in April 1785. "[S]alvation is in Christ Jesus alone," Rapp wrote; "my Jesus shone into my heart brightly as the word of life, and ... I needed nothing else since I had found Jesus" (translated and quoted in Arndt 1965:18). Such Christianity requires neither an ecclesiastical hierarchy nor sacraments; it is based on the individual's personal relationship with Christ. Moreover, like so much of German Pietism, it looks to the communal character of the early Christian church for its model.

Over the next two decades, Rapp and his growing body of followers continued to meet in each other's homes and villages, spreading the word of personal salvation through Christ. The church authorities, for their part, never allayed their efforts to suppress the heresy. Seeking only to "live as a congregation according to the ancient Christian religion of the first Christians" (translated and quoted in Arndt 1965:35), by 1803 Rapp and his group decided it was no longer possible to do so in their native land. George Rapp set out for America and in December made the first payment on a tract of land along the Connoquenessing Creek in western Pennsylvania where he was to establish the first town named Harmony. Two months later the first articles of association were drawn up for the Harmony Society, which by then numbered between 450 and 500 immigrants. The articles constituted the Harmony Society on a communal basis; all property was to be held in common and the needs of the members met by the society (Arndt 1965:70–72).

More important, the articles constituted a society in which the religious belief system circumscribed all aspects of cultural life—religion provided the society's *raison d'être,* it demanded the believers' exodus from their homeland, it motivated all their actions and their creations, and, ultimately, it assured the society's end. For twenty years following Rapp's arrival in America, the Harmony Society pursued a biblically mandated "wandering in the wilderness" (Rapp, translated and quoted in Arndt 1965:309), preparing the way for and awaiting the return of Christ to establish his New Jerusalem on earth. At each of two locations, first at Harmony and then at New Harmony along the Wabash River in southern Indiana, the Harmony Society established towns, planted vineyards, crops, orchards, and vegetable gardens, and erected houses, public buildings, mills, and shops. At both locations they prospered and then moved on in ten years. Finally, in 1824 Economy was established by the society's seven hundred members on the banks of the Ohio River twenty miles downstream from Pittsburgh, Pennsylvania. There George Rapp constructed his last garden, and there the Harmony Society remained. If any one thing characterized the society as members moved from one site to another in these early years, it was an increasing worldliness in material and economic life—expressed in town plan, architectural design, consumption patterns, and commercial and industrial contacts—coupled with an increasing otherworldliness in spiritual life—expressed in a shift to communal residence patterns and the introduction of celibacy.

George Rapp died in 1847, and still the Millennium of the Book of Revelation had not come. The society continued to prosper under Rapp's successors for a time, supplementing its agricultural and industrial production with investments in banks and railroads. By the end of the nineteenth century, however, the lack of charismatic leadership, the continued delay of the Millennium, a series of poor investments, and the decreasing numbers of the celibate society took their toll. In 1905 the three remaining Harmonists dissolved the society (Arndt 1980; Duss 1970). After a lengthy legal battle, in 1916 the Commonwealth of Pennsylvania was granted in settlement six acres of land within the town of Economy containing twenty of the most important Harmonist buildings along with a collection of 325,000 manuscripts and 18,000 original Harmonist artifacts. Today they form the core of the Old Economy Village museum and library.

George Rapp's house and garden occupy the block in Old Economy Village bounded to the east by Church Street, to the south by Thirteenth Street, to the west by Ohio River Boulevard (formerly Ohio View), and to the north by Fourteenth Street (formerly Main Street) (figures 6.1 and 6.2). The house and associated domestic outbuildings stand on the eastern 90 feet of the block, which measures 300 feet (north-south) by 380 feet (east-west). The garden covers the remainder of the block, approximately 86,700 square feet, or two acres. Currently, north to south and east to west paths mark the boundaries of four garden quadrants of unequal size; a large circular central element completes the composition.

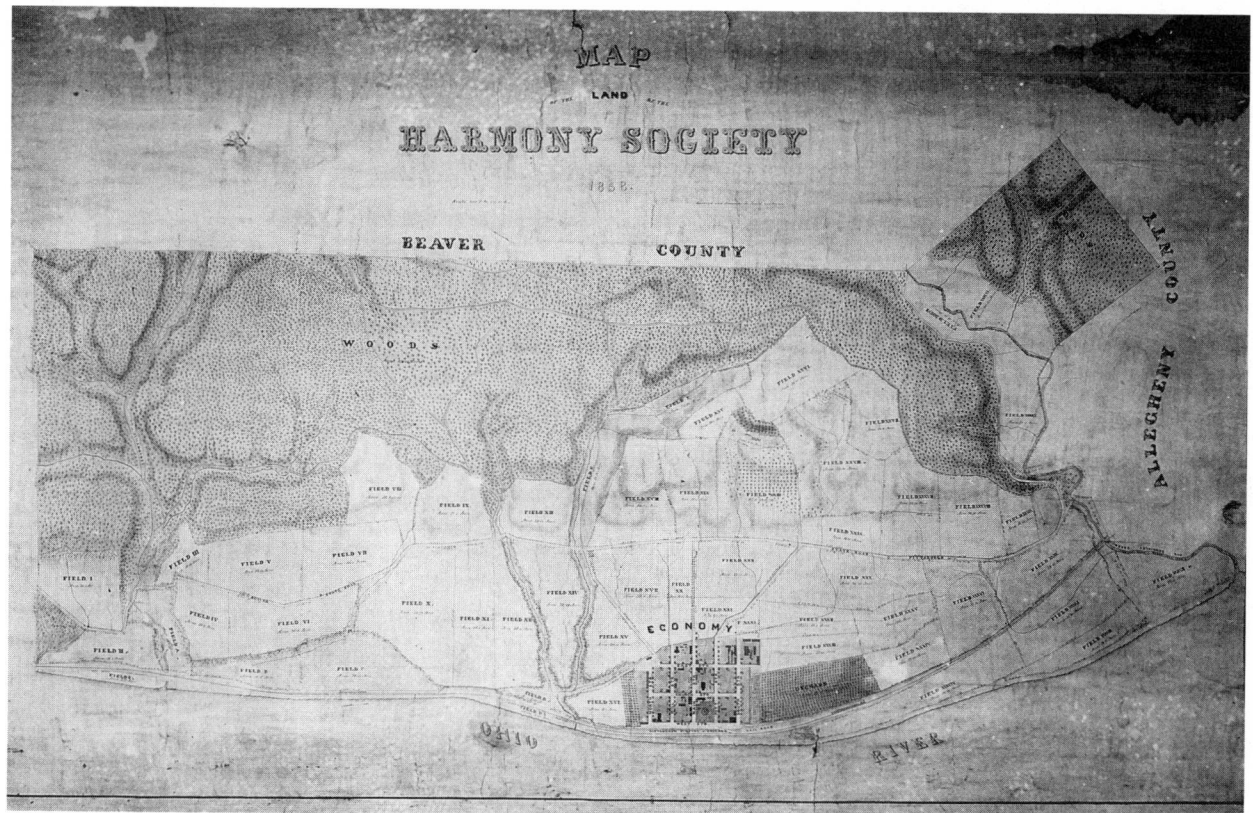

Figure 6.1. *Plan of the town of Economy and land of the Harmony Society, 1858. Photo by George E. Thomas, Clio Group, Inc. Courtesy of the Pennsylvania Historical and Museum Commission; Harmony Society Archives: Old Economy Village.*

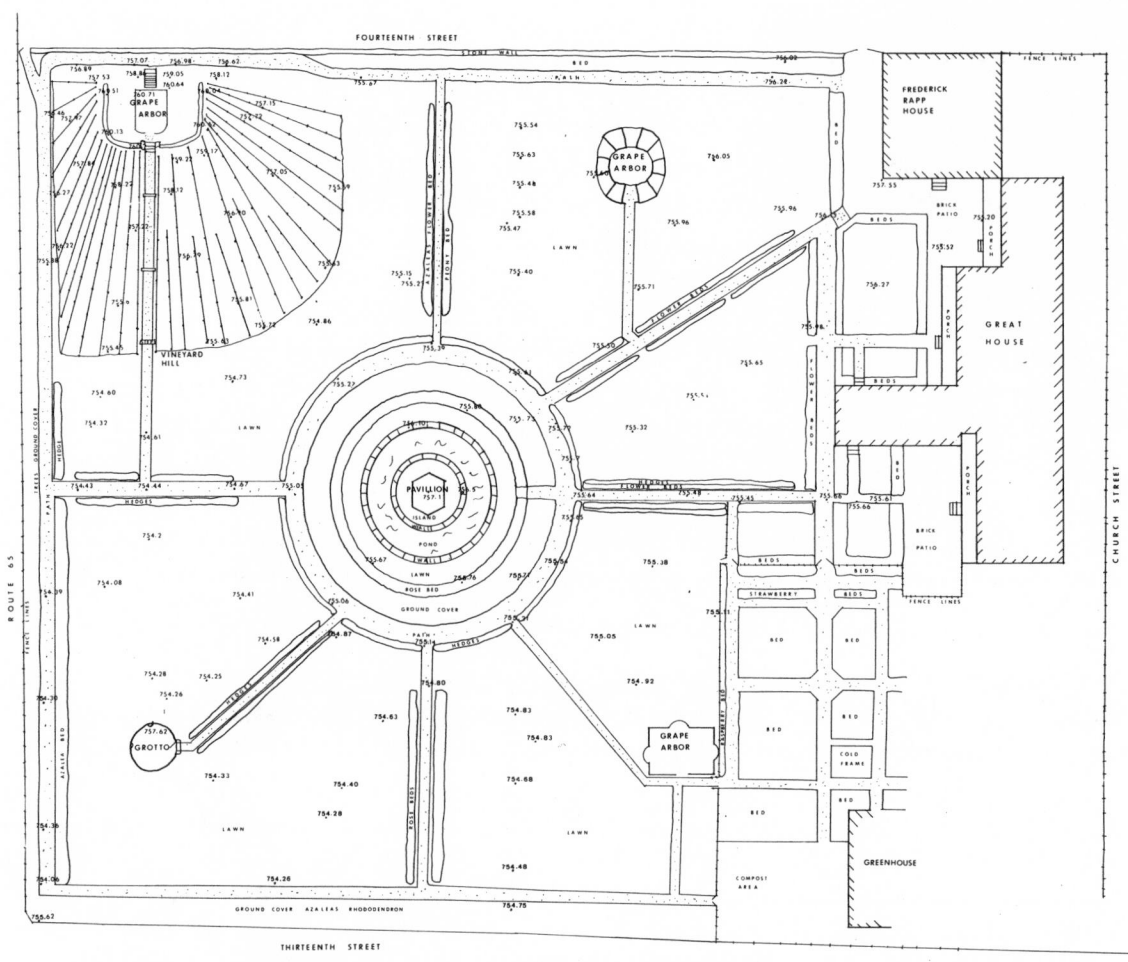

Figure 6.2. Plan of George Rapp's house and garden in Economy, 1989 (archaeological base map). Prepared by Conrad M. Goodwin and Lu Ann De Cunzo, Clio Group, Inc. Courtesy of the Pennsylvania Historical and Museum Commission.

Bounded by a stone wall on its north side and board fences to the south and west, the garden today combines historical and contemporary features (figures 6.3 and 6.4). A diagonal path lined with low boxwood hedges leads from the central pond to a rustic stone and thatch "Grotto" set amidst a scattering of trees in the southwest quadrant. The northwest quadrant rises to a mound, planted as a vineyard with the vines radiating from a central arbor atop the mound. A diagonal path bisects the grass-covered northeast quadrant, leading to a delicate frame arbor. The southeastern quadrant has similarly been planted in grass, with a scattering of fruit trees and an arbor. On an island in the central pond rises the classical hexagonal "Pavilion," a recreated statue of Harmony ornamenting its interior. Paths, rose beds, and boxwood hedges encircle the pond. Rapp's house further breaks the symmetry of the garden, lying mostly to the east of the northern quadrants. South of the house a vegetable garden has been planted, and east of this garden a carriage house and utilitarian yard have been restored.

Figure 6.3. George Rapp's garden. Looking northeast, toward the Rapp house, at the Einsiedeley (left foreground) and the Pavilion, 1988. Photograph by George E. Thomas, Clio Group, Inc. Courtesy of the Pennsylvania Historical and Museum Commission.

Figure 6.4. George Rapp's garden. Looking east-southeast from the summit of the vineyard mount toward the Rapp House, 1988. The Harmony Society Church steeple is visible above the roof. Photograph by George E. Thomas, Clio Group, Inc. Courtesy of the Pennsylvania Historical and Museum Commission.

Many of the century-old Harmony Society buildings stood dilapidated when the Common-wealth acquired Economy in 1916. By the 1930s their condition had worsened. In 1937, a thirty-year program of research and restoration was instituted under the direction of architect Charles Stotz, engineer Edward Stotz, and landscape architect Ralph Griswold. Working into the mid-1960s, the team led the restoration of Economy's historic buildings and landscape in what constituted, in its day, one of the most ambitious restoration programs of a historic American community.

Fifty years after the restoration of Economy began, a second course of restoration had become urgent. In 1987, the Pennsylvania Historical and Museum Commission initiated a comprehensive program of research and preservation studies prior to making any further restoration or interpretation decisions. Thomas and Newswanger Architects, a preservation architecture firm, and Clio Group, Inc., a historical and cultural resource consulting firm, headed a team that included twenty-one other consulting specialists to undertake this broad-ranging study of twenty historic structures and George Rapp's garden (see Clio Group, Inc. 1990; Wilmanns-Wells 1989).

Though well-maintained and popular with the visiting public as restored in the 1960s, research by museum staff suggested George Rapp's garden was not being accurately presented nor fully interpreted. Thus this latest research effort was designed to address both the physical history and cultural meanings of the garden. This chapter's authors—a historical archaeologist, a landscape historian, two architectural historians, and a cultural historian—led a team of archaeologists, horticulturists, landscape architects, and ethnobotanical analysts in developing an interdisciplinary research design aimed at unraveling the complex physical and cultural history of Rapp's garden.

The research design revolved around a series of questions. Interest centered on the physical garden and the history of its form, structure, organization, and contents. The first question, out of which many other questions arose, was what documentary, material, and archaeological resources survived relating to the history of the garden? Additional questions included: What could these resources tell us? Would it in fact be possible to reconstruct in detail Rapp's garden, both its configuration and plan and the specifics of plantings and their location? How close was the current configuration and planting scheme to that of George Rapp? What did Rapp's garden look like during his lifetime? How was it organized? What were its features? What were the plantings and where were they located? How did Rapp change them in the years between initial construction in 1824 and his death in 1847?

As researchers strove to determine what Rapp's garden was like in a physical sense, they also had to consider the layers of meaning associated with the garden, which served one or probably many roles and functions in Harmony Society culture. Surviving documentary and material resources were sought that illuminated the cultural and historical context of the Harmony Society, George Rapp, and his garden. Ultimately a second, and most significant, set of research questions was posed. What were the purposes, roles, and functions of the garden? Who used it? For what activities? What did the garden mean to George Rapp, to other members of the Harmony Society, and to outsiders who visited or otherwise knew it? What Harmonist beliefs and values were expressed, encoded, or symbolized in the garden's form, structures, organization, and plantings?

THE GARDEN OF GEORGE RAPP: FORM, ORGANIZATION, AND CONTENTS

Methodology

The epigraph opening this chapter, from a letter written by George Rapp, provides virtually the only statement by the Harmony Society leader of his concept and design for the garden. Other rich resources, however, amplify understanding by documenting in considerable detail the history of this extraordinary garden. Not the least of these resources is the garden itself, which, despite several restorations, still retains important features and evidence of its historical configuration. In addition, Harmony Society documents, including a collection of letters by George Rapp, contain details on the construction and planting of the garden in 1824 and 1825. Later society documents record plant orders and requests for cuttings from gardeners across the United States. Several visitors to Economy subsequently recorded descriptions and their impressions of the garden in accounts now preserved in published and manuscript form. Only a few significant graphic depictions of the garden survive from before the 1880s; these include an 1858 plan and at least one ca. 1870s photograph of the garden's northeast quadrant. Thereafter, photographers provided an incredibly complete visual record of the garden's later form and various restorations. Supplementing the record for this later period is the written and oral documentation of the restorations (Harmony Society Archives [HSA]; Pennsylvania Historical and Museum Commission [PHMC] Files). Finally, of course, there are the archaeological remains of each phase of the garden's ever-changing form.

The investigation of the garden centered on two principal activities: 1) documentation of the garden's existing physical conditions and components, and 2) excavation and recording of archaeological test units, followed by analysis of the findings. The archaeological team surveyed the garden and prepared a scaled topographic base map showing the locations of all extant garden features, such as walls, paths, structures, and planting beds (figure 6.2). In addition, a team of horticulturists and landscape architects undertook a census to identify all plants growing in the garden, including seasonal annuals and weeds. Trees and shrubs (woody plants) were plotted on the topographic base map; herbaceous plants were listed according to planting bed and keyed into the base map. As a final component of the physical documentation, an archival set of black-and-white photographs of the garden was produced along with a set of color slides.

Specific objectives guided development of the archaeological field testing plan. Previous testing (Warfel 1984) indicated that archaeological evidence of the garden's history prior to the extensive 1960s restoration did indeed survive. The identification of additional locations within the garden where archaeological resources survived intact—and of areas where recent restoration had resulted in substantial destruction of historical features and strata—thus formed the first objective. Second, researchers designed the archaeological field testing to yield specific information regarding the garden's form, features, plantings, and uses through time. This information would allow archaeologists to determine the potential of the archaeological resources to contribute to the comprehensive understanding of the garden's evolution in form, organization, and contents necessary for accurate restoration and interpretation.

A grid system oriented along the cardinal points provided horizontal control for the excavations. The control excavation unit placed in the southwest quadrant of the garden by Warfel (1984), in the vicinity of the "pile of stones in the midst of a . . . forest" (Rapp, in Arndt 1982:301), was re-excavated in order to correlate the earlier excavations with the current work and extended in order to sample the stratigraphy. A 55-by-3-foot trench was cut up the hill for the vineyard in the northwest quadrant, and two shorter trenches extended from it. Excavations in these locations sought evidence of the methods and chronology of the mound's construction and sought to identify patterns in the placement of earlier vine planting and postholes.

The original divisions of the garden and the evolution of circulation patterns as reflected in the placement of paths also interested the team and the Pennsylvania Historical and Museum Commission. To investigate the existing main north-south axial path, a 3-by-15-foot trench was excavated. Here researchers sought evidence of the history and construction of the paths and of the treatment of the paths' borders. To supplement these narrow trenches, a 10-by-10-foot areal excavation was placed in the northeast quadrant near Rapp's house in order to investigate this crucial transitional area between utilitarian houseyard and planned landscape. Finally, the "fountain and lake" at the garden's "middle point" (Rapp, in Arndt 1982:301) was tested by excavating a 3-by-35-foot trench originating at the existing pond wall and extending into the southeast garden quadrant.

In order to evaluate the potential to identify plants formerly growing in specific locations across the garden, the team collected one-liter and ten-liter soil samples respectively from planting holes, planting beds, occupation surfaces, and other features for phytolith and archaeobotanical analysis. The archaeologists, ethnobotanist, and phytolith analyst subsequently selected five flotation samples and fourteen phytolith samples for analysis.

The Documentary Evidence

Documentary research resulted in the identification of five major periods in the history of George Rapp's garden:

1) 1824–47   Original garden as designed, constructed, and maintained by and for George Rapp;

2) 1847–ca. 1892   Rapp's garden preserved by subsequent Society leaders following George Rapp's death;

3) ca. 1892–1922   Reinterpretation of the garden as a Victorian floral park, open to the public, by John Duss, band leader and Harmony Society trustee;

4) 1922–ca. 1938   Restoration of George Rapp's garden by the Garden Club of Allegheny County;

5) ca. 1938–present   Documentation and restoration under the direction of Ralph Griswold and Charles Stotz for the PHMC.

Such a periodization scheme should not, however, be construed to imply fixed periods in the garden's history devoid of change. On the contrary, the very nature of gardens and gardening implies constant change—a result of both the gardener's intervention and natural effects such as the changing of the seasons. Instead, the periods reflect times characterized by differences in the personnel responsible for the garden, differences that significantly influenced the garden's form, content, meaning, and level of maintenance. While recognizing the potential of an in-depth study of the evolution of this landscape (see for example Yentsch et al. 1987), emphasis in this chapter will be on the garden of George Rapp—the garden of 1824–47—the period that is most relevant to the Historical and Museum Commission's goal of interpreting the "life and thought of the Harmony Society."

Four principal types of primary documentary sources relate directly to George Rapp's garden: 1) correspondence between George Rapp and Frederick Reichert Rapp, his adopted son, written between August 1824 and April 1825 while George was directing the initial construction at Economy and Frederick remained at New Harmony in Indiana; 2) accounts of travelers to Economy to whom Rapp or one of his associates showed the garden; 3) correspondence between several Harmony Society members and outsiders regarding the purchase or exchange of plant materials; and 4) lists of plants growing in the New Harmony and Economy gardens.

Of these, the letters from George Rapp to Frederick alone reveal George's intentions as designer of the garden and offer direct insight into the process of developing and implementing its plan. The letters confirm that George Rapp was, in fact, principally responsible for the planning and construction of his garden. George speaks in the letters of the garden's plan, of progress in its construction, and of his hopes for receiving plantings from Harmony for it, but never of his thoughts on the garden's meanings or its relationship to his social philosophy or theology (Rapp, in Arndt 1982:98–509). This would not have been necessary, of course, with Frederick, as the two had previously been involved together in the construction of a garden in New Harmony.

Comparison of the Economy garden today with Rapp's detailed 1824 description of his plan for the garden's design reveals both elements that have been changed and those that have survived or have been reconstructed. Rapp's scheme was to create a quadripartite garden whose four quadrants would differ dramatically in character. One corner, with "a pile of stones in a forest," suggested a wilderness, while a vineyard created a cultivated landscape in another corner. These two quadrants he ultimately laid out farthest from his house, while immediately adjacent to it were the quadrants containing the orchard and flower beds, respectively.

Travelers' accounts of the 1820s through 1840s trace Rapp's progress in implementing his garden plans. Whereas his letters suggest he selected the essential plan early in the design process, the travelers' accounts give the distinct impression that the features of the quadrants and central element—the structures and most certainly the plantings—resulted from an evolving design over the course of a decade, from 1824 to the mid-1830s.

These accounts bring the garden to life and highlight further the differences between its original form, contents, and overall character and that of the restored garden of today. The earliest account, recorded in the late fall of 1825 by Friedrich List, reported:

> There is a wonderful garden in back of the presiding elder's [Rapp's] house, consisting of several acres with a vineyard, all kinds of flowers, orange, lemon, and fig trees, all kinds of American plants, cotton, tobacco, etc. The finest kinds of espalier fruit trees. One walks through arches of grapevines. The vines have grown nine to ten feet high in one year. There is a beautiful garden house with grass and foliage, papered inside, grass above; in the middle of the garden is a fountain. A Ceres [i.e., figure of Harmony] stands ready to be placed upon the 13-foot-high rock....The garden has prospered like a work of magic from nothing.... (translated and quoted in Arndt 1982:685)

The following spring, another German traveler, Bernhard, the Duke of Saxe-Weimar-Eisenach, visited Rapp and was also led through his garden.

> There is . . . a garden containing several acres with flowers and vegetables, as well as a vineyard, situated on a terrace-shaped half circle on the hill, ending in a bower. I especially admired the beautiful tulips of this garden in the midst of which is a round basin with a wonderful fountain. Mr. Rapp intends to build a temple here, in which he will place a statue of Harmony: the statue is now ready. It is the work of a carver in Philadelphia [William Rush] and is a colossal wooden figure. . . . In the garden are several cottages, one of them is roofed with sods, and has the shape of a pie. On the top is a suitable seat, where hereafter musicians are to play; within there is a temporary frame hall. Near the garden a green-house was built. . . . (translated and quoted in Arndt 1982:834)

By the time of George Featherstonaugh's visit to Economy in 1835, Rapp had successfully consummated his vision of the garden.

> [T]he spacious garden attached to Mr. Rapp's premises . . . contained more than half an acre of ground, was laid out in very narrow walks, separating beds crowded with vegetables, and was filled to repletion with fruit-trees of every kind—peaches, plums, apples on trellises, numerous varieties of pears, figs, and cherries, with raspberries in the greatest profusion. There was also a good, but unpretending conservatory, with oranges and lemons of a large size pendent from many of the trees, and various green-house plants in good order. In the center of the garden was a small temple, with pillars, surrounded with water, and a neat bridge thrown across it. . . . This exceedingly fruitful though rather too umbrageous garden was the only marked aristocratic feature about Mr. Rapp's premises: there was a general air about it which announced that it was not common property; but then every dwelling-house had its private garden, so probably its superior condition was as well the fruit of their attachment to him, as of his own taste and inclination. (Featherstonaugh 1970)

These and other travel accounts, along with information from other sources, provide firm evidence of the transformation of the garden's structures from temporary, frame enclosures to architectural monuments.

The accounts also document Frederick Reichert Rapp's role as the garden's architect-designer and engineer of its principal structures, such as the central fountain element. Both List and Bernhard mention the pond and fountain, the water supplied by a system of underground pipes leading down over one-half mile from springs outside of the town. George laid out this system soon after his arrival in Economy in August 1824 (translated and quoted in Arndt 1982:98). The water system played a role similar to the well-known Philadelphia system designed by Benjamin Henry Latrobe in 1799 to 1801 (Larner 1962:137), supplying many of the main buildings in Economy as well as the garden fountain. The Philadelphia Water-works may have provided a model for more than just the system of wooden pipes. The Centre Square Pump House by Latrobe comprised a small domed temple ornamented by William Rush's fountain statue of the "Nymph and Bittern." At Economy, Bernhard reported in 1826, Rapp intended to build a temple in the middle of the pond, "in which he will place a statue of Harmony" (translated and quoted in Arndt 1982:834). That statue too was carved of wood by William Rush and had been delivered in July 1825 (Arndt 1982:587). Significantly, Rush addressed his correspondence regarding the statue, and specifically his difficulties in designing it to function as a fountain, to Frederick (Arndt 1982:587). Furthermore, analysis of architectural drawings in the Harmony Society Archives at Old Economy has resulted in the tentative attribution to Frederick Rapp of a drawing of the domed temple (Drawing OE84.3.5; formerly no. 72; PHMC; HSA:OEV) built to house the statue in 1831. In May of that year, the *National Gazette* reported: "Mr. Rapp, of Economy, who is ever liberal in patronizing artists, has employed Mr. [Joseph] Woodwell [1807–98], to carve seven vases or urns, to represent a variety of fruits and flowers. The largest and most costly of these urns is to surmount, adorn and beautify a very handsome building [the domed temple] erected by Mr. Rapp; and the smaller ones are to cap the several arches over the passages leading to it . . ." (quoted in Arndt 1984:573).

By the summer of that same year, Rapp's "pile of stones in the midst of a small forest" had also been transformed into an architectural statement. Buckingham, who traveled to Economy in 1840 and was invited to accompany Rapp into his garden one afternoon, gave the best description of this structure during the leader's lifetime:

> At one quarter of the garden, Mr. Rapp pointed to a circular building of rustic masonry, composed of very large unhewn stones, rudely piled on each other, and covered with a sloping roof of straw-thatch, with rough bark door and portals, resembling the buildings called hermitages, often found in English grounds. On entering the interior, however, the visitor is pleasingly surprised to find an ornamented circular-room, with wrought ceiling, and ornamented panels; and in the centre of the whole, a well-executed female statue, meant as the personification of harmony, holding a lyre, and presiding as the genius of the place. [Note that the statue has been moved from its originally intended location in the domed temple]. Around the walls of the interior were several inscriptions; one of which was, "The Traveller's Disappointment," meaning to express the surprise intended to be occasioned by finding this statue and these ornaments within so rough an exterior; and another was "Harmony, founded by George and Frederick Rapp, Feb. 25, 1805." (Buckingham 1842:227)

An 1858 survey provides the earliest known rendering of the garden's plan (figure 6.5); the accompanying map depicts the Harmony Society's several-thousand-acre holdings at Economy. Although the garden appears as a square less than two inches in size on the original (currently in the collections of Old Economy Village, PHMC), it seems carefully rendered, though somewhat schematic, and illustrates the central pond with an island and paths dividing the garden into four quadrants. The thatched stone "hermitage" is suggested in the southwest quadrant, in a grove of trees. To the north, the vineyard mound is depicted in such a way as to suggest the vines were planted in concentric rings down its faces rather than in rays radiating from the summit. East of the vineyard, parallel dotted lines may indicate planting rows; an arbor and shrubbery or trees are also schematically outlined in the northeast quadrant. Paths, possible planting beds, and another arbor are sketched in the southeast quadrant.

Even more problematic than the diminutive drawing are typescript copies of plant lists and correspondence with professional and amateur horticulturists and botanists preserved in the collections at Old Economy Village. Should they be authenticated some day, they would not only identify plants Rapp grew in his garden, but also provide insight into the horticultural network in which he participated.

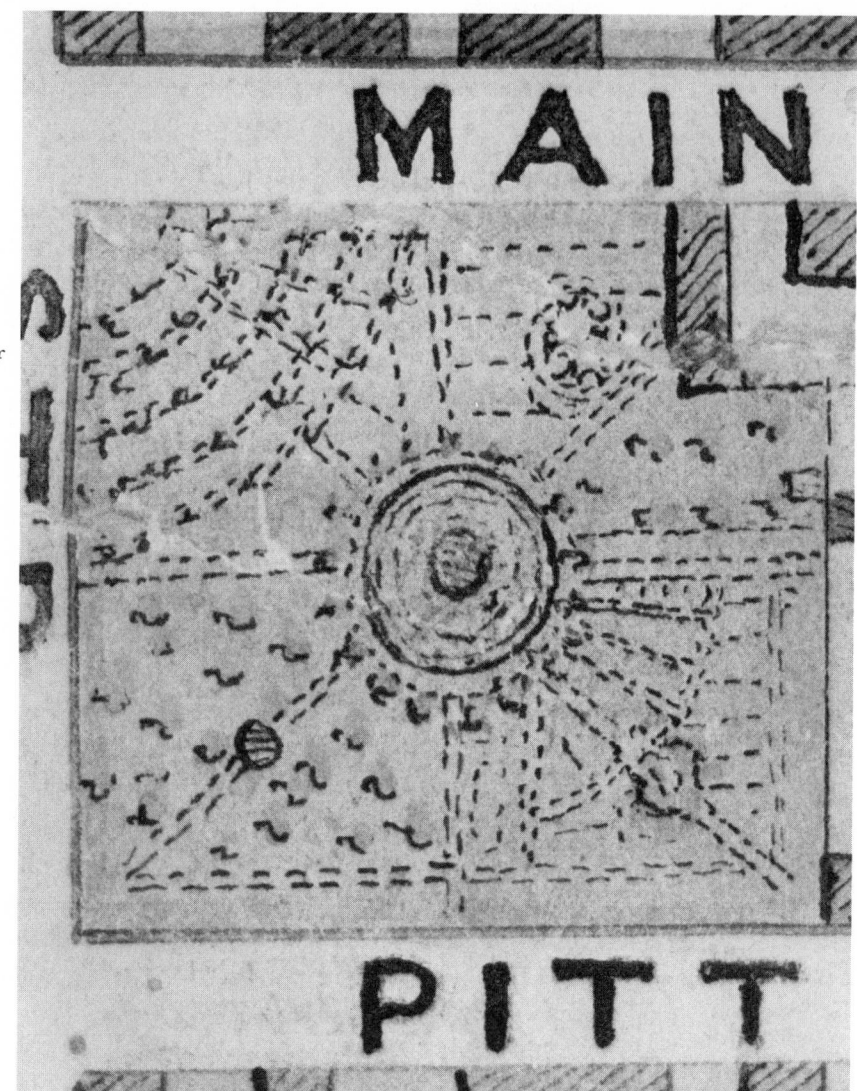

*Figure 6.5.
George Rapp's
garden at
Economy, 1858
(detail of figure
6.1). Rapp's
house stood just
off the bottom of
the view; Main
Street borders the
garden to the
north. Courtesy of
the Pennsylvania
Historical and
Museum
Commission;
Harmony Society
Archives: Old
Economy Village.*

The Archaeological Evidence

Historical documents identify some of the plants that enlivened the garden and illuminate aspects of the garden's form and structure. Truly understanding this garden, however, requires reconstructing in as much detail as possible its form, layout, structure, contents, and botanical organization and placement. Herein lies the key to the significance of archaeological techniques to the study of gardens and other cultural landscapes (Rubertone 1989:51). Despite the limited extent of the archaeological testing undertaken to date at Rapp's garden, the results indicate that archaeology offers the potential link between the written descriptions of the garden, the historical plant lists, the slim graphic evidence, and the exact location, design, and organization of specific plantings and garden features.

Most extensively tested was the vineyard mound rising in the corner of the northwest quadrant. Evidence of Rapp's earliest activities in the garden were preserved in this location, sealed beneath the fill from cellar excavations used to construct the vineyard mound (Rapp, in

Arndt 1982:301). Five small, shallow, bowl-shaped holes, 0.5–1.5 feet in diameter, had been filled with coal, ash, food bone, and other household refuse. They appear to represent individual stove-dumping episodes or the purposeful addition to planting holes of ash and bone as fertilizer and broken glass and ceramics for water retention or drainage. Although their function remains uncertain, they clearly resulted from Rapp's activities in the garden in the months before the vineyard mound was created in December 1824 (translated and quoted in Arndt 1982:98, 145, 158, 222).

George wrote Frederick Rapp on 1 December (see epigraph opening this chapter) that work on the vineyard mound was progressing; in a letter dated 13 December he reported, "I have had a hill for a vineyard made" (Rapp, in Arndt 1982:335). Thus Rapp's workers raised the vineyard mound over the course of approximately two weeks. The archaeological excavations revealed that construction debris and the household trash of Rapp and his work team were added to the growing hill along with the soil from the cellar excavations. The base deposit (0.3–0.7 foot thick where excavated) contained clay plugs, fractured building stone, and organic soils mixed with the yellowish-brown gravelly silt subsoils; the upper deposit (0.7–1.0 foot thick where excavated) lacked the clay, building stone, and organic soil. Shallow circular holes, lenses of domestic trash in soil matrices differing little from those of the surrounding deposit, and one more discrete trash-filled pit appeared at various places throughout the two deposits. These six features, often difficult to define during excavation, represent discrete dumpings of trash heaped on as the mound grew.

The limited test excavations revealed evidence of all three episodes of vine planting reported in the documents. Of the forty-four features encountered in the 1988 excavations, four postholes and fourteen plant and root holes appeared to at least predate the 1960s restoration and replanting. Patterns in the stratigraphic locus, size, alignment, spacing, form, and fills of all forty-four features suggest they represent the three documented planting episodes and perhaps other undocumented ones as well. Future excavations should clarify these planting sequences and result in a better understanding of the spatial patterning of the vines planted and the posts installed during each episode.

The excavation trench cutting across the existing north-south main garden path revealed the historical sequence of paths and their border treatments in this location and confirmed that the existing path does not directly overlie Rapp's original path. Again, due to the limited extent of the testing, the interpretations remain tentative but nevertheless suggestive. Below the existing peony bed bordering the path to the west, a 0.025-foot-thick lens of a pale yellow clayey soil may represent the remains of the earliest path. Stratigraphically and topographically, it lies deeper than the deepest paving level in the sequence beneath the existing path. This latter paving material, described as a very dark brown powdery loam, has been determined by phytolith analysis to comprise decayed bark (Piperno 1989). John Duss, who reinterpreted the garden in the 1890s and installed the first gravel paths, remembered bark paths throughout the garden as early as the late 1860s (Duss 1970). Thus near the end of Rapp's life or in the decade after his death, his yellow clay path was replaced by a less visually striking deep brown bark path laid just east of the original. Duss and subsequent restorers have preserved the location of the latter rather than the original in their reinterpretations of Rapp's garden.

East of the early clayey path, two bricks stacked in a backfilled hole and sealed by the bark path suggest a support for a trellis post. The feature reminds one of List's 1825 description of "walk[ing] through arches of grapevines" (translated and quoted in Arndt 1982:685). Four feet east of the brick trellis support, square to rectangular planting holes, 0.35–0.65 feet in size, had been cut into the early garden topsoil, forming a row bordering the path. The stratigraphy and topography suggest their contemporaneity with the clayey path and trellis.

The numerous reworkings and reorderings of the landscape elements encircling the central pond can be similarly traced in the archaeological record. Of special interest here is a 0.25-foot-thick deposit of yellow-orange sandy loam laid in a neatly excavated trench that cuts into the early-nineteenth-century land surface. Originating beneath the mid-nineteenth-century bark path found encircling the pond, this may represent another Rapp-era path, perhaps contemporary with that discussed above. These excavations suggest a path or possibly a path and adjoining planting bed extending over an eight-foot-wide area.

The 10-by-10-foot block excavation placed along the eastern edge of the northeast garden quadrant principally produced information regarding the later-nineteenth- and twentieth-century activities in this area, which included vegetable gardening, the demolition of a Rapp-period stable, and construction and ultimately demolition of a gardener's house. Despite this later activity, the excavations revealed evidence of the early-nineteenth-century garden in the form of a deposit of tilled topsoil. Even the small control unit excavated in the southwest garden quadrant, measuring only 2-by-3 feet in size, contributed to the developing understanding of George Rapp's garden. Here, near Rapp's "hermitage," a one-foot-thick, organically-enriched loam accumulated, such as would be expected in a forested area that annually contributed organic matter to the soil profile in the form of falling leaves. None of the travelers' accounts confirmed that Rapp's original intention to construct his "pile of stones" in the "midst of a small forest" had been carried out; the archaeological record suggests that it was.

THE GARDEN OF GEORGE RAPP
AND HARMONY SOCIETY CULTURE

Students of material culture, be they archaeologists, historians, art historians, architectural or landscape historians, folklorists, cultural geographers, or scholars in other disciplines, agree that material culture embodies something of the people who produced and used it—their activities, relationships, ideas and values, their lives, their culture. Numerous proposals have been offered as to just what is encoded in material culture and how it must be "read" in order to reveal its cultural meanings. Since Binford (1962) distinguished the technomic, sociotechnic, and ideotechnic functions of artifacts, others have examined their expression of world view (e.g., Deetz 1977) and of a culture's widely shared, basic beliefs, assumptions, attitudes, and values (Fleming 1974; Prown 1980, 1982), and their context-specific symbolic function as material metaphors (e.g., Hodder 1986, 1987). Yet other archaeologists and art historians interpret material culture as encapsulating moral, social, and ritual beliefs and relationships (Ray 1987; see also Gowans 1976; Leone 1977; Yamin and Yentsch 1989), and anthropologists, archaeologists, and folklorists alike have conceived of landscapes in particular as myths (Armstrong 1975; Glassie 1977; King, chapter 12, this volume).

To understand Rapp's garden as material expression charged with cultural meaning—as material metaphor, myth, symbol, performance, or ideology—team members turned to the religious, social, economic, and ideological contexts in which Harmony Society culture developed. In particular, attention was directed at the philosophy and religious beliefs of millennial communities and especially at their views on the landscape and nature; at George Rapp as spiritual leader and at his particular interpretation of the mysticism and pietism so widespread in the Germany of his time; at the Harmonists' cultural aesthetic and social traditions and the ways these traditions were expressed in and related to the landscape; and at worldly influences on the society, especially contemporary ideas on the order and meaning of nature, and how these ideas could or could not be integrated into the society's belief system.

The sources that Rapp may have drawn upon in designing his garden at Economy can be identified by examining the society's gardens at Harmony (1805–14) and New Harmony (1815–24), by studying the books and periodicals about garden design and horticulture in the Harmony Society library (of which only a fraction have survived), and by reviewing garden design as practiced in Germany and America in the late eighteenth and early nineteenth centuries. The correspondence files of the society contain a number of letters from botanists and plant dealers that shed light not only on Rapp's purchases but also on the network of connections from which he received ideas about garden design. The travelers' accounts already discussed not only describe the garden's form and contents, but also identify activities and events occurring in the garden and offer the travelers' interpretations of the cultural meanings and messages conveyed by the garden. Although Rapp wrote little explicitly about the symbolism and meaning of his garden, a review of his theological tracts, hymns, and poetry yielded important insight into his beliefs and symbolic vocabulary. Finally, secondary sources—the literature of Christian millennial utopianism, European and American landscape gardening, German traditional culture, and Enlightenment philosophy and science—provided both historical and cultural context and specific insight into forms, symbols, and their meanings.

As a committed millennial community, the Harmony Society focused its attention on those actions and events that pointed toward the Second Coming of Christ; this, they believed, would follow their wandering in the wilderness. Like other millennial communities, the society found inspiration in a vision of Christ's one-thousand-year reign of earthly harmony, freedom, and equality, expressed variously as a reconstituted Garden of Eden, the New Jerusalem, or the New Earth. Rapp's Harmony was to be an earthly paradise prefiguring the heavenly one that the faithful awaited in the Second Coming. The need to prepare the earth for the coming of the New Jerusalem governed the Harmonist attitude toward gardening. Like other emigrant millennial groups, they had to contend with the American wilderness and to reconcile it with biblical concepts and images. And like these other groups, the society expected its reward would be found in "a paradise improved," not in the natural state of the "waste and howling wilderness" (Nash 1967:36; Tichi 1979:15). The restoration of Eden, then, by the cultivation of the earth was the task set before them. The society's emigration to America seemed predestined as its members conceived of themselves as the righteous and of the New World as the regenerative New Earth of millennial prophecy.

Thus the Harmony Society grew in the context of a millennial movement that found expression internationally from the mid-seventeenth to early nineteenth centuries in the creation of new, often communal religious groups. Many sects in America embraced millennial thought and ideas about the reshaping of nature, including the Puritans, the Ephrata Cloisterites (Seventh Day Baptists), Oneida Perfectionists, the Moravians, the Zoar community, and later the various Mormon settlements (e.g., Hayden 1976:17–18; Leone 1977). For these millennial communities, so committed to the ideal of a natural paradise renewed, the symbolic role of the landscape was critical. The landscape imagery and symbolism George Rapp and other millennialists employed were, however, neither original nor unique to their theologies. Rather, these symbols were recombined, reinterpreted, and restated as material metaphors (Hodder 1987:3) comprising elements drawn from both secular and ecclesiastical contexts. Rapp's careful, conscious selection and combination of elements produced a garden that embodied not one, but many, metaphors, each meant to communicate its own messages.

From the Garden of Eden to the Garden at Gethsemane, the Christian church employed garden imagery extensively in symbolic expressions of theology and belief. The quadripartite plan Rapp adopted for his garden, for example, can be traced to the gardens of medieval monastic cloisters (Hennebo and Hoffman 1962–65). These gardens were invariably oriented with respect to the cardinal compass points, another element of church tradition recapitulated in the town plan, church, and garden plan at Economy.

Generally, the gardens of church tradition centered on a fountain. Water plays a fundamental role in this ecclesiastical imagery, for the image of salvation is linked to the water of baptism, representing the water of life. Scripture reinforced this symbolism. In the Apocalypse, the river of the water of life flows from under the throne in the new Jerusalem, and the salvation of the righteous is the reception of water from the fountain of life. The central pond in Rapp's garden was surrounded at an early date by conifers, botanically—or at least symbolically—related to cedars of Lebanon (PHMC, OEV Photo 235, 233, 748, 39), possibly in reference to Psalms 92:13, "the righteous will flourish like the cedar of Lebanon."

Similarly, the artificial vineyard mount of the northwest quadrant derives from a long ecclesiastical and secular tradition. A characteristic design element in medieval and Renaissance gardens, mounts acquired popularity in English gardens of the sixteenth and seventeenth centuries when their summits often featured arbors. Mounts both added variety to a flat topography and provided a view overlooking the garden. In the Bible, Jesus began his triumphal entry into Jerusalem from the Mount of Olives, the principal summit east of Jerusalem. Zion, the walled citadel of Jerusalem, was described as "His holy mountain upon which He has set His King" (Davis 1944:427, 431).

Rapp's mount, which looked out over the Ohio River to the west toward the setting sun, was planted not with olives but with another biblically resonant fruit, the grape. Grapes and viticulture symbolized fertility and signified a close union between Jesus and his disciples. Grapes had great economic and ornamental as well as symbolic value for Harmony Society members. They hung on trellises on most of the buildings, climbed pergolas and the trellises of the mount in the garden, and were grown in acres of vineyards outside the village. Viticulture formed one of the society's most important commercial activities. Perhaps better than any other feature of the garden, the mount with its vineyard strikingly represented the union of religious belief and worldly economy so integral to Harmonist art, life, and culture.

The foregoing discussion appropriately places Rapp's spiritualism and its symbolic expression through the material media of landscape and nature in the general context of the Christian ecclesiastical tradition. To truly understand him, his theology, the culture of his Harmony Society, and thus ultimately his garden, however, requires closer examination of his early life in Germany, the influences on his thought, and his personal expressions of his beliefs. Since George Rapp's ideology had been formed and his mission set out before he emigrated to America, the German mystic authors and the religious revivals, hermetic mysticism, and other separatist movements of his home region were obviously central to the development of his thought.

The 1760s through 1780s witnessed a revival of hermetic thought within the governmental and church districts of Rapp's own home town. The phenomenon indicated a growing dissatisfaction among the common folk with the coldness, formality, and hierarchy of the established Lutheran church (Kantzenbach 1984:12). The revival manifested itself in the preaching of sermons, distribution of texts, and renewed interest in earlier expressions of an emotionally rich, mysterious, fundamental, and, for some, intellectually engaging religion. One component of the revival centered on a painting by Johann Friedrich Gruber, the *Turris Antonia,* or *Tower of Antonia* (Harnischfeger 1980:136). Princess Antonia of Wurttemberg had commissioned the painting in the 1660s for a chapel near Stuttgart, about twenty-five miles from Rapp's home town. Didactic in function, it represents pictorially the secret, hermetic, cabalistic road to "initiation" and spiritual advancement of the self within the Christian framework (Harnischfeger 1980:42–46, 57–77). Surely Rapp knew this powerful image, which inspired eighteenth-century mystics as it had those of the seventeenth century (Breymayer and Haussermann 1977[1]:12; Scharfe 1968[5]:51, 291, 292).

The *Turris Antonia* features a circular garden with a central circular pool (figure 6.6). Christ stands upon a rock rising above the center of the pool. Over Christ hovers a symbolic female figure, the "Woman of the Apocalypse," who stands upon the moon, is clad in the sun, and has twelve stars around her head. In Revelation, she is identified as the woman who brought forth a son and fled into the wilderness (Revelation 12:1–6; see also Kring 1973:21). List's 1825 description of Rapp's garden (translated and quoted in Arndt 1982:685) notes a "13-foot-high rock" in the center of the pond, upon which the statue of Harmony was to be placed. Correspondence from Rush indicates the engineering difficulties he encountered in designing the statue as an operable fountain (Arndt 1982:587); it is perhaps for this reason that the "13-foot-high rock" was ultimately abandoned.

Figure 6.6. Turris Antonia. Reprinted from Ernst Harnischfeger, Mystik im Barock: Das Weltbild der Teinacher Lehrtafel. Urachhaus, Stuttgart, 1980, Plate 7, with permission from the publisher.

Radiating from the circular pool in the *Turris Antonia* are flower beds defined by a series of circular paths. These rings of flower beds are divided into twelve sections, each planted with a tree, next to which stands one of the twelve sons of Jacob (Fitzmeyer and Brown 1968:482–83). As previously noted, "cedars of Lebanon" appear surrounding the central pond in the earliest photographic views of Rapp's garden. The paths in the garden in *Turris Antonia* are painted yellow; archaeological test excavations in Rapp's garden tentatively identified yellowish sandy and clayey soils forming the earliest garden paths. A trellis planted with roses and grapevines surrounds the garden in the painting; similarly, in Rapp's garden in 1825, List speaks of "walk[ing] through arches of grapevines" (translated and quoted in Arndt 1982:685), while early photographs of the garden depict a trellis covered with grapevines surrounding the pond, broken by an arbor through which one passed to access the pond and Pavilion (PHMC, OEV Photo 4, 6, 40, 375). Finally, two architectural studies for the Pavilion attributed to Frederick Rapp survive in the Harmony Society Archives. One depicts the Pavilion as built (figure 6.7) (Drawing OE84.3.5; PHMC; HSA:OEV) with its domed roof reminiscent of that capping the classically inspired structure in the *Turris Antonia*.

Figure 6.7. Architectural study of the pavilion for George Rapp's garden at Economy. Attributed to Frederick R. Rapp. Drawing OE84.3.5. Photograph by George E. Thomas, Clio Group, Inc. Courtesy of the Pennsylvania Historical and Museum Commission; Harmony Society Archives: Old Economy Village.

While Rapp's garden may prove not to have been directly inspired by his memory of the *Turris Antonia,* his writings leave no doubt that his world view closely paralleled that expressed in the painting. From the form and symbol of his "Harmonie," from his use of the Virgin Sophia (Holy Wisdom) (Rapp: Hymn No. 343, HSA), and of the figure of Urania (Rapp: Hymn No. 260, HSA), from his interpretation of the importance of the Woman of the Apocalypse or Virgin in the Wilderness, from his mystic belief in the primordial unity of male and female and his advocacy of celibacy, and from his millennialist aspirations, it becomes clear that Rapp and his Harmony Society were associated with a particular religio-cultural conformation rooted in hermetic ideology. Equally clear is the fact that George Rapp ascribed symbolic meaning to his life, his congregation, and his world and that he perceived Nature and, especially, his own garden in this manner.

Rapp's hymns in particular provide a link between his religious world view and his garden. They portray Harmony as the guiding spirit of George Rapp's ideological life, a highly symbolic, deeply meaningful, active agent in the working out of his own and his congregation's salvation. Significantly, Rapp commissioned Rush to personify Harmony in a statue meant to occupy the central point in his garden, atop the pile of rocks in the central pool. Rapp refers to Harmony over and over again in his hymns.

> Behold, a cloud [Harmony] floats above you, high stand her blue strings, the winds are obedient to her . . . they hear song and sound of harp, harmonic and beautiful, melodiously united into the brotherhood's choir.

> Ascend, you lovely cloud to the higher circle of spirits of related persuasion, towards the Unity of the whole! Only for you and your peace cries my spirit! You have disclosed the secret of heaven to me! . . . Fulfill in me the works of salvation. . . . (Rapp: Hymn No. 209, HSA; translation by Wilmanns-Wells)

As endowed with symbolic meaning as Harmony, in Rapp's thought, was Nature.

> Your [Harmony's] prospects spacious and rich
> Meadows and fruited fields
> Equal to a paradise
> Under draping and arboring vines [bowers]
> All together. (Rapp: Hymn No. 56, HSA; translation by Wilmanns-Wells)

> Your ambrosian valley, full of honey, strengthening fragrances, all sorts of poppies, grapes and grape vines, and blossom-dusted wheat and rye, abundantly reelingly intertwined in friendship. . . . (Rapp: Hymn No. 236, HSA; translation by Wilmanns-Wells)

Thus was "paradise" prefigured not only in Rapp's garden but in the complete agricultural landscape of Economy. Nor was Rapp satisfied with this reification in garden and landscape of his paradisiacal vision. Rather he extended the metaphor further through performance. Travelers noted (Bernhard, translated and quoted in Arndt 1982:834; von Schweinitz, translated and quoted in Arndt 1965:447) and Rapp alludes in his hymns to the coming "all together" (see above, Hymn No. 56, HSA) of the congregation in the garden to sing, listen to music, worship, and celebrate. Rapp's lyrics served as part of a ritual reaffirming the dedication of the community to their religious (and secular) ideals of harmonious life in an ordered *Oekonomie* in preparation for Christ's Second Coming and re-establishment of heaven, paradise, on earth.

Not only did the garden "in performance" reinforce the communal commitment to the millennialist ideology, but it also served as a source of continuing personal inspiration for Rapp (see also Rapp: Hymn Nos. 207, 209, HSA).

> What do you
> seek here, inspired one?
> Primordial beginnings our thoughts are seeking here;
> Thoughts of new strength.
> How ever-greening are the expanses here;
> how cool the shade of the cedars . . .
> Here, here is the temple of the Godhead.
> (Rapp: Hymn No. 9, HSA; translation by Wilmanns-Wells)

George Rapp's religion was symbolic, mystical, mythic, and his writings demonstrate that he perceived Nature in these terms. The symbolic aspects of his garden may be viewed either as *retardataire,* harkening back to German iconography of the seventeenth century, or as a continuing example of a tenacious religious tradition.

But Rapp and his society were also innovative and original in the ways they reformed and adapted the symbolism to suit Rapp's goals in the American wilderness. For Rapp did not intend his garden to function solely as a religious metaphor. To speak metaphorically, as Rapp did, one might refer to several layers of the garden's associations, functions, and meanings laid one over the other, or perhaps more appropriately, numerous threads interwoven into a complex tapestry. In this ingenious interweaving lies Rapp's true accomplishment in the creation and performance of his garden.

An abiding commitment to its German cultural traditions forms one of the other layers or strands of Harmony Society culture encoded in both the society's landscape and its architecture. During the course of building Harmony, New Harmony, and Economy, Harmonist architecture was increasingly affected by exposure to American building practice. Yet the pattern of these changes is telling, as the Harmonists remained steadfastly true to German building practice in some areas while becoming quickly Americanized in others. Rapid Americanization was apparent in the Harmonists' use of materials, particularly as they took advantage of mass-produced building goods. If Harmonist buildings adopted an American formal skin, they nonetheless retained their German structure; construction technology remained fundamentally that of the German vernacular. Even the floor plans of the society members' homes built in Economy more than twenty years after their arrival in America remained the three-room German plan.

In the garden, the "pile of stones in the midst of a small forest" in the southwest quadrant was patterned after designs appearing in several German architectural and gardening publications of the late eighteenth century (*Gartenzeitung*; *Grohmann's Ideenbuch*). Stieglitz (1792–98:361) names this design the *Einsiedeley* (hermitage or shelter of the settler) and describes it thus:

> The Einsiedeley belongs to a lonely and vaguely melancholic region. . . . It can be a
> simple, crude little hut, round or square, whose windows are small and whose roof is of
> straw, carried on rough piers, and on whose walls one can trace the ravages of time and
> weather. It can variously take the form of a wood pile . . . or be assembled out of roots
> or the bark of trees can be nailed against it. It can depict a cavern or a mound, made up
> of earth and stone. Whether of stone or wood, it must demonstrate the greatest
> simplicity and neglect and no trace of artifice. . . . (translated by Lewis)

In one aspect, Rapp's building departed explicitly from Stieglitz's instructions. The encyclopedia recommended avoiding a tasteful and elegant interior ornamental program; "the momentary surprise" occasioned by the first entry into the building provided no compensation for the loss of character. The Rapps reproduced this building type in all three of their American towns; it derived from a European courtly or aristocratic garden and belonged to a secular tradition. As understood by contemporary German architects and designers, the *Einsiedeley* was meant to evoke, in a romantic sense of the sublime, a primeval place of shelter in the woods, suggesting the first dwelling of a settler. In religious terms, it also expresses the image of one who has taken refuge in the wilderness to isolate himself or herself as a hermit from society. The Harmony Society's own protracted wanderings unmistakably and purposefully paralleled the Israelites' forty years in the wilderness. Inevitably, this idea of the settler's first shelter also would have conjured visions of Adam and Eve's first shelter (Rykwert 1972).

In fact the *Einsiedeley,* set in a labyrinth in Harmony, the society's first town, provides perhaps the best example of the Harmonist allegorical program, because Rapp explained its symbolism himself. In 1811 he showed the labyrinth and its central *Einsiedeley* to a visitor, explaining, as the visitor later reported, that they "are emblematical. The Labyrinth represents the difficulty of arriving at Harmony. . . . At a distance [the *Einsiedeley*] has no allurements, but it is smooth and beautiful within, to show the beauty of harmony when once attained" (Melish, in Arndt 1980:457). At Economy, Rapp constructed two *Einsiedeleys.* One, in a labyrinth outside of town, was destroyed about 1860 and is not well documented. The other was moved from its place in a public town garden in New Harmony to Rapp's private garden in Economy, and from a labyrinth to a forest. A program of inscriptions was added to the interior walls (see Buckingham 1842:227, previously quoted on page 101 above). The role of the *Einsiedeley* and its meanings for Rapp, society members, and outsiders was changing. The *Einsiedeley* in Rapp's garden had evolved into a metaphor of the society itself, linking all three towns and their gardens. This last *Einsiedeley* memorialized the society's earthly history and did so in English for the outside world.

Other features, including the overall design of Rapp's garden at Economy, drew on German sources as well. Typical of an eighteenth-century picturesque mode of garden design, which featured both formal and naturalistic elements, the garden at Economy was already out of vogue by the second quarter of the nineteenth century in America. Thus, visitors termed it "rather baroque" (von Schweinitz 1831, translated and quoted in Arndt 1965:447) and reminiscent "of those at Hohenheim long since abandoned" (List 1835, translated and quoted in Arndt 1987:60).

Indeed, the entire cultural landscape created at Economy by the Harmonists symbolized the German homeland from which they were forced to flee. A contemporary German visitor referred to the society's move back from the Wabash to the "American Rhine," the Ohio River (Arndt 1987:427). Rapp's garden mount, a terraced vineyard, provided him with a prospect of the river and hills, along with the society's farmland and vineyards, a vista fundamentally similar to that gained when overlooking the landscape of the Wurttemberg region. The year before he died, George Rapp was visited by a German countryman, Franz von Loher. Discussing the New Earth, "when the hour is come," von Loher quotes Rapp as saying, "And in all this the German nation is marked: it will again be the greatest; it has been the most despised" (von Loher 1982:232).

The foregoing discussion hints at yet another layer or thread of meaning embodied in Rapp's garden: the traditional forms and symbols of the aristocracy and landed gentry of the Old and New Worlds pervade the garden. Even Antonia was a princess, and the influence of secular, palatial garden design is evident in the *Turris Antonia*. In replicating the forms and features of European and American estate and plantation gardens (see Berckhagen 1962; Carter 1977[1]:197; Hennebo and Hoffmann 1963; Hirschfeld 1779–85; McLean 1983:142–44; O'Malley 1986; Philadelphia Museum of Art 1976), Rapp's garden expressed economic and social advantage in a way that was familiar to him, his followers, and indeed the general European and American publics. Its overall quadripartite, geometric, and symmetrical plan recalled a garden style of earlier times, while at the same time it incorporated more current ideas. The differing treatment of each quarter introduced asymmetry and thus a naturalness to the plan. The quadripartite plan itself raises the possibility that the design of each quarter simultaneously expressed other themes—a traditional theme such as the four seasons or a more contemporary theme such as the four continents (Beiswanger 1983; Berckhagen 1962; Carter 1977; Hennebo and Hoffman 1965; Machor 1987; O'Malley 1986), in which the vineyard, for example, may represent Europe and the *Einsiedeley* the early American settler's hut. The travelers' accounts and early garden plant lists describe specimen plantings of native and exotic origins.

The garden struck one visitor as "marked[ly] aristocratic" (Featherstonaugh 1970), while another described Rapp as living "enthroned in a palace . . . [with its] broad magnificent garden" (List 1835, in Arndt 1987:60). Palace and garden are inseparable, the one dependent on the other for its existence and social meaning. The expression of social and economic position through the vehicle of an extensive and elaborate garden was not lost on the visitor, nor certainly on the Harmony Society member. To outsiders, then, Rapp's garden communicated economic success and social status in this world, not an obscure, mystical, otherworldly and thus suspicious religious fanaticism. Just such an image seems essential to the maintenance of the extensive economic interactions with the "outside world" on which the society relied for survival. Within the community, the association of this "aristocratic" garden with Rapp's home and the society members' familiarity with the garden through attendance at worship services held there served to further reinforce the internal social hierarchy on which the society was founded, despite its communal ideology.

The close relationship of house (or palace) and garden in the symbolic expression of social position can be seen clearly in Rapp's house. Its prototype was the symmetrical Georgian Palladian house with a center hall plan and attached flanking dependencies. Furthermore, it was executed in brick, the material of all but a handful of the more pretentious American buildings of the period. To furnish his house, Rapp wrote that he would "go to Pittsburgh with the girls to see what kind of taste the world now has [and] to choose the best" (translated and quoted in Arndt 1982:301). Consciously and purposefully, Rapp employed material culture to facilitate social and economic interaction within the community and with the world beyond.

On yet another level Rapp and the Harmony Society interacted with the "world." A profound transition in people's perception of nature was occurring in the first third of the nineteenth century, at the very same time Rapp was constructing his garden and composing his hymns on nature and divinity. Based on a "scientific" view of nature as a dynamic environment of complexly related organisms, this world view eventually challenged the traditional religious view of the universe. Despite the religious basis of Rapp's world view, he did not perceive these new ideas as a threat but rather embraced them from an early date. Harmony contained a botanic garden from which the society's physician was, by 1811, extracting specimens and arranging them according to the Linnaean system of taxonomic nomenclature (Melish, in Arndt 1980:457).

In Rapp's world, then, both religion and science contended, as he sought to impose a religious order over the natural world that science was helping him to classify and organize. For in the Harmonist view, scientific progress was not a tool with which to gain control of nature, but an instrument for confirming and upholding their religious understanding of the world. In this sense, then, Rapp's garden, definitely in the tradition of the horticultural showcase, was both botanic museum and Noah's Ark, summarizing and bringing together the fruits of creation, and preserving them through the millennium.

Contemporary ideas on "oeconomy," as expressed by Linneaus and others, also influenced Rapp's philosophy. The "oeconomy of Nature," the grand organization and government of life on earth, was designed to maximize production and efficiency. Such a model suited well the developing mechanistic, industrial society of nineteenth-century America. It suited Rapp as well; he embraced the new technology and modes of production. Economy consisted not only of vineyards and agricultural fields but also of cotton, woolen, and silk mills. Rapp believed that human creativity and industry glorified God (see both *Gedanken über die Bestimmung des Menschen* 1824 and *Feurige Kohlen* 1826); no conflict developed in his ideology between his New Earth millenarianism and his striving for material success in this world through commercial agricultural and industrial pursuits. Rapp resolved them in his belief system and in his garden. His garden embodied not only his vision of the Harmony Society's future post-millennial life but also the society's accomplishments in this life: an economic success dependent on the grapes, mulberries, apples, cotton, and tobacco represented among the garden's specimens.

This preliminary historical and archaeological study of George Rapp's garden at Old Economy Village makes it absolutely clear that Rapp's garden is as important and informative an object of Harmony Society material culture as the buildings, items of furniture, and manuscripts. Both consciously and unconsciously, Rapp embodied the essentials of his philosophy, world view, and traditional culture in the form, plant materials, and symbolism of the garden. The garden exquisitely expressed the Harmony Society's cultural, spiritual ideas on its relationship to God, nature, and to other peoples, incorporating a necessarily highly specific resolution of the tensions inherent in trying to live simultaneously in this world and the other.

Much of the carefully woven tapestry that was Rapp's garden remains to be reconstructed. Further research will allow some of the threads of meaning introduced here to be extended, new ones to be added, and perhaps require others to be rewoven. Truly "reading" this landscape requires a level of detailed knowledge of its structure, organization, and content not yet achieved. That the needed information survives—in the archaeological record, in the extant physical remains, and in the documents—is most remarkable, and that they be preserved is most essential. For only an interdisciplinary approach will reveal the many nuances of meaning the landscape incorporates of the worldliness and otherworldliness that was the Harmony Society.

ACKNOWLEDGMENTS

The research reported here was funded by the Pennsylvania Historical and Museum Commission as part of a comprehensive Historic Structures Report on Old Economy Village prepared by Thomas and Newswanger Architects and Clio Group, Inc. We thank the Pennsylvania Historical and Museum Commission for providing the opportunity to become involved with such an amazing site, and in particular Raymond Shepherd, director of Old Economy Village, who provided constant inspiration and the benefit of his rich knowledge of the Harmony Society and the sources; Karie Diethorn, Pat Belich and Ed Luketic of the Old Economy Village staff, who patiently led us through the garden and the archives; and Stephen Warfel, Ira Smith, John Callan, and Barry Loveland of the Historical and Museum Commission, who offered their support and assistance throughout the project. Valuable contributions to our thinking and our data base were also offered by Anne Yentsch, consultant on garden archaeology; Conrad M. Goodwin, archaeological field director; Naomi Miller, archaeobotanist; Dolores Piperno, phytolith analyst; and Clio Group, Inc., principals Tim Noble and Carl Doebley. This volume's editors, Rebecca Yamin and Karen Bescherer Metheny, offered thoughtful editorial assistance as we attempted to concisely and clearly integrate three years of research into a readable, chapter-length manuscript.

REFERENCES

Armstrong, Robert Plant
1975   *Wellspring: On the Myth and Source of Culture.* University of California at Berkeley Press, Berkeley.
Arndt, Karl J.
1965   *George Rapp's Harmony Society 1785–1847.* University of Pennsylvania Press, Philadelphia.
1980   *George Rapp's Separatists.* Harmony Society Press, Worcester, Massachusetts.
1982   *Harmony on the Wabash in Transition, 1824–1826.* Harmony Society Press, Worcester, Massachusetts.
1984   *Economy on the Ohio, 1826–1834, The Harmony Society During the Period of Its Greatest Power and Influence and Its Messianic Crisis.* Harmony Society Press, Worcester, Massachusetts.
1987   *George Rapp's Years of Glory. Economy on the Ohio, 1834–1847.* Peter Lang, New York.
Beiswanger, William L.
1983   The Temple in the Garden: Thomas Jefferson's Vision of the Monticello Landscape. *Eighteenth-Century Life* VIII(2):170–88.
Berckhagen, Ekhart
1962   *Deutsche Garten vor 1800.* B. Patzer, Hanover.
Binford, Lewis R.
1962   Archaeology as Anthropology. *American Antiquity* 28:217–25.
Breymayer, Reinhard, and Friedrich Haussermann, HSG.
1977   *Die Lehrtafel der Princessin Antonia: Kritische Ausgabe.* Berlin.
Buckingham, J. S.
1842   *The Eastern and Western States of America.* London.
Carter, Edward C., II, editor
1977   *The Virginia Journals of Benjamin Henry Latrobe, 1795–1798.* Yale University Press, New Haven.
Clio Group, Inc.
1990   Historic Structures Reports. Old Economy Village. Prepared for the Pennsylvania Historical and Museum Commission. Series in collections of Pennsylvania Historical and Museum Commission, Harrisburg.
Davis, John D.
1944   *The Westminster Dictionary of the Bible.* Revised by Henry S. Gehman. Westminster Press, Philadelphia.

Deetz, James
1977   *In Small Things Forgotten: The Archaeology of Early American Life.* Anchor Press, Doubleday, Garden City, New York.
Duss, John
1970   *The Harmonists.* 1943. Reprint. Harmonie Associates, Ambridge, Pennsylvania.
Featherstonaugh, George W.
1970   *A Canoe Voyage up the Minnay Sotor,* vol. 1. Reprint of undated edition. Minnesota Historical Society, St. Paul.
Fitzmeyer, Joseph. A., and Raymond E. Brown, editors
1968   *The New Testament and Topical Articles.* Vol. 2, *The Jerome Biblical Commentary,* edited by Raymond E. Brown, Joseph A. Fitzmeyer, and Roland E. Murphy. Prentice-Hall, Englewood Cliffs, New Jersey.
Fleming, E. McClung
1974   Artifact Study: A Proposed Model. *Winterthur Portfolio* 9:153–61.
Gartenzeitung
        Van Pelt Library, University of Pennsylvania.
Glassie, Henry
1977   Meaningful Things and Appropriate Myths: The Artifact's Place in American Studies. *Prospects* 3:1–49.
Gowans, Alan
1976   The Mansions of Alloway Creek. *RACAR: Revue de l'Art Canadien/Canadian Art Review* 3(2):55–71.
Grohmann's Ideenbuch für Liebhaber von Garten
1797–1808   Leipzig.
Harmony Society Archives (HSA)
        Pennsylvania State Archives, Harrisburg, Pennsylvania. Portions of the archives have been microfilmed.
Harnischfeger, Ernst
1980   *Mystik im Barock: Das Weltbild der Teinacher Lehrtafel.* Urachhaus, Stuttgart.
Hayden, Dolores
1976   *Seven American Utopias.* Cambridge University Press, Cambridge.
Hennebo, Dieter, and Alfred Hoffmann
1962–65   *Geschichte der deutschen Gartenkunst.* Three volumes. Broschek, Hamburg.
Hirschfeld, Christian L.
1779–85   *Theorie der Gartenkunst.* Five volumes. Leipzig.
Hodder, Ian
1986   *Reading the Past: Current Approaches to Interpretation in Archaeology.* Cambridge University Press, Cambridge.
Hodder, Ian, editor
1987   *The Archaeology of Contextual Meanings.* Cambridge University Press, Cambridge.
Kantzenbach, Friedrich Wilhelm
1984   Protestantische Geisteskultur und Konfessionalismus im 19 Jahrhundert. In *Probleme des Konfessionalismus in Deutschland seit 1800,* edited by Anton Rauscher. Ferdinand Schoningh, Paderborn.
Kring, Hilda Adam
1973   *The Harmonists: A Folk-Cultural Approach.* The Scarecrow Press and The American Theological Library Association, Metuchen, New Jersey.
Larner, John William
1962   Nails and Sundrie Medicines. *The Western Pennsylvania Historical Magazine* 45:115–38.
Leone, Mark P.
1977   The Role of Primitive Technology in 19th Century American Utopias. In *Material Culture: Styles, Organization, and Dynamics of Technology,* edited by Heather Lechtman and Robert S. Merrill, pp. 87–107. West, St. Paul, Minnesota.

Machor, James
1987   *Pastoral Cities: Urban Ideals and the Symbolic Landscape of America.* University of Wisconsin Press, Madison.

McLean, Elizabeth
1983   Town and Country Gardens in Eighteenth Century Philadelphia. *Eighteenth-Century Life* VIII(2):136–47.

Nash, Roderick
1967   *Wilderness and the American Mind.* Yale University Press, New Haven.

O'Malley, Therese
1986   Landscape Gardening in the Early National Period. In *Views and Visions: American Landscape before 1830,* edited by Edward J. Nygren, pp. 133–59. Corcoran Gallery of Art, Washington, D.C.

Pennsylvania Historical and Museum Commission (PHMC)
        Files and Manuscript Materials on Old Economy Village, Ambridge and Harrisburg, Pennsylvania.

Philadelphia Museum of Art
1976   *Philadelphia: Three Centuries of American Art.* Philadelphia Museum of Art, Philadelphia.

Piperno, Dolores R.
1989   Phytolith Studies at Old Economy Village. Ms. on file, Pennsylvania Historical and Museum Commission, Harrisburg.

Prown, Jules D.
1980   Style as Evidence. *Winterthur Portfolio* 15:197–210.
1982   Mind in Matter: An Introduction to Material Culture Theory and Method. *Winterthur Portfolio* 17(1):1–19.

Rapp, George
1824   *Gedanken über die Bestimmung des Menschen [Thoughts on the Destiny of Man].* Harmony Society Archives, Economy.
1826   *Feurige Kohlen [Flaming Coals].* Harmony Society, Economy.

Ray, Keith
1987   Material Metaphor, Social Interaction and Historical Reconstructions: Exploring Patterns of Association and Symbolism in the Igbo-Ukwu Corpus. In *The Archaeology of Contextual Meanings,* edited by Ian Hodder, pp. 66–78. Cambridge University Press, Cambridge.

Rubertone, Patricia E.
1989   Landscape as Artifact: Comments on "The Archaeological Use of Landscape Treatment in Social, Economic and Ideological Analysis." *Historical Archaeology* 23(1):50–54.

Rykwert, Joseph
1972   *Adam's House in Paradise.* Museum of Modern Art, New York.

Scharfe, Martin
1968   *Evangelische Andachtsbilder.* Veroffentl. Des Staatl. Amtes fur Denkmalspflege Stuttgart, Reihe C, Bd. 5 Volkskunde. Stuttgart.

Stieglitz, Christian Ludwig
1792–98 *Encyklopadie der burgerlichen Bakunst.* Five volumes. Leipzig.

Tichi, Cecelia
1979   *New World, New Earth: Environmental Reform in American Literature from the Puritans through Whitman.* Yale University Press, New Haven.

Von Loher, Franz
1982   Travel Account, 1846. *Western Pennsylvania Historical Magazine* (July):232ff.

Warfel, Stephen G.
1984   Archaeological Testing Report: 1984 Excavations at Old Economy Village, 36 BV 73. Ms. on file, Pennsylvania Historical and Museum Commission, Harrisburg.

Wilmanns-Wells, Christa

1989   George Rapp's Garden at Old Economy, Pennsylvania: Review and Commentary. Ms. on file, Pennsylvania Historical and Museum Commission, Harrisburg.

Yamin, Rebecca, and Anne E. Yentsch

1989   Interpretation in the Ethnographic Present: Morven, Princeton, New Jersey. Paper presented at the annual meeting of the Society for Historical Archaeology, Baltimore, Maryland.

Yentsch, Anne E., Naomi F. Miller, Barbara Paca, and Dolores Piperno

1987   Archaeologically Defining the Earlier Garden Landscapes at Morven: Preliminary Results. *Northeast Historical Archaeology* 16:1–29.

PART II

VERNACULAR AND SACRED SPACE

7

Social Relations
and the Cultural Landscape

J. Edward Hood

This chapter discusses the links between the physical landscape and culture. My intent is to argue that since the physical landscape is the context for the learning of culture and the material reproduction of society, it should be viewed as an important part of social relations. The landscape is "cultural" in that it physically embodies the history, structure, and contexts of human behavior in such a way that they are not readily separable from each other. Any understandings of the physical landscape, therefore, cannot be separated from the culture of the people who utilize it.

Culture is not a static thing but dynamic and changing, as are the landscapes discussed in this chapter. The study of landscapes provides one means for examining certain aspects of social relations. Landscapes should not be seen as passive or uninformative residues of human behavior.

CULTURAL LANDSCAPE

When discussing the term "landscape" there is often an implicit distinction between natural landscapes and those landscapes purposefully created by people. Analyses of the social intent of landscapes are often limited to more deliberate actions, such as the construction of formal gardens, estates, and urban planning. By "formal" or "planned," I refer to those landscapes that were pre-planned based on guide books or explicit premeditation and intent. Such landscapes include the formal gardens of the eighteenth-century North American Tidewater region (e.g., Kelso 1990; Leone 1984, 1987; Leone and Shackel 1990), and the intentionally informal, "naturalistic" landscape parks of England's gentry during the same time period (Williamson and Bellamy 1987:147–51). Social intent in formal landscape gardens is relatively clear; thus this form lends itself to analyses of the "meaning" of the landscape.

However, in between such formal planned landscapes and their symbolic opposite, "natural" landscapes, there is a very large category of spaces that have been increasingly referred to by such terms as houselots, yardscapes, streetscapes, vernacular landscapes, and so on (e.g., Beaudry 1986; Bouchert 1986; Jackson 1984; Paynter, Reinke, and Garrison 1987). These incidental spaces created by human activity are not necessarily explicitly purposeful or planned, but they can provide useful information for those wishing to study the relationship between social relations and material culture.

There has been much effort to conceptualize, define, and find methods to analyze landscapes (e.g., Beaudry 1986; Birks et al. 1988; Harvey 1973, 1985; Jackson 1984; Kelso and Most 1990; Norton 1987; Paynter, Reinke, and Garrison 1987; Rapoport 1982; Rowntree and Conkey 1980; Salter 1971; Sauer 1963). In fact, this topic has been the focus of much research in the fields of geography, cultural geography, and folklore studies (Lewis 1983 provides an overview of cultural landscape studies in these fields), as well as in historical archaeology (e.g., Anderson and Moore 1988; Beaudry 1986, 1989; Harrington 1989; Kelso and Most 1990; Mrozowski 1987; Paynter 1990; Reinke and Paynter 1984; Yentsch et al. 1987). One of my intentions is to present an archaeological perspective (archaeological in that it emphasizes the importance of material culture in human society) that does not segregate planned or formal landscapes from incidental and "natural" ones. Landscapes exist in a continuum of human perception and usage, and they can only be individually understood in the context of one another.

"Natural" is a construct people use to describe land that they feel has not been intentionally modified. Land that at one time was intensively utilized but has since fallen out of culturally recognized usage is often considered "natural." Separating natural landscapes from cultural ones is not an objective process. It is a matter of cultural definition and contextualization.

The regrowth of New England's forests is a good example of such a contextual definition of nature, with the species, condition, and distribution of second-growth vegetation a product of both past and present patterns of land utilization (Cronon 1983; Spurr and Barnes 1973). The transformation of New England's economy over the last three centuries, with the associated patterns of settlement, land use, and property holding, are at the core of this reappearance of a "natural" landscape. "Nature" can not be readily separated from "culture" in understanding this landscape, even if this landscape's physical manifestation consists entirely of trees and rocks. The same could be said of the "natural wilderness" that English explorers and immigrants encountered in North America. What they saw as untamed and wild was very much a managed environment transformed by millennia of Native American horticulture, gathering, and hunting.

Certainly, the physical landscape is in part the result of continuous abiotic and biotic processes that exist with or without humans. But even without direct physical contact from humans, landscapes are perceived and categorized into culturally relevant entities, even if these are "the edge of the Earth," "the unknown," "unexplored," "enemy territory," or "virgin land." Such categorizations can have tangible consequences for how that space is utilized, which in turn affects the behavior of those perceiving the landscape in that particular way. "The edge of the Earth" as a perceived place had very real emotional and physical consequences for European mariners during the fifteenth century and earlier.

123

Social
Relations
and the
Cultural
Landscape

In perpetuating or setting up an absolute dichotomy between cultural and natural, planned and incidental, we arbitrarily ignore the cultural and physical contexts that give meaning to "planned" landscapes such as formal gardens. A formal garden is culturally significant to its creators and observers because of its juxtaposition to what is seen as informal or unplanned (such as the yards and houselots associated with mundane activities). These two different types of landscapes are part of the *same* cognitive universe and have contextually specific definitions for each culture.

I define "landscapes" as the physical spaces perceived and utilized by humans both explicitly and implicitly. Perceptions of the "objective" qualities of the earth are a product of culture. Native Americans and English immigrants in New England confronted the same physical landscape, but each perceived a distinctly different thing. For the Native Americans, it was a productive realm that needed to be maintained both in ecological and spiritual balance; for the English, it was a "howling wilderness" that required "improvement" to bring it from a state of nature to one of productivity (Demos 1972:1–22; St. George 1982).

To better express how the physical landscape is incorporated into culture I have chosen to use the term "cultural landscape." This is one way of expressing how landscapes are created in terms of human use through action and perception and are loaded with cultural meaning in specific historical contexts. Cultural landscape can be extended to include all aspects of culturally defined space. This includes architecture and internal building space, gardens, yards, town organization, regional communication networks, fields, and wasteland. Each of these physical loci, as culturally defined space, has historically derived meanings. The landscape is not only a physical context that helps to constitute social relations, but it is also a meaningful context as well.

Learned understandings of the world (what is here defined as culture) (Barrett 1988; Bourdieu 1977, 1985:728–29; Giddens 1984; Hodder 1986:71–74) are in part created through experiencing the material world in which one grows up and carries out the mundane activities of life (Fletcher 1978; Harvey 1973, 1989; Hodder 1985:14, 1987; Kus 1982; Lane 1987; Miller 1987:81; Moore 1986; Rapoport 1982:66–68). The material world of dwellings, routes of movement, zones of resources, work areas, play areas, fields, and wilderness not only frames daily experience, but also provides the physical infrastructure with which material production is carried out (Harvey 1973, 1985, 1989; Paynter 1982).

The social ways that natural resources are accessed, the ways labor is deployed to provide the necessities of a society, and the ways that these products are distributed through a society constitute the process of *production*. Providing for material needs is not merely a material act; it is a social act. It does not take place apart from cultural understandings of what is needed, where it comes from, how it is obtained, how it should be distributed, and how and why it should or can be consumed (Harvey 1985:37, 1989; Marx [1867] 1967; Miller 1987:17–18; Mintz 1985; Speth 1983:xiii–xvi, 145–59; Wolf 1982).

Whatever the objective or functional organization of space within a society might mean in terms of rational economic models, this same spatial organization will have cultural meaning that is not necessarily reducible to function. This meaning, whatever it might be, is a critical aspect of the actual functioning of a given spatial organization in its specific cultural context (Harvey 1989; Hodder 1985:5, 1987; Tilley 1989). Meaning and physical context together help constitute social relations because individuals draw from a range of possible choices in pursuing their various interests and goals.

Elements of the production process, and of the landscape in general (such as fields, buildings, and roads), are material in form. They consist of what archaeologists often refer to as material culture and settlement pattern: "things" that are created by humans and that often survive through time. Because of its physical character, material culture can last longer than the initial behaviors that create it and often longer than the uses for which it was intended (Moore 1990). The materiality of the landscape lends an inertia-like conservatism to the spatial organization of society, as it does to both the process of production and to social relations.

As opposed to spoken words or actions, material objects can persist through time in their original form (Moore 1990). Such time depth can allow for the manipulation of meanings associated with those objects, providing a false historical precedent for new interpretations of meanings and associated social relations. Perceived time depth and reification of the meanings associated with material culture can have a traditionalizing effect, giving added strength to the new social relations associated with it (Hodder 1987; Rapoport 1982:60–61; Rowntree and Conkey 1980:462). The successive use of the landscape, by those who create it and by their descendants, provides few or no visible "breaks" in the continuity of its usage. As new functions and meanings are slowly attached to a landscape (for example, to cathedrals or public spaces), its actual physical constancy from the past can lend apparent social continuity through time. Such perceived continuity, or "tradition," can be a powerful means for justifying contemporary social relations.

Meanings supporting certain social relations can be imbued into objects and landscapes in order to help legitimate those social relations. People in positions of power and authority may often have greater ability to execute such transformations of meaning through the physical reorganizations of the landscape to better fit their particular interests. For such manipulations to be successful, however, such newly created landscapes must make some sort of meaningful sense to the society as a whole or be enforced by some means. Again, those with power, such as the state (Harvey 1985; Kus 1982) or members of the upper classes (Leone 1984; Williamson and Bellamy 1987), are in the best position to alter social meanings attached to the landscape by physically altering the landscape itself and by backing up this transformation through coercive means. The ultimate outcome of their actions, however, will be a product of both their efforts *and* the types of resistance and competition encountered (Harvey 1985).

Many material objects and aspects of the cultural landscape tend to be overtly "nonpolitical" in that they are part of the everyday, commonsense physical world, and thus tend not to evoke directly the specific social relations of which they are a part (Rowntree and Conkey 1980:474). At times, the meanings of objects can become overt and political, usually with more than one interpretation being viewed as correct. The fences and hedges used to enclose common fields and pastures in England during the seventeenth through the nineteenth centuries were seen by small landholders as more than a way of subdividing property and making agricultural production more efficient; these were the tools and symbols for the elimination of their economic livelihood. In resisting the new social and economic order being created through enclosure, small landholders and others defending traditional farming practices occasionally targeted the new fences and hedges for destruction. What had otherwise been a mundane aspect of the landscape became a powerful symbol, a symbol of social relations not separable from the landscape itself.

125
Social
Relations
and the
Cultural
Landscape

By viewing the landscape as not just a reflection of culture, not just a means for signaling status, and not just a functional arrangement of artifacts for articulating humans within their environment, one may take the stance that the landscape itself plays an important role in constituting human society. A society has many possible ways of articulating itself within the physical world. Ideals about landscapes are not directly translated into the physical world, but are used as parts of social strategies that result in landscapes containing complex and multivocal layers of meaning.

To help illustrate this point, I will compare three English cultural landscapes and discuss the connections between their physical histories and their social histories. These distinct regions experienced similar large-scale processes of change between the seventeenth and the nineteenth centuries. These changes largely entailed industrialization and the modernization of agricultural practices for specialized, extensive marketing (Butlin 1982; Thirsk 1985b; Wolf 1982). Despite similar economic conditions and a shared culture, each region went through distinct transformations resulting from the specific ways in which the social relations of each population were articulated within these regional landscapes.

The first two English landscapes to be discussed are in England and had a long history of continuous development and use. The third landscape to be considered is that of New England. There the lack of English cultural continuity created a substantially different physical and social context in which English social relations were carried out. The comparison of these landscapes helps reveal how important the landscape is to social relations and how people actively manipulate it as part of their social strategies. In each case the landscape played a specific role in constituting social relations and was actively manipulated in order to transform those social relations.

THE LANDSCAPES OF ENGLAND

England in the mid-seventeenth century was characterized by a number of regions defined by their geography and by the ways land was held and utilized within them (Thirsk 1984a, 1984b). Although there was great variability in land use and landholding practices within these regions (e.g., Underdown 1985), a number of large-scale patterns are discernible. At the most general level, the English landscape in the mid-seventeenth century could be broken up into three main regions (Thirsk 1984a:204–16, 1984b:xx–xxi; Williamson and Bellamy 1987:10–16).

The first region consisted of the Uplands, which generally had a scattered and low population density, with pastoral activities being the dominant agricultural practice (Hey 1984). The second region was the Open Field or "Champion" country (open, having few trees and relatively less hedges and walls; see Rackham 1986:4–5), typified by high population densities located in compact or nucleated villages lying at the center of large unfenced agricultural fields (see figure 7.1 for an example of a representative Open Field village).

Village residents held lands in the form of small intermingled parcels ("strips") within these large fields. There was often a high degree of community control over land use in the open fields that restrained the degree to which individuals could modify their land or its uses. Often some free access was available to certain types of materials found on "waste" lands within the towns, such as firewood and building materials (Mingay 1984; Orwin and Orwin 1967; Thirsk 1964). The third region was known as the Woodlands, consisting not of "woods" as we think of them in North America, but areas where the landscape comprised small enclosed fields, often bordered by thick hedge banks. These areas were typified by a relatively high population density located in scattered, often rambling villages (see figure 7.2 for an example of a Woodland village). Economic activities were generally mixed with a high proportion of intensive livestock management (Harrison 1984). This chapter will focus on two of these landscapes, the Open Fields and the Woodlands.[1]

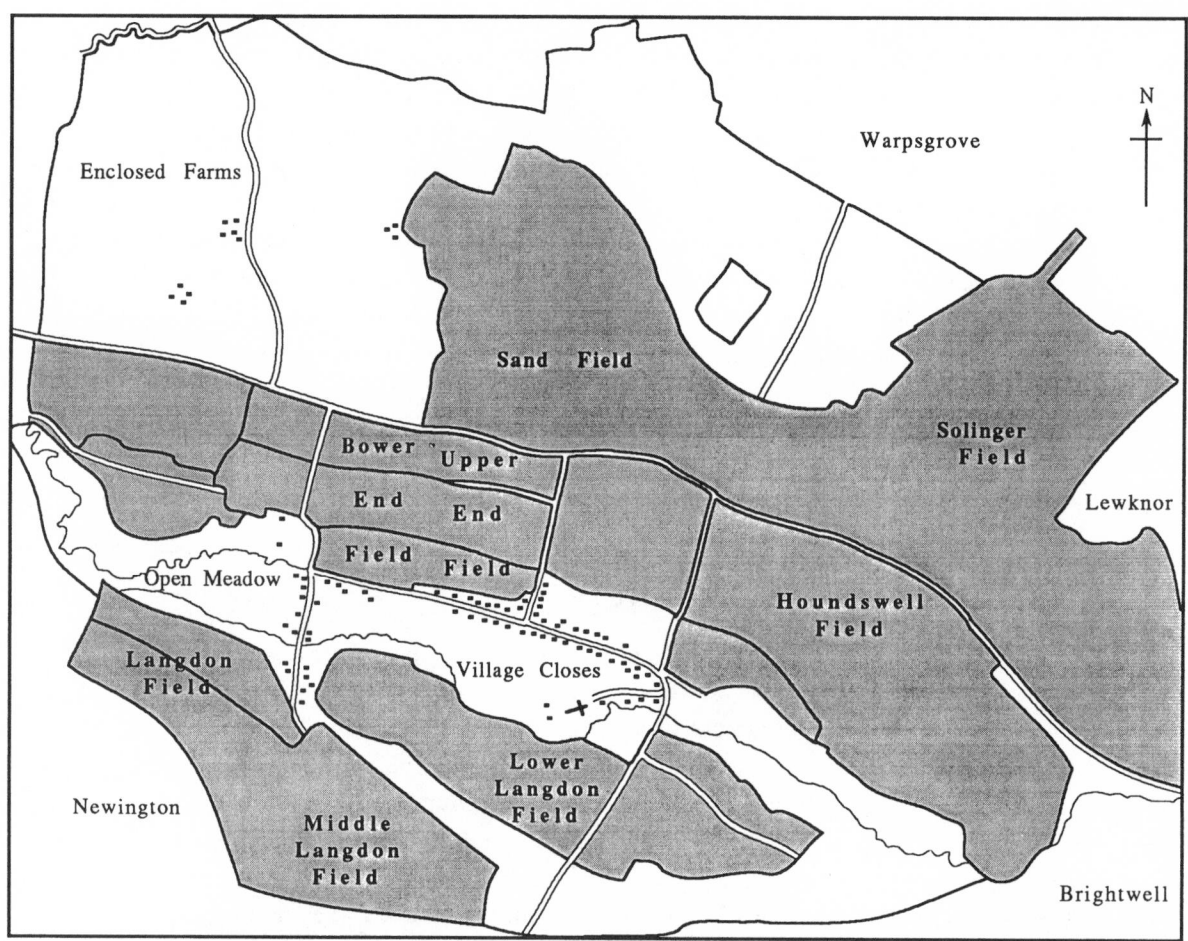

Figure 7.1. Example of an Open Field region township. Though great diversity existed between towns in the Open Fields regions, many shared the basic characteristics seen in this sketch of the township of Chalgrove, located in eastern Oxfordshire. In the center of the township is a nucleated settlement of houses and their lots ("closes"). Surrounding the closes are large, "open" fields divided into unfenced holdings, denoted by shading. In the northern part of the township three enclosed farms are seen lying adjacent to their lands (the boundaries of the farms are not depicted). After Gray 1915:20, a sketch made from the Chalgrove 1841 Tithe Apportionment Map.

127

Social
Relations
and the
Cultural
Landscape

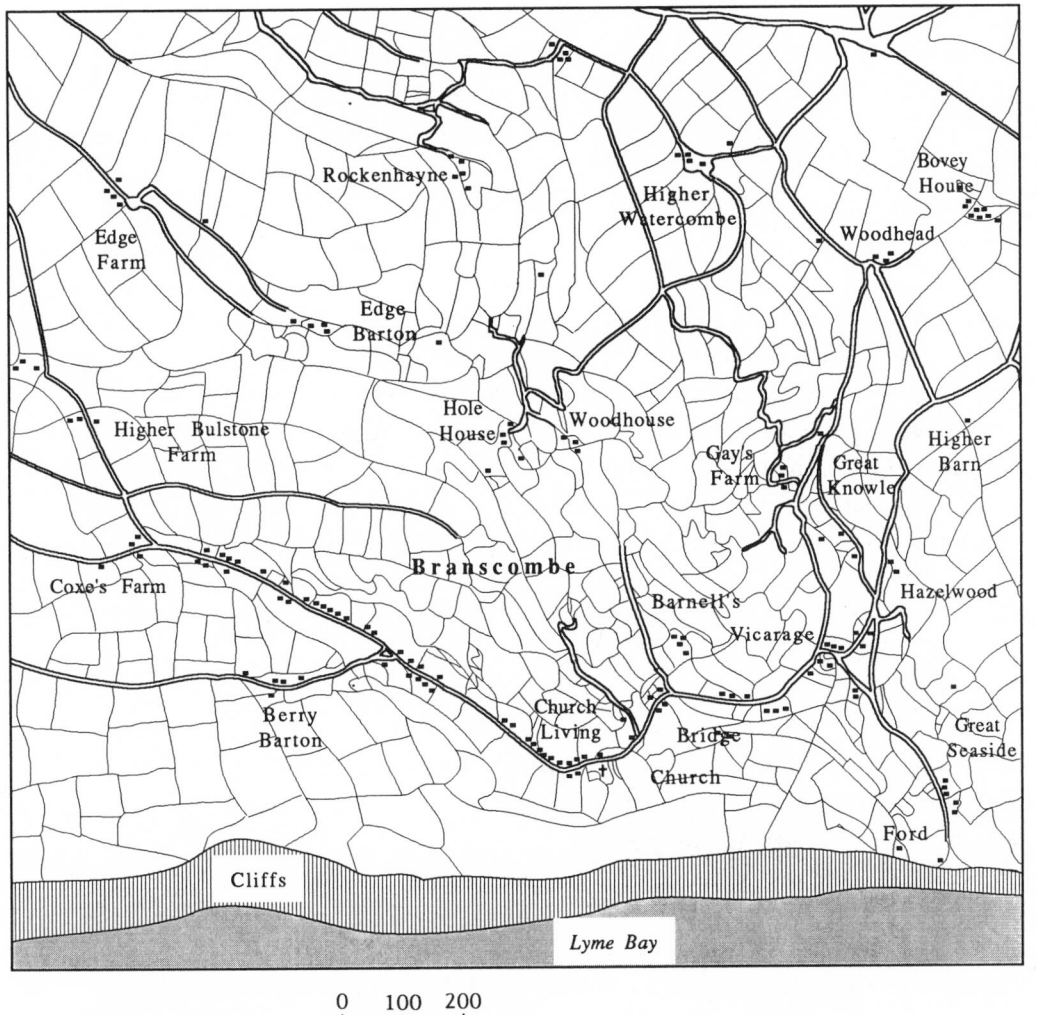

Figure 7.2. Map of Branscombe, a Woodland village in east Devon. Note the meandering and dispersed locations of the village houses and the small irregular field shapes. After Ordnance Survey of Great Britain, 1:25,000 series, sheets SY08/18, SY09/19, SY29/39.

The origins of these distinctive regions are the basis for an extensive body of research and debate (e.g., Aston 1985; Gray 1915; Hoskins 1955; Rackham 1986; Ravenhill 1972; Roberts 1987; Roberts and Glasscock 1983; Taylor 1975, 1983; Thirsk 1966; Titow 1965; Williamson and Bellamy 1987). Topography, geology, and environmental characteristics explain some of these regional distinctions, but it is also clear that these factors alone do not explain everything. Research on the English landscape has shown that cultural factors, including its medieval past (e.g., Aston 1985; Roberts 1983), have contributed to distinctions that endure into the present.

Recent work shows that the continuity of the structure of land-use patterns in some areas extends back at least into the second millennium B.C. Research in Devon by Andrew Fleming and others (Fleming and Collis 1973; Fleming and Ralph 1982) has shown that the structure of medieval field systems often followed that of pre-Roman times and that there were systems of land division (the exact social character of which is not understood) that extended at least seven kilometers in length as early as 1600 B.C. Tom Williamson and Liz Bellamy (1987:17–20) report the presence of similar systems of pre-Roman origin in East Anglia that more or less have helped to determine the structure of the modern landscape. At any particular time, the landscape of England was a palimpsest of continuous usage, no matter how dramatic the social transformations occurring at any one time.

Long-term processes of change during the fifteenth and sixteenth centuries led to increasingly swift transformations of social relations and patterns of landholdings and control after A.D. 1650 into a pattern that would last until the mid-nineteenth century and that still strongly influences the physical and economic character of England today (Thirsk 1984b, 1985b). In 1649, King Charles I was executed, striking a symbolic blow against the royalty and court gentry who had previously controlled the land and politics of England. Despite the restoration of Charles II in 1660, the Civil War of the 1640s had led to a reorganization of the regional gentries throughout the country, establishing a large and powerful landed class whose authority did not rise directly from association with the crown (Butlin 1982:29–31; Underdown 1985; Williamson and Bellamy 1987:123–24). The Glorious Revolution of 1688 firmly established the interests of this landed gentry, which dominated what had become the supreme governing body in England, Parliament (Hoskins 1955:118; Underdown 1985:208–10; Williamson and Bellamy 1987:123–24).

During this time period new practices of landowning and land use transformed the English landscape, often in the face of strong and sometimes violent opposition by the occupants of that landscape. Regional, national, and international market changes created new opportunities for the accumulation of wealth by the owners of large amounts of land. But the structure of England's post-medieval landscapes, and the land-use practices of its occupants, stood in the way of this desired "modernization." The particular relationships between landholding practices, land utilization, and the physical organization of the landscape in each region led to particular regional strategies for modernization ("improvement"), and to particular strategies for resisting many of the consequences of this improvement.

Agricultural Modernization of the Open Field Regions

The primary process of modernizing agricultural land use in the Open Field regions was that of enclosure. This entailed the reorganization of a town's lands from groupings of individuals' holdings scattered throughout the town in various communally controlled fields into single, privately controlled fields (Bowden 1985; Thirsk 1985a; Turner 1984a). Prior to enclosure, lands were communally controlled and held in subdivided but unfenced "open" fields that surrounded the village, usually nucleated in form (figure 7.1). Individuals' holdings, whether owned or rented (typically with long-term or semi-permanent leases), were often scattered throughout the various fields of the town. Such dispersal of holdings made their use relatively more difficult due to the amount of time spent traveling between each holding. The unfenced intermixing of holdings also made attempts to increase the productivity of the land through new methods, such as intensive fertilization, economically unattractive (Bowden 1985; Turner 1984a).

By breaking up these open fields and consolidating each landholder's parcels into continuous fields, and separating these from other lands by new fencing (enclosure), agricultural productivity per acre of land could be dramatically improved. Grain production was often increased on the order of 10 to 25 percent (Turner 1984a:39–41). Enclosure allowed better implementation of improved agricultural practices, reduced trespass, and often eliminated the need for leaving fields in fallow. In particular, increased specialization of land use was facilitated by this process. The end result of such improvement was increased profits for landlords and taxes for the government (Bowden 1985; Thirsk 1984a:192; Turner 1984a:38–41; Williamson and Bellamy 1987:97–101).

Enclosure had many detrimental effects as well, mainly on small landholders. These people had been able to make a living by farming their relatively small amounts of land and, importantly, by utilizing common grazing lands and accessing resources such as firewood, charcoal, and building materials from common and wasteland areas (Aston 1985:126; Mills 1980:101–5; Thirsk 1964:3).

Improving wasteland and taking it, along with the arable and pasture lands, from communal use and putting it into private hands was the primary purpose of enclosure (Turner 1984a:23–24, 58). The expense of reorganizing one's holdings into a single field, including the cost of fencing and improvements to the land, was quite high. Smaller fields cost relatively more per unit of fenced land than larger fields, thus putting a proportionally heavier cost on those who only held small amounts of land (Harvey 1970:71; Peters 1969:30; Turner 1984a:56–57; Williamson and Bellamy 1987:109–15). Small landholders who had been able to survive before enclosure could not sustain the capital outlays needed to make these adjustments to their holdings. In addition, they often could not afford the fertilizers and other products, such as building materials, that previously had been free or unnecessary. Improvement of agricultural land through enclosure did increase the profitability of farming, but these profits went to a relatively smaller group of people than that which previously had made a living from agriculture on this same land (Butlin 1982; Thirsk 1984a:192; Williamson and Bellamy 1987:100–115; Wrathmell 1980).

Enclosure often meant real economic loss and social disruption for many and was deeply resented by small landholders, who saw this as an attack on their way of life. Violent resistance to enclosure was often threatened and occasionally carried out via the pulling down or burning of enclosure fences and hedges (Harrison 1984:359–62; Underdown 1985). The primary method for surmounting such resistance was a request made by the largest landholders of a town to Parliament, asking for a legal, forcible enclosure of *all* the holdings within the town (Turner 1984a, 1984b).

By the late seventeenth century large landholders had considerable power and influence over Parliament and a more sympathetic Crown, which fostered an increasing rate of enclosure. Through the power of the state, the landowning gentry forcibly reorganized the English landscape. During the eighteenth and nineteenth centuries, 21 percent of the area of England was enclosed through such acts of Parliament (Turner 1984b:133). This transformation of the physical landscape was a fundamental part of the reorganization of English society from the remnants of the by then unprofitable medieval system of customary rights and obligations to a three-tiered system of landlord, tenant, and landless laborer (Johnson 1991; Mills 1980:130–35; Williamson and Bellamy 1987:102–3).

Agricultural Modernization of Woodland Regions: East Devon

The physical transformations of Woodland regions during this same time period were usually less dramatic than those in the Open Field districts. Nonetheless, Woodland areas also experienced major social and economic changes linked to the same national and international

129

Social
Relations
and the
Cultural
Landscape

transformations affecting Open Field communities. Since these transformations are generally less well understood than those of the Open Field regions, I will elaborate on the history and development of a town in the Woodland region of east Devon. Using as an example the town of Branscombe (figure 7.2), located on the south shore of east Devon, I intend to show how the particular landscape of this region helped shape its transformation during the same period that Open Field villages were experiencing similar modernization, but with dramatically different consequences for the landscape and social relations.

In the twelfth and thirteenth centuries, much of east Devon had a mixed arable and pastoral agricultural system based on both subdivided (or "open") fields and enclosed fields. These fields were for the most part irregularly arranged into small units and utilized for the practice of convertible husbandry, with fields rotating between crops and livestock raising (Fox 1975:183–86). During the fourteenth and fifteenth centuries this area increasingly was geared toward the raising of livestock, a practice associated with the growing number of smaller enclosed fields in Devon. By the sixteenth century east Devon had taken on its current appearance typified by small enclosed fields (Alcock 1975; Fox 1975).

The landscape of Devon was never static and was constantly adjusted to meet new conditions of production associated with new regional and local strategies for accumulating wealth. Land use was inherently shaped by the forms of previous landscapes, creating physical "traditions" that were closely intertwined with the cultural traditions of those who lived on and worked the land. As Underdown (1985) has discussed for this region, such traditions were variously interpreted and actively manipulated by the different classes of society. The physical landscape was very much a part of people's understandings of economy, legal rights, and acceptable social order.

The same economic processes of modernization affecting the Open Field regions after the mid-seventeenth century were also at work in Woodland regions such as east Devon. Here, land was already divided into small enclosures. The dispersed nature of landholdings and the irregular organization and small size of fields, however, made modernization of agriculture almost as difficult as it was elsewhere. Individual fields were, on average, less than three acres in size (Fox 1972:7), with some less than one acre (Hoskins 1940:5). All were surrounded by Devon Hedges consisting of thick earth and stone embankments with dense hedges and timber trees (Devon County Records Office [Devon C.R.O.] 1843; Hoskins 1940:5–6).

Despite substantial outward differences in appearance, modernization and rationalization of agricultural land in this region were similar to the modernization and rationalization of the Open Field regions in that they required the redistribution of land into more continuous holdings of appropriate size. Also, the medieval landholding practices of semipermanent leases were extinguished. In the Open Field regions this "modernization" of lease forms (to market-rate, short-term types of agreements) was usually accomplished automatically with an act of Parliamentary enclosure (Williamson and Bellamy 1987:114), something that could not readily be done in Woodland areas.

Unlike the Open Field regions, east Devon fields and farms needed to be improved by the *removal* of some hedges and the amalgamation of fields to make them more amenable to modern agricultural practices (Hoskins 1940:4–7). Rapid physical reorganization of east Devon fields was, however, essentially impossible due to the costs of removing the massive Devon hedges. Instead, those interested in modernizing land use manipulated the system of land leasing, shortening the terms of leases, when possible, to allow easier accumulation of land

and market-rate rentals (Hoskins 1940). Through this process many smaller farms were agglomerated into larger, more profitable farms (Alcock 1975; Hoskins 1940:11).

131
Social
Relations
and the
Cultural
Landscape

Lands owned by ecclesiastical institutions, such as the majority of holdings in Branscombe (Devon C.R.O. 1843; White [1850] 1968:378–79), generally were rented to local gentry and upwardly mobile "yeomen." Until 1800, leases held on ecclesiastical lands tended to be in the form of long-term rental agreements such as "copy hold" leases and leases of "three-lives," both of which could be extended more or less permanently through the payment of fines (for adding additional names or "lives" to the lease) (Clay 1985; Hoskins 1940, 1954:90–91; Underdown 1985:20–28; Williamson and Bellamy 1987:90–91).

Hoskins (1954:90–91) provides an example of how this system worked in the Devon town of Thorverton. In 1661 the Dean and Chapter of Exeter (an ecclesiastical institution, associated with Exeter Cathedral, that owned a substantial amount of land in Devon) had let out five farms and twenty-two houses and cottages in Thorverton to "a substantial yeoman" via copy hold and other long-term leases. The yeoman sublet these properties for what a Dean and Chapter surveyor felt was a profitable investment for the yeoman. Hoskins notes that this was a common method for "substantial yeomen," or "lesser gentry" as Underdown calls them (1985:21), to increase their wealth and landholdings.

William Marshall, an improvement-minded observer of late-eighteenth-century agriculture in Britain, wrote about the practice of subletting farms in east Devon and declared it to be "evil" and generally an unprofitable use of the land ([1796] 1970 [2]:111–12, 150). As a member of the gentry, he saw the old landholding and land-use practices as archaic and inefficient. Modernization of land use and private ownership or direct rental of optimal-sized farms were the appropriate means that "improvers" such as Marshall felt should be utilized. Either through enclosure or amalgamation, the "old ways" were to be eliminated and the doors opened for new ways to reap profit from the soil.

By 1841 most lands in Branscombe were being let-out on leases of twenty-one years (Devon C.R.O. 1843), a tenure relatively more amenable to the profitable collection of rents accruing from the modernization of land use than the older, longer-term leases. The Land Tax Assessments for Branscombe from the late eighteenth and early nineteenth centuries further attest that various members of the local gentry owned or rented large numbers of parcels within the town, and that control of these holdings changed hands with some frequency (Devon C.R.O. Land Tax Assessments 1780–1946).

The main method for modernizing land use was through the amalgamation of smaller fields and farms into larger contiguous groupings. This could be done several ways, though primarily it was accomplished through the acquisition of land adjacent to one's current holdings (with whichever rental agreement was in place) and then removing internal hedges, or, with less expense, by just removing gates or knocking holes through the hedges (Hoskins 1940:5–7, 1954:96–98). Associated with this practice was the separation of agricultural fields from the farmhouse of an amalgamated farm, and rental of the house as a cottage for laborers, with little or none of the farm land included in the lease (Alcock 1975:124–25; Hoskins 1940:7).

This trend led, in general, to an increasingly marginal lifestyle for many small land-holding tenants, an increase in the numbers of wage labor tenants, as well as growing poverty and emigration (Hoskins 1940:11, 1954:98–101). While the wealthy were able to acquire land and increase its profitability through modernization, their ability to completely transform the agricultural system for even greater profits was relatively limited. The physical structure of east Devon's small, hedgerowed fields made more massive transformations difficult and provided small landholders with some means to resist the process of modernization that entailed economic hardships for many throughout England.

Since the main landowner in Branscombe (the Dean and Chapter of Exeter) did not exert direct control over its lands in the town, but instead sublet them, there apparently was never a single person of landed authority in post-medieval and early modern Branscombe. There were, however, people who, by the strength of their positions as proprietors for large amounts of parish and freehold lands, were able to exert a strong influence over the village. These people accumulated wealth through the subletting of their large proprietorships in smaller parcels to other tenants. Manipulation of rental agreements, as well as marriage between land-controlling families (Devon C.R.O. Land Tax Assessments 1780–1946; Lysons and Lysons 1822:62–63, 133; Tomlinson 1985), allowed these proprietors to maintain and enlarge their estates and become "people of substance" (Tomlinson 1985:13). They modernized their holdings through seemingly "traditional" agricultural and rental practices without resorting to forceful means similar to Parliamentary enclosure. To do so would have been impossible due to the literally entrenched nature of Branscombe's landscape and the similarly embedded rights of small landholders.

Summary: Two Landscapes of England

For Branscombe, as elsewhere in England during the eighteenth and nineteenth centuries, increasing national market orientation and the modernization of agriculture were difficult as the social and material history of many villages defined a range of legitimate behavior that did not include evicting tenants *en masse* (except those owned entirely by a single landlord; see Wrathmell 1980). In Open Field regions where massive physical reorganization was feasible, tenants were "legally" forced off the land *en masse* through acts of Parliament.

A more conservative set of strategies seems to have been used in Woodland regions such as east Devon to extract surplus from agricultural and small crafts producers. Without abrupt disruptions of village life or agricultural practices, individuals manipulated the existing farms and field systems to create larger blocks of fields for improved agriculture. Simultaneously, a laboring class was created that did not have rights to access land or other resources and could be housed in the cottages snipped out of what previously had been small farms.

It would have been too difficult for the major landowners of Branscombe and other English villages with similar cultural landscapes to create large-scale transformations of their village's economies without protracted social struggle. Despite the fact that they owned the land, the landowners and proprietors were not able to easily remove their tenants, who maintained a relatively tenable economic position through an economy of mixed pastoral farming and small crafts production (Harrison 1984; Murray [1859] 1971:32; Tomlinson 1985). This relative economic independence was linked to the actual physical structure of the villages, fields, hedges, and roads of east Devon. To force change through large-scale legal acts in Woodland regions would have been extremely difficult, due to the fixity of the physical landscape and the social relations embedded in that landscape.

The act of physically transforming Open Field communities was relatively easy, forcing new landowning and use practices upon small landholders. The main forms of resistance to modernization available to small landholders in Open Field regions were court actions or the physical destruction of new enclosure fences. Both of these strategies were generally opposed by the state and were never sustained successfully for very long (Thirsk 1985a:381).

In implementing similar forms of accumulation in these two regions of England, distinct strategies were utilized that fit the extant physical and social conditions of each region. The new social relations and physical organizations of the landscape that resulted were specific to the histories of each region and the particular strategies utilized for accumulation (by landlords) and resistance to this accumulation (by small landholders). Because of the dynamic relationship between social relations and the cultural landscape, the *similar* social and economic transformations affecting the *different* regions of England created *dissimilar* social and physical conditions in each.

THE LANDSCAPE OF NEW ENGLAND

The English rapidly established colonies in North America beginning in the first quarter of the seventeenth century. These colonies, in the Caribbean, Virginia, and New England, had different characteristics (for an abundance of reasons that are beyond the scope of this chapter). New England, for example, emphasized the establishment of complete communities containing men, women, children, and many of the civic and social institutions of England. This settlement was very much a part of the large-scale economic transformations that were affecting England and the rest of Europe, changes that increasingly emphasized specialized market production and the free market selling of land and labor. In comparing the cultural landscapes of New England and England, I wish to emphasize that, though the creators of these landscapes shared the same culture, their use of the landscape was not uniform; it was dependent on the interactions of particular social relations in specific physical and historical contexts.

In New England there was no cultural continuity for English settlement and land use. Villages were created anew on land that had been previously occupied by Native Americans—people who had no direct cultural continuity with the English. These two groups interacted intensely, but in occupying Native American lands the English generally ignored Native American concepts of landownership and land use or considered them irrelevant to their own long-term goals. The immigrants made various attempts to replicate English society and economy through the duplication of political institutions, social classes, and often, in part, through the recreation of English landscapes. The varied backgrounds and goals of the English adventurers, merchants, and settlers, however, led to a diversity of settlement types (Fischer 1989; Garvan 1951; Powell 1965).

Despite the transplantation of English culture to the New World, "New" England never gained more than a superficial resemblance to its mother country. Fundamental to the creation of New England was a lack of physical structure for the institutions and understandings of English society to "work." In England land was a powerful and tightly controlled resource that served as the foundation for social hierarchy and the accumulation of wealth. The land was deeply marked by the daily rhythms of life and work in such a way that it was not readily separable in the minds of individuals from the inequality in the land's ownership that underlay the whole system. In New England such a cultural landscape simply did not exist, allowing for the possibility of a large range of new social and economic relationships to develop. People who had known only tenantry or small landholding could now become freemen and yeomen.

133
Social
Relations
and the
Cultural
Landscape

The making of the New England landscape was not a replication of the English landscape, but an active manipulation of the existing landscape based on individual and group goals embedded within understandings of social order and the possibilities for its physical manifestation. Given a lack of established physical infrastructure (landscape) and social hierarchy, the variables of regionality, class, gender, age, and other group affiliations provided individuals with the opportunity to interpret the New World in ways that were profoundly different, both among groups of immigrants and with England itself.

English settlers found New England to be a hostile and infertile land. To bring this land into a useful state of agriculture, two major transformations had to take place. First, Native American claims to the land had to be acquired or extinguished. Though the Native American system of land use was quite productive and efficient (Cronon 1983:34–53; Salisbury 1982:30–39), it could not support English society and economy. Native concepts of land ownership were particularly at odds with the way the English understood it, and the two fundamentally could not coexist (Cronon 1983:54–81).

Second, the land itself had to be "subdued" and brought into a state useful for English agricultural practices. This process was not merely practical in its execution but was symbolic in that the landscape had to be transformed into one that was culturally recognizable to the English. St. George (1982:161) discusses this symbolic transformation in terms of bringing land from a state of "nature" (in the view of the English) to one of "culture."

Beyond these initial stages of gaining control of the land, perhaps a more difficult problem for English immigrants as a group, or at least for their leaders and financial backers, was how to preserve in some form the structure of English society. The ready availability of land in New England helped to blur social distinctions as they existed in England (St. George 1982:159–60) and potentially allowed individuals to live outside of both the physical and social structure of English society.

The Nucleated Village in New England

Many of the initial settlements of New England (figure 7.3) such as Plymouth are described as nucleated villages (Garvan 1951:40). This village plan of closely clustered houselots surrounded by open agricultural fields (figures 7.1 and 7.4) (see Roberts 1987:6–9, 26–27) resembled the villages of the Open Field regions of England and is known to have been an *ideal*—if not always real—form for early New England settlements (Allen 1981; Carroll 1969:138–41; Massachusetts Historical Society 1871:474–80; Vaughan 1972:60–61).

Though each English nucleated village had its own peculiarities, this general form of settlement and associated land use (open, common fields) had relatively clear social consequences in the context of English medieval and post-medieval culture. Propinquity is the foremost of these, with the closeness and face-to-face character of house locations making constant personal contact and casual observation an aspect of everyday activities. Mills notes how the nucleated villages associated with open field agriculture allowed for a greater degree of control over the inhabitants by the local gentry. He sees the nucleation of houses as a means of indirect social control (1980:17–19, 128).

Despite the idealized status and initial use of nucleated villages at several settlements, including Plymouth, most early New England towns either started out dispersed or rapidly became dispersed (Allen 1981:5; Wood 1978, 1984:334). A major exception to this, however,

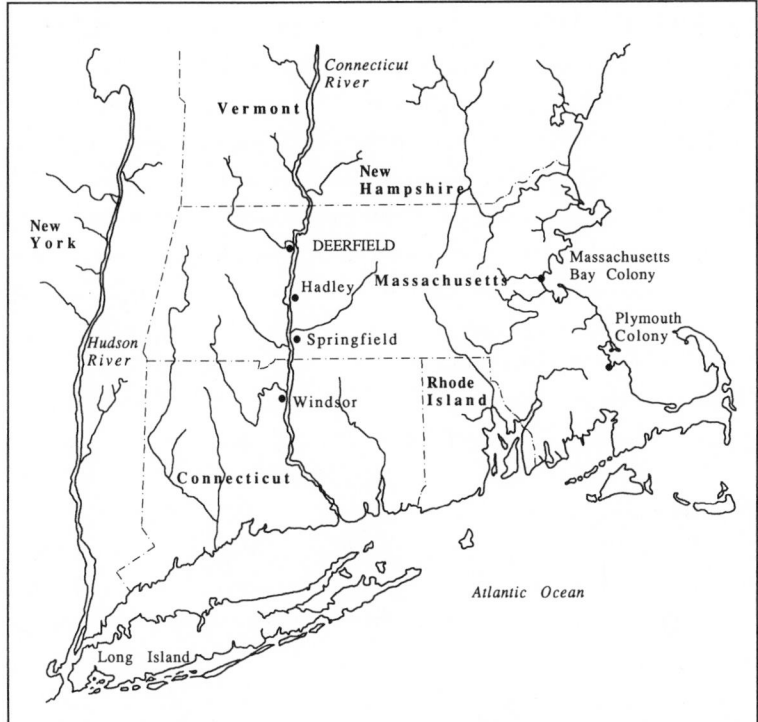

Figure 7.3. Map of southern New England.

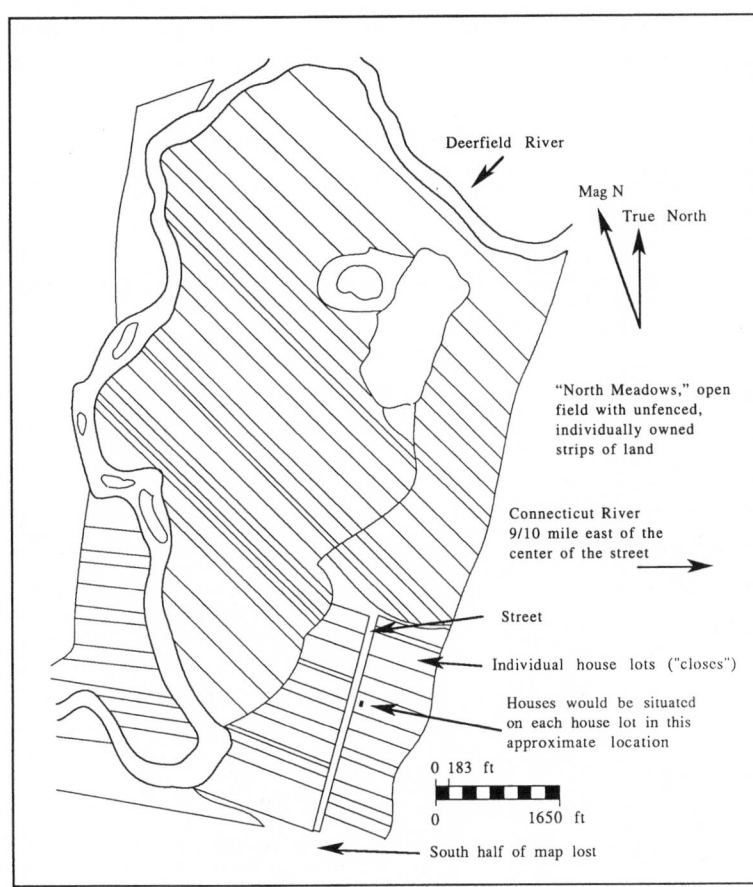

Figure 7.4. A nucleated village in the middle Connecticut River Valley. Based on a Plan of Deerfield made by the Proprietors Committee in 1671 prior to the town's actual settlement. Only the north half of the map has survived. Lands surrounding the village were utilized as common pasturage and woodlands. The layout of the village and north meadow fields still retains this basic plan today.

was the middle Connecticut River Valley where the nucleated village and open field form were used for at least eleven villages created during the period 1633–75. Settlements such as Windsor, founded in 1633, Springfield (1636), Hadley (1659), and Deerfield, which was laid out in 1671 (figure 7.4), were created with nucleated town plans and open fields that continued to be utilized into the early eighteenth century (Sheldon 1912; St. George 1988).

Joseph Wood has argued (1978) that nucleated settlements were not common in New England (a point contrary to most previous studies of the early New England village; e.g., Trewartha 1967:517–23) except in the middle Connecticut River valley. Wood cites a desire to utilize the valley's abundant meadow grasses for livestock raising as the primary reason for adopting this settlement form with its associated open fields. Though there is some validity to this point, there certainly could have been a number of ways for individuals to exploit these lands for livestock raising besides the open field–nucleated village. Also, grain growing was as much, if not more, of a hallmark of Connecticut River Valley agriculture as livestock raising during the early colonial period (Sweeney 1985:18).

Anthony Garvan (1951) links the use of nucleated town plans to the English colonization of a number of regions, including the Fens of East Anglia, the early-seventeenth-century Ulster plantations, and New England. Though he does not make a strong argument for why this settlement form was used specifically for the purposes of colonization, he is clear that it is associated with the early settlement of several English colonies. Brooke Blades more specifically argues that the nucleated village form was intentionally chosen for the purposes of colonization. He discusses how English plantation owners in early-seventeenth-century Ulster were attempting to replicate an English "cultural landscape" (1986:259–61). This landscape was not only meant to help repress indigenous Gaelic culture, but it was also meant to help maintain the social coherence of the English settlers on whom London investors in the Ulster plantations depended for a profit. Blades argues that the creation of an idealized English village form of compact, nucleated settlement was a "fundamental means of maintaining English cultural values" (1986:258).

Robert St. George (1988:338), Kevin Sweeney (1984, 1985), and Stephen Innes (1983) all discuss how the seventeenth- and eighteenth-century society of the middle Connecticut River Valley was built upon a system of aristocratic preference linked to an intricate web of kinship. By embedding unequal relations of power and wealth in material symbols that emphasized an organic community, ideal physical order, and even communality, these unequal relations could be maintained. St. George argues that the open field agriculture associated with these nucleated town plans was a key element in creating a unified society based on unequal access to resources and power (1988:346–47).

Central to any understanding of the English settlement of the Connecticut River Valley are the roles played by William Pynchon and his son John, who were the most important individuals among the region's elite. William founded the town of Springfield in 1636, and he and John served as the primary political and financial backers of most of the other new settlements in the Connecticut River Valley. With a network of kin they dominated the economic, political, judicial, religious, and military institutions of this part of Massachusetts Bay Colony throughout the latter half of the seventeenth century (Innes 1983; St. George 1988; Sweeney 1984, 1985).

Each new town created in the middle Connecticut River Valley had a committee of landowners, or "proprietors," who had a direct role in planning the layout of the towns. Some members of proprietors' committees came from other valley towns, but most were

137
Social
Relations
and the
Cultural
Landscape

from eastern Massachusetts Bay Colony where nucleated settlement was by and large not practiced. Others came directly from England where this form of settlement was beginning to be considered outdated by large landowners.

Though the documents regarding the creation of these towns have been researched and discussed in great detail by historians (e.g., Akagi 1924; Andrews 1889; Innes 1983; Judd [1905] 1976; Melvoin 1989; Sheldon [1896] 1983), nowhere are there found explicit directions by one of the Pynchons, or anyone else, about how to create a "nucleated" village. What are found are explicit directions about how to lay out homelots and field strips in a certain manner that, when viewed as a whole, entail a nucleated village with an open field system surrounding it.

Prior to its settlement, for example, the Deerfield Proprietors met in 1670 and appointed a committee that was empowered to lay out the town as they saw most fit. The committee was given the authority to:

> order the situation of the Town for the most convenience as in their discretion shall appear best [for] the whole tract, and the quality of each sort of land, and other accommodations considered, and appointing highways . . . and a place for the Meeting House, Church Officers lot or lots, . . . and to proportion each several sort of land there according to the quality thereof [so] that equity may be attentat [*sic*] to each proprietor according to their proportion in every sort of land dividable. John Pynchon, Esquire, is entreated, and empowered, at all his best opportunities to take his time to visit the Committee, and artist . . . and give them such advice in that work committed to them, as he shall judge most conducible to the good of the plantation. (Records of the Deerfield Proprietors, transcribed in Sheldon [1896] 1983:15–16)

It is not known what John Pynchon may have said to this planning committee regarding the layout of Deerfield, but it is important to note that he was by far the largest shareholder on the Proprietors' committee (which wrote the above quoted passage) (Records of the Deerfield Proprietors, transcribed in Sheldon [1896] 1983:16). After the creation and settlement of Deerfield, Pynchon rented out his lands in the new town in ways that would bring him a substantial return on his investments (see figure 7.4 for the presettlement plan of Deerfield) (Pynchon Account Books 1985a, 1985b, 1985c).

Though the Pynchons' involvement in creating the nucleated plans of the Connecticut River towns is clear, the proprietors of each town still had considerable influence in establishing their own particular version of this general design. What made this plan so attractive to the Pynchons and the town proprietors? It was not a standard form of New England settlement, and there were few existing models of other New England villages with similar layouts. Economic function is one explanation for such a settlement type, an argument that Wood has proposed for the Connecticut Valley settlements (Wood 1978). Certainly the lands here are more fertile than elsewhere in New England, but this type of land use would not have been the most lucrative for people such as the Pynchons and other regional investors, many of whom also had investments in the slave-based economies of the West Indies (Innes 1983:33–34).

Defense may have been an issue, though little direct conflict had occurred between the English and the local Native American populations prior to the creation of the earliest of these towns (to the south a war was fought against the Pequots in 1636–38, just after the founding of the first three nucleated settlements). The initial written directions by Deerfield's proprietors to lay out the town (Records of the Deerfield Proprietors, transcribed in Sheldon [1896] 1983:17–19) made no mention of defensive considerations, and the initial layouts of Hadley and Deerfield, for example, had no obvious defensive elements (Judd [1905] 1976; Melvoin 1989:53; Nostrand 1973; Reinke and Hood 1990; Sheldon [1896] 1983).

Not until the beginning of King Philip's war in 1675 (fought by the Native American inhabitants of southern New England in an attempt to stop further English encroachment in the region) did these towns erect palisades and fortify houses, measures that were not necessarily related to the layout of the towns. Even with these secondary defensive measures, defense against attacks by Native Americans was usually ineffective (Judd [1905] 1976; Reinke and Hood 1990; Sheldon [1896] 1983).

As discussed previously, open field agriculture in England was historically associated with nucleated settlement. The links between the two have been discussed at length by many (e.g., Gray 1915; Taylor 1975; Thirsk 1964, 1966), and there is some functional rationality for linking the two in terms of minimizing movement from home to dispersed field holdings (Chisholm 1972:117). Though the links between open field agriculture and nucleated settlement are historically strong and may make rational economic sense, they do not necessarily determine one another, and there are examples of one of these elements existing without the other (Garvan 1951; Hood 1990; Thirsk 1964, 1966).

Why would settlers create such a structured agricultural system that was increasingly seen as outmoded in England and even in New England in terms of more profitable forms of agriculture? I argue that it was in the interest of those who had large initial investments in the creation of these towns—the landed gentry such as the Pynchons and their close associates among town proprietors—to attempt to maintain stable, self-governing settlements. One way of doing this in a culturally unobtrusive and non-explicit way was through the use of the vaguely "traditional" nucleated village and open field agriculture.

By doing this, the towns could recreate a recognizable "English" form where the order of social and political hierarchy could be reproduced. Relevant political offices, including the proprietors and committees responsible for managing the common fields (such as fence viewers), could be utilized to maintain a socially stable and economically productive town. As St. George (1988), Sweeney (1984), and Innes (1983) argue, such political offices were almost completely dominated by the local gentry. This same gentry would also be most able to profit from the export of the town's agricultural goods and other products, which they dominated through the control of major entrepôts such as Springfield and even the West Indies (Innes 1983; Paynter 1982, 1985; St. George 1988).

The common field systems of these communities bound people into a defined range of agricultural activities. Individuals' lands were intermingled with one another and spread out through the common fields. All proprietors were required to maintain a proportion of the common field fence, which, in Deerfield, was approximately fourteen miles in circumference by the early eighteenth century (Sheldon 1912:243). The maintenance of this fence, and the regulation of dates for the opening of the fields for the common feeding of livestock, bound landholders (owners and tenants) together into a relationship that helped to maintain a self-regulating system of agricultural production. Though land was held privately and was bought and sold speculatively, it could not be easily segregated from the common fields for specialized use.

139
Social
Relations
and the
Cultural
Landscape

The relatively isolated location of these communities, far from the heart of the Massachusetts Bay Colony, provided a politically and socially unstructured environment for newcomers. The land was very rich and abundant, making it possible for individuals to establish profitable farms and settlements outside of the direct watch and control of colonial authorities. The organization of these communities with nucleated settlement and open field agriculture created a landscape that could help reproduce English society and its attendant social and economic hierarchy. It provided new settlers an opportunity for upward mobility, yet kept them within the economic interests of the growing colony and the regional gentry. These towns could politically, socially, and economically reproduce themselves with little direct manipulation by the colony. They would also provide a profitable return for those who helped create them and who controlled the flow of products to and from them.

For the inhabitants, these settlements may not have seemed dramatically different from any other New England or English village in which they had previously lived. The field systems and agricultural methods were certainly some version of what they were accustomed to, even if not in the exact configurations they had previously experienced. The unequal distribution of lands to people based on their existing wealth and status might have seemed odd, given the vast amounts of land available within these townships; indeed, much of the land was not parceled out until the mid- to late eighteenth century (Akagi 1924). But such inequality would still be a familiar part of their English cultural background and would have made sense given an understanding of landscape as something inherently owned, usually unequally. The face-to-face quality of living in a nucleated village, and the communal decision-making process regarding the use of the common agricultural lands, would further minimize the social discontinuities created by the clearly unequal distributions of land.

In this way the English cultural landscape of the middle Connecticut River Valley was created. It translated a "natural" landscape into one that helped reproduce English social and economic inequality. New England's landscape was not a reflection of the "mind-sets" of its English inhabitants as much as it was the product of their purposeful choices drawing on a range of possible cultural options regarding that landscape.

I have outlined one way of viewing the landscape. The particular stance argued here emphasizes the dynamic relationship between society and its physical, material context. Such an interactive relationship may be conceptualized through the idea of the "cultural landscape"—the physical spaces perceived and created by humans, imbued with meaning, and understood in culturally specific terms such that function and meaning are inseparable. The cultural landscape is the physical and symbolic arena for the social process of production, the accumulation of wealth, and the resistance to unequal accumulation. The cultural landscape contains and intertwines the material reproduction of society with the cultural understandings of that process. It is both a tool and the context of social change, being part of the constitution and daily reconstitution of society.

ACKNOWLEDGMENTS

I would like to thank Robert Paynter, Rita Reinke, Kevin Sweeney, Ritchie Garrison, Amelia Miller, and Susan McGowan for their guidance and help over the several years that I have participated in their research on Deerfield, Massachusetts, as well as for their comments on various parts of this chapter. The Department of Anthropology at the University of Massachusetts, Amherst, helped fund my research in Britain. I received the gracious help of a large number of people in Britain, particularly from Barbara Bender, Matthew Johnson, and the members of the Department of Archaeology and Prehistory at the University of Sheffield. I would especially like to thank Barbara Bender for her great efforts and assistance during my stays in London and Exeter and for introducing me to Branscombe. A number of individuals helped me with their comments and ideas on drafts of this chapter, including Martin Wobst, John Cole, Barbara Bender, Sheila Brennan, James Garman, Karen Bescherer Metheny, and Rebecca Yamin. The graphics were prepared by David Schafer. Any problems or faults with this chapter are, however, the responsibility of the author.

NOTE

1. Keep in mind that these regions are very broadly generalized and contain a great deal of internal variability. In defining them, some researchers emphasize agricultural practices (Thirsk 1984b), while others emphasize topographic characteristics and historical landscape organization (Rackham 1986:1–5; Williamson and Bellamy 1987).

REFERENCES

Akagi, Roy Hidemichi
1924   *The Town Proprietors of the New England Colonies.* University of Pennsylvania Press, Philadelphia.
Alcock, N. W.
1975   Fields and Farms in an East Devon Parish. *Reports and Transactions of the Devon Association for the Advancement of Sciences* 107:93–172.
Allen, David Grayson
1981   *In English Ways.* Institute of Early American History and Culture, University of North Carolina Press, Chapel Hill, North Carolina.
Anderson, Texas B., and Roger G. Moore
1988   Meaning and the Built Environment: A Symbolic Analysis of a 19th-Century Urban Site. In *The Recovery of Meaning: Historical Archaeology in the Eastern United States,* edited by Mark P. Leone and Parker B. Potter Jr., pp. 379–406. Smithsonian Institution Press, Washington, D.C.
Andrews, Charles
1889   *The River Towns of Connecticut: A Study of Wethersfield, Hartford, and Windsor.* Johns Hopkins University Studies in Historical and Political Science, Seventh Series, vols. 7–9, edited by Herbert Adams. The Johns Hopkins University Press, Baltimore.
Aston, Michael
1985   *Interpreting the Landscape.* B. T. Batsford, London.
Barrett, John C.
1988   Fields of Discourse: Reconstituting a Social Archaeology. *Critique of Anthropology* 7(3):5–16.
Beaudry, Mary C.
1986   The Archaeology of Historical Land Use in Massachusetts. *Historical Archaeology* 20(2):38–46.
1989   The Lowell Boott Mills Complex and Its Housing: Material Expressions of Corporate Ideology. *Historical Archaeology* 23(1):19–32.
Birks, Hilary, H. J. B. Birks, Peter Kalund, and Dagfinn Moe, editors
1988   *The Cultural Landscape: Past, Present and Future.* Cambridge University Press, Cambridge.
Blades, Brooke S.
1986   English Villages in the Londonderry Plantation. *Post-Medieval Archaeology* 20:257–69.

141

Social
Relations
and the
Cultural
Landscape

Bouchert, James

1986   Alley Landscapes of Washington. In *Common Places: Readings in American Vernacular Architecture,* edited by Dell Upton and John Vlach, pp. 281–91. The University of Georgia Press, Athens.

Bourdieu, Pierre

1977   *Outline of a Theory of Practice.* Cambridge University Press, Cambridge.

1985   Social Space and the Genesis of Groups. *Theory and Society* 14(6):723–44.

Bowden, Peter J.

1985   Agricultural Prices, Wages, Farm Profits, and Rents. In *The Agrarian History of England and Wales.* Vol. 7, *Agrarian Change 1640–1750,* edited by Joan Thirsk, pp. 1–118. Cambridge University Press, Cambridge.

Butlin, R. A.

1982   *The Transformation of Rural England ca. 1500–1800: A Study in Historical Geography.* Oxford University Press, Oxford.

Carroll, Peter

1969   *Puritanism and the Wilderness: The Intellectual Significance of the New England Frontier 1629–1700.* Columbia University Press, New York.

Chisholm, Michael

1972   *Rural Settlement and Land Use.* Aldine, Atherton, Inc., Chicago.

Clay, Christopher

1985   Landlords and Estate Management in England. In *The Agrarian History of England and Wales.* Vol. 7, *Agrarian Change 1640–1750,* edited by Joan Thirsk, pp. 119–251. Cambridge University Press, Cambridge.

Cronon, William

1983   *Changes in the Land: Indians, Colonists, and the Ecology of New England.* Hill and Wang, New York.

Demos, John

1972   Articles of Agreement Among the First Settlers of Springfield (1636). In *Remarkable Providences 1600–1760,* edited by John Demos, pp. 53–56. George Braziller, New York.

Devon County Records Office (Devon C.R.O.)

1780–1946   Land Tax Assessments for Branscombe. Devon County Records Office, Exeter, U.K.

1843   Tithe Map and Award for Branscombe. Devon County Records Office, Exeter, U.K.

Fischer, David Hackett

1989   *Albion's Seed: Four British Folkways in America.* Oxford University Press, New York.

Fleming, Andrew, and John Collis

1973   A Late Prehistoric Reave System Near Cholwich Town, Dartmoor. *Proceedings of the Devon Archaeological Society* 31:1–21.

Fleming, Andrew, and Nicholas Ralph

1982   Medieval Settlement and Land Use on Holne Moor, Dartmoor: The Landscape Evidence. *Medieval Archaeology* 26:101–37.

Fletcher, Roland

1978   Issues in the Analysis of Settlement Space. In *Social Organization and Settlement,* edited by David Green, Colin Haselgrove, and Matthew Spriggs, pp. 225–40. British Archaeological Reports, International Series No.47ii. British Archaeological Reports, Oxford.

Fox, H. S. A.

1972   The Study of Field Systems. *Devon Historian* 4:3–11.

1975   The Chronology of Enclosure and Economic Development in Medieval Devon. *The Economic History Review* 8(2):181–202.

Garvan, Anthony N. B.

1951   *Architecture and Town Planning in Colonial Connecticut.* Yale University Press, New Haven.

Giddens, Anthony

1984   *The Constitution of Society.* Polity Press, Oxford.

Gray, Howard
1915   *English Field Systems.* Harvard Historical Studies, vol. 22. Harvard University Press, Cambridge, Massachusetts.

Harrington, Faith
1989   The Emergent Elite in Early 18th Century Portsmouth Society: The Archaeology of the Joseph Sherburne Houselot. *Historical Archaeology* 23(1):2–18.

Harrison, Giles V.
1984   The South-West: Dorset, Somerset, Devon, and Cornwall. In *The Agrarian History of England and Wales.* Vol. 6, *Regional Farming Systems 1640–1750,* edited by Joan Thirsk, pp. 358–89. Cambridge University Press, Cambridge.

Harvey, David
1973   *Social Justice and the City.* The Johns Hopkins University Press, Baltimore, Maryland.
1985   *Consciousness and the Urban Experience.* The Johns Hopkins University Press, Baltimore, Maryland.
1989   *The Condition of Postmodernity: An Enquiry into the Origins of Cultural Change.* Basil Blackwell, Oxford.

Harvey, Nigel
1970   *A History of Farm Buildings in England and Wales.* David & Charles, Newton Abbot, U.K.

Hey, David
1984   The North-West Midlands: Derbyshire, Staffordshire, Cheshire, and Shropshire. In *The Agrarian History of England and Wales.* Vol. 6, *Regional Farming Systems 1640–1750,* edited by Joan Thirsk, pp. 129–58. Cambridge University Press, Cambridge.

Hodder, Ian
1985   Postprocessual Archaeology. In *Advances in Archaeological Method and Theory,* vol. 8, edited by Michael Schiffer, pp. 1–26. Academic Press, Orlando.
1986   *Reading the Past: Current Approaches to Interpretation in Archaeology.* Cambridge University Press, Cambridge.
1987   The Contextual Analysis of Symbolic Meanings. In *The Archaeology of Contextual Meanings,* edited by Ian Hodder, pp. 1–10. Cambridge University Press, Cambridge.

Hood, J. Edward
1990   Agriculture and Social Order in the Middle Connecticut River Valley during the Seventeenth Century. Paper presented at the annual meeting of the American Anthropological Association, New Orleans.

Hoskins, W. G.
1940   The Occupation of Land in Devonshire, 1650–1800. *Devon and Cornwall Notes and Queries* 21(1):2–12.
1954   *Devon.* Collins, London.
1955   *The Making of the English Landscape.* Hodder and Stoughton Ltd., London.

Innes, Stephen
1983   *Labor in a New Land: Economy and Society in Seventeenth Century Springfield.* Princeton University Press, Princeton.

Jackson, John Brinckerhoff
1984   *Discovering the Vernacular Landscape.* Yale University Press, New Haven.

Johnson, Matthew
1991   Enclosure and Capitalism: The History of a Process. In *Processual and Postprocessual Archaeologies: Multiple Ways of Knowing,* edited by Robert W. Preucel, pp. 159–67. Occasional Paper No. 10, Center for Archaeological Investigations. The Board of Trustees, Southern Illinois University.

Judd, Sylvester
1976   *The History of Hadley, Massachusetts.* 1905. Reprint. New Hampshire Publishing Company, Somersworth, New Hampshire.

Kelso, William M.
1990   Landscape Archaeology at Thomas Jefferson's Monticello. In *Earth Patterns: Essays in Landscape Archaeology,* edited by William M. Kelso and Rachel Most, pp. 7–22. University Press of Virginia, Charlottesville.

143

Social
Relations
and the
Cultural
Landscape

Kelso, William M., and Rachel Most, editors
1990   *Earth Patterns: Essays in Landscape Archaeology.* University Press of Virginia, Charlottesville.

Kus, Susan
1982   Matters Material and Ideal. In *Symbolic and Structural Archaeology,* edited by Ian Hodder, pp. 47–62. Cambridge University Press, Cambridge.

Lane, Paul
1987   Reordering Residues of the Past. In *Archaeology as Long Term History,* edited by Ian Hodder, pp. 335–56. Cambridge University Press, Cambridge.

Leone, Mark P.
1984   Interpreting Ideology in Historical Archaeology: Using the Rules of Perspective in the William Paca Garden in Annapolis, Maryland. In *Ideology, Power and Prehistory,* edited by Daniel Miller and Christopher Tilley, pp. 25–36. Cambridge University Press, Cambridge.
1987   Rule by Ostentation: The Relationship Between Space and Sight in Eighteenth-Century American Landscape Architecture in the Chesapeake Region of Maryland. In *Method and Theory for Activity Area Research: An Ethnoarchaeological Approach,* edited by Susan Kent, pp. 604–33. Columbia University Press, New York.

Leone, Mark P., and Paul A. Shackel
1990   Plane and Solid Geometry in Colonial Gardens in Annapolis, Maryland. In *Earth Patterns: Essays in Landscape Archaeology,* edited by William M. Kelso and Rachel Most, pp. 153–67. University Press of Virginia, Charlottesville.

Lewis, Peirce
1983   Learning from Looking: Geographic and Other Writing about the American Cultural Landscape. *American Quarterly* 35(3):242–61.

Lysons, Daniel, and S. Lysons
1822   *Magna Britannia: Being a Concise Topographical Account of the Several Counties of Great Britain.* Vol. 6, *Devonshire.* Thomas Cadell, London.

Marshall, William
1970   *Marshall's Rural Economy of the West of England,* vol. 1–2. 1796. Reprint. Augustus M. Kelly Publishers, New York.

Marx, Karl
1967   *Capital,* vol. 1. 1867. Reprint. International Publishers Co., New York.

Massachusetts Historical Society
1871   Essay on the Laying Out of Towns. In *Collections of the Massachusetts Historical Society.* Vol. 1 (fifth series), *The Winthrop Papers,* pp. 474–80. Massachusetts Historical Society, Boston.

Melvoin, Richard
1989   *New England Outpost: War and Society in Colonial Deerfield.* W. W. Norton & Co., New York.

Miller, Daniel
1987   *Material Culture and Mass Consumption.* Basil Blackwell, Oxford.

Mills, Dennis
1980   *Lord and Peasant in Nineteenth Century Britain.* Rowman and Littlefield, Totowa, New Jersey.

Mingay, G. E.
1984   The East Midlands: Northamptonshire, Leicestershire, Rutland, Nottinghamshire, and Lincolnshire (Excluding the Fenland). In *The Agrarian History of England and Wales.* Vol. 6, *Regional Farming Systems 1640–1750,* edited by Joan Thirsk, pp. 89–128. Cambridge University Press, Cambridge.

Mintz, Sidney
1985   *Sweetness and Power: The Place of Sugar in Modern History.* Elizabeth Sifton Books, Viking, New York.

Moore, Henrietta
1986   *Space, Text and Gender: An Anthropological Study of the Marakwet of Kenya.* Cambridge University Press, Cambridge.
1990   Paul Ricoeur: Action, Meaning and Text. In *Reading Material Culture,* edited by Christopher Tilley, pp. 85–120. Basil Blackwell, Oxford.

Mrozowski, Stephen

1987   Exploring New England's Evolving Urban Landscape. In Living in Cities: Current Research in Urban Archaeology, edited by Edward Staski. *Special Publication Series* No. 5:1–9. Society for Historical Archaeology.

Murray, John

1971   *Murray's Handbook for Devon and Cornwall.* 1859. Reprint of *The Handbook for Travellers in Devon and Cornwall.* David and Charles Reprints, Whitstable, U.K.

Norton, William

1987   Abstract Cultural Landscapes. *Journal of Cultural Geography* 8(1):67–80.

Nostrand, Richard

1973   The Colonial New England Town. *The Journal of Geography* 72(7):45–53.

Orwin, C. S., and C. S. Orwin

1967   *The Open Fields.* Third Edition. Clarendon Press, Oxford.

Paynter, Robert

1982   *Models of Spatial Inequality: Settlement Patterns in Historical Archaeology.* Academic Press, New York.

1985   Surplus Flow Between Frontiers and Homelands. In *The Archaeology of Frontiers and Boundaries,* edited by Stanton Green and S. Perlman, pp. 163–211. Academic Press, Orlando.

1990   Afro-Americans in the Massachusetts Historical Landscape. In *The Politics of the Past,* edited by Peter Gathercole and David Lowenthal, pp. 49–62. Unwin Hyman, London.

Paynter, Robert, Rita Reinke, and J. Ritchie Garrison

1987   Vernacular Landscapes in Western Massachusetts. Paper presented at the annual meeting of the Society for Historical Archaeology, Savannah, Georgia.

Peters, J. E. C.

1969   *The Development of Farm Buildings in Western Lowland Staffordshire up to 1880.* Manchester University Press, Manchester, U.K.

Powell, Sumner Chilton

1965   *Puritan Village: The Formation of a New England Town.* Anchor Press, Doubleday, Garden City, New York.

Pynchon Account Books

1985a   James Osborne, Creditor. In *The Pynchon Papers.* Vol. 2, *Selections from the Account Books of John Pynchon, 1651–1697,* edited by Carl Bridenbaugh and Juliette Tomlinson, pp. 298–302. The Colonial Society of Massachusetts, Boston.

1985b   Samson Frary of Pacomtuck, Debtor. In *The Pynchon Papers.* Vol. 2, *Selections from the Account Books of John Pynchon, 1651–1697,* edited by Carl Bridenbaugh and Juliette Tomlinson, pp. 298–302. The Colonial Society of Massachusetts, Boston.

1985c   Phillip Mattoune (rental agreement). In *The Pynchon Papers.* Vol. 2, *Selections from the Account Books of John Pynchon, 1651–1697,* edited by Carl Bridenbaugh and Juliette Tomlinson, pp. 298–302. The Colonial Society of Massachusetts, Boston.

Rackham, Oliver

1986   *The History of the Countryside.* J. M. Dent & Sons Ltd., London.

Rapoport, Amos

1982   *The Meaning of the Built Environment: A Nonverbal Communication Approach.* Sage Publications, Beverly Hills.

Ravenhill, W. L. D.

1972   The Form and Pattern of Post-Roman Settlement in Devon. *The Devon Archaeological Society Proceedings* 7:83–94.

Reinke, Rita, and Ed Hood

1990   Report on the Hadley Palisade Project. On file, Hadley Historical Commission, Hadley, Massachusetts.

Reinke, Rita, and Robert Paynter

1984   Archaeological Excavation of the Surroundings of the E. H. Williams House, Deerfield, Massachusetts. University of Massachusetts Archaeological Services, Amherst, Massachusetts.

145

Social
Relations
and the
Cultural
Landscape

Roberts, Brian

1983   Of Landscapes and Words. In *Villages, Fields and Frontiers: Studies in European Rural Settlement in the Medieval and Early Modern Periods,* edited by Brian Roberts and R. Glasscock. British Archaeological Reports, International Series, No. 185:21–42. British Archaeological Reports, Oxford.

1987   *The Making of the English Village.* Longman Scientific and Technical, Harlow, U.K.

Roberts, Brian, and R. E. Glasscock, editors

1983   *Villages, Fields and Frontiers: Studies in European Rural Settlement in the Medieval and Early Modern Periods.* British Archaeological Reports, International Series, No. 185. British Archaeological Reports, Oxford.

Rowntree, Lester, and Margaret Conkey

1980   Symbolism and the Cultural Landscape. *Annals of the Association of American Geographers* 70(4):459–74.

Salisbury, Neal

1982   *Manitou and Providence: Indians, Europeans, and the Making of New England, 1500–1643.* Oxford University Press, New York.

Salter, Christopher, editor

1971   *The Cultural Landscape.* Duxbury Press, Belmont, California.

Sauer, Carl O.

1963   The Morphology of Landscape. In *Land and Life: A Selection From the Writings of Carl O. Sauer,* edited by John Leighly, pp. 315–50. University of California Press, Berkeley.

Sheldon, John

1912   The Common Field of Deerfield. *History and Proceedings of the Pocumtuck Valley Memorial Association* 5:238–54. Published by the Association, Greenfield, Massachusetts.

Sheldon, George

1983   *A History of Deerfield, Massachusetts.* 1895–1896. Reprint. Pocumtuck Valley Memorial Association, Deerfield.

Speth, John

1983   *Bison Kills and Bone Counts: Decision Making by Ancient Hunters.* University of Chicago Press, Chicago.

Spurr, Stephen, and Burton Barnes

1973   *Forest Ecology.* The Roland Press Company, New York.

St. George, Robert Blair

1982   "Set thine house in order": The Domestication of the Yeomanry in Seventeenth Century New England. In *New England Begins: The Seventeenth Century.* Vol. 2, *Mentality and Environment,* edited by Jonathan Fairbanks and Robert Trent, pp. 159–88. Museum of Fine Arts, Boston.

1988   Artifacts of Regional Consciousness in the Connecticut River Valley, 1700–1780. In *Material Life in America: 1600–1860,* edited by Robert Blair St. George, pp. 335–56. Northeastern University Press, Boston.

Sweeney, Kevin

1984   Mansion People: Kinship, Class and Architecture in Western Massachusetts in the Mid-Eighteenth Century. *Winterthur Portfolio* 19:231–56.

1985   From Wilderness to Arcadian Vale: Material Life in the Connecticut River Valley, 1635–1760. In *The Great River: Art & Society of the Connecticut Valley, 1635–1820,* edited by Gerald Ward and William Hosley Jr., pp. 17–27. Wadsworth Athenaeum, Hartford, Connecticut.

Taylor, Christopher

1975   *Fields in the English Landscape.* J. M. Dent & Sons Ltd., London.

1983   *Village and Farmstead: A History of Rural Settlement in England.* George Philip, London.

Thirsk, Joan

1964   The Common Fields. *Past and Present* 29:3–25.

1966   The Origin of the Common Fields. *Past and Present* 33:142–47.

1984a   *The Rural Economy of England: Collected Essays.* The Hambledon Press, London.

1985a   Agricultural Policy: Public Debate and Legislation. In *The Agrarian History of England and Wales.* Vol. 7, *Agrarian Change 1640–1750,* edited by Joan Thirsk, pp. 298–388. Cambridge University Press, Cambridge.

Thirsk, Joan, editor
1984b   *The Agrarian History of England and Wales.* Vol. 6, *Regional Farming Systems, 1640–1750.* Cambridge University Press, Cambridge.
1985b   *The Agrarian History of England and Wales.* Vol. 7, *Agrarian Change, 1640–1750.* Cambridge University Press, Cambridge.

Tilley, Christopher
1989   Interpreting Material Culture. In *The Meanings of Things: Material Culture and Symbolic Expression,* edited by Ian Hodder, pp. 183–94. Unwin Hyman, London.

Titow, J. Z.
1965   Medieval England and the Open-Field System. *Past and Present* 32:86–102.

Tomlinson, Margaret
1985   *Three Generations in the Honiton Lace Trade.* The Sovereign Printing Group, Sidmouth, U.K.

Trewartha, Glenn T.
1967   Types of Rural Settlement in Colonial America. In *Readings in Cultural Geography,* edited by Philip L. Wagner and Marvin W. Mikesell, pp. 517–38. University of Chicago Press, Chicago.

Turner, Michael
1984a   *Enclosures in Britain: 1750–1830.* Macmillan Press, Ltd., London.
1984b   The Landscape of Parliamentary Enclosure. In *Discovering Past Landscapes,* edited by Michael Reed, pp. 132–66. Croom Helm, Kent, U.K.

Underdown, David
1985   *Revel, Riot and Rebellion: Popular Politics and Culture in England 1603–1660.* Clarendon Press, Oxford.

Vaughan, Alden, editor
1972   *The Puritan Tradition in America 1620–1730.* University of South Carolina Press, Columbia.

White, William
1968   *White's Devon.* 1850. Reprint of *History, Gazetteer and Directory of Devonshire.* David and Charles Reprints, Newton Abbot, U.K.

Williamson, Tom, and Liz Bellamy
1987   *Property and Landscape: A Social History of Land Ownership and the English Countryside.* George Philip, London.

Wolf, Eric
1982   *Europe and the People Without History.* University of California Press, Berkeley.

Wood, Joseph
1978   *The Origin of the New England Village.* Ph.D. diss., Department of Geography, Pennsylvania State University. University Microfilms, Ann Arbor.
1984   Elaboration of a Settlement System: The New England Village in the Federal Period. *Journal of Historical Geography* 10(4):331–56.

Wrathmell, Stuart
1980   Village Depopulation in the Seventeenth and Eighteenth Centuries: Examples from Northumberland. *Journal of Post-Medieval Archaeology* 14:113–26.

Yentsch, Anne E., Naomi F. Miller, Barbara Paca, and Dolores Piperno
1987   Archaeologically Defining the Earlier Garden Landscapes at Morven: Preliminary Results. *Northeast Historical Archaeology* 16:1–29.

8

"One of the Best Farms in Essex County": The Changing Domestic Landscape of a Tenant Who Became an Owner

Sara F. Mascia

This chapter presents a methodological approach for examining the transition from farm tenancy to ownership in mid-nineteenth-century New England as this shift is reflected in the documentary and archaeological record.[1] New England farm tenancy is a subject largely overlooked in the past by scholars, who have placed more emphasis upon the study of the independent farm owner (e.g., Bidwell and Falconer 1925; Danhof 1969; Russell 1976). The practice of rental tenancy in New England played an important role in the nineteenth-century rural economy. An examination of the rise from rental tenancy to ownership from an archaeological and documentary perspective will provide a greater understanding of nineteenth-century New England and the reality of rural farm life.

For the farmer, the position of either tenant or owner should have direct archaeological correlates because that position will directly demonstrate his or her ability to alter the landscape and purchase consumer goods. The change in position from tenant to owner is not merely a rise in economic status. The difference in this case is not simply an elevation in wealth that will manifest itself in the accumulation of consumer goods that eventually become part of the archaeological record. The tenant who becomes an owner will be more likely to first invest in changes and improvements to the farm that provides his or her livelihood and only later purchase various consumer items reflecting a higher position. It follows that to approach an understanding of this change of status, three areas should be examined closely: 1) the changes and improvements to the physical layout of the farm over time; 2) the location and shifting of activity areas and building use over time; and 3) the patterns of refuse disposal in the farmyard over time. A full understanding of the spatial and physical changes to the farm's domestic compound is necessary to achieve this goal.

This methodological approach is presently being tested at the Spencer-Pierce-Little farm in Newbury, Massachusetts. The Spencer-Pierce-Little property has a long history of land tenure beginning in 1635. The plan of study offered in this chapter will be used specifically to examine the transition from tenancy to ownership on the Spencer-Pierce-Little property in the mid- to late nineteenth century. In many respects the site provides an ideal location from which to examine this problem. Edward H. Little became a tenant farmer in the early 1850s when he leased the Spencer-Pierce property from the heirs of John Pettingell. By working the land on the three-hundred-acre parcel and investing in outside pursuits, he and his family managed to save enough money so that in 1861 he was able to purchase the property (Beaudry 1987:14; Essex County Registry of Deeds, Book 268:240, Book 631:111, 112, Book 634:7). The archaeological record at the site, like its documentary history, also has proved exceedingly rich and complicated; future archaeological research will be aimed at recovering details of the changing use of the land over time and how this relates to changes in property ownership and household membership, shifting agricultural practice, and changes in agricultural and household technology.

Following is a discussion of the origin and history of land tenure in the United States. This section provides an interpretive context for an archaeological examination of rental tenancy in the northeastern United States. After this, the proposed method of study will be examined with regard to its expected archaeological correlates. Finally, the research framework will be examined using data compiled from the Spencer-Pierce-Little site.

AGRICULTURAL LAND TENURE

Farm tenancy has been defined as "an institution which provides for getting the land into the hands of those who are in a position to cultivate it but not buy farms" (Goldenweiser and Truesdell 1924:19). The study of agricultural land tenure is important because a majority of the nineteenth-century United States population depended upon agricultural production for its livelihood. Traditionally the subject of land tenure in United States history has been examined from historical and economic perspectives (e.g., Cummings 1978; Currie 1981). Recently, however, there has been a trend to look beyond the obvious economic impacts of tenancy to the larger framework of its social, political, and ideological impact upon the people engaged in its practice (Heskin 1983; Orser, Nekola, and Roark 1987).

In a culture with a land-based economy, the land system becomes the decisive force behind the type of society that can exist (Clawson 1968:1). The land tenure system defines the formal and customary arrangements that determine access to and control over resources and opportunities in rural areas (Cummings 1978:3). The land is the essential ingredient to the agrarian world. It affects the amount of agricultural production, establishes status, and forms claims on the owner to participate in the social and political world around him or her (Cummings 1978:31).

The "agricultural ladder" is one theory that attempts to explain the levels of advancement in the agrarian world (table 8.1) (Bertrand and Corty 1962:35; Goldenweiser and Truesdell 1924; Harris 1953; Orser, Nekola, and Roark 1987; Wehrwein 1925). According to this theory, the common farm laborer is at the bottom of the ladder, the tenant farmer is in the middle, and the independent owner-operator is at the top. A landless person attempts to pass through each level until he or she achieves the highest level, which is ownership. To reach the highest level on the ladder was one form of the American dream in the nineteenth century (Bertrand and Corty 1962:111; Heskin 1983). In examining the progress of individuals climbing the "agricultural ladder," it becomes evident that the highest rung cannot be reached by all who are participating in this process. Many who do participate in agricultural activity achieve only one level on the "ladder." For example, the laborer may always remain a laborer without ever achieving ownership. Likewise, a tenant might become an owner, remain a tenant, or even be reduced to a laborer. For Edward H. Little of the Spencer-Pierce-Little farm, the shift from tenant to owner moved him to the top of the "agricultural ladder." His increased participation in the local political, economic, and social world, recorded in contemporary documents, also marked his ascension to the upper rung of the ladder.

149
One
of the
Best Farms
in Essex
County

HISTORY OF LAND TENURE IN THE UNITED STATES

A simple definition of tenancy is the occupation of land and/or property. A more specific definition, the practice of paying rent to occupy land, is the interpretation used for the purposes of this study. The history of land tenure in the agrarian United States is central to the examination proposed here. Its roots and subsequent development are crucial to the understanding of the tenured farm, the farm family, and their many social, political, and economic connections.

Colonial Period

Current national land policies of the United States are historically associated with English law and result from early attempts by the colonies to disassociate themselves from European feudalism (Harris 1953:vii, 355). Colonial settlers, especially in New England, traveled to

Table 8.1
The Agricultural Ladder

Owner/Operator
Mortgaged Owner
Farm Manager (Wage Operator)
Tenant
cash renter [a]
share/cash renter [b]
sharecropper [c]
share tenant [d]
Farm Laborer (Wage Laborer)

SOURCES: Bertrand and Corty 1962:108, 113; Goldenweiser and Truesdell 1924:102, 117; Heskin 1983:6; Orser 1991:41–42; Wehrwein 1925:74.

[a]Cash renters paid a predetermined amount of cash to the landlord in return for land and housing; theoretically, as Orser notes (1991:42), the tenant was then free to dispose of the crop as he or she wished.

[b]Under share renting, the landlord supplied the tenant with land, housing, and fertilizer; the tenant supplied the labor, seed, and everything else necessary to farm the land. The landlord received a share of the crop based on the proportion of fertilizer supplied to the farmer.

[c]Sharecroppers received a portion of the crop from the landlord in return for their labor.

[d]Under this agreement, the tenant paid a predetermined share of the crop to the landlord in return for housing and land; the tenant provided everything else to farm the land.

the New World for a variety of reasons. Chief among these was the desire to own property. With the enclosure of the English countryside, the practice of primogeniture, and the religious persecution present in England in the seventeenth and eighteenth centuries, many found the prospect of coming to the New World a promising one (Cosgrove 1984; see also Hood, this volume).

The English land system that they left behind was based upon European feudalism. Today many are under the misconception that the present United States land system is one that grew out of the English system of the seventeenth and eighteenth centuries. This belief, although partly correct, is not wholly accurate. By examining briefly the two major agricultural systems present during the colonial period, a clearer understanding of the origins of our present system will emerge.

The two systems examined are those of the corporate colony of Massachusetts and the royal colonies of Virginia and New York. The land systems of the three colonies were distinctive until the time of the American Revolution (Harris 1953:80). Following the European feudal system, land rights in Virginia and New York were based upon the establishment of large manorial estates. Although little land was leased in the colonies during this period, this type of land distribution was regularly practiced in Virginia and to a lesser degree in Maryland (Clawson 1968:26). With the overwhelming demand for cash crops, owners with large properties would lease parts of their land just to get it under cultivation (Harris 1953:341). The majority of landowners, however, would hire laborers or pay for a man's passage in return for his service (Harris 1953:80). Service to the landowner was the key to this system.

In New England a different system was established, and it is this system that has had the most influence over the development of United States land policies. In this case it is true that "land institutions may have unique features growing out of historical patterns of settlement and/or conquest which are tied to value systems grounded in religious, social, political, and cultural antecedents" (Cummings 1978:13). As an example, the corporate colony of Massachusetts and the creation of the New England town system will be briefly examined (Harris 1953:278). The first grants were awarded to the settlers as a group, who then, as a group, laid out a controlled settlement upon the land (see Hood, this volume). A complete town system consisted of the town plot (a common, streets, and homelots), adjacent land for farming, meadowlands for pasture, and woodlands for raw materials and additional pasture (Harris 1953:278). In New England the settlers worked together to develop a system of small farms operated and occupied by the owner, who engaged in subsistence agriculture and not cash crop economics.

A national land policy was created in the years following the Revolution. The policy harbored certain fundamental principles established in New England, including:

1) the right to tax
2) the right to judge
3) the right to eminent domain
4) the right of police power (regulation of fences, hunting, fishing, etc.)
5) the right to escheat
6) the right to sell and/or rent
7) an effective system of sale
8) the condition that non-resident owners will not be taxed at a higher rate than resident owners
9) the property of those dying intestate will be divided equally among all children.
   (Harris 1953: 310; Stewart 1967:9)

In the late eighteenth century most communities passed legislation barring entails (the practice of including in legal documents a provision that the property is to be inherited by a person and his or her descendants and never divided) and primogeniture (the practice wherein a property is entailed to the oldest son and passed down through the line of direct male descendants). Some of these vestiges of English land traditions still continued on a small scale in pockets around New England into the mid-nineteenth century. Unfortunately for tenants, a segment of the population that had demanded "representation," no secure system of rental tenancy was established (Heskin 1983:4).

151
One
of the
Best Farms
in Essex
County

The Nineteenth Century: Tenancy and the "Agricultural Ladder"

As tenancy grew more common in the nineteenth century, the northern middle states began to break up their land for rental farms. New England also had a thriving tenant population. The southern colonies, with their reliance upon the institution of slavery, did not engage in rental tenancy to the same degree as the North until after the Civil War. Most new immigrants coming to the United States would begin as tenants with the hope of eventually owning a farm in the north or in the newly opened western states and territories (Goldenweiser and Truesdell 1924:117). The United States in the nineteenth century was still overwhelmingly rural despite its rapidly growing urban populations. The virtues of the farmer and of farm life were extolled by admiring ministers, writers, physicians, and poets during the middle of the century (Russell 1976:317; Wright 1981:75). It was at this time that the goal of owning a farm became an American dream.

The belief that tenancy is a stepping stone to ownership is one that is deeply embedded in the American land system. The notion of the desirability of ownership was reinforced via the many technological innovations of the nineteenth century, the growing number of "progressive" farmers, and what Hayden refers to as the "domestic revolution" (Hayden 1981; McMurray 1988:3; Russell 1976:321).

New nineteenth-century industrial technology helped to ease the pressure of farming large tracts of land with little manpower. For example, the steel plow and the cotton gin freed what little manpower there was for other activities. Farmers could now participate in a variety of economic enterprises, broadening the scope of farm activities to include blacksmithing, hiring out to plow other farmers' fields, road building, wall building, etc. (Russell 1976:322).

The large number of agricultural journals that appeared in the mid-nineteenth century attest to the growing number of "progressive" farmers who were now involved in the rural reform movement (the process of turning the farm into a business) (McMurray 1988:vii, 3). These farmers were participating in a larger network that linked all members of the agricultural world (McMurray 1988:vii). Agricultural journals provided information on crops, farmhouse architectural plans, and new inventions that were available to all levels of society, especially the small farmer (McMurray 1988:3–4, 225; Russell 1976:345).

The domestic reform movement, strongly associated with the rise of industrial society, represents the freeing of the family, particularly the farm wife, from participation in agricultural activities (Hayden 1981; McMurray 1988:87–128; Russell 1976:337). In the early to mid-eighteenth century, cheese manufacture, butter churning, cooking, clothing manufacture, and laundering were the main tasks of the farm wife (McMurray 1988:91). As the work of the farmer eased, the work of the wife remained the same. McMurray points out that writers in agricultural journals and progressive women such as Harriet Beecher Stowe began to examine the activities of the farm wife with an eye to reform (McMurray 1988:87–128). The rearrangement of domestic space (including the relocation of the kitchen to the back of the house), the hiring of servants to do the wife's work, and pressure on the farmer to take over certain chores (milking and collecting eggs) were extolled by these writers as a way to ease the burdens of the farm wife (Hubka 1984:147–50; McMurray 1988:87–128).

Ownership and Tenancy

Ownership is a coveted position. With it comes the right to hold title to property, the right to agricultural produce grown on the property, and a well-established social status that includes the right to contribute to the community as well as a sense of responsibility (Goldenweiser and Truesdell 1924:13). Farm owners' participation in local politics, church activities, and local economic enterprises can be observed through the documentary record. Community involvement is encouraged by the sense of security that comes with ownership. There are many types of owners, including the owner/operator, the retired farmer, the widow, the investor, and the owner who operates only a portion of his or her property. The last four are the most common types of rural landlords. Owners who are landlords may have additional income-producing ventures (e.g., trade, commerce) within the community that are not based directly on agriculture.

The whole system of rental farming is one that does not allow for security. The property is always held by a superior, there may be no incentive to improve the farm, the tenant holds a low social position, and the tenant's main motivation is to extract as much as possible from the soil, often to the detriment of the landscape (Goldenweiser and Truesdell 1924:15). If a tenant plans to purchase the property he is renting, he may understand that his ability to turn a profit without depleting his resources is the most efficient way to achieve ownership. Without this profit there will be little hope of improving his position and becoming an owner (Stiverson 1977:86). The ineffectiveness of the lease system is another driving force behind the desire to own. The tenant may have a definite contract in the form of a recorded agreement for a fixed time period. If not, an oral or unwritten agreement that has no definite termination date may be in effect (Heskin 1983:19).

In New England the primary form of tenancy was cash rental.[2] The tenant would pay the owner a predetermined sum for the use of the owner's property. This lease was usually one that defined a specific time period (Probyn 1881:502). The most relevant landlord/ tenant relationship for the purposes of the research outlined here is that of the absentee landlord and cash renter.

Analytical Frameworks and Archaeological Research

Only a few historical studies of tenancy have been conducted in New England, most notably the work conducted by Stephen Innes, who based his research on tenancy in eighteenth-century Springfield, Massachusetts, solely upon account books (Innes 1978). Other scholars have begun to re-examine the New England farm from a new perspective (Atack and Bateman 1987; Barron 1985; Boxley 1985; Clark 1990; McMurray 1988); the farmer is no longer viewed by all as independent and solely subsistence-oriented, but rather as someone involved in a variety of economic pursuits. Virtually no attempts have been made to study tenancy in New England through the archaeological record, however. A common occurrence in the archaeological literature is the mention of the practice of tenancy at a site studied for other purposes (e.g., Bowen 1988:167).

The Hamlin site, excavated by Louis Berger and Associates, Inc. (1986), is a notable example of research conducted at a rural farm site in the Northeast. Although not a tenant farm site, an analysis of rural consumer behavior at the Hamlin farm makes this study one of the most relevant in recent years. At the Hamlin farm, wealth was expressed not in purchased material goods but rather in changes and improvements to the farm site itself. The concept of the farm as a symbol of status is relevant to the study of rural farm sites as a whole and has direct application for understanding changes that occur during the shift from tenancy to ownership.

Recently, a growing number of historical archaeologists have begun to examine farm tenancy in other regions (e.g., Catts and Custer 1990; Orser 1990). The majority of this work has been concentrated in the American South (e.g., Adams 1990; Orser 1988; Otto 1977, 1980; Singleton 1985, 1988). A recent issue of *Historical Archaeology,* devoted exclusively to southern plantations and farms (Orser 1990), provides comparative data and several analytical frameworks that are useful to the study of tenancy. The majority of related archaeological research in the American South, however, focuses on the ante- and postbellum plantations, systems of land tenure that are very different from New England rental tenant farming.

Despite the contextual differences, these studies have something to offer to comparable work in New England. One of the more relevant tenancy studies to the research presented in this chapter is that of Charles Orser, who has outlined a way for archaeologists to examine tenancy with regard to the material basis of the postbellum tenant plantation (Orser 1988; Orser, Nekola, and Roark 1987). His emphasis upon settlement, housing, and material possessions with regard to their spatial, temporal, and cultural characteristics is one that provides an example for researching two economically and socially distinct groups of people. Orser examined the layout of the plantation upon the landscape during the ante- and postbellum periods in the context of two different labor systems (slave labor versus tenancy in its various forms). He also used the physical remains of these systems to examine the hierarchy (laborer versus owner) present on the plantation both before and after emancipation. Orser defines his work as "plantation archaeology," or "a kind of historic sites archaeology that focuses upon the diverse ethnic, occupational, social, spatial, and economic aspects of plantation organization" (1988:10). In doing so, he is able to examine the plantation as a single functioning unit over time, rather than as the locus of separate and perhaps unrelated activities that are not tied into the overall site.

This type of framework, placed in the context of New England tenant farming, allows the examination of the farm's physical remains in the context of a functioning whole. The physical layout of the farm and any alterations of the landscape made by the tenant farmer and owner farmer can be studied in much the same manner as that proposed by Orser. Tenant archaeology can thus shed light upon the use of space and the different social, economic, political, and occupational makeup of those living on the farm. With these goals in mind, the following methodology is proposed for the examination of tenancy and ownership in nineteenth-century New England.

A METHODOLOGICAL APPROACH
TO THE STUDY OF TENANT FARMING
AND OWNERSHIP IN NEW ENGLAND

In order to examine how this rise up the agricultural ladder is represented on farm sites, the researcher must conduct intensive documentary research of primary sources relating to the tenant and must examine the variety of secondary sources pertaining to agricultural practices. The same genealogical, or "life history," approach (Beaudry and Mascia 1989) should be applied to the archaeological record through detailed analysis of site formation processes. The outcome of the research will be the creation of a series of maps that cover the time period in question (before tenancy, during tenancy, during ownership). This research can show that the changes that are involved in the rise from tenant to owner are represented in both the documentary and archaeological records. One purpose for the development of this framework is to allow for the study of farm sites that do not have a rich documentary assemblage.

Documentary Research

The first phase of research should include the examination of the documentary data relating to the property owners and tenants. The documents examined typically fall into five groups: 1) primary government and legal documents (vital records, census records, tax records, probate records, maps); 2) family or farm documents (personal diaries, farm and/or household accounts, letters, and specific materials unique to the farm); 3) newspapers and journals; 4) photographic evidence; and 5) any relevant secondary documentary sources (agricultural, town, and family histories).

The primary documents will provide data regarding the occupants of the farm and possibly information about the layout and topography of the farm as well. The secondary documents will allow for an understanding of the economic, political, and social environment of the time. Possible applications of this research to an archaeological site will be discussed later in this chapter. Through written documents, an understanding of the many different factors that have influenced patterning in the archaeological record (sex, ethnicity, age; economic, political, and occupational status) will permit a more accurate reconstruction of the past (Otto 1980:3–4).

Archaeological Research

It is argued here that the type of labor system, tenant or owner, will have definite archaeological correlates that can be recovered during excavation.[3] This research begins with historical maps that are used to locate any buildings, outbuildings, and field boundaries for the periods of tenancy and ownership under study. Following this, or if no maps exist, the researcher should make a detailed record of the existing landscape. This involves a detailed topographical survey and, if possible, the use of aerial photography to view the surrounding area as well as the site itself. These data will be analyzed for evidence of vegetation and field patterns, including nonextant boundary divisions. If soil maps of the area exist, additional information on soil fertility, drainage patterns, and any other characteristics of soils on the property can be gathered. A vegetation survey should be conducted over the course of a year in order to collect information on and samples of the full range of plant species that grow on the site. Tree coring can also be employed to date the variety of species present. This will help to construct a comparative collection of present-day plant specimens as well as provide samples for pollen and phytolith analysis. This collection is also useful for the interpretation of excavated botanical remains. Traditional field walkovers and surface collections should also be undertaken at this time.

155

One
of the
Best Farms
in Essex
County

The excavation of the domestic compound should follow the examination of the existing landscape. The emphasis of this research will be on distinguishing the archaeological patterns that reflect the overall land-use patterns at the farm site. Investigators should identify: 1) the physical layout of the farm and any improvements made over time; 2) the activity areas of the farm and their changing locations, including building use over time; and 3) refuse disposal in the farmyard with any associated patterns over time.

The recovery of archaeological evidence of improvements to the farm, which may include the installation and/or abandonment of various features (i.e., walkways, wells, sheds, barns, cisterns, and refuse dumps), may help link these activities to the occupation of the farm by the tenant or owner. The farmstead is laid out for the use, convenience, and efficiency of the farmer. The location of activity areas, and the change in location of these areas over time, can be examined with respect to the occupation of the site by both the tenant and owner.

Understanding and interpreting refuse distribution will help to view the overall layout of the farmyard both temporally and spatially. The key to this research will be distinguishing archaeological patterns that reflect the periods of tenancy and ownership. The transition from tenancy to ownership may be visible in the archaeological record if these data are examined closely. Spatial analysis of the artifact distribution patterns in activity areas surrounding the house should be completed and included in the mapping process. To tie all of the research goals together, the creation of a series of maps that cover the time period in question will help reveal both large- and small-scale evidence of land-use patterns that cannot be found in the documents alone.

The documentation of changes within the domestic compound will be the key to understanding the effects of rising up the agricultural ladder. Examination of artifacts as indicators of a rise in status is a technique that has long been applied in archaeological research. In historical archaeology, with the help of documentary material, this has become a standard research practice. Works such as Miller's "Classification and Economic Scaling of Nineteenth-Century Ceramics" (1988) have provided archaeologists with a model for understanding how changes in status are reflected in the archaeological record through one highly visible form of material culture. This type of study may help to identify a difference in the status of individuals and/or a change in the economic status of a single individual.

However, despite the utility of this type of study, ceramics are not the only form, or even the preferred form, of material culture used to convey status (cf. Friedlander 1991; Louis Berger and Associates, Inc. 1986). Other types of status markers should be examined, particularly in the case of a change in status from tenant to owner. As mentioned above, this transition is not merely a rise in economic status, and the archaeological evidence should be examined with this in mind. Once the tenant establishes ownership of the property, he or she will have the freedom to invest in changes and improvements to the farm that provides his or her livelihood. Only after the improvements are made to the farm will the owner be likely to purchase various consumer items reflecting a change in status. Therefore, the traditional indicators of a rise in status do not readily apply in this situation. The difference in this case is not simply an elevation in wealth but rather an investment in the future of the farm. Archaeological data should be examined in order to determine this difference.

As a case study I turn to the Spencer-Pierce-Little farmstead in Newbury, Massachusetts, where rental tenancy was practiced during the nineteenth century.

NEWBURY, NEWBURYPORT, AND THE SPENCER-PIERCE-LITTLE FARM

The town of Newbury was founded in 1635 when a group of twenty-three Ipswich men settled along the Parker River, in an area since referred to as the "old town" (Coffin 1845:2; Labaree 1962:2–3; Smith 1854:8). Here, the mouth of the nearby Merrimack River is protected by Plum Island, a point of land running parallel to the coast, thus creating a sheltered port with riverine and ocean access. For this reason, Newbury was associated with a variety of mercantile enterprises from the earliest period of settlement. The land surrounding the two rivers also proved to be ideal for farming. The first settlement, which was set up around a large green, was granted recognition by the General Court in Boston when it allowed the settlers the right to send representatives to participate in that organization (Smith 1854:9). Each settler was granted from four to over a thousand acres (1854:13).

By 1638 the population had grown so much that many moved away from the green and the "old town" to settle next to the "waterside" of the Merrimack River. After 1642 increased immigration and a relaxation of trade taxes brought a new group of people to the "waterside" (Smith 1854:17). These new settlers were engaged in mercantile pursuits. The Merrimack quickly became the main source of revenue for the "waterside" inhabitants while the residents of the "old town" continued to focus on agriculture (1854:24).

A clear separation between the "old town" and "waterside" existed and was permanently demarcated in 1763 when the "waterside" residents petitioned to be incorporated as a separate town. From the time the petition was granted in 1764, the dramatic maritime history of the "waterside," now Newburyport, overshadowed its parent town. Fishing, and then shipbuilding and trading, brought great wealth to the port town.

Newbury, because of its proximity to Newburyport, grew by association and through this link was exposed to the larger national and international community. Merchants from Newburyport, after finding the growing town too crowded, would purchase a "country farm" in Newbury as a retreat and/or investment (Clawson 1968:27; Smith 1854:20). In a seacoast town, merchants often engaged in land speculation and trade with agricultural producers in order to increase their wealth (Clawson 1968:27). Although the Newburyport maritime industry peaked in the late eighteenth century, many merchants still engaged in real estate speculation throughout the nineteenth century. This practice contributed to the expansion and endurance of rental tenancy. Many of the merchants would purchase property and rent to tenants who would manage the farm in such a way as to ensure that the property value would steadily increase (Goldenweiser and Truesdell 1924:13). During the nineteenth century the Spencer-Pierce-Little property was tenured under a secure lease system. This form of tenure was one that was mutually beneficial to both the merchant/owner and the tenant.

157

One
of the
Best Farms
in Essex
County

The Spencer-Pierce-Little Farm and Its Owners

The Spencer-Pierce-Little property (figure 8.1) has been occupied since 1635 when John Spencer, one of the town founders, was granted a four-hundred-acre parcel of upland and a four-acre lot in town (Beaudry 1987:7, 1989a:4; Grady and Remsen 1992:17).[4] The site comprises fallow and cultivated fields, salt marsh, woodland areas, and the farmyard. Within the farmyard stands the Spencer-Pierce-Little house (figure 8.2), built ca. 1690 of fieldstone with molded brick Artisan Mannerist detail (Grady and Remsen 1992:13–14). The attached wood-frame tenant farmer's house, surviving outbuildings, and large open fields communicate to the visitor an impression of the site's lengthy agricultural past.

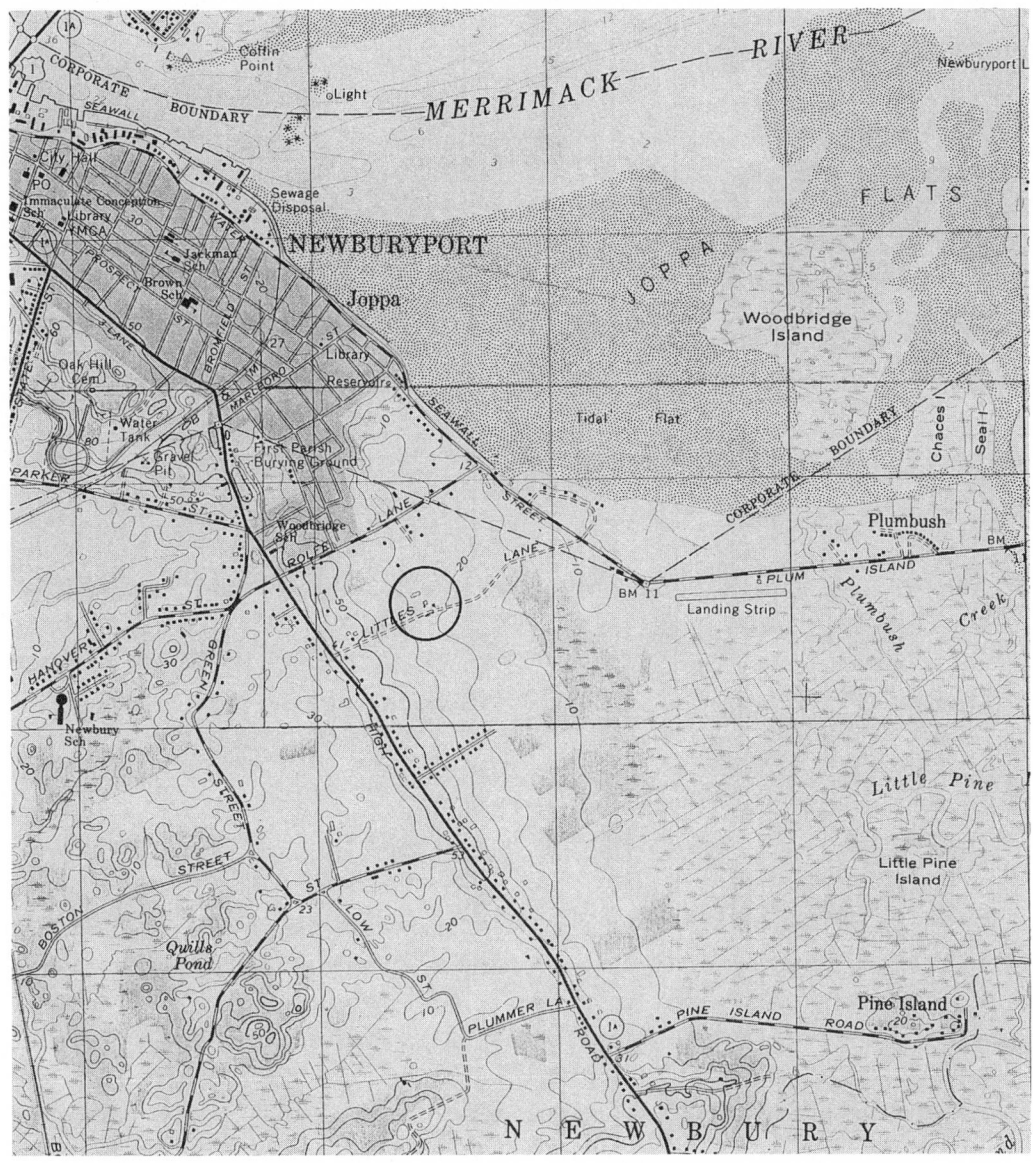

Figure 8.1. Portion of United States Geological Survey Topographic Map, Newburyport East, Massachusetts– New Hampshire Quadrangle, 1966. 7.5 Minute Series. Scale 1:24,000. Site location is indicated by a circle.

Figure 8.2. View of the Spencer-Pierce-Little house from the southeast, ca. 1890. The photograph shows the original stone house with a wood addition to the left and the tenant house to the far right. Courtesy of the Society for the Preservation of New England Antiquities, Boston.

John Spencer (1604–48), the site's first owner, arrived in Ipswich, Massachusetts, in 1634 on the *Mary and John* (Boyer 1977:143). Spencer established the farm as a commercial venture, raising livestock on the property during his tenure (Grady and Remsen 1992:17). His involvement in cattle raising is recorded in a deposition given by William Osgood in a 1659 Newbury witchcraft case. Osgood states that nineteen years earlier, in 1640, "he being then building a barn for Mr. Spencer [and] John Godfrey being then Mr. Spencer's herdsman," Godfrey told a group of men "that he had gotton [*sic*] a new master against the time he had done keeping cows" (Dow 1911[2]:160). Godfrey's reference to a new master that he "knew not" and his inability to answer questions about "him" led Osgood to conclude that he had signed a pact with the devil.[5] The deposition is important because it reveals that Spencer had hired Godfrey as a herdsman, thus beginning a long history of tenant farming at the site.

Spencer was turned out of the Puritan town in 1637 for his support of Anne Hutchinson, a banished advocate for a less rigid religious code, and he soon returned to England where he died in 1648 (Beaudry 1987:8; Coffin 1845:12; Grady and Remsen 1992:17; Smith 1854:14). The four-hundred-acre parcel was left to his nephew, also named John Spencer, who sold sections of the property to pay taxes and eventually sold the remainder, some three hundred acres, to his uncle, Daniel Pierce Sr., with the provision that "the yearely rents during the time that Thomas Coleman hath in the farm yet to come, which is two years, . . . [be] reserved &

159

One
of the
Best Farms
in Essex
County

excepted unto the use of the said John Spencer" (Dow 1911[1]:285). This reference indicates that Thomas Coleman was a tenant on the land in 1651 and may have been there as early as 1645 when he is mentioned as "having taken a farme" (Beaudry 1989a:5; Currier 1896:30).

When Daniel Pierce Sr. acquired the property, including "all housing, barnes, cowhouses, orchard, garden and fences," it was transferred to the new owner by means of twig and turf, a symbolic action wherein a twig and some soil are literally handed from the old owner to the new (Salem Registry of Deeds, Ipswich Series, Book 1:96, 133). Pierce brought to the farm his first wife, Sarah, and their three children, Daniel Jr. (b. 1638), Joshua (b. 1642), and Martha (b. 1648 or 1649). In 1654 Sarah Pierce died and Daniel married his second wife, Anne Lowell Milward. Anne, the widow of a local mariner, had two children by her first husband (Rebecca and Elizabeth). Daniel and Anne had one daughter, Sarah. The Pierce household, then, consisted of the six children, servants or slaves, as well as Daniel and his wife.

Daniel Sr. died in 1677, and the farm was inherited by his son, Daniel Jr. In his will, Daniel Pierce Sr. entailed the estate to ensure its inheritance through his male descendants and also stated that his wife, Anne, "shall injoy her former libertyes in the house during her life" (Essex County Registry of Probate:21151). His probate inventory lists the farm, 20 acres of upland, 33 acres of meadow, a malt house, the "furniture" for the maltings, 3 horses, 40 head of cattle, 160 sheep, 18 pigs, a wide variety of dairying utensils, other farm vehicles and equipment, and "Negros" valued at £60 (Essex County Registry of Probate:21151).

Daniel Jr. continued to grow barley for his father's malt house in Newburyport, raised livestock on the farm, and rented land to tenant farmers under a sharecropping system of tenancy (Dow 1911[3]:130–32). John Webster, a former apprentice to Daniel Pierce Sr., stated in a 1680 deposition that a Captain Vinson was living on Pierce land. In the same case, Richard Knight stated that Henry Jaques, Richard Pettengell, and Joseph Dummer also lived on the property (Currier 1896:34–35).

Architectural evidence suggests that Daniel Jr. built the ca. 1690 stone-and-brick cruciform-plan structure that stands today. The first mention of the house appears in the will of Daniel Jr., dated 1701. Daniel died in 1704, leaving his estate, now much larger than his father's, to his male heirs; his will directed that they "shall not sell any part" of "the ffarme [of] my Honoured ffather (deceasd) bought of Mr John Spenerd [sic]." He also made provisions for his wife, Elizabeth, leaving detailed instructions that allowed her to live in the "stone house" with their son, Benjamin (b. 1668), who was principal heir and executor of his father's estate (Essex County Registry of Probate:21153).

The property passed out of the Pierces' hands in 1778 when Nathaniel Tracy, a Newburyport merchant, purchased the house. This began a new phase of ownership by Newburyport merchants that continued until 1827 (Grady and Remsen 1992:9, 31). Nathaniel Tracy was the son of Patrick Tracy, one of Newburyport's most prominent merchants (Labaree 1962:10–11). Tracy was a privateer during the American Revolution and in fact outfitted the first American privateer vessel, which set sail July 1775 (Hurd 1888:1748). He amassed a vast fortune while capturing over 100 British ships worth over 3,950,000 in specie (gold or silver coin) and lived on a lavish and grand scale until he went bankrupt in 1786 after an especially ambitious business deal went sour (Currier 1896:37–38; Hurd 1888:1748; Lee 1921:63). The Tracys retired to the Spencer-Pierce-Little farm, where they were visited by many travelers, most notably Thomas Jefferson and John Quincy Adams, whose visits are recorded in their personal diaries (Grady and Remsen 1992:34). Architectural evidence suggests that Tracy remodeled the house's interior in late Georgian fashion and rebuilt the central chimney. Following Tracy's death in 1796, his widow, Mary Lee Tracy, sold "the farm whereon I now live" to Offin Boardman for $12,800 (Essex County Registry of Deeds, Book 162:144).

Offin Boardman, also a merchant of local prominence, built two additions to the Spencer-Pierce-Little house: the tenant house, constructed in 1797, and the west wood addition, built ca. 1800 (Grady and Remsen 1992:9). Boardman lived on the farm until his death in 1811, at which time he was declared insolvent. The farm was subsequently conveyed by his executors to John Pettingell, with Sarah, Boardman's widow, retaining dower rights (Essex County Registry of Deeds, Book 200:236).

An overall plan of the property's metes and bounds and a detailed plot plan of the domestic compound were made at this time (figure 8.3). The plans identify the function of buildings and different areas in the yard and fields. Fifteen structures are listed on the plan of the domestic compound:

1. Stone house
2. Wood part of dwelling house
3. Scullery
4. Farm House (tenant farmer's house)
5. Poultry house
6. Wood House Old
7. Hog house
8. Poultry house in Garden
9. Grainery
10. Stable
11. Barn
12. Cider House
13. Shed
14. Sheep pen and Shed
15. Linter [lean-to] or shed.

Spatial divisions within the property are identified as:

1. Front Yard
2. Flower Garden
3. Back Yard
4. Nursery and Garden
5. Cow Yard
6. Yard between Cider house and Sheep pen
7. Passage way to Orchard and Barn
8. Garden
9. Fruit Garden
10. Orchard
11. Gates. ("Plan of the 'Homestead' of Boardman's Farm Surveyed October 1812 by Paul Titcomb"; Archives, Society for the Preservation of New England Antiquities [SPNEA Archives])

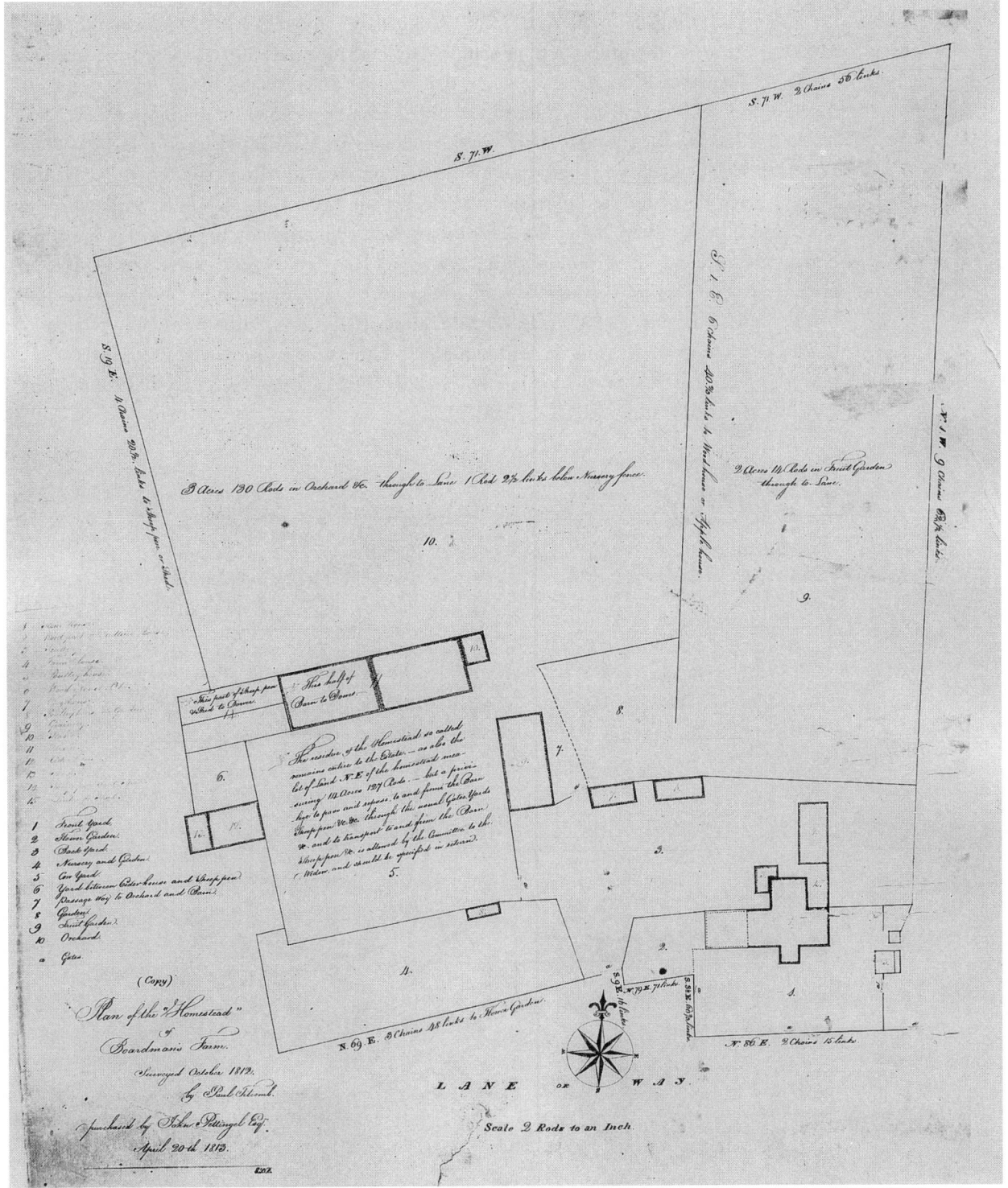

Figure 8.3. "Plan of the 'Homestead' of Boardman's Farm Surveyed October 1812 By Paul Titcomb." The key to the left indicates buildings and landscape features by number. Courtesy of the Society for the Preservation of New England Antiquities, Boston.

The final merchant owner was John Pettingell, who died in 1827 (Grady and Remsen 1992:39). At present, nothing in the documentary evidence indicates that Pettingell lived on the farm. The records do show, however, that he leased the tenant house to a number of different individuals, none of whom had any long-term investment in the property. According to one local historian, who published the following unconfirmed account in 1894: "Mr. Pettingell was much astonished to find that his tenants were using one room in the mansion-house as a receptacle for their corn during husking, another room as a poultry yard, where in were several large turkeys being fatted for the market, while the porch, the chief glory of the house, was piled nearly to the top with cider apples . . ." (Jones 1894:79; see also Grady and Remsen 1992:39). After Pettingell's death, the property was managed by his heirs, who also had numerous tenants, including Edward H. Little (figure 8.4). Little eventually purchased the property from the Pettingell family in 1861; at the time of purchase, Little had been a tenant on the property for approximately ten years (Essex County Registry of Deeds, Book 268:240; Book 631:111, 112; Book 634:7).

Figure 8.4. Edward Henry Little (1819–1877). Courtesy of Mrs. Nancy Noyes.

163

One
of the
Best Farms
in Essex
County

The Little family papers include richly detailed records of crops grown at the farm between 1850 and 1870 and additional information regarding farm and household management by the Little family (SPNEA Archives). As a tenant and owner, Edward H. Little profited from a dairy business and grew a variety of vegetables (e.g., onions, potatoes, squash) to be sold in Newburyport with the help of a number of laborers who lived on the farm. Edward Francis and Daniel Noyes Little inherited the farm after their father, Edward H. Little, died in 1877. Edward and Daniel began a business of importing draft horses from the Midwest, continuing the practice of commercial husbandry on the farm.

Throughout most of the twentieth century, the Spencer-Pierce-Little farm was occupied by female descendants of Edward Little; they continued to rent portions of the property to tenant farmers. In 1971, Agnes and Amelia, granddaughters of Edward H. Little, deeded the farm to the Society for the Preservation of New England Antiquities (SPNEA), retaining a life interest. Following Amelia's death in 1986, SPNEA "initiated a long-term project aimed at eventually opening the site as a museum after extensive research into the property and its occupants, as well as conservation and architectural study of the house proper, furnishes the basis for a comprehensive and sensitive interpretation of the site to the public" (Beaudry 1989a:11; see also Beaudry 1987:14, Grady and Remsen 1992). SPNEA has continued the tradition of leasing the farm out to various tenants.

Summary

The Spencer-Pierce-Little property has remained essentially intact from 1651 to the present. Because the property was not significantly reduced and/or altered, it provides an excellent opportunity to examine a working farm and its associated activities over time. Several aspects of the site's history are of particular interest.

First, the Spencer-Pierce-Little farm has operated as a mixed commercial agricultural enterprise throughout its history. Types of livestock raised on the property from the early seventeenth century to the present include cows, oxen, pigs, sheep, and horses. The Spencers are known to have raised cattle, while the Pierces raised sheep and produced grain crops (e.g., barley for malting). The Littles used the farm for dairying and market gardening; later, they raised draft horses, but returned to market gardening in the early to mid-twentieth century.

Second, the site has been continuously farmed by tenants and laborers living on and/or working the land. The site therefore provides an ideal case study for examining the nature of tenancy and ownership. The Little family, in particular, lived on the farm for an extended period of time; thus the changes in behavior associated with the rise from tenancy to ownership should be visible archaeologically.

As Cummings notes, "Land tenure institutions do not exist in isolation . . . they are influenced by labor, capital, product markets, and a wide range of other institutions" (1978:14). This is reflected in the different types of commercial activities pursued on the site over time as well as in the changes made to the farm by Edward Little when he assumed ownership of the property. The changing world of the nineteenth century and its associated economic, social, and political movements (e.g., the progressive farm movement) undoubtedly influenced the behavior of the site's inhabitants; we would expect these influences to be reflected in the archaeological record as well.

Finally, this case study may provide a more realistic understanding of the nature of rural farm life. New England farming traditionally has been examined with regard to its roots in

England and the subsequent development of a market economy (e.g., Bidwell and Falconer 1925; Danhof 1969; Rothenberg 1985; Russell 1976). Studies of nineteenth-century New England agriculture were focused on the so-called sudden "shift" away from the self-sufficient farmer to a market economy; in this model, the farmer no longer focused his energies on subsistence but rather on a multipurpose enterprise (e.g., Barron 1985). The history of the Spencer-Pierce-Little farm refutes this notion of a sudden change in the nineteenth century, as all along the owners and tenants were engaged in a variety of nonsubsistence-related pursuits. This may not have been an unusual practice throughout New England, especially with regard to tenant farmers, who often needed additional sources of income. More likely, it seems that a gradual "shift" in the focus of farm production occurred due to a number of outside influences. The economic decline in the Northeast during the nineteenth century also was a factor that influenced farmers with regard to the use of the farm and land. For tenants, investment in expensive, long-term changes would not be a priority, whereas owners would be looking toward the future.

Current research at the Spencer-Pierce-Little site is discussed below with these issues in mind.

THE SPENCER-PIERCE-LITTLE PROJECT

The Spencer-Pierce-Little property, now approximately 230 acres in size, has been the focus of long-term archaeological research since 1986. The overall research design for the site proposes two levels of investigation: 1) at the scale of the homestead or homelot, and 2) at the larger scale of the farmstead (Beaudry 1987). The former involves detailed, microscale investigation of evidence that can be related to the household (Beaudry 1984, 1986, 1988, 1989a); methods for investigation at the level of the farmstead are more extensive in scope.

Documentary Research

Following an examination of available primary documents, the majority of the ongoing documentary research for the Spencer-Pierce-Little Project has focused on the Little family papers and photographic data housed at SPNEA headquarters in Boston. The Little family papers were separated into two categories relating to the family and the farm. Account books are well known for their contribution toward understanding rural life (Bowen 1988:164; Innes 1978); Edward H. Little's farm accounts have likewise proven to be very helpful for research on the transition from tenancy to ownership. His accounts helped to establish an understanding of the variety of activities that took place on the farm, including the types of crops grown, the variety of animals present, the types of items purchased for farmwork, food/animals purchased for household consumption, labor employed, and labor hired out. More important, the accounts recorded any changes in activities once Little became the owner of the farm. The actual accounts are in booklets and on hundreds of individual pieces of paper. Because of the impracticality of using each piece of paper, the annual accounts, completed each January, were the focus of this research.

The family photographs, which date to the period of ownership by the Littles, have provided pictorial evidence of changes to the farm environment, including information on the location and types of outbuildings, treatment of the "public" and "private" areas of the farm, and visible changes to the complex as a whole. These data, together with earlier sketches and drawings of the farm and the archaeological data, will help us to construct a series of maps and images that reflect the changes in the domestic farm landscape over time.

165

One
of the
Best Farms
in Essex
County

Farm journals and newspapers will also be examined for the time period in question. During the 1991 field season, hundreds of copies of the *Massachusetts Ploughman* were discovered in the attic of the house. Edward H. Little had a subscription to this agricultural newspaper from the 1850s until his death in 1877. This journal, like many other contemporary farm journals, included information about new farming practices, new strains of plants and animals, new inventions to make work easier and more efficient, and some references to the social and political world of the farmer. Little was also a member of the Essex Agricultural Society and received its journal. While reading through the Essex Agricultural Society's papers and journals, it was discovered that Little became a trustee for the society not long after he became the owner of the farm.

Secondary sources include a variety of histories of Newbury, Newburyport, and the farm. The documentary research will also be extended in the future to involve a more detailed examination of the rural community surrounding the property as well as the maritime community of Newburyport. Examining the farm as a functioning unit whose social and economic development depended upon specific land-use practices will help to reconstruct the activities of both household members and those who labored on the farm as tenants.

As mentioned earlier, an important part of the documentary research revolves around the study of Little's account books. Another set of account books, kept by Bartlett Currier while a tenant farmer on the Spencer-Pierce-Little property (1830–38), will also be examined.[6] Preliminary examination of Currier's accounts shows that they are more detailed than Little's and include complete year-end inventories of the stock and all agricultural products sold. These accounts provide data regarding seasonal farm activities as well. Future research may thus provide comparative data with which to examine the accounts of Edward H. Little as a tenant and owner, data which may reveal any significant changes in agricultural production, in stock purchased and sold, and in seasonal farm activities.

Finally, the documents show that Edward Little's rise in status was clearly reflected in his public life. Following his purchase of the farm, Little held a series of offices in the town of Newbury, including selectman, assessor, and overseer of the poor. He became a large stockholder in the First National Bank of Newbury, a trustee of the Institution for Savings, a mortgage lender, and, in the 1870s, part owner of the ship *Exporter* (Little Family Papers, SPNEA Archives). Little's rising social status, particularly in terms of his role in the community, will be examined further as part of this project.

Archaeological Research

Archaeological work conducted on the property to date includes a limited examination of the farmyard in 1986, continued examination of the yard during a Center for Archaeological Studies Summer Workshop in 1987, and excavation of the areas surrounding the farmhouse during subsequent Boston University Summer Field Schools (1989–93) (figure 8.5) (Beaudry 1987, 1989b, 1991). Additional archaeological research on the property has included field walkovers, archaeobotanical analysis, and the commencement of the overall topographical analysis. A tree coring program was initiated during the summer of 1992 by Julie Hansen. Analysis of archaeological material collected from the site is continuing at the present time. Excavated faunal material has been partially analyzed by David B. Landon (Landon 1991), some floral remains have been examined by Sally Pendleton (Pendleton 1990), and pollen analysis is being conducted by Gerald Kelso.

A starting place for the research on tenancy and ownership is the 1812 plat map that was discovered in the Little papers (figure 8.3). The locations of outbuildings and fields are noted on the map, providing a view of the farm as it existed prior to the Little occupation. Following the three areas of inquiry outlined for this study, the archaeological data will be carefully examined for evidence of the various changes and improvements to the farm, including the features on the property that were installed and/or abandoned during the nineteenth century. Some of the features discovered archaeologically include a cistern, sheds, walkways, wells, and refuse dumps. The waste and water management systems are of particular interest to this research as some may also be related to the progressive farm movement that Edward H. Little was most certainly interested in as an owner. The 1812 plan also suggests that the property served multiple agricultural purposes, providing tillage, pasture, salt marsh, and wood lots; changes in land-use practices associ-

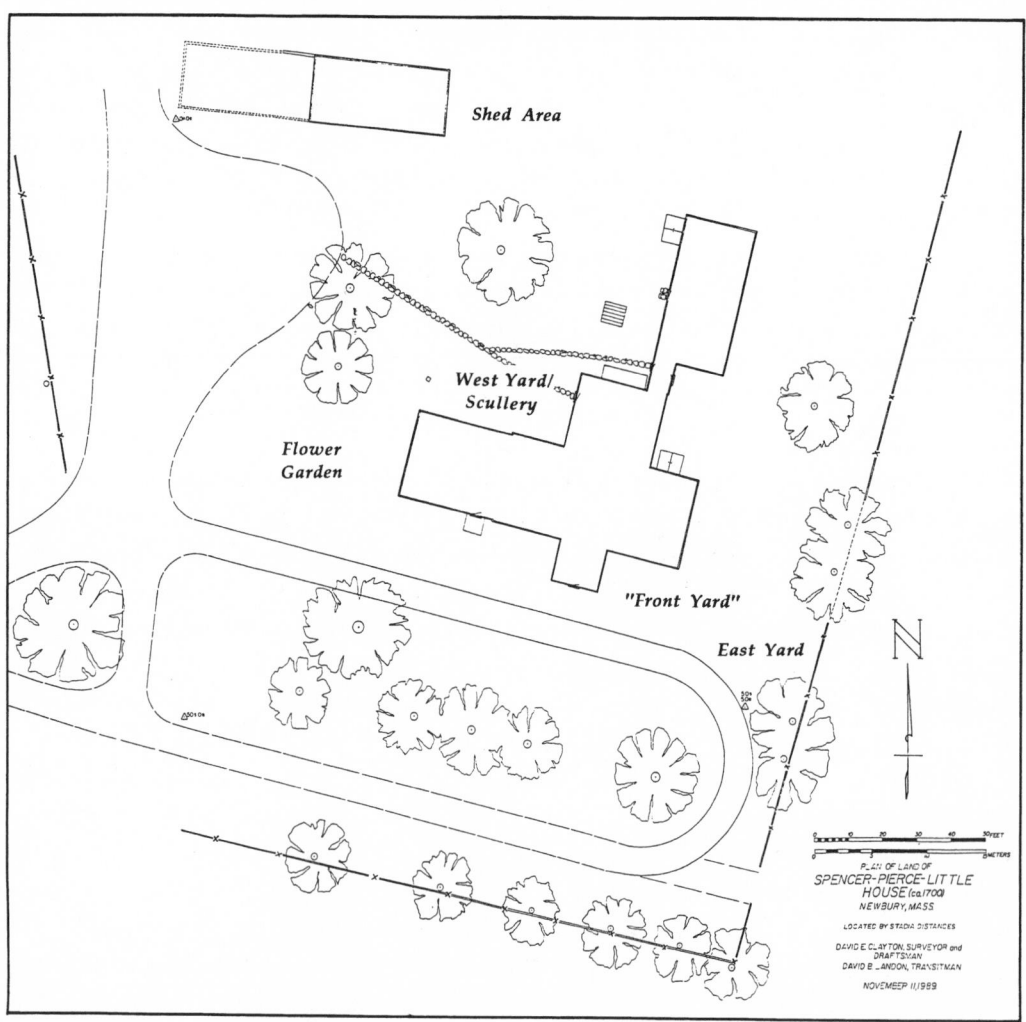

Figure 8.5. Plan of the domestic compound at the Spencer-Pierce-Little farm indicating yard areas investigated archaeologically.

ated with tenancy, and especially Little's rise from tenant to owner, may be preserved in vegetation and field patterns or they may be evident in soils or archaeobotanical analyses.

Edward Little's rise up the agricultural ladder is represented first and foremost by improvements that he made to the farm once he purchased the property. His introduction of an improved water management system for the kitchen of the house reflects this upward movement. A large brick cistern with its associated pipes was discovered in 1990 adjacent to the kitchen of the stone house (Beaudry 1991:19). The cistern was installed next to the kitchen and connected to the roof gutter system by a downspout. It was used to collect runoff from the roof and had a second pipe that was used to bring water into the kitchen by means of a hand pump. The construction of the cistern has been dated to the mid- to late nineteenth century.

Edward Little made a conscious effort to move all areas representing farm activity to the rear of the house or behind a tree line planted to separate the farm's work areas from the areas that would likely be seen by visitors (figure 8.6). Results of tree coring conducted in 1992 show that some of the trees planted along the drive to screen off the fields date from the period after Little purchased the farm, and three of the trees tested in front of the stone house date from the 1850s (Julie Hansen 1992, personal communication). In addition, many of the buildings shown on the 1812 plat map were removed by the late nineteenth century.

Along with the installation of the cistern in the area outside of the kitchen (to the west), Little may also have covered an early-eighteenth-century cobbled workyard and the foundation of a scullery depicted on the 1812 map, thus indicating a change in activity in this area (figure 8.7) (Beaudry 1991:18–19). The cistern was installed on the site of the earlier structure; most of the debris from the demolition of the scullery was removed at this time.

167

One
of the
Best Farms
in Essex
County

Figure 8.6. View of the tree-lined driveway at the farm, looking west, ca. 1985. Photograph by David Bohl. Courtesy of the Society for the Preservation of New England Antiquities, Boston.

Figure 8.7. View from the west of the Spencer-Pierce-Little house and tenant house, ca. 1885. This is the earliest view of the rear of the house and the workyard. Photograph by Wilfred A. French. Courtesy of the Society for the Preservation of New England Antiquities, Boston.

Excavations were conducted in the area of the wood house, or shed, a structure identified on the 1812 map. The remains of what may be a crude outbuilding foundation were found, but these remains lie above strata containing early- to mid-nineteenth-century artifacts (Beaudry 1989b:3). Documentary evidence suggests that a succession of structures, including sheds, stables, and a carriage house, existed here (Little Family Papers, SPNEA Archives). Additional excavation is required to identify each individual structure and to understand completely the sequence of construction. Preliminary analysis shows that by the late nineteenth century this area was used for dumping trash from either the main house or the tenant farmer's house. Large quantities of redware and other utilitarian ceramics (mostly yellowware and stoneware), glass fragments (from bottles, drinking vessels, and windows), nails, horse and ox shoes, metal tool fragments and hardware, and other artifacts were found in this location. A photograph from the late nineteenth century shows that a large fence or windbreak, running east-west, was constructed nearby (figure 8.8). While it is still unclear whether it was the Littles or their tenants who used the area behind the fence for trash deposition, the fence almost certainly was constructed by Little and, as such, the fence is another indicator of the reorganization of space within the domestic compound by Edward Little.

169

One
of the
Best Farms
in Essex
County

Figure 8.8. View from the southwest of the Spencer-Pierce-Little house and tenant house. The fence between the tenant house and the carriage house is visible to the left in the photograph. Courtesy of the Society for the Preservation of New England Antiquities, Boston.

Photographic evidence has shown that the yard area to the east of the house, depicted as a highly utilitarian work space on the 1812 map, was a manicured lawn in the late nineteenth century (SPNEA Photo Archives). This area, formerly the location of the poultry house, produced enormous quantities of household refuse when excavated, all of which date from the early to mid-nineteenth century. The fact that the poultry house was torn down sometime after 1812 (the date of the map on which it is depicted) and that trash disposal ceased here by the middle of the nineteenth century suggests that there was a shift in the treatment and use of the space around the house.

The analysis and interpretation of refuse distribution at the Spencer-Pierce-Little site is the final area to be examined. Distribution maps of the farmyard showing both temporal and spatial distinctions will be created following completion of the artifact analysis. This analysis will be closely linked to the examination of changing activity areas. For example, the yard surrounding the wood house became an area of refuse disposal in the late nineteenth century. The domestic compound is seen as a key to this research and will be examined closely in order to distinguish archaeological patterns in the hope of understanding the use of space by the tenant and, later, the owner.

The changes that have been identified through archaeology and documentary research thus far, though preliminary in nature, attest to Little's primary concern as an owner, that of making improvements to the farm. The farm itself was his mark of status, and his obituary in 1877 is an indication of his success. The author of the obituary stated that Little's farm was "One of the best farms in Essex County, or in fact, The Commonwealth" (*Newburyport Herald* 1877), thus symbolizing Little's achievements as a tenant turned owner.

Conclusion

This aspect of the Spencer-Pierce-Little study is in its initial stages; hence, much of what is offered here is programmatic, consisting essentially of what is proposed rather than a detailed presentation of what has been done. It is hoped that the study outlined here will nonetheless provide a different look at the New England farm. An examination of the practice of rural tenancy is crucial to our understanding of nineteenth-century New England, yet this subject has received little attention. Evidence from the Spencer-Pierce-Little site clearly shows the manipulation of the immediate domestic compound by Edward Little; these alterations reflect his change in status, both economically and socially, from tenant to owner. This case study, though preliminary, provides a basis for comparative research and hopefully will encourage scholars to look at the role of tenancy so that we may develop a greater understanding of rural life.

NOTES

1. Portions of this chapter were originally presented as conference papers co-authored with Mary C. Beaudry (Beaudry and Mascia 1989; Mascia with Beaudry 1989). See Mascia 1994 for a detailed analysis.

2. Following the Civil War another form of tenancy—sharecropping—gained prominence in the South. Orser (1991:41) offers a succinct definition of sharecropping as "a system wherein farmers receive a portion of the crop they produce in return for their labor." For other forms of tenancy in the postbellum South, see table 8.1 and Orser 1991:42. After the war many former slaves were in a position of having to establish their own economic livelihood. For many, farming a portion of the plantation became their only means of survival. Plantation owners were still cultivating a cash crop that was thought by many to be a means to move up economically (Goldenweiser and Truesdell 1924:9).

3. The following section is derived in part from the overall research plan created by Mary C. Beaudry for the Spencer-Pierce-Little site (see Beaudry 1989a and Beaudry and Mascia 1989).

4. Much of the genealogical research presented here was conducted by Anne Grady. Her research notes are on file at the Society for the Preservation of New England Antiquities, Boston, Massachusetts.

5. For additional information regarding John Godfrey's witchcraft trials, see Demos 1982:36–56.

6. Richard Cunningham, a descendant of Bartlett Currier, has graciously loaned the account books kept by Currier; copies are in the possession of the author.

REFERENCES

Adams, William H.
1990   Landscape Archaeology, Landscape History, and the American Farmstead. In *Historical Archaeology on Southern Plantations and Farms,* edited by Charles E. Orser Jr. *Historical Archaeology* 24(4):92–101.

Atack, Jeremy, and Fred Bateman
1987   *To Their Own Soil: Agriculture in the Antebellum North.* Iowa State University Press, Des Moines.

Barron, Hal S.
1985   Staying Down on the Farm: Social Processes of Settled Rural Life in the Nineteenth Century North. In *The Countryside in the Age of Capitalist Transformation,* edited by Stephen Hahn and Jonathan Prud, pp. 327–42. University of North Carolina Press, Chapel Hill.

Beaudry, Mary C.
1984   Archaeology and the Historical Household. *Man in the Northeast* 28:27–38.

171

One
of the
Best Farms
in Essex
County

1986   The Archaeology of Historical Land Use in Massachusetts. *Historical Archaeology* 20(2):38–46.

1987   Limited Archaeological Reconnaissance of the Spencer-Pierce-Little House Property, Newbury, Massachusetts. Center for Archaeological Studies, Boston University, Boston, Massachusetts.

1988   Archaeology of the Spencer-Pierce-Little House Property, Newbury, Massachusetts. Interim Report No. 1. Center for Archaeological Studies, Boston University, Boston, Massachusetts.

1989a   The Spencer-Pierce-Little House and Lands in Time and Mind. Paper presented at the annual meeting of the Society for American Archaeology, Atlanta, Georgia.

1989b   Archaeological Research at the Spencer-Pierce-Little Farm, 1989. *Context* 8(1–2):1–3. Center for Archaeological Studies, Boston University, Boston, Massachusetts.

1991   Beyond the Kitchen Door: The 1991 Field Season at the Spencer-Pierce-Little Farm. *Context* 9(3–4):18–19. Center for Archaeological Studies, Boston University, Boston, Massachusetts.

Beaudry, Mary C., and Sara F. Mascia

1989   Stability in Change: Archaeological Glimpses of an Agricultural Landscape over Three Centuries. Paper presented at the annual meeting of the Council for Northeast Historical Archaeology, Morristown, New Jersey.

Bertrand, Alvin L., and Floyd L. Corty, editors

1962   *Rural Land Tenure in the United States: A Socio-Economic Approach to Problems, Programs, and Trends.* Louisiana State University Press, Baton Rouge.

Bidwell, Percy W., and John J. Falconer

1925   *The History of Agriculture in the Northern United States 1620–1860.* Carnegie Institute, Washington, D.C.

Bowen, Joanne

1988   Seasonality: An Agricultural Construct. In *Documentary Archaeology in the New World,* edited by Mary C. Beaudry, pp. 161–71. Cambridge University Press, Cambridge.

Boxley, Robert F.

1985   Farmland Ownership and the Distribution of Land Earnings. *Agricultural Economics Research* 37(4):40–44.

Boyer, Carl, editor

1977   *Ship Passenger Lists: National and New England (1600–1825).* Published by the compiler, Newhall, California.

Catts, Wade, and Jay F. Custer

1990   Tenant Farmers, Stone Masons and Black Laborers: Final Archaeological Investigations of the Thomas Williams Site, Glasgow, New Castle County, Delaware. Delaware Department of Transportation Archaeological Series No. 82. Center for Archaeological Research, University of Delaware.

Clark, Christopher

1990   *The Roots of Rural Capitalism: Western Massachusetts, 1780–1860.* Cornell University Press, Ithaca, New York.

Clawson, Marion

1968   *The Land System of the United States: An Introduction to the History and Practice of Land Use and Land Tenure.* University of Nebraska Press, Lincoln.

Coffin, Joshua

1845   *A Sketch History of Newbury, Newburyport, and West Newbury from 1635 to 1845.* S. G. Drake, Boston.

Cosgrove, Denis

1984   The Geometry of Landscape. In *The Iconography of Landscape: Essays on the Symbolic Representation, Design and Use of Past Environments,* edited by Denis Cosgrove and Stephen Daniels, pp. 254–76. Cambridge University Press, Cambridge.

Cummings, Ralph W.

1978   *Land Tenure and Agricultural Development.* University of Wisconsin, Madison.

Currie, J. M.

1981   *The Economic Theory of Agricultural Land Tenure.* Cambridge University Press, Cambridge.

Currier, Bartlett
1830–38 Account Books. Originals owned by Richard Cunningham, Newbury, Massachusetts. Copy of original in possession of the author.

Currier, John J.
1896 *"Ould Newbury": Historical and Biographical Sketches.* Damrell and Upham, Boston.

Danhof, Clarence H.
1969 *Change in Agriculture: The Northern United States, 1820–1870.* Harvard University Press, Cambridge, Massachusetts.

Demos, John Putnam
1982 *Entertaining Satan: Witchcraft and the Culture of Early New England.* Oxford University Press, New York.

Dow, George F.
1911 Records and Files of the Quarterly Courts of Essex County, Massachusetts. Essex Institute, Salem, Massachusetts.

Essex County Court Records
James Phillips Duncan Library Manuscript Collection. Essex Institute, Salem, Massachusetts.

Essex County Registry of Deeds
Salem, Massachusetts.

Essex County Registry of Probate
Salem, Massachusetts.

Friedlander, Amy
1991 House and Barn: The Wealth of Farmers, 1795–1815. *Historical Archaeology* 25(2):15–29.

Goldenweiser, E. A., and Leon E. Truesdell
1924 *Farm Tenancy in the United States: An Analysis of the Results of the 1920 Census Relative to Farms Classified by Tenure Supplemented by Pertinent Data from Other Sources.* Government Printing Office, Washington D.C.

Grady, Ann, and William Remsen
1992 Historic Structure Report: Spencer-Pierce-Little House, Newbury, Massachusetts. Two volumes. Society for the Preservation of New England Antiquities Conservation Center, Waltham, Massachusetts.

Harris, Marshall
1953 *Origin of the Land Tenure System in the United States.* The Iowa State College Press, Ames.

Hayden, Dolores
1981 *The Grand Domestic Revolution: A History of Feminist Designs for American Homes, Neighborhoods, and Cities.* The MIT Press, Cambridge, Massachusetts.

Heskin, Allan David
1983 *Tenants and the American Dream: Ideology and the Tenant Movement.* Praeger Publishers, New York.

Hubka, Thomas C.
1984 *Big House, Little House, Back House, Barn: The Connected Farm Buildings of New England.* University Press of New England, Hanover, Massachusetts.

Hurd, D. Hamilton
1888 *History of Essex County, Massachusetts.* J. W. Lewis and Company, Philadelphia.

Innes, Stephen
1978 Land Tenancy and Social Order in Springfield, Massachusetts, 1652–1702. *William and Mary Quarterly* (Third Series) XXXV:33–56.

Jones, Alvin Lincoln
1894 *Under Colonial Roofs.* C. B. Webster, Publishers, Boston.

Labaree, Benjamin
1962 *Patriots and Partisans: The Merchants of Newburyport 1764–1815.* Harvard University Press, Cambridge, Massachusetts.

173

One
of the
Best Farms
in Essex
County

Landon, David B.

1991   Zooarchaeology and Urban Foodways: A Case Study from Eastern Massachusetts. Ph.D. diss., Department of Archaeology, Boston University.

Lee, Thomas A.

1921   The Tracy Family of Newburyport. *Essex Institute Historical Collections* 57:57–74. Newcomb and Gauss, Salem, Massachusetts.

Louis Berger and Associates, Inc.

1986   The Hamlin Site, 1780 to 1856: A Study of Rural Consumer Behavior. Report on file, Bureau of Environmental Analysis, New Jersey Department of Transportation, Trenton.

Mascia, Sara F.

1994   Climbing the Agricultural Ladder: An Archaeological and Documentary Case Study of the Transition from Tenant to Owner on a New England Farmstead. Ph.D. diss., Department of Archaeology, Boston University. University Microfilms, Ann Arbor.

Mascia, Sara F., with Mary C. Beaudry

1989   Archaeological Approaches to the Study of an Agricultural Landscape: The Spencer-Pierce-Little Farm, Newbury, Massachusetts. Paper presented at the annual meeting of the Eastern States Archaeological Federation, East Windsor, Connecticut.

McMurray, Sally

1988   *Families and Farmhouses in Nineteenth Century America: Vernacular Design and Social Change.* Oxford University Press, New York.

Miller, George L.

1988   Classification and Economic Scaling of Nineteenth-Century Ceramics. In *Documentary Archaeology in the New World,* edited by Mary C. Beaudry, pp. 172–83. Cambridge University Press, Cambridge.

Newburyport Herald

1877   Newburyport, Massachusetts.

Orser, Charles E., Jr.

1988   *The Material Basis of the Postbellum Tenant Plantation: Historical Archaeology in the South Carolina Piedmont.* The University of Georgia Press, Athens.

1991   The Continued Pattern of Dominance: Landlord and Tenant on the Postbellum Cotton Plantation. In *The Archaeology of Inequality,* edited by Randall H. McGuire and Robert Paynter, pp. 40–54. Basil Blackwell, Cambridge, Massachusetts.

Orser, Charles E., Jr., editor

1990   Historical Archaeology on Southern Plantations and Farms. *Historical Archaeology* 24(4).

Orser, Charles E., Jr., Annette M. Nekola, and James C. Roark

1987   Exploring the Rustic Life: Multidisciplinary Research at Millwood Plantation, a Large Piedmont Plantation in Abbeville County, South Carolina, and Elbert County, Georgia. Archaeological Services Branch, National Park Service, Atlanta.

Otto, John Solomon

1977   Artifacts and Status Differences: A Comparison of Ceramics from Planter, Overseer, and Slave Sites on an Antebellum Plantation. In *Research Strategies in Historical Archeology,* edited by Stanley South, pp. 91–118. Academic Press, New York.

1980   Race and Class on Antebellum Plantations. In *Archaeological Perspectives on Ethnicity in America: Afro-American and Asian American Culture History,* edited by Robert Schuyler, pp. 3–13. Baywood Publishing Company, Inc., Farmingdale, New York.

Pendleton, Sally

1990   The Plant Remains from the Spencer-Pierce-Little Kitchen: A Historical Ethnobotanical Analysis. M.A. thesis, Department of Archaeology, Boston University.

Probyn, J. W.

1881   *Systems of Land Tenure in Various Countries.* Cassell, Peter Galpin & Company, New York.

Rothenberg, Winifred B.

1985   The Emergence of a Capital Market in Rural Massachusetts 1730–1838. *Journal of Economic History* 45:781–808.

Russell, Howard

1976   *A Long, Deep Furrow: Three Generations of Farming in New England.* University Press of New England, Hanover, New Hampshire.

Salem Registry of Deeds

Salem, Massachusetts.

Singleton, Theresa A.

1988   An Archaeological Framework for Slavery and Emancipation, 1740–1880. In *The Recovery of Meaning: Historical Archaeology in the Eastern United States,* edited by Mark P. Leone and Parker B. Potter Jr., pp. 345–70. Smithsonian Institution Press, Washington, D.C.

Singleton, Theresa A., editor

1985   *The Archaeology of Slavery and Plantation Life.* Academic Press, Orlando.

Smith, E. Vale

1854   *History of Newburyport from the Earliest Settlement of the Country to the Present Time.* Damrell and Moore, Boston.

Society for the Preservation of New England Antiquities Archives (SPNEA Archives)

Harrison Gray Otis House, Boston, Massachusetts.

Stewart, Charles Leslie

1967   *Land Tenure in the United States: With Special Reference to Illinois.* Johnson Reprint Corporation, New York.

Stiverson, Gregory A.

1977   *Poverty in a Land of Plenty: Tenancy in Eighteenth-Century Maryland.* The Johns Hopkins University Press, Baltimore.

Wehrwein, George

1925   Tenancy in Farm Land Tenure. *Journal of Land and Public Utility Economics* 1(1):71–82.

Wright, Gwendolyn

1981   *Building the Dream: A Social History of Housing in America.* The MIT Press, Cambridge, Massachusetts.

9

Farmers and Gentlemen Farmers: The Nineteenth-Century Suburban Landscape

Rebecca Yamin and Sarah T. Bridges

New Jersey's identity rests with its farming tradition. Known as "the Garden State," the association of agriculture with New Jersey extends back into colonial times and continues virtually to the present. However, since the nineteenth century, this tradition, though widespread, has not been distributed uniformly throughout the state. The dispersed pattern of relatively large farms characteristic of some counties (for example, Monmouth County) was very different from the pattern of much smaller but intensive operations characteristic of other parts of the state. The Henry Hopper farm in Fair Lawn, Bergen County, represented the latter type. Within easy reach of New York City, especially after the introduction of trolley and rail transportation in the nineteenth century, the Hopper farm, like many farms similarly located, specialized in market gardening targeted for urban consumption (see Manning 1984 for a discussion of this pattern in New Jersey). The Hopper farm was part of what John Stilgoe (1988) calls the "borderlands": areas that were neither urban nor truly rural.

Stilgoe and other scholars have recently given serious attention to the nineteenth-century process of suburbanization that was closely associated with the elaboration of public and private transportation systems. In his book entitled *Borderland: Origins of the American Suburb, 1820–1939,* Stilgoe describes this distinctive landscape as a place "where houses are so far apart that even in winter they cast shadows only on their own lots; the borderlands are ordered about a horseback and carriage pace, not a pedestrian one: the borderlands are distant enough from cities to be free of pigeons . . . [and] people enjoy the rain because they keep gardens; trees offer a sense of privacy, of distance, of nature as the limit above which no structure, except church spires, may reach" (Stilgoe 1988:11).

At the outset of the Hopper house project, it was not obvious that the Hopper farm was part of this borderland landscape. Focusing on the site as an isolated problem, as the place that would be destroyed by pending construction of a highway interchange, we thought of it simply as a nineteenth-century farmstead. The macro-landscape outside the "dooryard" did not seem particularly pertinent nor even accessible.

The site was delimited by twentieth-century commercial and residential developments. Its value initially appeared to lie in its potential to provide micro-landscape (settlement pattern) and material-culture information on a household from a virtually extinct farming tradition in this particular community.[1] That this farming tradition was associated with the nineteenth-century suburbanization process did not become clear until we tried to explain the discrepancies between the oral histories collected on the house and its various occupants and the documentary evidence. It is this explanatory process, and the special role of oral history, that this chapter addresses.

THE HOPPER ARCHAEOLOGICAL SITE

In its dilapidated state, the Hopper house property appeared to epitomize the nineteenth-century past (figure 9.1). Locally, it was known as one of the town's last farmsteads, a fragment and a symbol of a bygone way of life. A planned New Jersey Department of Transportation (NJDOT) project led to an evaluation of the house and immediate environs for inclusion in the National Register of Historic Places. Although the standing structure was not found to be eligible, preliminary archaeological testing identified *in situ* structural and artifactual remains that were subsequently determined eligible for listing in the National Register by the New Jersey State Historic Preservation Officer (SHPO) for the information they could yield on nineteenth-century domestic lifeways in rural Bergen County (Bureau of Environmental Analysis 1986).

The Henry A. Hopper archaeological site was named for the man who built a house on the property in ca. 1855 and died there in 1912. The standing structure was supposedly not

Figure 9.1. The Hopper house, 1989. Photograph by Emmett Francois.

the original, but a replacement built after a fire destroyed most of the earlier house in ca. 1890. The DOT archaeologists argued that the fire was one of the things that made the site so valuable. Artifacts were recovered from a cellar hole associated with a portion of the house not replaced after the fire. These represented the "accumulation of acquired possessions up to a particular moment"—a "time capsule"—a rare occurrence on an archaeological site (Bureau of Environmental Analysis 1986:31).

The Hopper site was considered significant for other reasons as well: the presence of personal items along with kitchen-related artifacts in the deposits could provide information on the status and material culture of the Hopper family, and analysis of the entire artifactual assemblage could yield important information on the economic effect of twentieth-century suburbanization on a rural northeastern New Jersey farmstead. Thus, the emphasis of the eligibility determination was on the continuity and change in household history and in local social and economic history over a century of occupation.

But underlying the stated research goals was the implied significance of Henry A. Hopper—the sheriff of Bergen County in 1862, a freeholder from 1865 to 1871, and a representative to the state legislature in 1870. This was not just the house of any farmer; it was the property of one of Bergen County's leading citizens, someone worth knowing about and someone about whom there would surely be an oral tradition as well as substantial documentary evidence.

The Hoppers were among the first Dutch families to settle Bergen County. Andries Hopper, who came to New Amsterdam in 1652, was granted the privileges of a small burgher in 1657; he engaged in trade and served as commissary of wares for the Dutch West India Company. In 1655 he was transferred to Bergen where he was appointed secretary and attorney general of the colony (Ackerman 1947).

The Hoppers who developed the property on Fair Lawn Avenue were among the fourth, fifth, sixth, and seventh generations of the family to live in this country. Just before 1920, the property passed out of the Hopper family to another farm family, the Crouchers, who remained on the land for only two generations. In 1953 Percy and William Croucher Jr. sold the farm to the Frank A. McBride Company, a development company. Under the McBride ownership, the house was used for offices and the adjacent land for truck storage. Several of the outbuildings housed a construction and landscaping business. The land at the back of the property (north) became part of the celebrated Fair Lawn Industrial Park. When it opened in 1954, this development of modern facilities, warehouses, and laboratories covering 190 acres was described by the sitting New Jersey governor, William Meyner, as "a model industrial community which gracefully fits into the plan for suburban living" (*The Shopper and News Beacon* 1954).

ORAL HISTORY

When we began to study the Hopper house, we expected a rich local history and oral tradition to accompany the local written records and stately house shown in Walker's 1876 *Atlas of Bergen County* (figure 9.2). We expected a house "transmuted into a symbol," as Anne Yentsch (1988) has phrased it, with stories of one idealized historic figure translating into a broad and generalized local social history. To our surprise, we found something quite different.

Figure 9.2. "Residence of Henry A. Hopper, Esq." Walker's Atlas of Bergen County, 1876.

Our major oral informant was James R. Croucher. A long, open-ended interview was conducted with Croucher before the excavation began, and conversations continued during and after the fieldwork. Croucher grew up in the Hopper house. To him it was not the Hopper house at all but the "Croucher homestead," the place to which his grandfather, William Croucher, brought his wife and six children to start anew in 1919. The oldest sons, Percy and William, were in business with their father. They lived in separate quarters on either side of the house, with their father and mother in the middle, at least for a time.

James Croucher was the baby in Percy's family of five. He was born in Fair Lawn in 1934, his oldest sibling being thirteen years his senior. Croucher fondly remembered growing up on the farm. There were eleven in the household; all the males worked in the fields. With the farmhands, who also lived in the house, as many as fourteen waited to bathe in the only bathroom (installed in the 1920s) at the end of a hot summer afternoon. Family gatherings were boisterous affairs; an unmarried aunt once danced on the porch, to the outrage of some of the Dutch Reformed families in the neighborhood.

But Croucher also remembered feeling inferior to the children from Radburn, the white-collar community down the road. Established in 1928, Radburn was a planned community that eventually attained international recognition as a model town "for the motor age." The well-known social philosopher, Lewis Mumford, among others, served on its planning board. One scholar described Radburn as "the first planned community to consider the automobile a vital part of the American way of life, but one that should not be permitted to dominate the landscape" (Schaffer 1980:54). For Croucher, Radburn was the place where kids played baseball all day while he labored on the farm; Radburn kids went east to Ridgewood High, a fashionable community, while the farm kids went west to the high school in Paterson, a city in decline. Croucher also felt pressure to prepare for a life off the farm. He wanted to be a dairy farmer, but his father encouraged him to work in a garage and finally to go to college to become a pharmacist. The elder Croucher clearly anticipated the sale of the farm, an event which finally came in 1952. It was the next-to-last farm to be sold for commercial development in Fair Lawn.

Croucher could not have been a more cooperative informant or more enthusiastic about the project; he visited the site daily, sometimes more than once. But he knew absolutely nothing about the Hoppers. Their connection to the site did not exist for him and certainly did not interest him. If he found us excavating layers beneath the twentieth-century topsoil, he would say something like, "Oh, that's a Hopper layer, isn't it?" and disdainfully turn away to lead anyone who was willing through the vacant house, regaling them with Croucher history. The lack of a Hopper myth seemed odd for a house associated with one of Bergen County's leading nineteenth-century citizens. The house did have a ghost story, recounted by a New Jersey congressman who kept an office there after the Crouchers sold it, but it was about a ghost without an identity, the generic old house ghost who could be heard going up and down the stairs.

Croucher's aunt, Marian Blake, another willing informant, did remember something of the Hoppers. She was five years old when her family came to Fair Lawn from Long Island in 1919. According to her, the old house her family bought was in disrepair. Garret Hopper, one of Henry's sons, lived with his childless and "crazy" wife in the eastern half; the rooms were filthy and the floors were collapsing. This is a very different picture of Garret than the one painted in a contemporary source, Francis A. Westervelt's *History of Bergen County* (1923). "When his father died," wrote Westervelt, "Garret Hopper became the owner of the farm, of which he had been for many years the manager, and under his direction, it continued to be known as one of the finest truck farms in Bergen County" (1923:260).

What Marian may have remembered was Eliza Hopper's side of the house. Henry's fourth wife outlived him by a year, not dying until 1913. Her half of the house may have been vacant until it was sold to the Crouchers in 1919. Marian's memory, however, was right on target for the location of the well, which her family filled up with household goods, including an old-fashioned Victrola and a sewing machine, when they moved out in 1930.

Thus, our two major oral informants raised questions about the actual significance of the Hoppers in the local community. Jim Croucher's lack of knowledge suggested that, in spite of Henry Hopper's civic responsibilities, he and his family were neither very well known nor very important; Marian Blake's memories suggested that the lifestyle of the Hoppers might have been impoverished or even slightly disreputable.

THE DOCUMENTARY EVIDENCE

Written histories of Bergen County (Clayton 1882; Van Valen 1900; Westervelt 1923) refer to Henry and the Hopper family as prominent in the county and community; however, these sources provide few details beyond a basic genealogy and a listing of the public offices

Henry held for mid–life years. The agricultural census data for the years 1850–80 provide interesting insights into changes in the house and into Henry's property holdings. The "cash value of farm" was recorded for all farmers in Saddle River Township, of which Fair Lawn was part until 1924. We compared the mean and median values for farmers in the township to the value of Henry A. Hopper's farm (table 9.1). Henry was in no way the richest farmer in Saddle River; nor was he the poorest. Even when his additional properties (maps show other small holdings along Small Lots Road) and their values are considered, the total value of his holdings lay somewhere in or below the middle.

We learn from the census data that, as would be expected, Hopper improved his lot during his adult life. In 1850, when his farm's value was less than the mean or median, he was thirty-one years old; in 1870, when its value reached its highest ($34,000) and exceeded the mean by $20,000, he was fifty-one. However, by 1880, Henry's fortunes had begun to fade. By this time Hopper was married to his fourth wife and was father to eight children. Henry not only gave land away to grown children, but an 1880 deed records the sale of a 33-acre tract.

The decline in Hopper's fortunes in the latter years of the nineteenth century suggested a possible reason for his minor role in history "as remembered" (to the Croucher family); for an explanation, we turned to the broader context of the community in which he lived.

The landscape history of Saddle River/Fair Lawn indicates that as early as the 1830s, when Henry Hopper's father first acquired the farmstead, conditions within the community (location and transportation corridors and systems) seemed to fit Stilgoe's characterization of a "borderland." By looking at a series of nineteenth-century maps of Bergen County, the forces affecting the transformation of farmlands into suburban borderlands can be traced.

The 1861 Hopkins map shows the Erie Railroad running in a northeasterly direction, to the west of Small Lots Road and west of the Passaic River. The Erie Railway, which began as the Paterson and Hudson Railroad in 1831, replaced the Paterson and Ramapo Railroad in 1853 (Chamber of Commerce 1954). The Paterson and Ramapo Railroad provided a direct link between Jersey City and Suffern and ran through Fair Lawn. Added to this later in the century were the steam and electric mainline spurs and street or interurban railways. The 1913 Bromley map (figure 9.3) shows a northwest branch of the Erie Railway crossing Small Lots Road to the east of the Hopper property and the interurban trolley running just west of the northwest corner of the property. Croucher remembered walking in the abandoned right-of-way for the trolley tracks.

Table 9.1
Mean, Median, and Range of Cash Value of All Saddle River Farms Compared to Henry A. Hopper's Farm

Year	N	Mean	Median	Range	Henry A. Hopper
1850	77	$7,619	$7,000	$2,000–25,000	$6,000
1860	116	$7,011	$5,500	$300–30,000	$10,000
1870	94	$14,057	$10,000	$400–110,000	$34,000
1880	97[a]	$11,873	$9,000	$300–75,000	$20,000

SOURCE: U.S. Agricultural Census, 1850–1880, New Jersey State Archives, Trenton.
[a]There were 120 farmers in the 1880 census; of these, the entries for 23 were illegible.

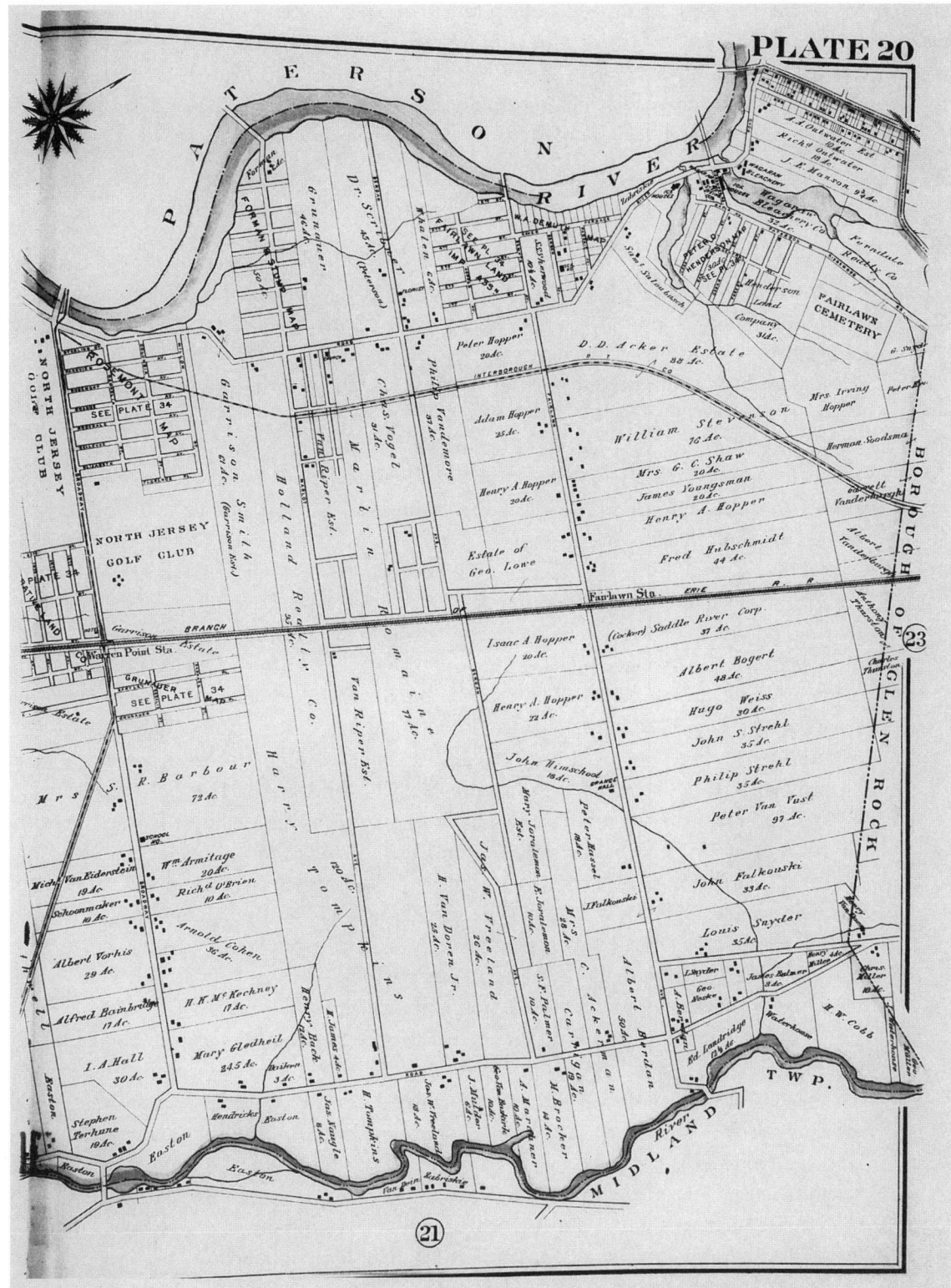

Figure 9.3. Bromley's Atlas of Bergen County, 1913, showing the Henry A. Hopper property along Small Lots Road.

The two maps also show a configuration of properties very different from the spreading acreage traditionally associated with New Jersey farms. The long, narrow Hopper lot is sandwiched between other similarly narrow lots along the road edge. Even the original name of the road, Small Lots Road, which apparently goes back at least to the beginning of the nineteenth century, reflects the size of the farm lots in this area.

MEANING IN THE SUBURBAN LANDSCAPE

Seen in the context of a suburban landscape, Croucher's disinterest in the Hoppers can be explained. In the twentieth century, Croucher contrasted his small-scale farmstead home with the more lavish suburban houses in the new settlement of Radburn. The fact that the Hoppers were early suburbanite homesteaders was not particularly exceptional to Croucher; he viewed them as no more than small dirt farmers who were forced to leave the land in relative poverty.

More important, we can begin to understand what the Hopper site represents in terms of nineteenth-century demographic trends, economic development, and community structure. Recent examination of the early years of the suburbanization phenomenon by historian Henry Binford notes that improvements made to roads and bridges during the Federalist period provided the framework for the movement of goods into the cities in the Jacksonian era. People in the inner suburbs—those just beyond the urban center—took on the task of moving, selling, and processing agricultural products, while production continued in the outer suburbs, which looked much as they had before: "The scattered centers, the absence of dense settlement, the fuzziness of boundaries, the bucolic appearance of the landscape—all these bore a resemblance to the country. To many outside observers, the suburbs of this period seemed an economic backwater. Hardly anyone outside the fringe understood what had happened there since the late eighteenth century" (Binford 1985:43).

Thus, nineteenth-century Fair Lawn, New Jersey, farms were a critical part of the overall economy of the New York metropolitan area. Well within twenty miles of New York City, the small farms along Small Lots Road supplied the urban populations with necessary agricultural products (figure 9.4). The mid-nineteenth-century Fair Lawn farmer, therefore, was not the same as his eighteenth-century counterpart. The Hopper farm was oriented to production for urban consumption. These farmers were the area's first suburbanites, then, not the white-collar commuters who came later in the twentieth century.

Both Binford (1985:60) and Bender (1978:100) argue that through the middle of the nineteenth century, state and regional leadership from these early suburban communities remained locally based. Officeholders were drawn from the two groups at the top of the social hierarchy—the old farm and artisan families and the prosperous fringe entrepreneurs—who were joined in large, intermarried households (Binford 1985:60). Both Andries Hopper and Henry Hopper exemplify this pattern.

In the late nineteenth century, as power and status within the emerging political structure shifted to individuals with translocal rather than local connections, the Hoppers lost their rank within the social hierarchy. Henry's son, Isaac, was the county's tax collector, but he was not a representative to the state legislature as his father and grandfather had been before him.

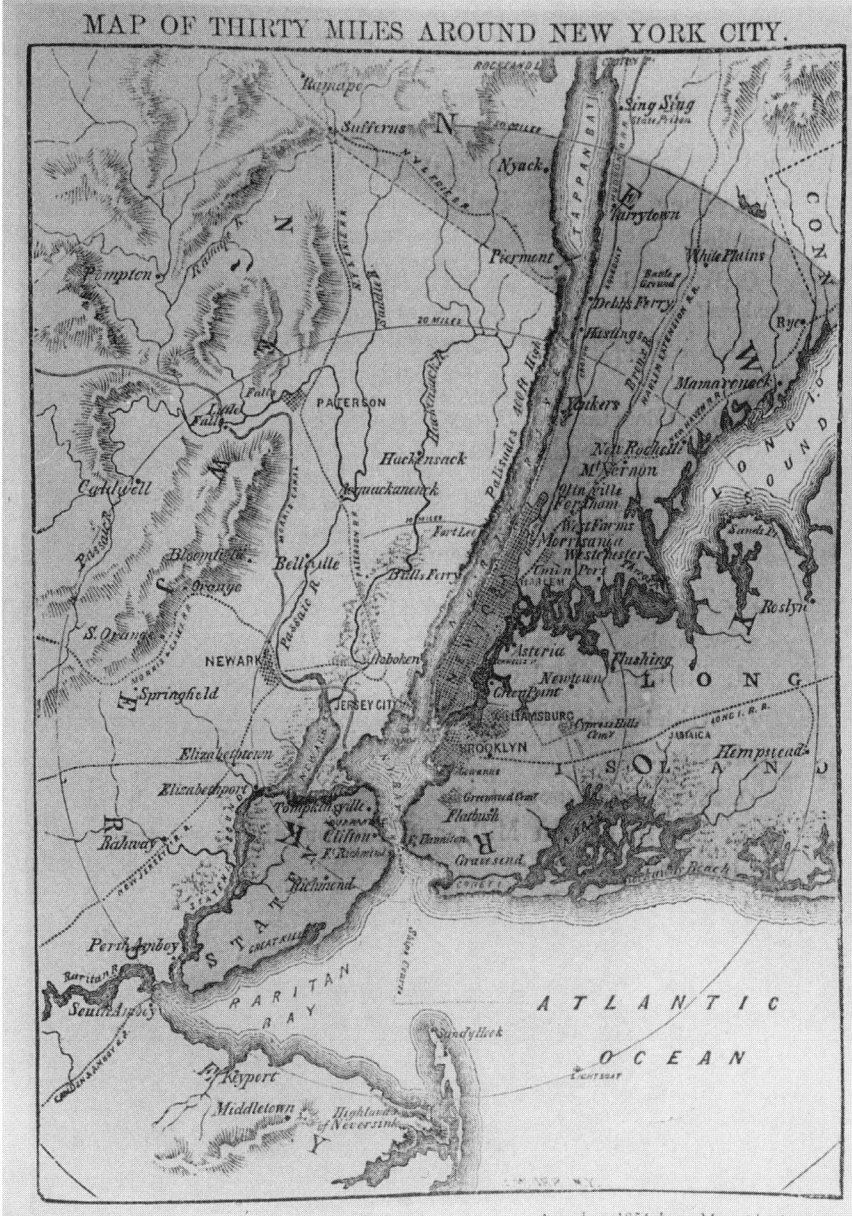

Figure 9.4. "Map of Thirty Miles Around New York City," from James Monteith's Youth's Manual of Geography, 1854 (Stilgoe 1988:47). Fair Lawn is east of Paterson. Printed with permission of Yale University Press.

As early as 1854, James Monteith addressed the significance of the borderlands in his Youth's

Perhaps the most telling demonstration of Henry Hopper's role as a suburbanite, rather than as a rural farmer, is the representation of his house that appears in Walker's 1876 *Atlas of Bergen County* (see figure 9.2). It is a house that fits the gentleman farmer ideal, described by John Stilgoe as an alternative to the slovenly farms that were held up as examples of moral decay in the 1870s and 1880s. It is clear from Stilgoe's illustrations (reproduced here as figures 9.5 and 9.6, drawn from the didactic periodicals of the day), that even though Hopper was a full-time farmer, his house met the specifications for a gentleman farmer and a representative of moral rectitude.

Figure 9.5. *"The Thrifty Farmstead," from Periam and Baker's The American Farmer's Pictorial Cyclopedia, 1884 (Stilgoe 1988:77). Printed with permission of Yale University Press.*

Figure 9.6. *"The Gentleman Farmer's Seat," from Scharf's Westchester County (Stilgoe 1988:104). Printed with permission of Yale University Press.*

Note the striking similarity between specific components of the 1876 rendering of the Hopper house (figure 9.2) and the gentleman farmer's spread shown in figure 9.6. In both, elegantly attired people are shown enjoying a well-groomed yard surrounded by a picket fence. In the illustration entitled "The Gentleman Farmer's Seat," a woman stands in a doorway while several others stand in the yard; in the Walker rendering someone is sitting on the porch. A porch, seen on both houses, was an essential part of the borderland house as were trees, also conspicuous in both illustrations. For Andrew Jackson Downing, the most important criterion for choosing a site for a country seat was to "secure a position where there is some existing wood and where the ground is so disposed as to offer a natural surface for a fine lawn" (Downing [1883] 1974:161). Farm buildings are shown clustered and separated from the fenced-in area associated with the houses in both illustrations; men in work clothes are shown outside the fence.

Andrew Jackson Downing was an outspoken proponent of country living. In his book *Country Houses,* published in 1850 and reprinted nine times before the end of the Civil War, he argued that "the solitude and freedom of the family home in the country . . . preserves the nation, and invigorates its intellectual powers" (quoted in Marsh 1989:509). According to an article by Margaret Marsh about the social construction of domestic space in American suburbs from 1840 to 1915, Downing centered his hopes for the continuance of American democracy in America's countryside, a sentiment that was echoed in the works of Nathaniel Hawthorne and Henry David Thoreau, both of whom distrusted urban civilization. The farmer attached to the city and the urbanite commuting to the country had equal roles in this idealized way of life.

To a great extent Hopper's house met the specifications for the "perfect borderland house" as described by Downing and other contemporary writers. For instance, as pointed out by Stilgoe (1988:102), Zebulon Baker argued in 1857 that "every freestanding house ought to have windows carefully placed to admit as much sunlight as possible . . . windows should nearly reach the ceiling, in order that light might come in from above the eye. Moreover, large windows correctly sited would admit the life-giving fresh air absolutely necessary to sound health, particularly the health of children." Both the upstairs and downstairs windows in the Walker rendering of the Hopper house fit this description as do the attic dormers, also a valued feature of the day. Other requirements were the porch, which, in Herman Melville's words of 1856, "[combined] the coziness of in-doors with the freedom of outdoors," and the color, which, according to Downing, should be "soft and quiet shades" (quoted in Stilgoe 1988:103).

Marsh's study of changes in domestic architecture in this period (1989) also throws light on the Hopper house as it appeared in the 1876 atlas and on the changes made to the structure after the 1890 fire. In a study of 151 house designs from pattern books and house magazines for the periods 1860–80 and 1900–12, Marsh shows that the typical house of the earlier period protected the family's privacy and encouraged intrafamilial separation (1989:515). In addition to a formal entry hall, houses of the earlier period generally had a parlor and separate sitting room on the first floor, and gender-specific rooms, such as a study or library for men and a sewing room (upstairs) for women. Separate bedrooms and a playroom for the children were located upstairs. Domestic servants lived either on the floor with the family or in the attic. Hopper's mid-century house fits this form. In contrast, the addition of the west wing at the turn of the twentieth century reflects what Marsh calls "the new domesticity" (1989:525). Family togetherness became more important; one living room was meant to bring everyone together.

Marsh argues that the earliest migrations of urbanites into the suburbs were made by men who wanted to remove their wives and children from the moral and physical miasma of the metropolis. Women liked the advantages of the city with its "access to social life, material goods, and educational opportunities for children" (1989:509). However, as the cities became less habitable (as they became clogged with traffic and crowded with newly arrived immigrants) and suburbs became more accessible (with the advent of omnibus, trolley, and rail systems), women, as well as men, saw the advantage of suburban living. Under these changing conditions, Marsh claims, "women began to make incursions into men's spheres and men began to take a greater interest in the home" (1989:513). The built-in restrictiveness of commuter schedules and the more limited responsibilities of working for someone else freed men to participate in what became a new domestic ideal expressed in a new domestic architecture.

During the last third of the nineteenth century and well into the twentieth century, the idealized, open borderlands began to show signs of deterioration. Manufacturing entered these towns and threatened their semibucolic tranquillity with mill town squalor. Anxious to preserve their ideal of respectable, cherished borderlands, suburban advocates devised environmental strategies—a "frosting of the suburbs"—with careful planting, innovative grid-and-cluster patterns, protective covenants, and, finally, entire planned communities, all situated within the existing natural landscape (Stilgoe 1988). Radburn, in Fair Lawn, is a perfect example of this phenomenon. It was designed as more than a garden city; it was an orderly, planned community in which each parcel of land was to fill a specific purpose in a balanced urban-rural environment.

Immediately adjacent to Radburn stood the Hopper/Croucher home, a remnant of Downing's invigorating and highly respectable (nineteenth-century) suburban/agrarian development. For mid-nineteenth-century Fair Lawn, the open land-use pattern of the Hopper farmstead setting represented a suitable middle-class alternative to the nearby stratified and decaying urban settlements. But by the time the Crouchers took possession of the property in the 1920s, the Hopper farm no longer represented the ideal settlement mode. Rather, it stood in sharp contrast to the burgeoning and more structured suburban communities with their grids, tiny lots, and central domestic control. In fact, the Hopper farm might have soon become an exemplar of class division within the rural community.

Just as the juxtaposition of the Hopper farm and Radburn represented more than a local phenomenon, Croucher's version of the Hopper house history was representative of more than local or even recent history. The historian Carl Ryant has made the point that a comparison of oral interviews with the written record may reveal questions left unasked (Ryant 1988:564). Croucher's ignorance of the Hoppers seemed to us peculiar; that the legends he told us were of his own family rather than about the Hoppers was disappointing. However, upon further examination we realized that his perspective reflected the diminishing role of civic leaders in suburbanized Saddle River—the disappearance of the big fish in a little pond. We had been blinded by our own bias toward the old as being the most important. Other historians have noted the strength of oral history to "redress class, race, and gender imbalances in traditional documentary historical records" (Jones and Osterud 1989:556). For us, as historical archaeologists, oral history may also redress our tendency to look at sites in a time frame restricted by diagnostic artifacts. In the case of the Hopper house site, at least, a much longer time frame provides a more meaningful context for analysis of historical and archaeological data.

THE ARCHAEOLOGICAL EVIDENCE

The structural evidence and associated artifactual deposits on the Hopper property suggested that an earlier, smaller house had been incorporated into the house built by Henry Hopper in 1855. Eighteenth-century artifacts were recovered from an excavation unit against the northeast corner of the standing structure and around the edges of the east wing cellar foundation (figure 9.7). The foundation stones of the northeast corner appeared to be more rough-hewn than the rest of the center block. A close examination of that section of the cellar also suggested that it was part of an earlier structure. As shown in figure 9.7, the earlier structure would have been about thirty-five feet long and sixteen feet wide. It had a central stairwell and a hatch in the middle of the southern wall. The cistern inside this structure was probably added when the larger house was built in the middle of the nineteenth century; instead of being a stone-lined hole dug into the ground, this cistern had been built up from the inside and buried in earth.

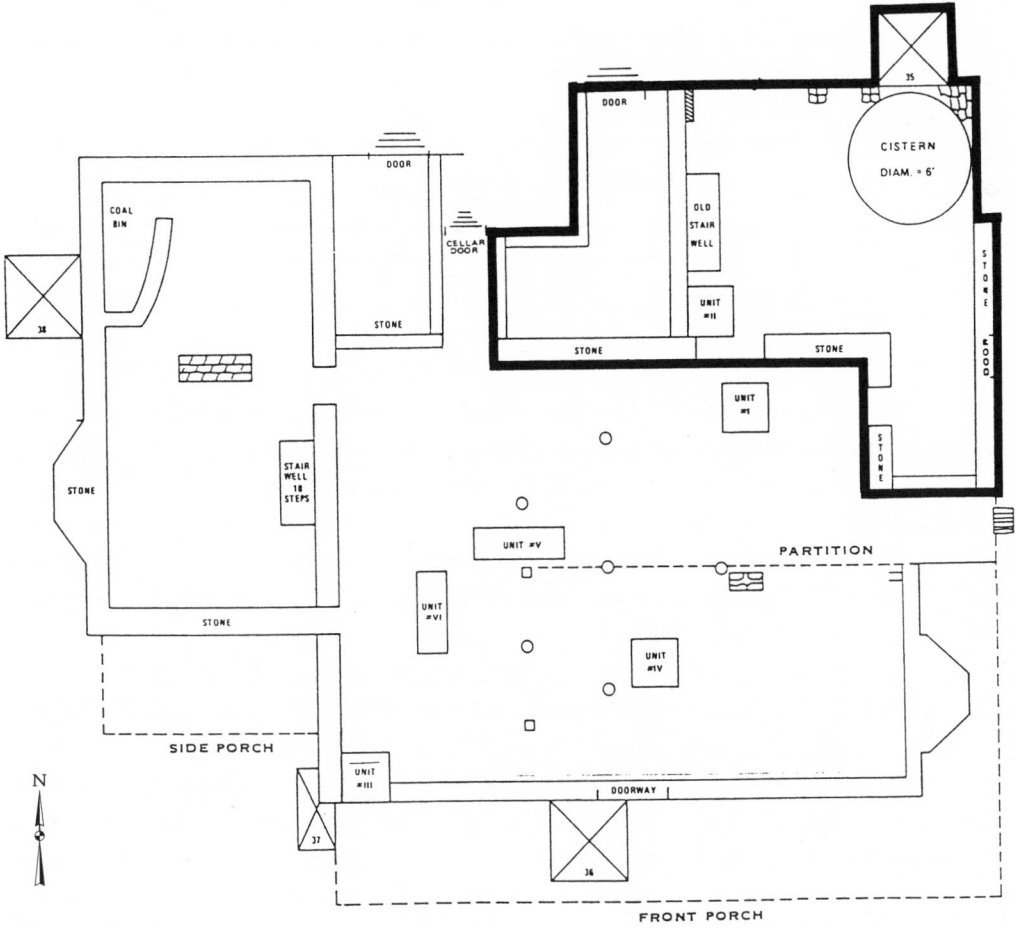

Figure 9.7. Detail of the Hopper house showing the outline of the earlier house (upper right) within the 1855 foundation.

In the style of other early Dutch houses in the neighborhood, the earlier house was most probably made of stone. When the original house was dismantled, the stones may have been reused to build the foundation of the 1855 house. This would explain why even the below-ground foundation stones of the house were so carefully cut, an unusual feature in area cellars (Mary Crain 1989, personal communication). In his genealogy of the Hopper family, Ackerman (1947) mentions that Andrew Hopper, Henry A. Hopper's father, lived on the same site as his son and that his house had burned. There was some evidence of burning in one of the layers excavated in the unit next to the northeast corner. Although we cannot be sure that this smaller structure was the elder Hopper's homestead, the evidence, including the artifacts damaged by fire, is compelling.

Archaeological evidence demonstrated that the center block and east wing, including its ell extension, were built at the same time. They do not, however, appear to have been destroyed at the same time. Close examination of the Walker rendering shows a porch or door overhang on the back of the east wing. The extension, which is described in a secondary source, had apparently been removed by 1876 when the drawing was made. A thin layer of burned debris on top of the ell foundation also suggested that the ell's superstructure was not extant at the time of the ca. 1890 fire that destroyed the wing.

Interestingly, the east wing was only partially replaced after the fire. The functions of its various rooms were evidently transferred to other parts of the house: the small, post-fire addition to the east side included a dining room connected to a kitchen and bedrooms above. The placement of these rooms within the main body of the house rather than in a wing extension reflected the previously discussed trend toward more centralized living spaces.

By contrast, the new west wing, which archaeological evidence showed to postdate the fire, provided a completely separate living space, probably for Garret Hopper and his wife. It was arranged in the modern fashion, with a single living room, dining room, and kitchen on the first floor and several bedrooms above. The multiple parlors that characterized the mid-nineteenth-century house were out of fashion by the turn of the century and the west wing was designed in the new style. More important, the ideal of a separate living space suggests that extended families were also out of fashion. Garret Hopper and his wife apparently preferred to live in their own space, rather than living with Hopper's parents, while he managed his father's farm. To create space, the small knoll on which the original house sat was expanded. Excavation in the front yard exposed a thick layer of fill (debris from the fire) used to create a level lawn in front of the west wing.

Our analysis of the artifacts recovered at the Hopper house reflected a concern with the identification of traits or features that might be distinctive of a borderland site and that might be expected of a household the status of which declined over time. The two major artifact-bearing deposits that were investigated (two fills associated with the wing that burned off the house in about 1890, and a midden behind the kitchen door, apparently deposited in the early 1870s) were both unusual. Neither seemed to reflect the more familiar selective nature of an archaeological assemblage where only things that are broken get thrown out. The fills associated with the fire (one in the cellar foundation and one used to alter the grade of the front yard) included the things—ceramics, glass, architectural remains, buttons, and a few other personal items—that were in the wing when it burned. The kitchen midden appeared to represent a house-cleaning episode. Practically all the ceramics in the midden dated from the period 1828–48, even though associated diagnostic glass dated from a later period. Apparently, some time in the 1870s, someone threw away the old dishes, presumably because they had been replaced with new, more fashionable ones. However, although they were deposited in the 1870s, these ceramics represent choices made in an earlier period and may thus be compared to those found in the cellar foundation. This comparison allows us to consider the Hopper house ceramics as a possible reflection of changing socioeconomic status through time.

Although Miller (1991) has warned against comparing ceramic indices from one period to another because the prices of all wares, including CC ware (creamware), fell over time, indices were calculated and used in combination with other measures. Tables 9.2 and 9.3 show the results. As can be seen, the mean value for the ceramics from the kitchen midden was higher than the mean value for the ceramics from the cellar foundation. The relative ceramic index (a rank order, weighted-mean calculation based on Miller's hierarchical arrangement of deco-

Table 9.2
Ceramic Index Calculations for the Kitchen Midden at Henry A. Hopper's Farm

Form	Type	Index Year	Value	#	Product
Plates 10-9"	Edged	1838	1.33	10	13.30
10-9"	Underglazed lined	1833	1.67	2	3.34
10-9"	Painted	1838	2.17	4	8.68
10-9"	Willow	1836	2.50	9	22.50
10-9"	Transfer printed	1838	2.67	23	61.41
10-9"	Flow print	1846	2.64	9	23.76
Total				*57*	*132.99*
Average Value			*2.33*		
Cups London	Painted	1838	1.50	1	1.50
London	Painted	1838	3.00	4	12.00
Total				*5*	*13.50*
Average Value			*2.70*		
Bowls	Sponged	1855	1.11	1	1.11
	Painted	1836	1.80	1	1.80
	Printed	1838	2.80	3	8.40
	Flow Print	1838	3.25	1	3.25
Total				*6*	*14.56*
Average Value			*2.43*		
Mean Value			*2.49*		

NOTE: Mean Ceramic Date: 1864; *Terminus Post Quem:* 1879.

Table 9.3
Ceramic Index Calculations for the Cellar Fill at Henry A. Hopper's Farm

Form	Type	Index Year	Value	#	Product
Dishes 10"	White granite	1880	2.11	23	48.53
Cups London	White granite	1880	1.82	3	5.46
Bowls	White granite	1880	2.34	10	23.40
Total				*36*	*77.39*
Mean Value			*2.15*		

NOTE: Mean Ceramic Date: 1893; *Terminus Post Quem:* 1885.

rated whiteware from least expensive to most expensive) was also higher for the kitchen midden (55.18) than for the ceramics from the cellar fill (38.35). Both calculations suggest a higher value for the ceramics from the kitchen midden than from the cellar foundation.

The quantity and variety of ceramic vessels represented in both deposits were also compared. A total of two hundred vessels were identified in the kitchen midden representing seven different forms (cups, plates, saucers, bowls, serving dishes, a platter, and a colander). Only sixty vessels were identified in the cellar fill, including four different forms (plates, bowls, cups, platters) plus a tea set. The mid-century Hopper household owned a Union pattern transfer-printed dinner set, many additional transfer-printed pieces from several dinner sets, and at least ten patterns of flow blue (from one set or possibly several). No dinner sets were identified from the fire-associated fills. Instead, sherds from unmatched white granite vessels were recovered; the tea set was soft paste porcelain decorated with a gold band.

If dishes are accepted as an expression of status, it does appear that the socioeconomic position of the Hoppers fell between mid-century and the end of the century, but conclusions must be considered tentative. Farmers expressed status in many different ways in New Jersey (see Louis Berger and Associates, Inc. 1986 for an interesting discussion of this phenomenon) and much more work needs to be done in this area.

Even more tantalizing is the possible recognition and definition of a characteristic suburban or borderland pattern. It is hoped that as more borderland sites are identified and analyzed, those comparisons can be made.

THE MACRO-LANDSCAPE

Unlike most of the chapters in this volume, the landscape examined here was not limited to the site (or sites) under study. What might be called the macro-landscape provided a context for understanding a site that otherwise did not make much sense. Inconsistencies in the oral history led us from a narrow perspective limited by the boundaries of the Hopper property to a broader temporal-spatial analytical framework. Within this broader perspective, phenomena in the written record that had been inexplicable began to make sense. That Henry Hopper's obituary, for instance, described him as "a remarkable old man. . . . Until several weeks ago, he seemed to be enjoying the best of health, frequently claiming that he had neither ache nor pain and was ready for every meal served in his home . . ." hardly seemed to be a dignified tribute to a leading citizen (*Paterson Press Guardian,* Notices, Book 6, 4 December 1912), but by 1912 Hopper's mid-century civic contributions had lost their value. His farm—his life—was a symbol of the past; it could be denigrated or ignored.

That the Hopper farm was more truly a manifestation of a nineteenth-century suburban ideal than a rural one explains the farm's small size and the size of the surrounding plots. It even explains the origin of the name "Small Lots Road" for a feature in the landscape that, until the early nineteenth century, had been a nameless link between two north-south connecting roads.

As a methodological component of historical archaeology, oral history is useful for much more than locating outbuildings or deriving genealogies. Directed questions and responses and the analysis of oral accounts may provide subtle nuances that otherwise might be missed by even the most careful reading of letters and memoirs. Critical analysis of Croucher's testimony revealed an eloquent bias in these data. It was the edge in Mr. Croucher's voice when he talked about "the kids from Radburn" that led us to focus on the juxtaposition of the farm and the planned community across the road. It was his lack of interest in the Hoppers that helped us to find out who the Hoppers really were.

NOTE

1. See John Stilgoe, *Common Landscape of America, 1580 to 1845* (1982), for a discussion of the micro- and macro-landscapes of the farmyard and community or region.

REFERENCES

Ackerman, Herbert Stewart
1947   *The Genealogy of the Hopper Family.* Privately published. On file, The Johnson Free Public Library, Hackensack, New Jersey.

Bender, Thomas
1978   *Community and Social Change in America.* The Johns Hopkins University Press, Baltimore.

Binford, Henry C.
1985   *The First Suburbs: Residential Communities on the Boston Periphery, 1815–1860.* University of Chicago Press, Chicago.

Bromley, G. W.
1913   *Atlas of Bergen County,* vol. 2. Philadelphia.

Bureau of Environmental Analysis
1986   An Archaeological Investigation of the Route 208, Section 3P Project, Fair Lawn Borough, Bergen County, New Jersey. New Jersey Department of Transportation, Trenton.

Chamber of Commerce
1954   Fair Lawn, New Jersey. On file, Fair Lawn Public Library.

Clayton, W. Woodford
1882   *History of Bergen and Passaic Counties.* Everts and Peck, Philadelphia.

Downing, Andrew Jackson
1974   *Rural Essays.* 1883. Reprint. Da Capo Press, New York.

Hopkins, G. M.
1861   *Map of Bergen County, New Jersey.* Philadelphia.

Jones, LuAnn, and Nancy Grey Osterud
1989   Breaking New Ground: Oral History and Agricultural History. *Journal of American History* 76(2):551–64.

Louis Berger and Associates, Inc.
1986   The Hamlin Site, 1780 to 1856: A Study of Rural Consumer Behavior. Report on file, Bureau of Environmental Analysis, New Jersey Department of Transportation, Trenton.

Manning, Alice
1984   Nineteenth Century Farmsteads on the Inner Coastal Plain of New Jersey. In *Historic Preservation Planning in New Jersey: Selected Papers on the Identification, Evaluation, and Protection of Cultural Resources,* edited by Olga Chesler, pp. 42–92. Office of New Jersey Heritage, Department of Environmental Protection, Trenton.

Marsh, Margaret
1989   From Separation to Togetherness: The Social Construction of Domestic Space in American Suburbs, 1840–1915. *Journal of American History* 76(2):506–27.

Miller, George L.
1991   A Revised Set of CC Index Values for Classification and Economic Scaling of English Ceramics from 1787 to 1880. *Historical Archaeology* 25(1):1–25.

New Jersey State Archives

1850–80   Agricultural Census for Saddle River Township, Bergen County, New Jersey. On file, New Jersey State Archives, Trenton.

Paterson Press Guardian

1912   Obituary of Henry Hopper. Notices, Book 6, 4 Dec. 1912.

Ryant, Carl

1988   Oral History and Business History. *Journal of American History* 75(2):560–66.

Schaffer, Daniel

1980   Lessons in Land Use: Radburn and the Regional Planning Association of America. In *Planned and Utopian Experiments: Four New Jersey Towns,* edited by Paul A. Stellhorn, pp. 53–74. New Jersey Historical Commission, Trenton.

The Shopper and News Beacon

1924–74   On file, Fair Lawn Public Library.

Stilgoe, John R.

1982   *Common Landscape of America, 1580 to 1845.* Yale University Press, New Haven.

1988   *Borderland: Origins of the American Suburb, 1820–1939.* Yale University Press, New Haven.

Van Valen, J. M.

1900   *History of Bergen County, New Jersey.* New York Publishing Company, New York.

Walker, A. H.

1876   *Atlas of Bergen County.* Published by C. C. Pease, successor to A. H. Walker. Reading Publishing House, Reading, Pennsylvania.

Westervelt, Francis A.

1923   *History of Bergen County, New Jersey, 1630–1923.* Lewis Publishing Company, New York.

Yentsch, Anne E.

1988   Legends, Houses, Families, and Myths: Relationships Between Material Culture and American Ideology. In *Documentary Archaeology in the New World,* edited by Mary C. Beaudry, pp. 5–19. Cambridge University Press, Cambridge.

10

Charleston Townhouses: Archaeology, Architecture, and the Urban Landscape, 1750–1850

Martha A. Zierden and Bernard L. Herman

The urban archaeology of Charleston spans the cultural ecology of artifice and nature, reflected in artifacts as inconspicuous as minor flora and as grand as the walled domestic compounds of the urban gentry. The artifacts of landscape formation in Charleston, as elsewhere, resulted from and included construction of public and private dwellings, functional and physical definition and segregation of activity areas (Herman 1989), physical changes to the terrain (Mrozowski 1987:3), and the allocation and regulation of shared resources, livestock maintenance, food procurement, and sanitary waste management (Calhoun et al. 1984; Fries 1977; Honerkamp and Council 1984; Leone et al. 1989; Mrozowski 1987; Ostrogorsky 1987; Reitz and Zierden 1991; Rosengarten et al. 1987; Trinkley 1989). The study of historical urban land use must consider the relationship between the social and symbolic functions of urban space and the reflection of those functions in the spatial, architectural, archaeological, and documentary records (Herman 1984; Mrozowski 1988:19; Rothschild 1985:163).

Although, to some extent, Charleston's historical landscape appears to be intact, its study involves documentary research, archaeological excavation at urban sites, and the analysis of standing structures. The archaeological data were drawn primarily from a series of excavations by The Charleston Museum. These excavation projects were undertaken intermittently since 1975 and under the purview of a research design since 1981. Close to twenty sites have been examined; the level of effort at these sites ranged from limited testing to data recovery. The evidence gained through field archaeology has been applied to the interpretation of standing structures. Similarly, the analyses of historical plats and probate inventories yield bodies of information that augment both the archaeological and architectural records. Read together, the archaeological, documentary, and architectural records reveal complex patterns. Each body of evidence provides specific insights into how and why the urban landscape has evolved in the ways it has. Each genre of historical evidence is limited by the intentions that gave it expression; not all forms of expressive culture were generated to the same purpose. What exists, however, is a vast body of information connected by the systemic relationships inherent in the communicative essence of community and culture. The challenge is to link systemic relationships with the physical processes of landscape formation.

The evidence reveals at least four systemically defined historical processes at work in the formation of the Charleston landscape. Each of these processes contributed to the physical definition of the urban terrain, as well as to city society and economics, and consisted, in turn, of multiple secondary processes. Mundane actions with intended results, such as earth moving and building, or with unconsidered consequences, including aspects of deforestation, refuse disposal, or animal slaughtering, signify the operation of broader, often related social and economic processes. Beginning with land clearing and moving toward urban household organization, the following categories constitute the processes of urban landscape formation:

1) Conversion: the alteration of the natural terrain and changes inflicted on fauna and flora through the appropriation and modification of native environmental features to cultural purposes. In its simplest sense, conversion represents the reduction of the natural world through human agency. Conversion entails such actions as clearing land for building, reducing timber to lumber, and filling marsh to create usable ground. Conversion also includes such tasks as dividing and naming land. In sum, it is the rendering of the natural world to cultural ends.

2) Accommodation: the modification of expressive behaviors to meet natural and cultural environmental limitations. Intemperate climate, scarce local resources, and unimprovable terrain present obstacles that cannot be overcome entirely by human agency. While people generally rely on conversion to realize landscape formation goals, they also accommodate themselves to environmental constraints. Such constraints are not always natural in origin. For example, the septic pollution of potable water sources and the rise in disease-bearing vermin populations are both products of the conversion process that are typically mediated by a combination of conversion and accommodation. Similarly, the need to express certain types of social relationships within a constricted setting requires accommodation.

3) Intensification: increased functional demands on limited urban lands. Intensification results in such phenomena as architectural infill (for example, converting open yards into building lots or building in the gaps between freestanding structures), repeated and rapid reutilization of urban land, and the multiple occupation of individual sites. Intensification may also lead to or result in functional transformations in urban land use such as the shift from domestic to industrial activities. This aspect of intensification involves secondary processes of segregation and specialization.

4) Regulation: the constant organization and reorganization of human space with two major dimensions. First, regulation entails the imposition of community standards, such as those related to fire prevention or household sanitation, on group and individual environments. Regulation in this sense implicitly accedes to the collective nature of the landscape. Second, regulation also refers to individually enacted landscape processes such as enclosure, domestic centralization, and privatization. These are all part of the broader category of actions taken to govern social interaction in the context of domestic relations and private property.

The goal of this chapter is to illustrate how these processes influenced the formation of Charleston's historical urban landscape between 1750 and 1850. Through the discussion of seven domestic sites, we will describe the larger urban landscape represented by the documentary and architectural records.

THE SITES

Archaeological research in Charleston, much of it done in compliance with state and federal laws, has encompassed a range of commercial, residential, public, and industrial sites, many of them multicomponent and multifunctional. Most of the sites are located in the densely occupied city core (figure 10.1). The sites most appropriate to the present landscape analysis are the residential townhouses. Seven excavated townhouse sites, first occupied in the late eighteenth century by middling merchants or elite planter-merchants, provide a solid data base for elucidating historical processes.

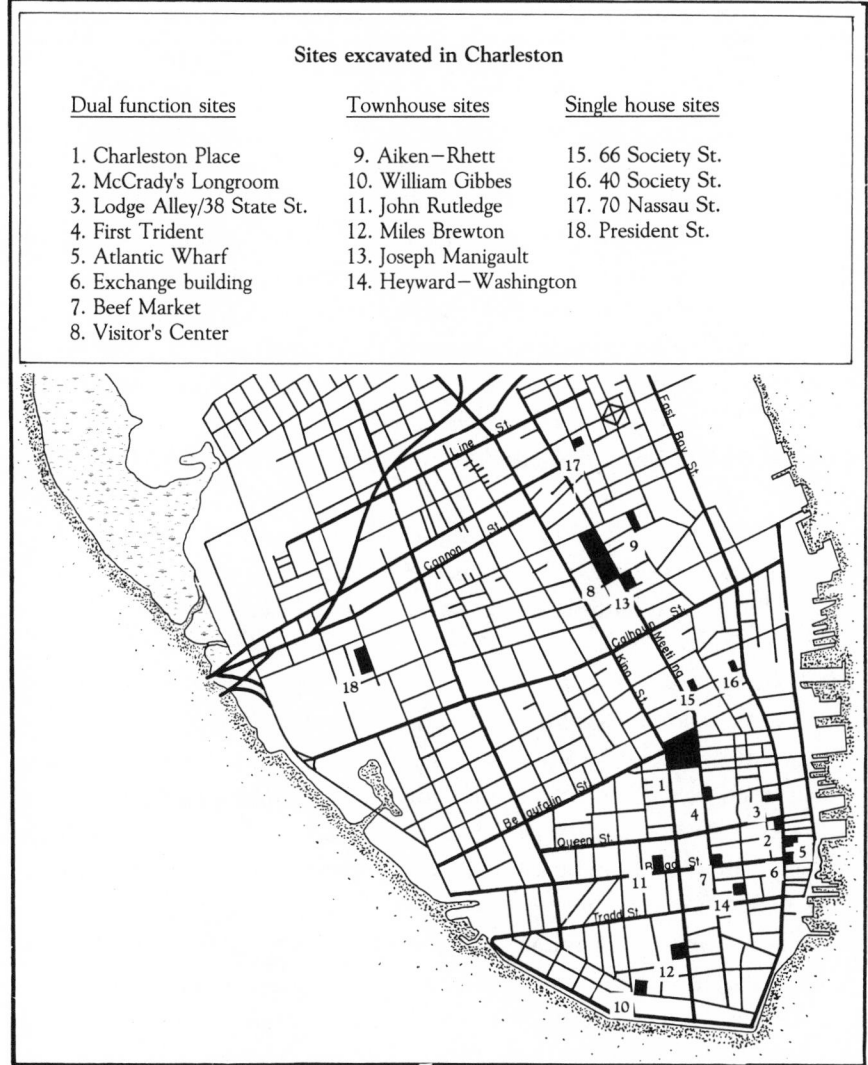

Sites excavated in Charleston

Dual function sites	Townhouse sites	Single house sites
1. Charleston Place	9. Aiken–Rhett	15. 66 Society St.
2. McCrady's Longroom	10. William Gibbes	16. 40 Society St.
3. Lodge Alley/38 State St.	11. John Rutledge	17. 70 Nassau St.
4. First Trident	12. Miles Brewton	18. President St.
5. Atlantic Wharf	13. Joseph Manigault	
6. Exchange building	14. Heyward–Washington	
7. Beef Market		
8. Visitor's Center		

Figure 10.1. Map of peninsular Charleston, showing the location of excavated sites.

The seven sites share several physical characteristics common to the general architectural character of the city. First, each property conforms to its historical property lines and contains original standing structures. These include a main house and a variety of outbuildings, making it possible to locate and assess the excavation units relative to other site features. Second, the retention of original, clearly marked property boundaries suggests that all refuse recovered was generated by the site occupants and was not discarded from other sources, a situation difficult to presume on other urban sites in Charleston and elsewhere (Garrow 1984; Zierden and Calhoun 1986). Third, each of the sites was owned and occupied by the same family, in contrast to urban rental property. The below-ground evidence parallels the architectural evidence; the clarity and integrity of the often complex archaeological record at these sites are relatively good. Their continuous use as residential properties to the present day facilitates study of the domestic evolution of the sites. Five of the sites were the townhouses of wealthy, influential, slaveholding families with large resident slave populations; two others were associated with nineteenth-century merchants considered middle class by Charleston standards (Smith 1987).

Discussing the sites as a single entity masks differences among them. Principally, the quantity, location, and purpose of archaeological excavation varied widely, though the data from each site were used to address similar research questions within a comparative framework. Three of the townhouse sites were first developed in the eighteenth century. John Rutledge, a lawyer, planter, and framer of the Constitution, erected his house in 1763 on a previously improved lot along the city's main thoroughfare. In the 1850s the house was purchased and remodeled by one of the city's wealthiest real estate investors, Thomas N. Gadsden. Limited testing (96.5 square feet) was conducted in 1988 in conjunction with restoration of the house as an inn. Five excavation units were located adjacent to the outbuildings and in the rear yard (Zierden and Grimes 1989).

William Gibbes commissioned his house in 1772 along the southern border of town. Gibbes was a successful merchant and factor, and his house has remained an urban gentry residence to the present day. Three units (75 square feet) were excavated in the center rear yard in 1986 prior to swimming pool construction by the present owners (Zierden et al. 1987).

The Miles Brewton house, built in 1769 by a wealthy merchant and slave trader, has remained in family hands as a residence. Excavations were conducted to explore the evolution of the property and to mitigate impacts to the site as the house and grounds underwent extensive renovation. Excavations exposed 491.25 square feet in two separate projects (1988 and 1990, respectively) (Zierden 1990); thirty-four excavation units were placed in all areas of the site, including the front yard, main house, workyard, and formal garden (figure 10.2).

Two additional townhouses, both located in Charleston Neck, a suburban area originally outside the city limit, were built in the early nineteenth century. The Aiken-Rhett house, built in 1817, was owned from 1820 to 1882 by the William Aiken family. Aiken was a wealthy businessman, planter, and politician, and an early investor in the South Carolina Railroad. The house passed from his descendants to The Charleston Museum, where it is operated as a historic house museum. Limited testing, confined to six units in the rear yard (225 square feet), was undertaken to assess the integrity of the archaeological record for listing in the National Register of Historic Places (Zierden, Calhoun, and Hacker 1986). The Joseph Manigault house, located two blocks away, was built as a townhouse for a planter

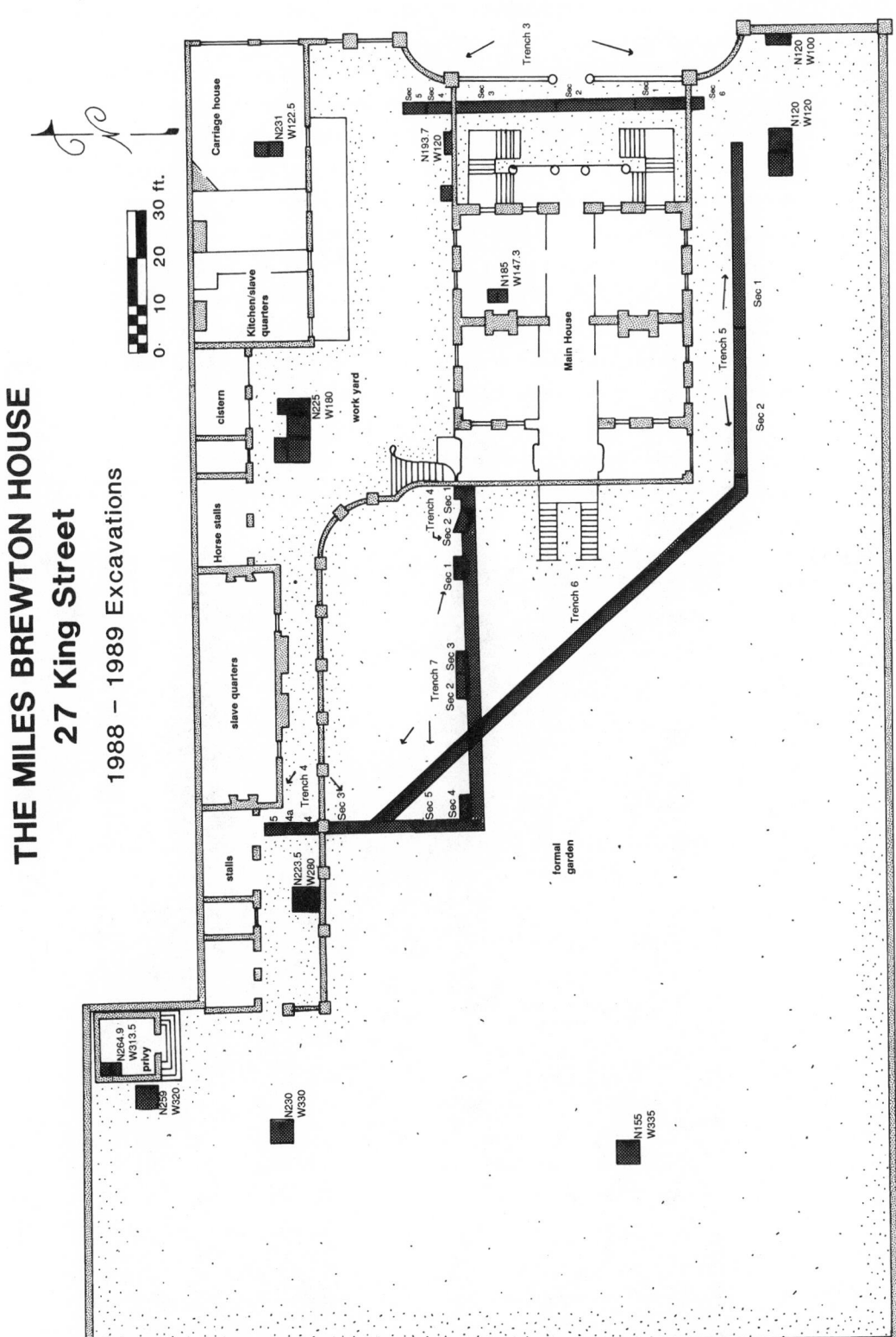

Figure 10.2. Site map of the Miles Brewton house, showing main house, outbuildings, and enclosing walls.

family in 1803. After its sale in 1852, the property suffered a series of detrimental uses, including sale and subdivision of portions of the yard and destruction of all outbuildings. These changes compromised major portions of the archaeological record. Testing, including ten units (167 square feet) in the vicinity of the main house, was conducted in 1990 to assist in the accurate restoration of the front facade and workyard (Zierden 1992).

The five elite townhouses share several features. With the exception of the Rutledge house, all were raised on previously unimproved lots in what were considered suburbs of the eighteenth- and early-nineteenth-century city. The dwellings are all urban mansions designed as variations on double-pile Georgian plans locally referred to as double houses (figures 10.3 and 10.4). Their polite, formal qualities extend to the geometrically genteel organization of yards and outbuildings. The spacious lots contained a number of specialized outbuildings, including, but not limited to, kitchens, stables, carriage houses, wells, privies, and slave quarters. Between thirteen and twenty slaves lived in these compounds along with the owner's family. The elite townhouses stand in visual, as well as physical, contrast to the middle-class sites. The latter are characterized by dwellings only one room wide (known in Charleston as single houses), constricted lots, and attenuated outbuildings combining multiple functions or sharing uses with neighbors along an adjoining property line.

Figure 10.3. The Heyward-Washington house, 1772, is a classic example of a Georgian double house. Collections of The Charleston Museum.

A. Dwelling House, two Stories with garret and cellar of wood and covered
   with Shingles on a brick foundation.
B. Kitchen and Wash room, two Stories of brick and covered with shingles
   with cellar.
C. Carriage house of wood.
D. Stable of wood.
E. Other offices and Out houses.
F. Garden.
G. Well and pump.
H. Houses on the adjoining lots of brick and covered with shingles.

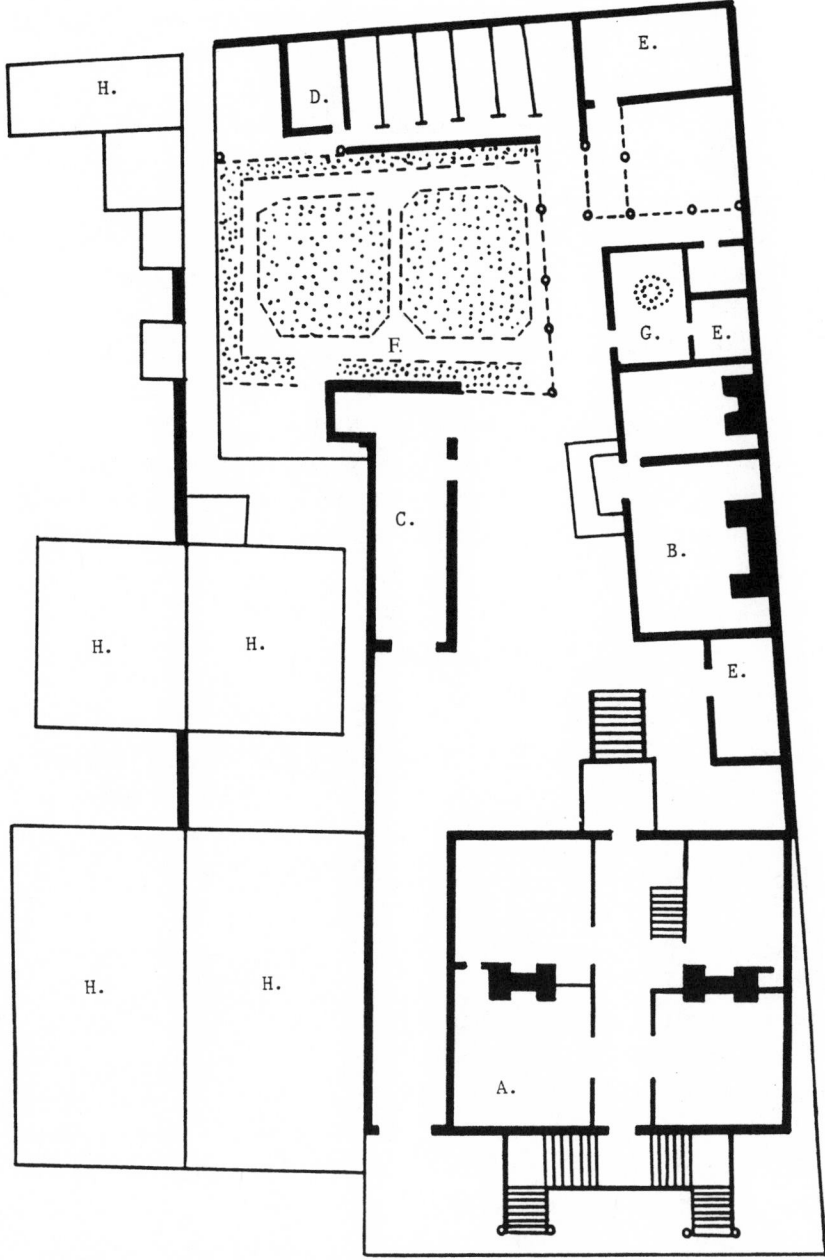

*Figure 10.4. Gabriel Manigault house and lot, East Bay Street, 1787. Built as a full Georgian "double house,"
the Manigault mansion complex included the full complement of domestic support buildings associated with
lowcountry plantations. Recorder of Deeds, Charleston, Book T-6, following p. 54. Redrawn by S. DeChard.*

In other Atlantic seaboard cities, residents of these houses might be considered lower-level members of the gentry. David Smith (1987) suggests that Charleston's particular economic history both contributed to and reflected its distorted class structure, which was characterized by a peculiarly underdeveloped middle class. The pervasive presence of African-American slave labor and resulting stiff competition from "low cost high skilled slave mechanics" (Smith 1987:20) stifled the development of the white working class and middle class. Even moderately successful small proprietors often employed slaves. Those who achieved wealth reinvested their capital in land and slaves, economically and socially styling themselves as urban planters rather than as merchants or industrialists.

The Ansonborough residents represent these struggling small-time city planters and minor merchants. Two archaeologically tested "middle-class" sites, at 66 and 40 Society Street, are located in a late-eighteenth-century residential suburb ravaged by fire in 1838. The small lots contain brick single houses built in 1839 and outbuildings with consolidated functions. Both properties were owned by, or rented to, a series of merchants and artisans, most of whom experienced financial difficulties during their tenure. Testing was conducted at these sites in 1987 and 1989, respectively. Five units (54.4 square feet) were dug at 66 Society Street and one unit (15 square feet) at 40 Society Street; both excavations were located in the center of the small rear yards, at the request of Historic Charleston Foundation, prior to property renovations (Zierden 1989; Zierden et al. 1988). As a whole, excavations at these sites produced detailed stratigraphic profiles and sequences; pollen, floral, and faunal samples; cultural materials from a variety of functional and temporal strata; and architectural remains. Each class of data contributed to the elucidation of historical process. When "read" in conjunction with documentary and architectural "texts," the townhouse sites enable us to construct a "narrative" about the processes of urban landscape formation.

CONVERSION

Conversion of the native terrain, flora, and fauna of what would become Charleston began with the arrival of the first European and African settlers and the mapping and division of the land. The imposition of an abstract geometric grid on the native terrain represents the obvious first step of the conversion process. The urban plan of Charleston, known as the "Grand Modell" (figure 10.5), consisted of a large central square formed at the intersection of the two principal thoroughfares that effectively divided the city into four quadrants (Smith and Smith 1917:22). The Grand Modell itself incorporated an even older fortification plan, parts of which remain evident in the present configuration of streets. The most significant features of the Grand Modell reveal it to be part and parcel of the so-called Georgian "mindset" widely discussed in vernacular architecture studies (Deetz 1977; Glassie 1975) and architectural history (Reed 1983). In the development of city form, Charleston's Grand Modell stood as an interchangeable element in the larger context of British provincial town planning throughout the Atlantic basin in the eighteenth-century age of mercantilism (Corfield 1982).

The idea of a mathematically regular form superimposed over the natural topography confronted and organized the irregularities of nature. The resulting product was a city form incorporating all the qualities of bilaterally symmetrical design and its attendant values of social hierarchy, political authority, and centralized economic power. Affluent builders, such

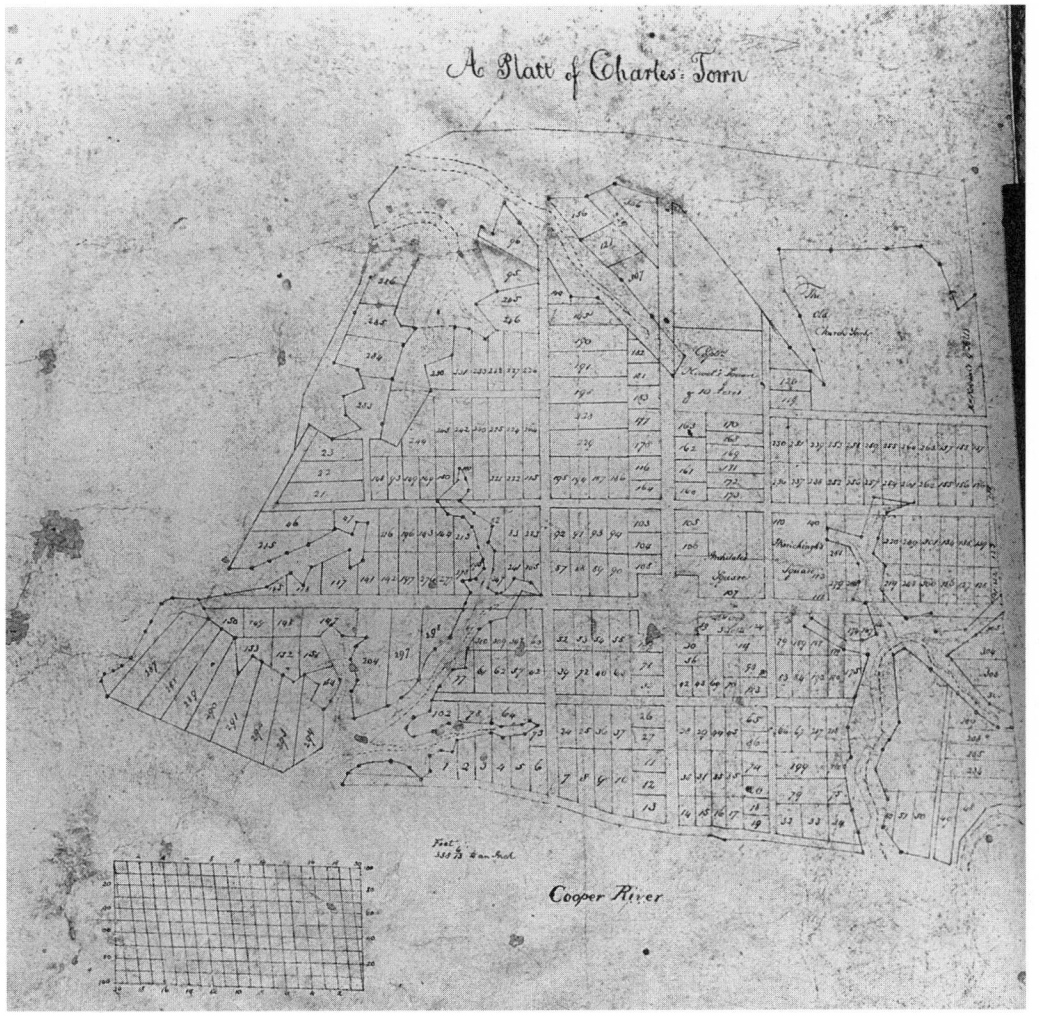

Figure 10.5. The earliest surviving copy of the Grand Modell. Courtesy of the South Carolina Historical Society.

as those associated with the sites discussed here, developed their houselots within the grid; they often did so by replicating the aesthetics and politics of geometry within the more intimate but no less public domestic spaces they inhabited. The external grid of the street with all of its prescribed passages and landmarks resonated in the plans and internal hierarchies of Charleston townhouses.

As the Grand Modell filled and its occupants divided and subdivided their lots, other property holders acquired lands along the edge of the city. Plats were drawn and the urban fabric extended outward. Property maps for early Charleston suburbs typically illustrate lesser grids of streets and building lots laid over streams, wetlands, and pre-existing plantations. Sometimes these ancillary grids continued the old street patterns, relentlessly pushing on with a geometrically inspired implacability constrained only by the rivers forming the peninsula upon which the city was founded. Elsewhere, new additions to the city core moved off at odd angles, all the while adhering to the geometrical regularity characteristic of the larger plan. The specific limitations of the local native environment, which would affect the reality of Charleston's urban aspect, did not impede the vision of the first city planners. Streams and tidal ditches were topographical nuisances to be filled and developed as city growth intensified.

The imposition of the grid represented only one early step in the conversion process. Once the surveyors had substituted an academic, mathematical reality for the natural one, landowners and city residents still had to develop the parcels that constituted the greater city form. The malleability of the native landscape in this process cannot be overestimated. Building streets, cutting native timber and scrub, filling marshes and creeks, fencing lots, and erecting buildings were actions that transformed landscape into cityscape. The key elements in the conversion process were traversing, bounding, and improving the landscape. While we observe these elements in the pattern of streets and squares as well as in the built environment, it is archaeological data—particularly the palynological record—that provide the most compelling evidence of the chronology and degree of conversion.

Ongoing analysis of the botanical remains, seeds, and wood charcoal at Charleston sites provides scattered, albeit tantalizing, clues to environmental change. The analysis of pollen recovered at the John Rutledge and Miles Brewton houses revealed changes relative to those sites and to the surrounding environs (Reinhard 1989, 1990). Zones predating construction of the John Rutledge house (ca. 1763) contained pollen derived from a hardwood forest environment, with a low level of weeds and grasses that colonize a disturbed, or cleared, environment. The above zone, when interpreted with those associated with Rutledge's occupation in the 1770–80s, revealed a deforested area in which disturbance plants largely replaced forest vegetation. Because the pollen spectrum can reflect arboreal species from as far away as a few miles, the data suggest environmental changes more widespread than those caused by the construction of a house on a single lot (Karl Reinhard 1988, personal communication). Analysis of nine samples from the Miles Brewton site produced a more varied and complex picture, but the basic trends noted for the Rutledge site stand. The location of the Brewton site next to a large marshy area that was gradually filled between 1750 and 1820 is also reflected in the pollen spectrum. The dramatic decline in tree species associated with moist areas suggests the draining and/or filling of low-lying areas in Charleston. Through analysis of seeds, coal, and wood charcoal, Michael Trinkley has also found evidence of deforestation and the filling of low-lying areas, as well as increased amounts of disturbed or cleared land colonized by weedy species in the late eighteenth century (Trinkley 1989).

The lower levels dating from construction of the John Rutledge house contained two wetland weedy plants, bulrush (*Scirpus* spp.) and bedstraw (*Galium* spp.), as well as an "aggressive" colonizer of disturbed areas, chenopod (*Chenopodium* spp.) (Trinkley 1989). The First Trident site, a marshy lot filled in the eighteenth century to create commercial real estate, contained other colonizers common to vacant ground: vetch (*Vicia* sp.), wildbean *(Stropostyles helvoia),* Paspalum (*Paspalum* sp.), Fabaceae, and Brassicaceae. These families consist of weedy plants that fruit in the late summer or fall. The bulk of these were associated with a 1790s zone (Trinkley 1983). Evidently, dramatic deforestation of the Charleston area occurred between 1760 and 1800. This is further reflected in rising prices for firewood during that period (Weir 1983:44). The conversion of native timber for fuel and building materials resulted in the widespread deforestation of the surrounding countryside with obvious palynological effects.

The eighteenth-century buildings of Charleston bear out the palynological evidence and provide specific correlates to the archaeological record. If we look at the incidence of building activity, we see that the architectural development of Charleston, as with every other American landscape, occurred in cycles. This phenomenon can be traced to a variety of sources ranging from broad-based economic changes to shifting attitudes about the physical organization of domestic life. The first general building cycle associated with Charleston and the process of conversion is characterized by buildings that retained stylistic ties to the trans-Atlantic mercantile community of predominantly British provincial towns. While African, French, Dutch, and German influences were present and clearly affected elements of building style and taste, the basic visual quality of the domestic architecture in Charleston and other American ports up to the mid-eighteenth century remained consistent with the vernacular building traditions found throughout the English-speaking towns and cities of the Atlantic basin. These building forms included the neoclassical city mansions belonging to wealthy merchants, a kind found from the Carolina lowcountry to the seaports of northern New England and Great Britain (Bold 1990; Smith 1983). There were also minor rowhouses, one or two rooms in plan and two to three stories in height; commercial residences with ground-floor, street-front shops and backlot and upper-story living quarters; and freestanding dwellings built in the local idiom of vernacular farmhouses. All these forms made Charleston visually sensible not only in the general context of the Atlantic world but also in the regional context of Carolina society and material life. That coherence was achieved even as the native environment was leveled and filled. If we reduce the conversion process to an equation of paired oppositions, we can note quite simply and concretely that the landscape that was discovered raw and natural ended up domesticated and refined.

ACCOMMODATION

Vertebrate faunal assemblages from Charleston sites most clearly reflect accommodation to local resources. A dependence on beef, as well as utilization of a variety of wild species indigenous to the local environment, characterized subsistence practice in Charleston. Urban citizens relied more heavily on domestic fauna—mammals and birds—than did their rural neighbors. This may be due to the function of the market in the urban setting, making domestic meats more readily available (Reitz 1986). Many types of wild game would have been more difficult for the average urban citizen to obtain (Reitz 1987). The result is that native game may have assumed a distinctive urban social prestige. Wild game, the stuff of rural subsistence, in an urban setting may well have been the cosmopolitan delicacies of urban gourmets.

Evidence clearly indicates the maintenance of livestock within urban domestic compounds, despite the presence of a specialized meat market at the corner of Meeting and Broad Streets. Analysis of beef element distribution between residential sites, markets, dumps, and places of public entertainment suggests that owners of public facilities depended heavily on the market for their meats. In contrast, much of the cattle bone found on residential properties resulted from on-site slaughter. Significantly, home butchering may have been more prevalent on elite sites (Reitz and Zierden 1991). Documentary sources suggest that the maintenance of livestock, particularly cattle, persisted into the twentieth century. Occupants of the Aiken-Rhett and Miles Brewton townhouse sites are known to have maintained cattle in addition to poultry. The presence of resident livestock and domestic fowl paints a portrait of many Charleston sites as urban plantations accommodating and combining the mentalité of both city and country life.

One of the most striking aspects of accommodation involved the fit of plantation and urban mercantile architectural forms onto the deep narrow lots of the city. By the late eighteenth century, three building forms dominated Charleston's domestic architecture: single houses, double houses, and paired houses. Of the three, the building type most closely associated with the streetscapes of Charleston was the single house: one room wide and two deep with the narrow gable end fronting the street and a piazza facing the yard. While one architectural historian suggests that "single houses were sensitive compromises between the public need for urban density and the private desire for domestic seclusion" (Severens 1988:7), the actual genesis of this building form is far more complex and illustrates the process of accommodation.

The origins of the single house can be traced to several forces—each representing a specific set of needs ranging from the business of interaction to the social organization of slavery. The single house at the end of the eighteenth century served more than just the functions of privacy recognized by Severens. In the earlier decades of the colonial period, the domestic fabric of the city's architecture had been considerably more diverse and more in keeping with a broader trans-Atlantic English tradition of provincial ports and market towns. The need for buildings combining commerce and residence existed within a diverse architectural repertoire. The most common solution possessed a street-level, one-room shop with a general living space behind and "best" room and chambers above. In mid-Atlantic cities, for instance, pairs of dwellings with shared passageways to the backyard composed the majority of lower- and middle-class townhouses. In Charleston, the earliest generation of single houses accommodated commercial and domestic functions. The narrow street elevation was fitted with a sidewalk-level door into the business premises while a second, internally placed entry gave admittance into the house itself. Although details of appearance diverge from English and other American seaport parallels, the actual disposition of public and private rooms is remarkably similar (Giles 1990; Laithwaite 1984). Even in newly rebuilt towns of the early eighteenth century such as Gravesend, sited on the Thames downriver from London, where builders erected abutting houses they maintained the practice of segregated entries into the commercial and domestic areas of the house. Builders in late-eighteenth-century Philadelphia similarly designed their houses to accommodate dual functions.

Late-eighteenth-century surveyors' plats of Charleston sites clearly illustrate the commercial component influencing single house design. A King Street plat shows the buildings constructed on two deep, narrow lots fronting King Street just above Blackbird Alley (figure 10.6). The architectural organization of each lot included a major street-front building with a ground-floor, front commercial room, and rear and second-story living quarters. The plan of the southernmost of the two King Street buildings contained two spaces: the front business room with direct street access and a rear room that served as either an extended counting room or, more likely, as a dining room. Access into this space was gained either from the front room or through a side door opening off of a narrow side yard and driveway. Adjacent to this three-story structure stood a two-story wood combination house and counting house. Although the plan of the northernmost building reflects the center-passage form we most often associate with the Charleston single house, the pattern of curbside access into the front room and entry into the back room obtained either internally across a stair passage or from a side yard represents the accommodation of commercial and residential functions into the architectural improvements made on Charleston's city lots. The same is true of the backlots, both of which are fitted out with kitchens, washhouses, and other structures.

Charleston backlot development, and the growing preference for single houses, suggests that the process of accommodation drew on a second source. For all its urbanity and the close commercial and cultural contacts with Europe and the West Indies, Charleston stood as a gateway to the plantation landscapes of its own hinterland. The dominant architectural expressions of the lowcountry plantation gentry followed a predilection for large, modish Georgian houses placed in contrived settings, flanked by dependencies, and served by a multitude of lesser buildings ranging from kitchens to slave quarters (Upton 1986:206–8). The great plantation owners were often the great city house proprietors, and the most resonant theme for the organization of the urban environment drew on images of plantation living and architecture. Others have characterized the architectural compounds of Charleston gentry as urban plantations (Wade 1964), but the precise architectural relationship between hinterland and downtown has never been explored. Still, if we strip the lowcountry plantations of all their agricultural buildings, what remains is an architectural core defined by service spaces such as kitchens, washhouses, quarters, dooryards, and gardens. This set of architectural functions is fully represented in a plat of Thomas Bradford's Church Street lot (figure 10.7). The big house with its gable to the street shows its formal public face, while functions of increasing dirtiness—descending from kitchen to privy—range back along a workyard. Behind and to the side of the entry and workyards Bradford finished his lot with a large garden gridded into squares and traversed by paths.

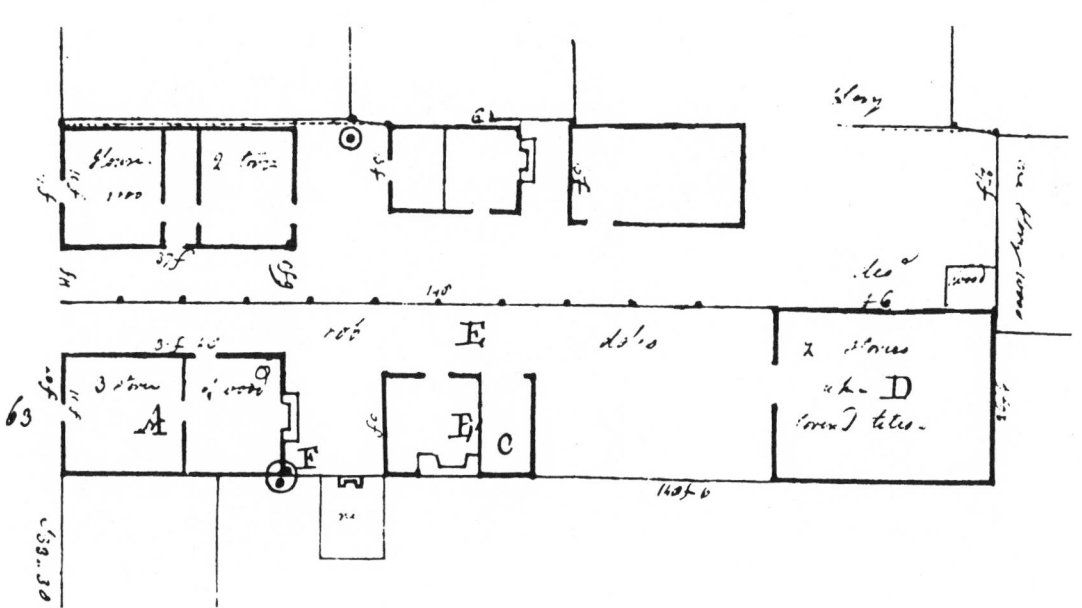

Figure 10.6. Plan of lots and buildings on King Street above Blackbird Alley, 1799. The two houses illustrated in the surveyor's drawing clearly indicate the existence of gable doorways opening onto King Street. While the uppermost house follows the plan of a center-passage single house, the lower dwelling reflects a lesser known two-room arrangement. McCrady Plat Collection, South Carolina Department of Archives and History, microfilm reel 3180, plat 536.

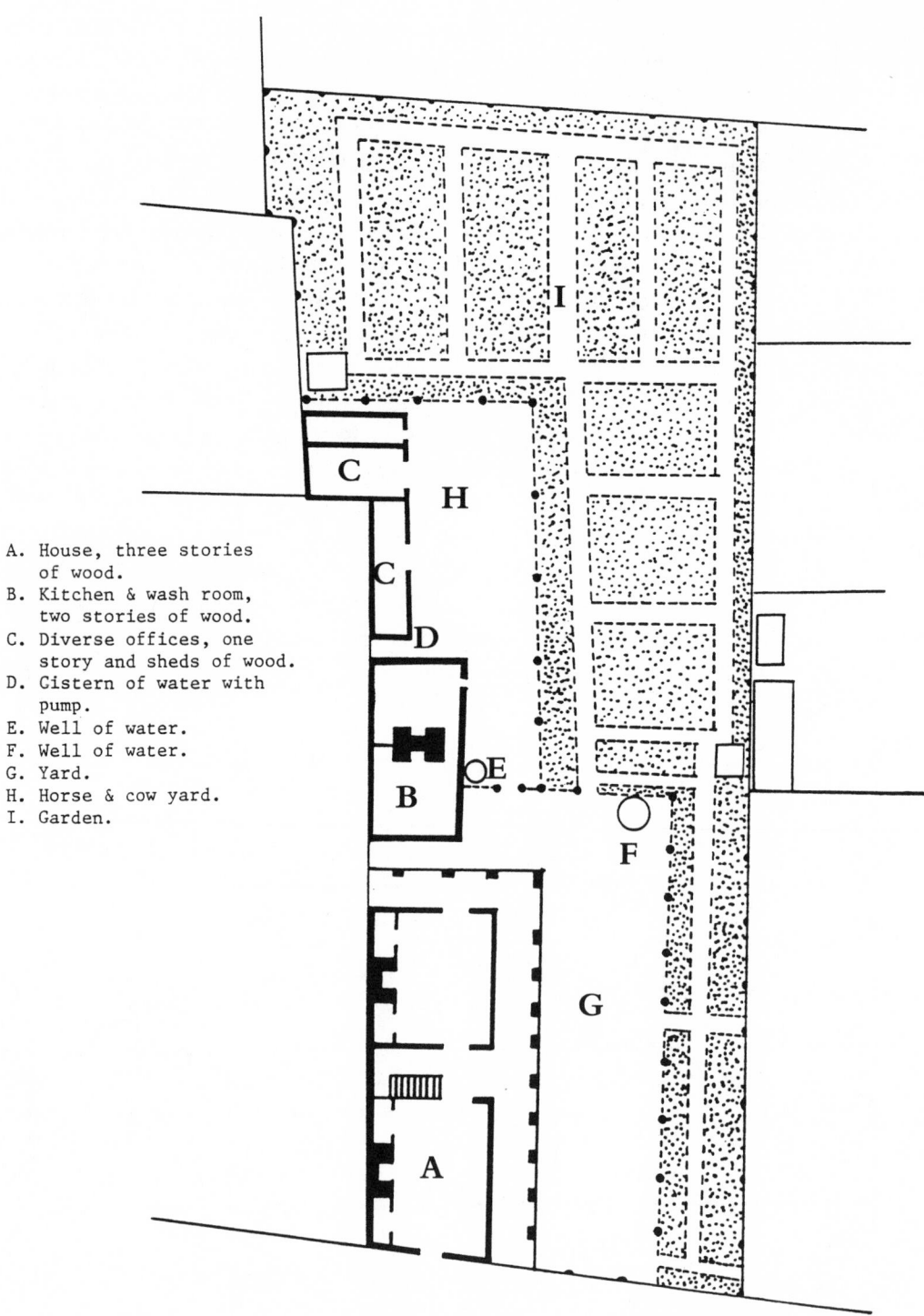

A. House, three stories of wood.
B. Kitchen & wash room, two stories of wood.
C. Diverse offices, one story and sheds of wood.
D. Cistern of water with pump.
E. Well of water.
F. Well of water.
G. Yard.
H. Horse & cow yard.
I. Garden.

No. 76 Church Street

Figure 10.7. Thomas Bradford house and lot, Church Street, 1802. The Bradford complex contained the architectural and spatial elements of a well-developed single-house lot. Recorder of Deeds, Charleston, Book I-7, following p. 39. Redrawn by S. DeChard.

Bradford's house, like the two on King Street, contained a ground-floor, front commercial space or office. Access into the house was gained either through the front (business) or via one of two routes into the back (household). Visitors to the household gained admittance from the street onto a piazza and from there into an entry passage or they walked around the back gable and entered the dining room and pantry. They could also arrive by carriage or horse, turn into the yard, dismount, and then step up onto the piazza. Others, whose business was not with the big house, passed beneath the gaze of the house residents and stopped at the kitchen or passed through a gate into the rear workyard containing washhouse, sheds, and the privies. Of particular note are the access points into Bradford's formal garden. The garden, which covered more than half the area of the lot, could be entered only by one of three gates—each of which opened onto the house and dooryard. The garden, which fronted the quarters and other backbuildings, was kept separate by a low fence. The overall effect evinced all the hierarchical relationships and segmented experiences of the backlot dwellers that characterized eighteenth-century southern landscapes from Maryland through the Carolinas (Isaac 1982; Upton 1986).

Thus, the Charleston single house stands as a solution accommodating two very different architectural agendas: the commercial needs of urban ports and market towns and the cultivated manners and affectations of elite, white, lowcountry plantation culture. Peter Coclanis has characterized the single house with its gable end to the street as representing a type of withdrawal from the public eye (Coclanis 1985). While there is more truth to this characterization in the mid-1800s than in earlier decades, it fails to hold up when we look at Charleston in the context of a larger urban culture. Single houses were essential to the organization and success of the Charleston landscape. On the one hand, they created private processional displays in the public eye within the confines of congested lots; on the other, they provided for the aggressive transactions of the mercantile world. Accommodation—the modification of cultural expression to meet a full range of environmental limitations—was enacted in the synthesis of urban mercantilism and plantation society within the constricted confines of the city's lots.

INTENSIFICATION

As the city developed and grew through the early nineteenth century, the process of landscape intensification increasingly characterized the organization and textures of Charleston. Architecturally, intensification resulted in a number of highly visible cityscape formation processes, especially enclosure and infill. Enclosure refers specifically to the construction of private barriers in the city that not only blocked and channeled physical access into private compounds but also increasingly denied visual access. Enclosure with wooden fences in the eighteenth century gave way to brick walls rising six feet and more above grade in the nineteenth century.

The Miles Brewton house embodies a highly developed example of urban enclosure that increasingly characterized the mid-nineteenth-century streetscapes of Charleston (figure 10.8). The front of the house, elevated on an above-ground basement, is separated from the street by eight-foot brick walls and a wrought-iron gate. The *chevaux de frise* (a coil of spiked wrought iron) was added to the gate after the Denmark Vesey slave insurrection of 1822. Further, the front entrance is separated from the side yards by equally imposing brick walls. A visitor approaching the house may only advance as far as the front portico, where he or she is visible from the house, yard, and street. Excavations of builder's trenches revealed that these flanking walls were added in the 1820–30s. Further, close examination of the brickwork indicates the solid brick wall along the front sidewalk replaced a more open brick-and-wrought-iron fence. Based on the discovery of a well-defined postmold and posthole beneath this wall, it appears that the brick-and-wrought-iron fence replaced a more informal wood post-and-rail fence (figure 10.9) (Zierden 1990).

Thus, the archaeological and architectural research at the Brewton House suggests that this model evolved through the eighteenth and nineteenth centuries. Likewise, renovation of the Aiken-Rhett compound in the 1850s incorporated elements of an earlier kitchen and stable, with extensive and stylish modernization to the privies and enlarged slave apartments, "Gothic" livestock sheds, and an eight-foot-high brick wall. Additional archaeological evidence of renovations includes large pits filled with construction rubble often containing datable artifacts (Zierden 1990; Zierden, Calhoun, and Hacker 1986).

The construction of brick walls paralleled the growing practice of siting single houses front to back so that the view from the piazza of one house looked to the near windowless rear wall of the next. The necessity for stair windows and the etiquette of urban enclosure

Figure 10.8. Front view of the Miles Brewton house, showing front entrance, wrought-iron fence, side-enclosing walls, and (right) second floor of kitchen/slave quarters in the workyard. Photo by Terry Richardson. Collections of The Charleston Museum.

Figure 10.9. Posthole/ postmold beneath the brick wall between the formal garden and workyard at the Miles Brewton house. Note that the soils of the postmold are present within the brick foundation. Evidence for repair of the brick wall is visible above the postmold.

gave rise to so-called "north wall manners" that required occupants and neighbors to look neither out nor in the landing window.

A plat for a row of Meeting Street properties in Ansonborough reveals the typical early-nineteenth-century arrangement of crowded backbuildings and walled lots. Significant components of these deep and narrow lots are the fenced gardens noted at the rear of each lot. These fenced and walled gardens sited as far as possible from the street express the enclosed aspect of the Charleston cityscape (figure 10.10). While blocks of single-house elevations front the street, the backlots consist of a green and private core. Although the interior of the block is green, it too is made up of a series of gardens visually and physically screened from one another. The overall effect is one of intimate and private open-air settings situated in the segmented landscape of the urban core. In essence, back gardens provided secluded spaces for private promenades; they created private spaces for what, in other cities, constituted aspects of public behavior enacted through personal display and emulation. An 1813 survey for a Queen Street property clearly shows the extent to which the enclosed aspect of Charleston houselots could be maintained (figure 10.11). At the street stood a two-story wooden house with back kitchen, privy, and yard. A second complex occupied the backlot behind the first and consisted of a similar set of buildings. Each of the two dwelling groups possessed a well-defined yard and was separated front to back by a brick wall. The hindmost of the two complexes incorporated a separate fenced garden at the very rear. Access to the two lots was gained through side-by-side entries into passages or driveways opening onto Queen Street and separated from each other by a fence.

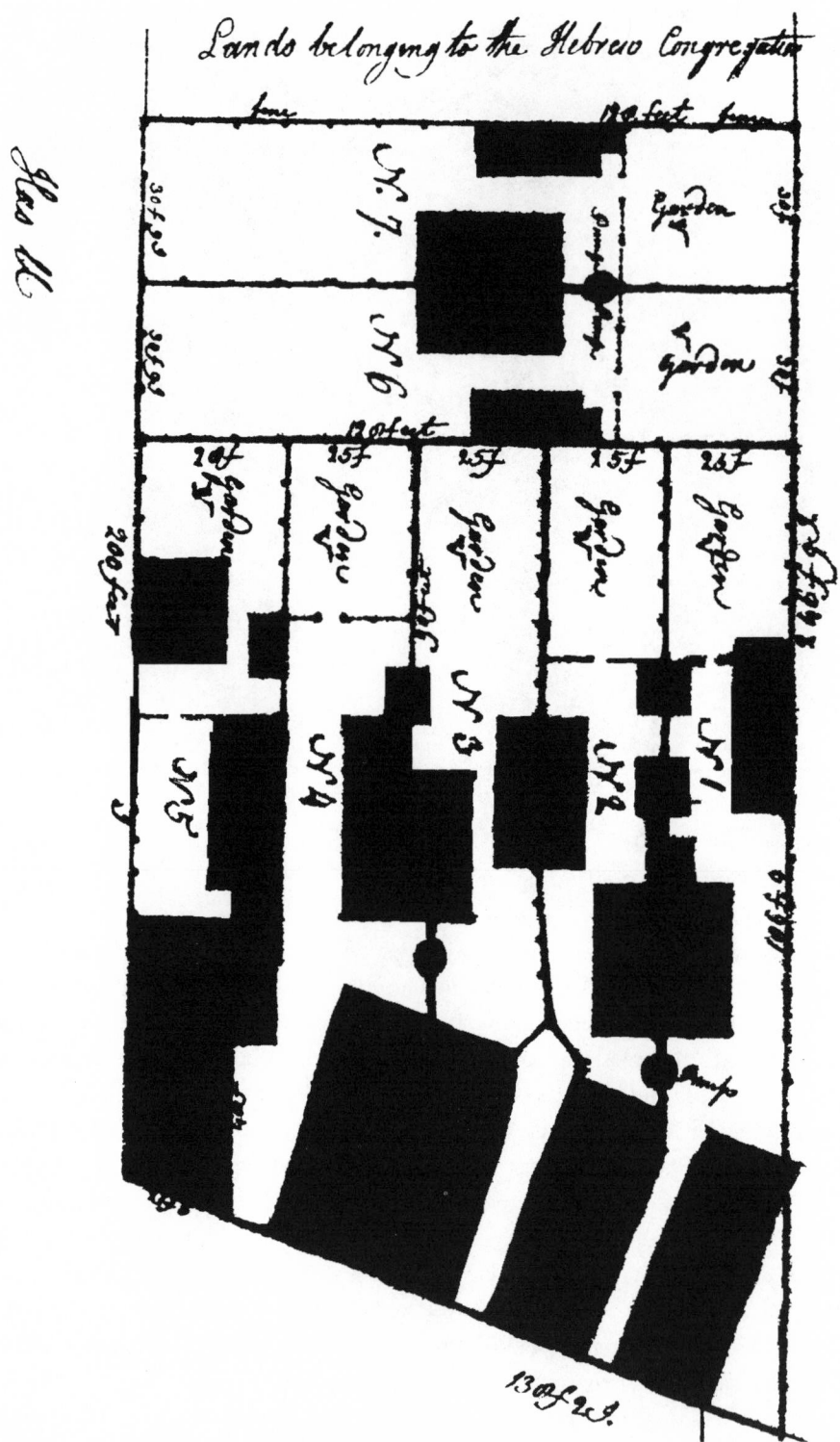

Figure 10.10. Lot plans for Ansonborough, Meeting, and Hasell Streets, 1802. Clearly rendered in this survey of seven lots are the gardens situated at the back of each property. Each garden is fenced off from the domestic compound located behind the house. McCrady Plat Collection, South Carolina Department of Archives and History, microfilm reel 3195, plat 182.01.

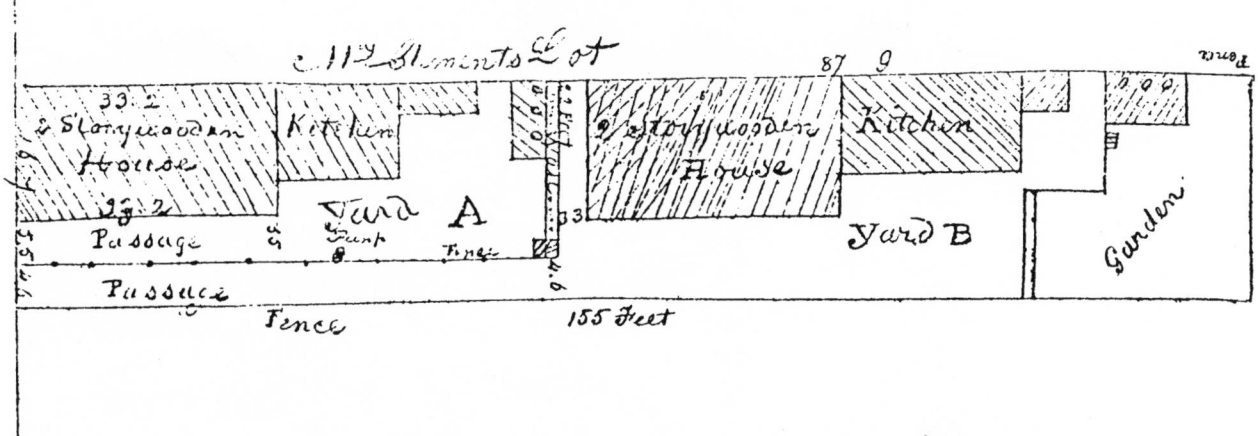

Figure 10.11. Queen Street, 1813. James McDowall's property was developed with two single-house complexes situated behind the other. Side-by-side passages divided by a fence led from the street to the yard. Each of the two-story wooden houses possessed an attached kitchen as well as privy along the rear property line. Note that the rear house and lot includes a garden—an amenity missing from the front lot. Recorder of Deeds, Charleston, Book E-8, following p. 455.

Intensification also produced clear archaeological evidence for lot fencing and walling as well as yard paving. The enclosure of the urban compound is paralleled in the paving of the workyards, following intensive refuse disposal in those areas. At the Miles Brewton house, refuse disposal was concentrated in the workyard adjacent to the outbuildings from the time of the initial occupation of the house (figure 10.12). Over the next 75 years, 2.5 feet of refuse accumulated in this area. The lowest zone contained some domestic refuse and large brick fragments in a matrix of mixed sand, reflecting the construction of the house and outbuildings. This zone contained evidence of an outdoor hearth, full of the debris of social activity, such as pipe stems and wine bottle fragments. This hearth may predate Brewton's occupation of the lot or may be associated with Brewton's resident slaves. The overlying layers of brown sand accumulated in a series of sheet deposits and small trash pits. Associated with these deposits were flecks of charcoal, large quantities of animal bone, and domestic artifacts of all types, including ceramics, glass, and personal items. Most of these materials were very fragmented, suggesting heavy traffic and trampling. The faunal assemblage contained bones that were rodent- or dog-gnawed, suggesting that following their casual disposal they lay on the ground surface long enough to be tasted by urban foragers. Vermin species were also recovered from these soils. Additionally, the soil matrices contained oyster shells and building debris—primarily brick and mortar. The qualities of these soils imply intensive refuse disposal and heavy use (Zierden 1990).

The stratigraphy in the workyard contrasts with that of the garden. There, a large quantity of artifacts dating from the 1770s was deliberately tilled into the planting beds. Unlike the workyard materials, these were large, with many broken *in situ* or reconstructable vessels, and were deposited in a relatively short time period. The animal bones were also relatively intact. This deliberate deposit was designed to enrich the soil and improve drainage (William

Figure 10.12. Stratigraphy of the Miles Brewton courtyard.

Kelso 1990, personal communication). Following the initial deposit, only occasional sherds were cast into the garden with the edges of this defined space being the exception.

Refuse disposal in the workyards reached a "critical mass" in the early 1800s. In the Miles Brewton courtyard, the upper zones of refuse were first covered with irregular lenses of tabby (lime and crushed oyster shell) mortar and then finally paved with brick and slate. Datable artifacts indicate that the paving occurred around 1840. Refuse was then disposed of elsewhere on the site or carted off-site. The total accumulation of soil in the workyard for the next 150 years amounted to six inches or less. The post-1840 soils primarily contained architectural debris with relatively little kitchen or organic refuse (Zierden 1990). The paving of the Miles Brewton workyard was far from an isolated event. The work spaces behind the Rutledge and Aiken-Rhett houses were also paved in the 1840s–50s (Zierden and Grimes 1989; Zierden, Calhoun, and Hacker 1986). Similarly, numerous early-nineteenth-century plats depicting properties in the more congested neighborhoods of the city clearly label paved yards.

Very little post-1840s refuse was recovered from the Gibbes and Rutledge sites, and later deposits at the Brewton and Aiken-Rhett houses were confined to secondarily used features such as privies and building foundations. Whenever possible, refuse disposal was concentrated near the outbuildings. The rear yards of the Aiken-Rhett and Miles Brewton sites, a workyard and formal garden respectively, were virtually free of refuse (Zierden 1990;

Zierden, Calhoun, and Hacker 1986). The more constricted Rutledge yard revealed some refuse in the center of the yard; the artifacts were basically the same type and size but the stratigraphy was less than half the depth at the kitchen building and contained fewer and smaller sherds (Zierden and Grimes 1989). The problem of refuse disposal was even more critical on smaller lots like those at 66 and 40 Society Street. Here lack of space precluded separation of a workyard and garden. Excavations in the centers of these rear yards revealed a complex and congested combination of zones and large trash pits dating from the first half of the nineteenth century (Zierden 1989; Zierden et al. 1988).

An 1810 surveyor's plat for a group of four tenements on Meeting Street, adjacent to the courthouse square, illustrates the practices of walling and paving the workyards behind the house (figure 10.13). Each of the three-story brick houses possessed a rear yard of nearly fourteen hundred square feet, over half of which was covered by backbuildings, including kitchens, quarters, offices, and necessaries. The remaining 47 percent of the yard area was paved and visually screened from its neighbors to the rear and sides by division walls and outbuildings. A second example from the core of the city clearly delineates these properties. John Duncan's three-story, street-front building includes an open, ground-floor commercial room and upper-story living apartments (figure 10.14). A covered passage leads from curbside to a paved backyard furnished with brick sheds, "kitchen & wash room" with slave quarters above, and water cistern and privies located adjacent to each other. At the very rear of the yard stood a "store 2 & 1/2 Stories with cellars of brick cover'd with tiles." In the structural organization of yards in the city, Duncan's commercial premises filled the area occupied by the back garden on other lots with a warehouse 91 feet long and spanning the full width of the 25-foot-wide property. The comparison to a single house lot, like Samuel Prioleau's on Church Street, is particularly striking because the three functional zones of the property are so clearly revealed: street front and house, domestic yard and backbuildings, and back garden (or, in Duncan's case, back warehouse) (figure 10.15). The creation of paved yards and enclosed lots in the context of regimented functional zones represents a theme we will return to in our discussion of the regulation process. Lots like John Duncan's typically represent long-term site occupation where various backbuildings are added to the complex and other buildings are modified and improved.

A second formation process in the urban landscape is that of infill. As part of the intensification process, infill resulted in the creation of even more congested urban lots. Behind both single and double houses, auxiliary structures were arranged within a fenced or walled compound. Slave quarters, kitchen, stables, well at mid-lot, and privy in a rear corner were essential elements of the urban plantation compound. The maintenance of gardens and livestock required additional features. While variation in the size, content, and arrangement of these structures existed, they nonetheless were considered basic functional components for urban life and were present in some form. The support structures were often aligned along one or both walls to the rear of the house, and the working yard typically was segregated from formal gardens.

By the 1830s, Charleston townhouse owners increasingly crammed their backlots with greater numbers of backbuildings. The most common practice involved adding an increasing number of functionally specific types of domestic support structures. One of the most complete examples of this house-centered infill strategy was a house on Coming Street platted in

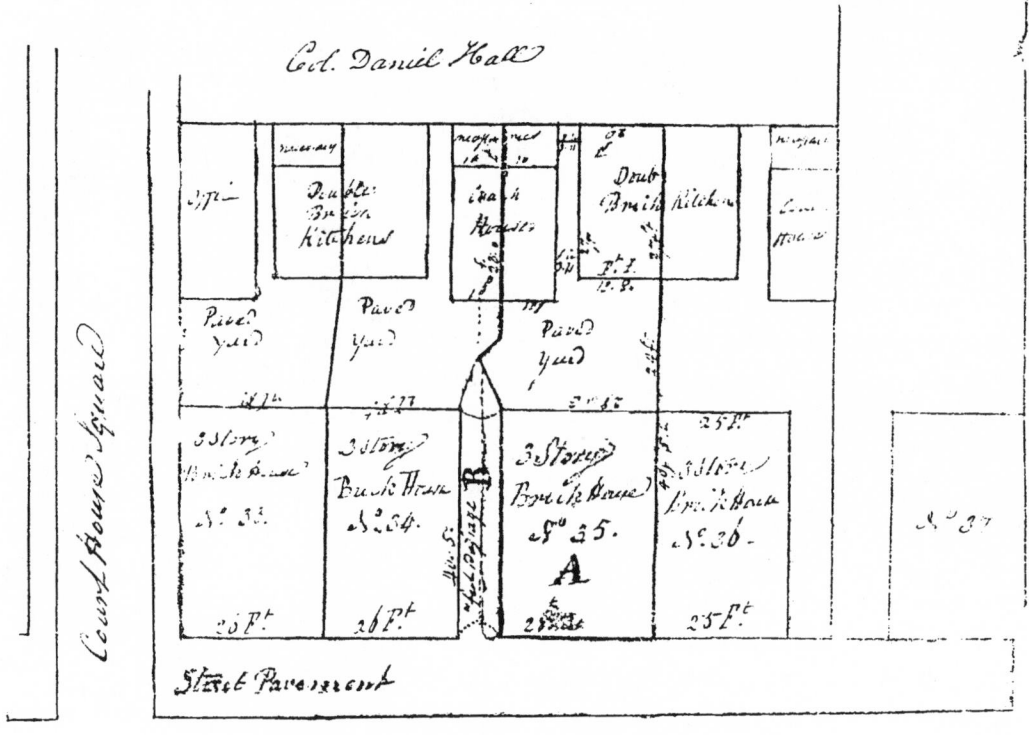

Figure 10.13. Meeting Street tenements adjacent to Court House Square, 1810. The four dwellings recorded in this survey consist of two sets of paired houses sharing party walls. Several examples of this arrangement survive in the city, including the nearby Blake Tenements and Catfish Row. Recorder of Deeds, Charleston, Book B-8, following p. 4407.

the 1840s. The dwelling at the head of the lot followed the familiar single-house arrangement. The view from the piazza encompassed both public street and private drive as well as flower garden planted against the adjoining property. Behind the formal street facade, the Coming Street property contained a variety of work and storage spaces. The range of rooms and buildings progressing to the rear of the lot began with a pantry and ended with the euphemistic "temple," or double privy. Between these two extremes in the food spectrum stood a store room, servants' hall, bathing room, kitchen, washhouse, and poultry coop. Spread against the rear property line were the wood house, stable, and carriage house. The backbuilding complex faced inward to a yard or court visually and physically separated from the adjacent property. The key features of the infill process here included the creation of multiple structures, each with specifically designated household functions. Compared to a Church Street property surveyed in the late 1700s, the Coming Street complex is considerably more congested with tightly defined functional zones around each structure. The infill process illustrated by the Coming Street property clearly approaches a maximum segregation

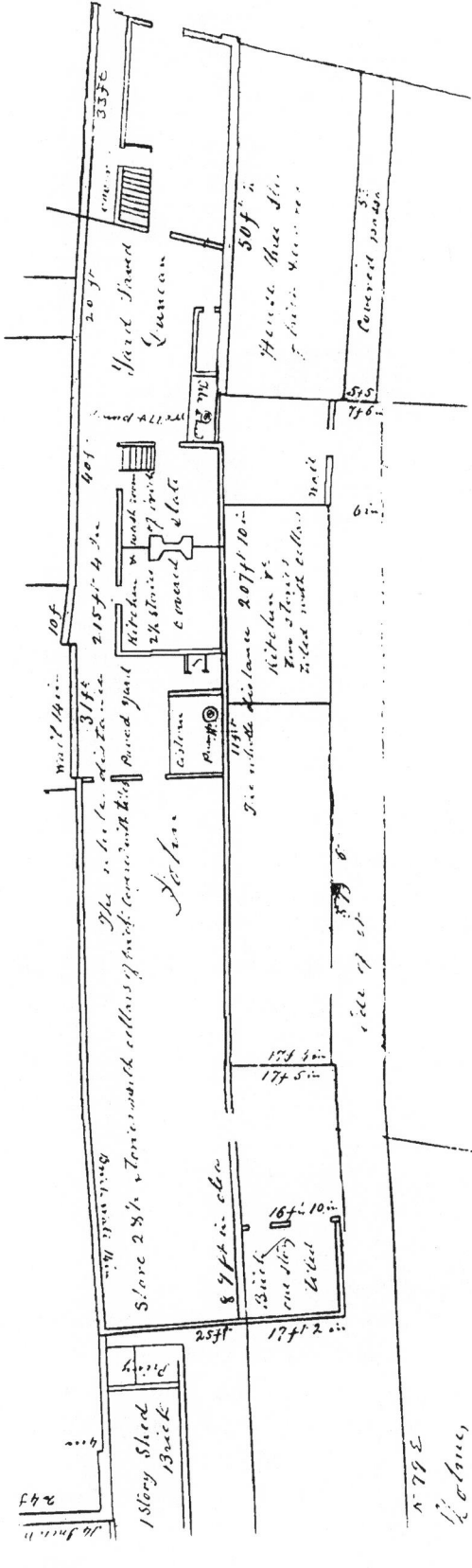

Figure 10.14. John Duncan's house and lot, 1866 copy of ca. 1800 original. Located near the Cooper River waterfront, Duncan's architectural landscape comprised a three-story house with a ground-floor commercial room and upper-story apartments, kitchen and washhouse, a two-and-a-half story store "with cellars of brick cover'd with tiles." The store, which covers nearly half of Duncan's lot, defined the space behind the house as commercial as well as domestic. McCrady Plat Collection, South Carolina Department of Archives and History, microfilm reel 3180, plat 524.

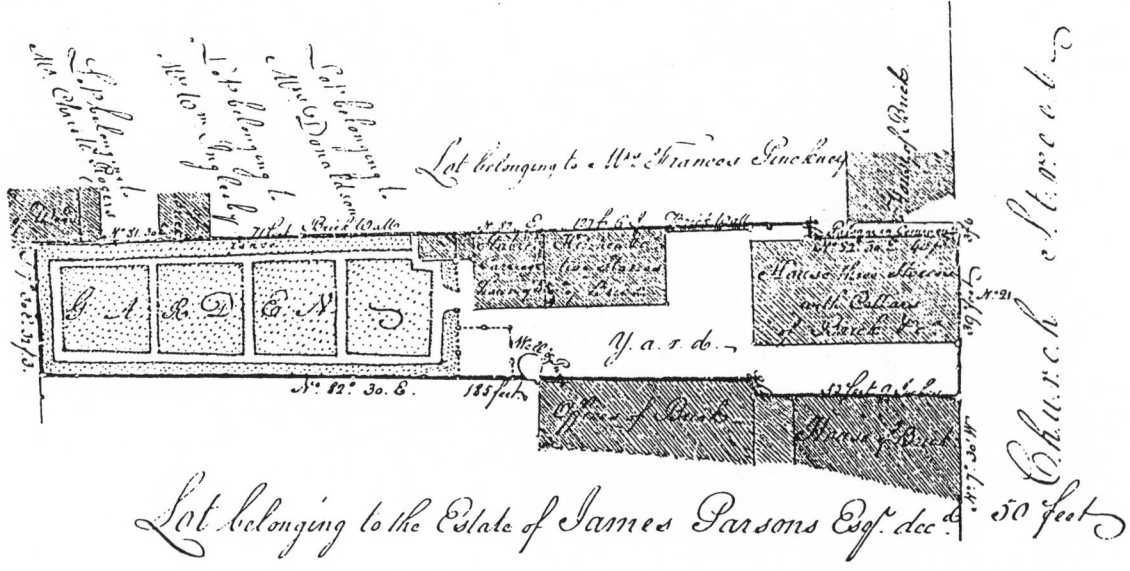

Figure 10.15. Samuel Prioleau's estate, Church Street, 1792. Prioleau's backlot, unlike John Duncan's, remained entirely domestic in character. Behind the house and fronting the yard ranged a kitchen and carriage house. The rear of the lot consisted of a neatly designed formal garden screened from the workyard by a fence and divided by walking paths into four squares. As with many Charleston lots in the late eighteenth and early nineteenth centuries, a privy occupied one corner of the garden. Recorder of Deeds, Charleston, Book G-6, following p. 498. Redrawn by S. DeChard.

of domestic space. The level of spatial definition reflected by the Coming Street property was not unique to Charleston or to urban settings. Farmers in the mid-Atlantic region and New England, for example, also bought into a vision of spatial consolidation and functional specificity (Garrison 1991; Herman 1987; Hubka 1984; McMurry 1988).

Not all Charleston builders modified the urban domestic landscape by adding more and more outbuildings. Some property owners, like Matthew Webb on King Street, pursued a strategy of subdividing their deep lots into a number of individual house compounds (figure 10.16). Webb's subdivision of his King Street property is particularly notable for the manner in which he crowded four domestic groupings into a single parcel just 27 feet wide and a full 233 feet deep. At the sidewalk stood a two-story wood house in front of a combination kitchen, washhouse, and quarters in a walled backyard. The size of the yard and the house's position at the head of the lot clearly indicate its primacy in the context of Webb's property. From King Street, access was provided beneath a covered entrance into a six-foot wide "Alley or Passage in common to & for the use of the four Lots." The second and third lots in from King Street contained a pair of back-to-back two-story wooden "tenements." A kitchen and washhouse combination was provided for both dwellings, but the foremost of the two also received two smaller sheds. Finally, at the very back of the lot in the corner farthest from the King Street sidewalk entry, stood a two-story wood dwelling. Unlike the houses on the front three parcels, the hindmost house possessed no service buildings other than a small unlabeled shed wedged into the corner created by a property wall and the rear gable of the dependency on the adjacent Webb parcel.

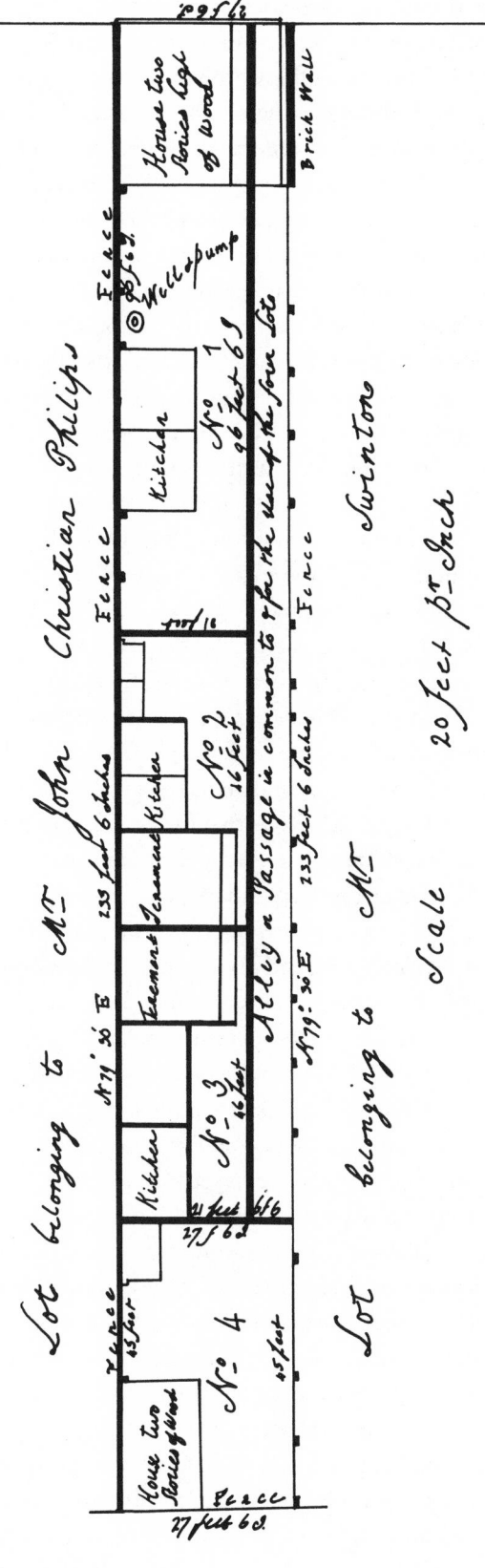

Figure 10.16. Matthew Webb's King Street property, 1796. The Webb lot shows the narrow, sometimes extraordinarily deep lots associated with Charleston single houses. Webb chose to develop his property with a number of tenements set one behind the other. His strategy resulted in an arrangement not unlike a private alley. Compare Webb's lot development with those of Samuel Prioleau, John Duncan, and James McDouall. Recorder of Deeds, Charleston, Book D-7, following p. 62. Redrawn by S. DeChard.

Webb's King Street property reflects a type of subdivision infill that has almost vanished from the Charleston landscape. The practice of backlot development is a common feature in urban plans from northern New England to the Carolina lowcountry as well as in English provincial towns of the seventeenth through nineteenth centuries. In Philadelphia, for example, the many side streets, courts, and alleys reflect the development of housing and other urban uses in the core of larger blocks. Similarly, in cities like Fredricksburg, Virginia, and Wilmington, Delaware, lots that run from a major thoroughfare back to a parallel secondary street and are anchored architecturally at both ends represent a commonsensical approach to development within the constraints of the urban landscape. In Charleston, the practice of infilling single parcels with multiple houselots occurred in the context of single house development. Charleston was not a city where public alleys and courts cut into the heart of the urban grid, creating more (and more congested) living areas. Charleston alley developments were most often characterized by private access. The difference between Webb's King Street property and the Coming Street compound lay in the exploitation of urban land as an economic resource. Webb clearly saw his as urban capital and developed it accordingly within the single house idiom; the owner of the Coming Street lot viewed his in the idiom of the urban plantation and provided himself with the many lesser buildings requisite to the symbolic organization of the Charleston backcountry.

Infill as part of the intensification process typically occurred through a series of building episodes resulting in the architectural transformation of the backlot. The third example discussed here turns from the documentary evidence for infill to that contained in the buildings themselves. The archaeology of architecture reveals strata and chronologies both similar and parallel to those associated with below-ground archaeological features. The examination of the backbuildings at the Aiken-Rhett site reveals two major stages in the property's physical history. First, there are the backbuildings as constructed at the time of the initial development of the Judith Street block; second, there are the major improvements made little more than a decade later; and third, there are the improvements made in the 1850s.

Built as a double house (a dwelling designed on a center-passage, double-pile plan), the Aiken-Rhett complex included two facing backyard dependencies. A one-story carriage house and stable stood adjacent to the Elizabeth Street side of the property. The brick building incorporated direct access onto the street as well as a small, heated ground-floor room for stablehands or coachmen. A two-story brick kitchen, washhouse, and quarter faced the stable across the yard. The design of this building adhered to the favored form of such structures in early-nineteenth-century Charleston as represented in similar backbuildings on the adjacent property. The ground-floor plan incorporated a kitchen nearest the house, a partitioned stair to the second-floor quarters, and a washhouse or laundry. The five-bay yard elevation of the backbuilding included three separate entries—one into each of the three functional zones. Chimney piles were located on the interior of the back wall abutting the neighboring lot. Upstairs the quarters consisted of two heated common rooms and four unheated chambers. Windows were unglazed and secured with shutters swinging outward on strap hinges. Two more unheated rooms for quarters were carved out of the attic level.

The renovation of the backbuildings on the Aiken-Rhett property did nothing to improve the quality of life for the enslaved inhabitants, but it did significantly alter the way in which the rear yard was infilled and enclosed. The old stable building was raised to two stories and doubled in length from 36 to 72 feet. The original stable, which had been built as a one-story structure, 20 by 36 feet, contained a harness room, carriage bay, and horse stalls. The doubled length limited the function of the old structure to carriage and harness storage while creating new stabling facilities for six horses. Each horse received its own 5-by-7-foot stall and feeding trough. The upstairs of the carriage house contained a large open hayloft located over the new stabling area and slave quarters over the old carriage house. Most notable in the extended carriage house were the efforts taken to cut the yard off from the street. Street openings in the old carriage house were sealed, effectively walling in the Aiken-Rhett workyard. The blank Elizabeth Street wall was relieved visually with a pointed arch blind arcade on the second floor. Even the stall vents on the first floor were designed with jogged offsets that admitted air from the street but prevented both people and horses from looking out or passersby from reaching in.

The kitchen, which began as a two-story structure with the customary cooking and washhouse functional division below and quarters above, was extended in a fashion similar to the enlargement of the carriage house and stable. The changes to the second-floor quarters were particularly notable in two respects. First, the old arrangement of quarters divided by a front to back stair and entry was removed. The new second-floor plan developed around a stairwell opening onto a long passage that ran along the front of the building. The shuttered, but unglazed, windows overlooking the workyard below admitted light and air to the quarters across the passage by means of interior windows and transoms. In a manner typical of antebellum Charleston backbuildings, the Aiken-Rhett kitchen and quarters possessed no windows or openings providing direct access by sight or sound to the neighboring backlot. All but one of the quarters contained a fireplace, and each possessed a door with evidence of locks or shot bolts that could be secured from within. The new quarters seem to exhibit a level of improvement over the older pattern of a small heated room with smaller unheated chambers found in Charleston backbuildings. Larger rooms, however, more likely signified denser living accommodations as the functional range of the carriage house and kitchen expanded.

The yard was completed with a tall brick wall surrounding the entire lot and a pair of gates at the very back of the property, which opened onto Mary Street. The construction of elaborate brick privies, chicken coop, and cow shed in the 1830s added highly specialized outbuildings to the working yard. Visual and physical separation from the street, expanded service structures, new backyard amenities, and extensive paving and drainage systems in the Aiken-Rhett compound all reflect on the larger process of intensification and, as we shall see, on a pattern of an ever more narrowly regulated urban landscape.

Archaeological excavations within the 1850s kitchen addition suggest that an underlying earlier drain system was part of the 1830s renovations. A large circular pit full of brick and slate rubble encountered in excavations behind the stable also documents this construction period. The additions and changes to the outbuildings also are reflected archaeologically. The antebellum refuse that accumulated around the kitchen was covered by the addition to the kitchen and stables, and by the paving of the courtyard between the two dependencies (in brick, laid in a herringbone pattern). By this time, the bulk of domestic refuse was carted off-site, but a significant amount of household trash and debris still accumulated behind the new kitchen addition. A new yard drain was constructed in this period. Built of brick and capped with slate, this elaborate feature incorporated a watering basin for animals and an entry vault that probably served as a privy for resident slaves. This privy/vault was abandoned in the 1890s and capped with lime (Zierden, Calhoun, and Hacker 1986). Ghosting along the stucco of the rear kitchen wall suggests that this feature was enclosed with a small lean-to. William Aiken, recognized as an innovative and progressive thinker in other areas, evidently expressed his desire for municipal sanitation and efficiency in the design and amenities of his lot.

The architectural and archaeological evidence for intensification expressed in the Aiken-Rhett complex can be observed throughout Charleston. Even in the oldest colonial sections of the city, the aspect of mid-nineteenth-century urban sensibilities colors our impressions of the eighteenth-century townscape. Where early nineteenth-century watercolors depict open urban vistas and post-and-rail fences separating private yards from public thoroughfares, we now see high brick walls and congested lots. But even our sense of the nineteenth-century past is incomplete. The modern visitor encounters backbuildings with grassy lawns and glazed windows, where the early-nineteenth-century slaves labored in a trash-strewn yard and slept fitfully in their crowded quarters with the buzz of mosquitoes in their ears.

REGULATION

Charlestonians, like other urban dwellers of early America, sought to regulate their environment in a variety of ways. The common point of conflict was, as Dell Upton has disarmingly termed it, the tension between the "messy" and the "neat" city (Upton 1994). Platted, bounded, and segregated, the Charleston landscape was constantly contested. Poor sanitation practices, ranging from open cesspits to carrion rotting in the streets, nurtured a wide range of diseases. The stress generated among the white populace by possible insurrections from the African-American majority (as well as the anxiety created among African-American citizens by reprisals and restrictions) encouraged a mentalité and material culture of social withdrawal. Regulation, whether public or private, corporate or individual, describes the process of imposing order on the ways in which people use the landscape relative to one another and to the urban corporation as a whole. As with the preceding discussion of urban landscape formation processes, we will focus briefly on just two elements of regulation: sanitation and segmentation.

Through the nineteenth century, Charlestonians remained concerned with health and sanitation problems resulting from diminished native resources and increased population pressure (Pease and Pease 1985). Accordingly, they sought to regulate both public and private landscapes. Cisterns built to collect rainwater and brick drains designed to remove wastewater are tangible archaeological evidence of attempts to make the yard more livable. The Brewton yard contained evidence of an extensive drain network first constructed in the 1770s and expanded in the early nineteenth century. The drain fill was full of small lost artifacts and small fish bones. Evidently, fresh fish were cleaned and scaled adjacent to the kitchen and the remains washed into the drain (Zierden 1990). The drain at the Aiken-Rhett house, part of 1850s renovations, connected a watering basin for animals and a privy vault for slave use before continuing beyond property boundaries (Zierden, Calhoun, and Hacker 1986). The Gibbes house also had a drain system, though less elaborate and less extensive (Zierden et al. 1987).

Attention to sanitation is also reflected in changing refuse disposal practices at the elite townhouse sites. Excavations at the Aiken-Rhett house revealed that refuse was concentrated near the outbuildings rather than generally dispersed across the yard (Zierden, Calhoun, and Hacker 1986). Extensive excavation at the Miles Brewton site provided further details on this pattern. Refuse was concentrated in the vicinity of the kitchen and near the house from the period of initial occupation through the early nineteenth century. Refuse from the mid- to late nineteenth century was deposited farther to the rear of the workyard behind the privy or, most likely, carted off-site (Zierden 1990). The Rutledge site exhibited an even more dramatic example, where 3.5 feet of refuse built up between 1750 and the 1840s, when the yard was paved with brick; after the latter renovation, less than 6 inches of soil and refuse accumulated (Zierden and Grimes 1989).

Faunal analysis has also provided information on urban sanitation. One aspect of the urban-rural contrast model is a greater percentage of commensal (non-food) taxa in the city. Such animals as rats, birds, cats, and dogs constitute 4.3 percent of rural faunal assemblages and 10.6 percent of urban ones, suggesting that vermin were more closely associated with human activity areas in the city (Reitz 1986). The urban elite sites contain a lower percentage of vermin, however, possibly indicating a more sanitary environment or the cleanliness associated with the site amenities that only an elite economic class could afford.

Segmentation (Castille et al. 1982:5; Herman 1989) enabled householders to refine and signify the socially efficient use of available land. The grand Georgian townhouses examined in this study may be viewed as "architectural pronouncements of social order" comparable to the great plantation houses built throughout the eighteenth- and early-nineteenth-century Tidewater South (Isaac 1982:39). The larger double houses were often elevated with an above-ground basement that cooled the house, gave protection from flooding, raised the main living quarters above street level, and provided the image of social distance. The sense of distance was further enhanced by the presence of formal entrances and forbidding brick walls or wrought-iron fences that often stood between the double houses and streets (Coclanis 1989:8; Weir 1983).

The study of standing single houses in the context of their lots and neighboring houses suggests three areas of inquiry parallel to archaeological issues: extended household and lot organization, the functional segmentation of urban household and commercial space, and the process of urban enclosure. By the early nineteenth century, for example, many eighteenth-century buildings on Church Street were modified to remove their commercial rooms and to receive new connecting back buildings. The first change reflects a growing segregation between work space and domestic space, while the latter change describes a consolidation of household functions under a single roof and a growing sense of room specialization. By 1840, when Ansonborough was being rebuilt following a devastating fire, fully developed single houses in detached rows were standard.

The shift to the single house by the mid-nineteenth century reflects one trait in the standardization of the built environment. The social and domestic sensibilities encoded in the single house extended to the regulation of broader categories of social relationships. In plan, the extended single house consisted of a series of interconnected functional zones that communicated with one another and the street via a number of routes. The main house abutted, but did not front, the street. Access from the street into the single house therefore followed one of two routes: from the sidewalk onto the piazza, or from the sidewalk and street down the carriage way. In all instances, the organization of the single house unit ran from street to backyard in a pattern of decreasing formality and increasing dirtiness. These linked domestic spaces exist in and define a highly stratified and processional urban plantation landscape (Upton 1994; Wade 1964). These patterns are reflected archaeologically as intrasite variations in the depth and complexity of stratigraphy, as well as in artifact (cultural and organic) density.

An accelerating response to population pressure, health, and sanitation concerns was a shift to centralized control, either private or municipal, over the basic necessities of daily life. Specifically, the eighteenth century featured individual household-level responses to such basic needs as water procurement, trash disposal, and sanitary waste management. These adaptive strategies are visible in the archaeological record in the form of wells, trash pits and sheet deposits, and privies, respectively. Wells, pits, and privies were used secondarily for refuse disposal.

The antebellum years witnessed major changes in the social, economic, and technological systems of the United States. Industrial development was a key factor in these changes, and cities were the center of these events. In order to capture new commerce and industry, cities strove to establish and maintain images of health, attractiveness, and modernization. The pressure of competition made the provision of services such as lighting, disease prevention, water, and street maintenance a necessity (Goldfield 1977:67). Fear of epidemics and efforts toward the prevention of disease resulted in municipal water and sewage systems and trash pickup. This began in 1826 in Charleston but took the remainder of the century to achieve full realization. Stopgap measures for Charlestonians included wells converted to cisterns and regular cleaning of privy vaults (Goldfield 1977:69; Honerkamp, Council, and Will 1982:159; Rosengarten et al. 1987).

The archaeological evidence for these changes differs from the evidence of earlier periods. As a consequence, a disorganization characterizes the archaeological record of intensely utilized urban sites (Honerkamp and Council 1984). A lack of domestic refuse, the presence of a large amount of coal in jumbled zone deposits, and the presence of pipes and pipe trenches are archaeological correlates of this period, as are abandoned privies full of household refuse.

The regulated urban landscape of the single house compound is further distinguished by constriction and segmentation. Access in and out of the single house yard, either via the piazza or carriage way, was beneath the gaze of the controlling and authoritative occupants. The threshold where the lot met the street was the narrowest point of open space. Thus, the greatest physical constriction occurred at its most vulnerable and most public point, symbolizing a tightening, monitoring, and regulation of movement. Domestic space in the city as a whole became increasingly segmented and partitioned into discrete areas. These qualities, as evidenced in the archaeological record, were further emphasized by the construction of brick partition walls. The construction of elaborate urban plantation compounds with clustered buildings, visually screened domestic vistas, and paved, trash-free yards grew increasingly common in nineteenth-century Charleston. Together, these observable trends reflect broader patterns in the standardization and regulation of the urban landscape.

Responding to daily needs and confined to a finite amount of space, Charlestonians turned their single houses sideways, built kitchens and stables behind them, and put as much distance as possible between their wells and privies. When urban density made these sanitation efforts ineffective, residents constructed cisterns and drain systems, and paved offensive areas in close proximity to the dwelling. Where possible, refuse disposal and other maintenance activities were segregated in side portions of the yard.

J. B. Jackson offers a definition of landscape as "a composition of man-made spaces on the land," and then expands his formula characterizing landscape "not as a natural feature of the environment but a *synthetic* space, a man-made system of spaces superimposed on the face of the land, functioning and evolving not according to natural laws but to serve a community—for the collective character of the landscape is one thing that all generations and all points of view have agreed upon" (Jackson 1984:7–8). The collected evidence of landscape formation in Charleston embraces the totality of shaped land, of "land modified for permanent human occupation, for dwelling, agriculture, manufacturing, government, worship, and for pleasure—not by chance, but by contrivance, by premeditation, by design" (Stilgoe 1982:3). Because the character of landscape is reducible to individual actions and perceptions in community contexts, landscape studies, archaeology included, require the recognition of the interplay between the historical self and community: "an understanding of landscape expression requires a method of identification; a means whereby we identify authors *in* the landscape. It requires too a method of explanation; a means whereby we explain the process in which ideas become contexts for the making of the landscape" (Samuels 1979:73). Thus, historical landscapes, urban and rural, stand as vast texts subject to the contributions of many authors, the interpretations of many readers, and the discourses of many critics.

Urban landscape archaeology in Charleston finds its purpose in the discovery of form and pattern in "shaped land," the explanation of discovered patterns, and interpretations of the processes and meanings worked into the land. Landscape archaeology forces us to extend the concept of site beyond an aggregate of related archaeological features or above-ground remains within a specific spatial context to encompass the totality of the environment. It is the archaeology of "man-made spaces on the land." We might imagine urban landscape archaeology working at intrasite/intersite analyses on a grand scale. The archaeological interpretation of city environments also springs from the consideration of the social and cultural construction of urban spaces as they shape and are shaped by the experience of being in the city. Urban landscapes concretely express complex historical processes and reflect the social relationships that inform the appearance and meaning of the urban environment. The questions we ask of urban landscape archaeology are typically larger in scope than those usually associated with site-specific research. On the one hand we maintain our commitment to recovering the specifics of individual phenomena in detail; on the other we struggle to push our comprehension of singular phenomena into the apprehension of community environmental action and reaction. The discovery of singular phenomena leads to the broader search for how and why people have shaped the physical environment in the ways they have. Urban landscape archaeology, therefore, is about how people "thought" the environment. It is subject to what we can term a material culture approach to history (Herman 1992).

Our purpose here has been to describe and discuss some of the landscape formation processes involved in the historical "thinking" and contemporary reading of the urban environment of Charleston, South Carolina, from the colonial period through the mid-1800s. Townhouse studies in Charleston have provided information on adaptation to the conditions of the urban environment. The urban landscape—the portion of a city comprehended in a single view—ranged in its perspective from slave quarters in prisonlike walled domestic compounds to the rooftop vistas and waterfront promenades enjoyed by the city elite. All those views, from the most wretched to the grandiose, represented parts of a complex whole, and the social meanings at either end of the spectrum were therefore equally comprehensible though inequitably shared. Urban landscape behaviors, from trash disposal to courtyard planning, address the recognition of far-reaching, interconnected patterns linking the landscape formation processes of conversion, accommodation, intensification, and regulation to the culture and character of a complex urban ecology.

REFERENCES

Bold, John
1990   The Design for a House of a Merchant. *Architectural History* 33:75–82.
Calhoun, Jeanne, Elizabeth Reitz, Michael Trinkley, and Martha Zierden
1984   Meat in Due Season: Preliminary Investigation of Marketing Practices in Colonial Charleston. *Archaeological Contributions* 9. The Charleston Museum, Charleston.
Castille, George, David Kelley, Sally Reeves, and Charles Pearson
1982   Archaeological Excavations at Esplanade Avenue and North Rampart Street, New Orleans, Louisiana. Ms. on file, U.S. Department of the Interior, National Park Service, Atlanta.
Coclanis, Peter A.
1985   The Sociology of Architecture in Colonial Charleston: Pattern and Process in an Eighteenth Century Southern City. *Journal of Southern History* 18:607–23.
1989   *The Shadow of a Dream: Economic Life and Death in the South Carolina Lowcountry 1670–1920.* Oxford University Press, New York.
Corfield, P. J.
1982   *The Impact of English Towns, 1700–1800.* Oxford University Press, Oxford.
Deetz, James
1977   *In Small Things Forgotten: The Archaeology of Early American Life.* Anchor Press, Doubleday, Garden City, New York.
Fries, Sylvia Doughty
1977   *The Urban Idea in Colonial America.* Temple University Press, Philadelphia.
Garrison, J. Ritchie
1991   *Landscape and Material Life in Franklin County, Massachusetts, 1770–1860.* University of Tennessee Press, Knoxville.
Garrow, Patrick H.
1984   The Identification and Use of Context Types in Urban Archaeology. *Southeastern Archaeology* 3(2):91–96.
Giles, Colum
1990   Making a Georgian Suburb. *The Architect's Journal,* 8 May 1990:44–53.
Glassie, Henry
1975   *Folk Housing of Middle Virginia: A Structural Analysis of Historic Artifacts.* University of Tennessee Press, Knoxville.
Goldfield, David R.
1977   Pursuing the American Dream: Cities in the Old South. In *The City in Southern History,* edited by Blaine Brownell and David Goldfield, pp. 52–90. Kennikat Press, Port Washington, New York.
Herman, Bernard L.
1984   Multiple Material/Multiple Meanings: The Fortunes of Thomas Mendenhall. *Winterthur Portfolio* 19(1):67–86.
1987   *Architecture and Rural Life in Central Delaware, 1700–1900.* University of Tennessee Press, Knoxville.

1989   Rethinking the Charleston Single House. Paper presented to the Vernacular Architecture Forum, St. Louis, Missouri.

1992   *The Stolen House.* University Press of Virginia, Charlottesville.

Honerkamp, Nicholas, and R. Bruce Council

1984   Individual Versus Corporate Adaptations in Urban Contexts. *Tennessee Anthropologist* IX(1):22–31.

Honerkamp, Nicholas, R. Bruce Council, and M. Elizabeth Will

1982   An Archaeological Investigation of the Charleston Center Site, Charleston, South Carolina. Ms. on file, U.S. Department of the Interior, National Park Service, Atlanta.

Hubka, Thomas

1984   *Big House, Little House, Back House, Barn: The Connected Farm Buildings of New England.* University Press of New England, Hanover, New Hampshire.

Isaac, Rhys

1982   *The Transformation of Virginia, 1740–1790.* Institute of Early American History and Culture, University of North Carolina Press, Chapel Hill.

Jackson, John Brinckerhoff

1984   *Discovering the Vernacular Landscape.* Yale University Press, New Haven.

Laithwaite, Michael

1984   Totnes Houses, 1500–1800. In *The Transformation of English Provincial Towns, 1600–1800,* edited by Peter Clark, pp. 62–98. Hutchison, London.

Leone, Mark, Elizabeth Kryder-Reid, Julie H. Ernstein, and Paul A. Shackel

1989   Power Gardens of Annapolis. *Archaeology* 42(2):34–39, 74–75.

McMurry, Sally

1988   *Families and Farmhouses in Nineteenth Century America: Vernacular Design and Social Change.* Oxford University Press, New York.

Mrozowski, Stephen

1987   Exploring New England's Evolving Urban Landscape. In Living in Cities: Current Research in Urban Archaeology, edited by Edward Staski. *Special Publication Series* No. 5:1–9. Society for Historical Archaeology.

1988   Historical Archaeology as Anthropology. *Historical Archaeology* 22(1):18–24.

Ostrogorsky, Michael

1987   Economic Organization and Landscape: Physical and Social Terrain Alteration in Seattle. In Living in Cities: Current Research in Urban Archaeology, edited by Edward Staski. *Special Publication Series* No. 5:10–18. Society for Historical Archaeology.

Pease, William H., and Jane H. Pease

1985   *The Web of Progress: Private Values and Public Style in Boston and Charleston, 1828–1843.* Oxford University Press, New York.

Reed, Michael

1983   *The Georgian Triumph, 1700–1830.* Routledge and Kegan Paul, London.

Reinhard, Karl

1989   Parasitological and Palynological Study of Soil Samples from the John Rutledge House. In Investigating Elite Lifeways through Archaeology, edited by Martha Zierden and Kimberly Grimes. *Archaeological Contributions* 21:166–74. The Charleston Museum, Charleston.

1990   Pollen Analysis of the Miles Brewton House, Charleston, South Carolina. Ms. on file, The Charleston Museum, Charleston.

Reitz, Elizabeth

1986   Urban/Rural Contrasts in Vertebrate Fauna from the Southern Coastal Plain. *Historical Archaeology* 20(2):47–58.

1987   Vertebrate Fauna and Socioeconomic Status. In *Consumer Choice in Historical Archaeology,* edited by Suzanne Spencer-Wood, pp. 101–19. Plenum Press, New York.

Reitz, Elizabeth, and Martha Zierden

1991   Cattle Bones and Status from Charleston, South Carolina. In *Beamers, Bobwhites, and Blue-Points: Tributes to the Career of P.W. Parmalee,* edited by Bonnie Styles, James Purdue, and Walter Klippel, pp. 395–408. Illinois State Museum Publications.

Rosengarten, Dale, Martha Zierden, Kimberly Grimes, Ziyadah Owusu, Elizabeth Alston, and Will Williams III

1987   Between the Tracks: Charleston's East Side during the Nineteenth Century. *Archaeological Contributions* 17. The Charleston Museum, Charleston.

Rothschild, Nan A.

1985   Spatial Aspects of Urbanization. *American Archaeology* 5(3):163–69.

Samuels, Marwyn S.

1979   The Biography of Landscape: Cause and Culpability. In *The Interpretation of Ordinary Landscapes: Geographical Essays,* edited by D. W. Meinig, pp. 51–88. Oxford University Press, New York.

Severens, Kenneth

1988   *Charleston Antebellum Architecture and Civic Destiny.* University of Tennessee Press, Knoxville.

Smith, Alice R., and D. E. Huger Smith

1917   *The Dwelling Houses of Charleston, South Carolina.* J. B. Lippincott, Philadelphia.

Smith, David

1987   Dependent Urbanization in Colonial America: The Case of Charleston, South Carolina. *Social Forces* 66(1):1–29.

Smith, J. T.

1983   The Eighteenth Century Background to Newfoundland Houses. In Dimensions of Canadian Architecture, edited by Shane O'Dea and Gerald Pocius. *Selected Papers* 6:34–43. Society for the Study of Architecture in Canada.

Stilgoe, John R.

1982   *Common Landscape of America, 1580 to 1845.* Yale University Press, New Haven.

Trinkley, Michael

1983   Analysis of Ethnobotanical Remains. In An Archaeological Study of the First Trident Site, edited by Martha Zierden, Jeanne Calhoun and Elizabeth Pinckney. *Archaeological Contributions* 6:88–96. The Charleston Museum, Charleston.

1989   Ethnobotanical Analysis of Samples from the John Rutledge House. In Investigating Elite Lifeways through Archaeology, edited by Martha Zierden and Kimberly Grimes. *Archaeological Contributions* 21:155–65. The Charleston Museum, Charleston.

Upton, Dell

1986   *Holy Things and Profane: Anglican Parish Churches in Colonial Virginia.* Architectural History Foundation, MIT Press, Cambridge, Massachusetts.

1994   Another City: The Urban Cultural Landscape in the Early Republic. In *Everyday Life in the Early Republic,* edited by Catherine E. Hutchins, pp. 61–117. Henry Francis DuPont Winterthur Museum, Winterthur, Delaware.

Wade, Richard C.

1964   *Slavery in the Cities: The South, 1820–1860.* Oxford University Press, New York.

Weir, Robert M.

1983   *Colonial South Carolina: A History.* KTO Press, Millwood, New York.

Zierden, Martha

1989   Management Summary: Test Excavations at 40 Society Street, Charleston, South Carolina. Ms. on file, The Charleston Museum, Charleston.

1990   Excavations at the Miles Brewton House, 1988–1990. Notes on file, The Charleston Museum, Charleston.

1992   The Front Yard and the Work Yard: Archaeology and Interpretation at the Joseph Manigault House. *Archaeological Contributions* 22. The Charleston Museum, Charleston.

Zierden, Martha, and Jeanne Calhoun
1986   Urban Adaptation in Charleston, South Carolina. *Historical Archaeology* 20(1):29–43.

Zierden, Martha, and Kimberly Grimes
1989   Investigating Elite Lifeways through Archaeology: The John Rutledge House. *Archaeological Contributions* 21. The Charleston Museum, Charleston.

Zierden, Martha, Jeanne Calhoun, and Debi Hacker
1986   Outside of Town: Preliminary Investigations of the Aiken-Rhett House. *Archaeological Contributions* 11. The Charleston Museum, Charleston.

Zierden, Martha, Jeanne Calhoun, Suzanne Buckley, and Debi Hacker
1987   Georgian Opulence: Archaeological Investigation of the Gibbes House. *Archaeological Contributions* 12. The Charleston Museum, Charleston.

Zierden, Martha, Kimberly Grimes, David Hudgens, and Cherie Black
1988   Charleston's First Suburb: Excavations at 66 Society Street. *Archaeological Contributions* 20. The Charleston Museum, Charleston.

11

The Construction of Sanctity: Landscape and Ritual in a Religious Community

Elizabeth Kryder-Reid

Anyone who has ever excavated a garden should be able to tell you that you do not find much. That is, you do not find much in the way of ceramics, bones, glass, and the other sorts of debris that generally litter domestic sites. If there has been little disturbance, you may find soil features such as planting beds and root holes, and perhaps if the preservation is good, you may find seeds and microfloral remains. If the garden was elaborate, there may be surviving topographic features such as ramps, falls, and mounts, and even remnants of statuary or foundations of structures like pavilions, dove-cotes, springhouses, and temples. But the garden is not the place to dig for artifacts. It is perhaps for this reason that in recent years landscape archaeologists have been drawn to diverse theoretical strains to make sense of their excavated data. It may also be, however, that the imperative to understand these sites and explain their meaning lies in the nature of the subject of landscape itself.

The archaeology of landscapes is, after all, the archaeology of space—specifically the human shaping, perception, and use of that space. The topic demands a variety of inquiries, from the consideration of those designing, constructing, and controlling the space to the nature and meaning of the social interactions taking place within it. The study of landscapes strikes at the core of how we make sense of our world: how our lives are permeated by our physical environment, perhaps as fundamentally as by the language we speak. Landscape archaeology questions not only the meaning and symbolic significance conveyed by acts such as the cultivation of plants, but also how our actions and interactions with our surroundings shape who we are. It examines how the organization of sight, the control of movement, and the structure and pattern of space construct our subjectivity—our sense of who we are and how we relate to one another and to the world around us.

In this study, these questions are applied to a property in Annapolis, Maryland, owned by the Redemptorists, a congregation of priests and brothers known officially as the Congregationis Sanctissimi Redemptoris (Congregation of the Most Holy Redeemer, or C.Ss.R). Since 1853, the Redemptorists have resided on the former property of Charles Carroll of Carrollton, Maryland, a signer of the Declaration of Independence (figure 11.1). The Redemptorists' occupation of the property is recorded both in the physical changes to the landscape, changes recovered by four seasons of excavations (1987–90) by Archaeology in Annapolis, an archaeology project sponsored jointly by Historic Annapolis Foundation and the University of Maryland at College Park, and in twelve volumes of *Chronicles,* a collection of documents that records in diary-like entries the daily activities of the congregation's life.[1] The *Chronicles* primarily detail the ministry and daily life of the house—the comings and goings of the priests, the celebrations of significant anniversaries, activities of the parish—but include accounts of the changing landscape as well. Details such as storm damage, building projects and repairs, plantings, and harvests are interspersed with descriptions of the use of the property for outdoor liturgies, funerals, garden parties, recreation, and meditation. The wealth of documentary and archaeological material presents an excellent opportunity to use landscape archaeology as an avenue for cultural analysis and, more specifically, to apply the notion of landscape and ritual as communicative languages through which meanings are constructed.

Figure 11.1. St. Mary's parish church and rectory viewed from Spa Creek showing the former house and gardens of Charles Carroll of Carrollton, now owned by the Redemptorists.

To begin, I should like to ask a question: What is the problem of landscape archaeology for which the idea of "ritual" offers a solution? One response is that in the process of interpretation an archaeologist must begin with mute objects, however much they are articulated by texts, and give them the voice(s) of their original cultural contexts. For archaeologists this complicated business of deciphering cultural meaning requires them to build associations among objects (or other forms of material culture) and between objects and people. One way to understand these associations is to presume certain cultural universals, such as the essential symbolic nature of human thinking. This symbolic thinking may be as strict as Levi-Strauss's premise that humans process their experiences into named categories that are composed of oppositions, but it may also be taken on a more general level. I draw here on the words of anthropologist Edmund Leach (1968:524): "All of us in our daily lives manipulate the symbols of an intricate behavioral code, and we readily decode the behavioral messages of our associates; this we take for granted. . . . Our day-to-day relationships depend upon a mutual knowledge and mutual acceptance of the fact that at any particular time any two individuals occupy different positions in a highly complex network of status relationships. . . ." Leach goes on to suggest that ritual is the social communication aspect of behavior that, in a sacred or secular context, articulates and affirms these status differences. Anthropologists such as Robertson-Smith (1894), Durkheim (1915), and Radcliffe-Brown (1952) have long highlighted the ways in which rituals strengthen the bonds between individuals within a social group by symbolizing the underlying values of that group. Others, such as Tylor (1871), Frazer (1922), and Malinowski (1948), have seen ritual as a means by which individuals understand and make peace with their place in the unexplainable and often unpredictable world. Rituals, for Levi-Strauss, are those events in which participants pass to the desirable or "winning" side of an opposition, whether between profane and sacred or dead and living. In doing so, rituals may resolve contradictions and heal social or physical wounds (Levi-Strauss 1966:32). Each of these views has been highly effective in explaining the persistence and ubiquity of rituals throughout the world, but they have been less successful in recognizing and explaining the dysfunctional, disruptive, and transformative aspects of ritual. In short, they have trouble explaining change.

In response, Geertz (1973) and others have developed and applied a more dynamic view of ritual, which argues that one cannot separate the more functional social structural aspects of ritual from their meaningful cultural aspects. In this seemingly minor twist on a classic Durkheimian functionalism lies a profoundly different way of understanding material culture. In a Geertzian analysis, sacred objects, and their enaction through ritual, are not simply society rationalizing itself, but instead are the means by which society constructs itself. This point may seem a difference of semantics, but the theoretical bases of the two viewpoints are fundamentally opposed.

In a functionalist view the symbols, myths, and rituals are a means by which society reinforces its social structure and negotiates tensions or contradictions within the group. The symbolic forms are seen as "expressions" of that which already exists—the society. The alternative view maintains that symbols cannot be "expressive" because it is through symbols and symbolic action that the subjectivity of the individual and the identity of the larger group is constructed. The acts of speaking, moving, perceiving, worshipping, etc., are not expressing an existing reality but instead are "performative." The drama of the ritual infuses the stage and the props with meaning, and the space and objects in turn structure the acts and perceptions of the actors. Understanding this recursive, reifying relationship between the material and mental world is the challenge of the archaeology of landscapes.

For the purposes of this analysis, the active and recursive relationships among the Redemptorists, the rituals they perform, and the space within which they perform them are taken as the cultural context that makes the landscape meaningful. That the space changed over the course of the years between 1853 and 1950 is hardly surprising, nor is the observation that the community's identity, structure, and daily life changed as well. What is of interest, however, is that the transformations that took place—even those that appear to be radical—were never seen as contradictory or controversial. This chapter argues that these changes were negotiated, affirmed, and legitimated in part through the physical space and the rituals enacted within it.

THE REDEMPTORISTS: THE NINETEENTH CENTURY

Gone were the Carrolls. Silent were their halls
Beside the Severn: yea the strife was o'er,
New pilgrims walked by Maryland's green shore
And preached the Love which human souls enthralls.
Then rose Religion's sacred temple walls,
Here in their cells these pilgrims node and bore
Abroad, the honey of both love and lore.

(Anonymous 1928:32)

The Redemptorist Congregation, founded in Germany in 1732, established its first American province in northern Ohio and Michigan in 1832. After seven years, the priests settled in Pittsburgh; one year later, a house was established in Baltimore. In 1852, the Redemptorists were preparing to move their novitiate (a school for candidates' preparation for orders) out of Baltimore when the Carroll property became available. The Carroll house, built originally in 1721 and expanded in the 1770s and 1780s, was selected for the new site, and the Redemptorists took residence in 1853 (Borgmann 1904:13). The introduction to the *Chronicles* describes the Redemptorists' primary ministry as the care of Catholics in the city.[2] Their responsibilities have included the St. Mary's parish, a novitiate from 1853 to 1862 and from 1867 to 1907, a "major seminary" or "Theologate" (1862–68), St. Mary's primary and secondary school, and various foreign and domestic missions. Daily life within the community was defined by a hierarchy, despite the Rule's dictum that the members "be uniform in all things" (Redemptorists 1939:26).[3] Within each house the rector or superior was the ultimate authority, assisted by a minister. The ordained fathers stood next in precedence, ranked in seniority by date of their professions (Redemptorists 1939:257). The students (novitiates and chorists) ranked next, followed lastly by the lay brothers.

Redemptorist community life was based on the professed vows of poverty, chastity, and obedience, and of perseverance in the congregation until death (Anonymous 1928:34), yet the landscape they inherited in 1853 was almost antithetical to their avowed identity. Carroll had presented himself as a wealthy, educated member of the aspiring political and economic elite. In contrast, the Redemptorists rejected all that Carroll's worldly, individualistic, publicly oriented terraced garden displayed. They were poor whereas he was wealthy; they were communal whereas he was individualistic; they were private whereas he was public; and they were distant from the strongly Protestant and secular town where Carroll had striven to be accepted. The landscape that the Redemptorists inherited was, in essence, in direct opposition to their professed ideology and prescribed way of life. For example, the priests had all taken vows of poverty, yet they were to live in a mansion valued in 1798 at $2,900 (Elder 1975:71) and in 1930 at $20,372 (Worden n.d.). The Redemptorists were Catholics who had devoted their lives to religion, yet they lived in the midst of a Protestant stronghold.[4] The congregation was a closed community, yet the site they occupied had been listed as one of the four most prominent landmarks on the 1781 map of Annapolis and had been groomed as a showpiece of wealth and taste. Finally, the first members were a group of twenty-two men resolved to live as a community, yet they were living in a house planned to be the city seat of a single family. If these characterizations are accurate, then one may conclude that in 1853 the Redemptorists were presented with a series of contradictions. This study of the congregation's shaping of the land is an examination of its resolution of these contradictions through rituals and the stage upon which they were enacted.

The symbolic approach taken here holds that the material world and mental world are integrally entwined and that the changes in the physical world of the Redemptorist community reflected and reified its changing social relations and ideology. By the very form of the landscape and the enactment of that space, young men entering the house were taught to be novitiates and, should they succeed, eventually priests. This "enactment" often took the form of ritual in the sense that, whether through formal liturgy or prescribed duties, all the labors of the priests and brothers were intended to be devotional. There was no division between "work" and other activities of the routine; hoeing the garden was as much a devotional act as prayer, and morning spiritual exercises were as necessary as meals. For instance, the congregation's historian (Borgmann 1904:35) described the construction of the rectory in which five hundred thousand bricks were unloaded by hand and forty thousand cubic feet of soil were excavated for the foundations: "Many a young man, whose tender hands had never touched a pick or shovel, exerted all his strength to remove the hard ground . . . and, though fingers sometimes bled . . . labor was consecrated by prayer." These rituals and their landscape settings were integral to the process of becoming and being a Redemptorist.

Community

Perhaps the most formative aspect of Redemptorist life was the creation of community. Entering the congregation meant taking on the name and title of the family—brother or father. The tension between this corporate identity and the individual adolescents and young men who entered as students was mediated by the daily practice of the regimen, or Rule. According to this Rule, all work was dedicated to the glory of God and to the perseverance of the congregation. The material culture and setting of the routine were part of the construction of this identification with the community. Students were required to wear the same habits (figure 11.2) and "under linens" in order to preserve poverty and the communal life *("Ne paupertati ac vitae communi offeratur damnum eodem vestitu et lintea utentur omnes subjecto")* (Visitatio Canonica, 2 December 1861). The few possessions owned by the Redemptorists

Figure 11.2. Redemptorist Fathers gathered in the garden with St. Mary's church in the background. Courtesy of the St. Mary's Parish Archives.

were held in common: excavations revealed an assemblage of coarse earthenwares and un-decorated institutional tablewares, predominantly ironstone. Items commonly thought of as "personal," such as thimbles, knives, brushes, and snuff, were dictated in the Rule to be "put in a place accessible to all" (Redemptorists 1939:145).

The uniformity of dress and possessions reflected a behavioral code that permitted little individual expression. The daily regime, including meditation, communal meals and worship, study, and manual labor, was completed in silence. Talking, at least under the first rector, Father Rumpler, was allowed only during "an hour of fraternal conversation" (Borgmann 1904:25). The rector and his "prefects" enforced the rules of the congregation, which prescribed that "No one is allowed to enter the room of another and have a mere conversation" and that all correspondence be monitored (Visitatio Canonica, 28 February 1882). Even "free days," granted at the disposal of the rector, only permitted students to take picnics to the farm, go boating, or participate in other communal recreation.

The organization of the architecture and landscape was transformed into a setting for a cooperative, communal life. On the first two floors of the Georgian-style Carroll house partitions were removed to create large spaces for communal worship, work, eating, and schooling.

> *Dommus ita est ordinata ut in Superiore parte sacellum domesticum praeparetur in quo apervandum sit Sanctissimum Sacramentum et peragenda varia ac exercitia devotionis et communia et privata. In parte domus inferiori Refectorium cum Culina, in caeteris vero partibus at Collegium pro recreatione instituenda et variis conventibus, a Regulis praescriptis peragendis sicut et (cubiculis privatis) cubicula privata disposita sunt.* (Redemptorists, *Chronicles,* April 1853)

> [T]he house was so arranged that in the upper part a domestic chapel might be prepared in which the most holy sacraments could be observed and various exercises of devotions be carried out both communally and privately. In the lower part of the house there was a refectory with a kitchen, whereas in the other parts [there was] a College [Common room] for the institution of recreation and various assemblies prescribed by the rules; similarly, certain rooms were arranged for private use.

On this stage the daily routine was played out as each morning the community assembled at matins before the day's assigned tasks, and each night after compline as the Redemptorists returned to their private cubicles on the third floor. The dispersal and gathering of the individual bodies created a rhythm and structure that bound the community and reified their relationships to one another.

The Redemptorists' labor during the day was similarly a routine of forming and re-forming for common tasks in common spaces. A map compiled from excavations and nine-teenth-century sources (figure 11.3) depicts the Redemptorist landscape as a functional and communal space. Unlike Carroll's design for pleasure and public display,[5] the space was organized to fulfill the needs of the community: there was a vineyard and wine cellar to the west, an arbor to the east, and a farmyard and boating facilities to the south. The area that had been Carroll's private, formal, terraced garden was used no differently by the Redemptorists than the rest of the area around the house. Excavations on the lowest terrace, which had been graced by Carroll's two classical brick pavilions, revealed the remains of a wooden springhouse. Excavations along the waterfront recovered part of a wooden chicken coop.

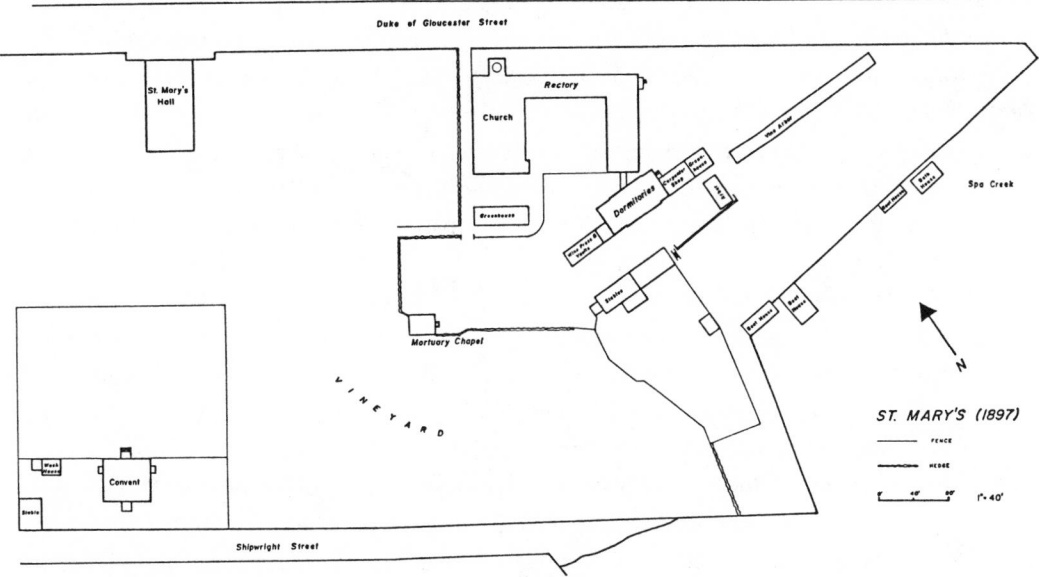

Figure 11.3. Map showing the St. Mary's site in 1897 with numerous outbuildings built in the former Carroll terraced garden.

Furthermore, access through the Redemptorists' landscape was dictated by the work to be performed rather than by the creation of vistas for personal enjoyment. Whereas Carroll had separated his work space from his ornamental landscape, the Redemptorist trod the same paths whether bringing in the grape harvest, going out to tend flower and vegetable plots, feeding the chickens, or returning from a swim in the creek. Carroll created a geometrically regular landscape (Leone and Shackel 1990) that, when viewed from the water, framed the house as its central focal point. In contrast, the Redemptorists' property was a jumble of barns, outbuildings, religious statuary, and fields. Once in the garden, Carroll's visitors could approach the house only by surmounting a series of ramps and terraces. The sequence of visual and physical barriers reflected the differential access accorded to different members of society. For the Redemptorists, access was determined by the strict requirements of the students' and priests' daily regimen. For instance, the Rule lists it as a "Grievous Fault. . . . To go out into the garden, kitchen, the Refectory, or the balcony, without the Superior's leave" (Redemptorists 1939:181).

Within this setting, the labor itself was a consecration of communal identity. The chronicler writes:

> *Vix notare necesse est paupertatum in omnibus regnasse nihilominus omnes quam maxima animi pace ac tranquillitate perfunctantur, quum in hac domo omnia. . . . Regulis magis conformiter peragere valerens.* (Redemptorists, *Chronicles,* introduction)

> It is scarcely necessary to note that poverty reigned in everything. . . . Nonetheless everyone enjoyed the greatest possible peace and tranquillity of spirit/mind because [insofar as] they were able to do so, [they] performed everything in this house in conformity with the rules.

Much of that labor was devoted to fashioning the built forms that in turn structured the daily movement, views, and formations of the occupants. The *Chronicles* contain numerous references to painting, cleaning, and even major building projects. Referring to the construction of the rectory, a marginalia note added to the 1862 *Chronicles* recounts that "[i]n May the students and novices began to inhabit the new house. The labors of Frs. Rosenbaum & Bone & Werner & Strict are ever worthy of remembrance. Plastering (at least pitching mortar into crevices), lathing, painting, etc. were ordinary occupations. Studying was out of the question. The new house has been solemnly blessed by Rev. P. Provincial before anyone was permitted to inhabit it." An area was set aside for a "Novice Garden," where in 1868 the congregation history records: "To promote the health of the young men, Father Anwander had part of the garden divided into plots, one of which was assigned to each student for cultivation of flowers or other plants he might fancy. It afforded unspeakable delight to the good Rector to see the success of some in raising flowers; or that of others, more given to utility in their views, in the cultivation of beans, peas, or corn" (Borgmann 1904:55). Other agricultural duties were practiced in the community's fields, where the students harvested grapes in the vineyard and other crops grown at the farm just outside of town. In the practice of these rituals, whether the harvest in the fields or the liturgy in the chapel, the novices were trained to be Redemptorists. Through participation in these communal acts, the members reinforced the solidarity of the group and the relation of the members to one another. The rituals coalesced the labor, the landscape, and the ideology into the very actions by which these men became Redemptorists.

Poverty

If the basis of the congregation was its community, the most identifiable characteristic of the Redemptorists' daily life was the realization of the vows of poverty. The Rule states that "it is forbidden to any member of the Congregation to have any *peculium,* or private possession of money or other things" (Redemptorists 1939:141). The vow of poverty was the locus for a whole array of associations related to denial of the body so as to enrich the spirit. Celibacy reserved all passion for the Redeemer. Lack of attachment to things left the young novices open to receive and value gifts of the spirit. In a sense, worldliness was removed so that "otherworldliness" could be the sole focus of the men. The philosophy of asceticism is best summarized by the congregation's historian:

> Many of these young men, nay boys of sixteen to eighteen, had left homes which every comfort rendered sweet. They had left loving parents and affectionate sisters and brothers to consecrate themselves heart and soul to their Divine Master. . . . With manly courage they embraced the austerities of the religious life, remembering that, only by suffering and self-denial, could they become true disciples of their Redeemer, and true apostles. Thus we find delicate youths undergoing hardships that might be found unbearable even by the robust. (Borgmann 1904:24-25)

The rituals enforcing this ideal of an impoverished body and enriched spirit were, as in the case of community, part of the immediate landscape and daily regimen. Poverty as an ideal was enacted in the dress, possessions, and daily regimen of the novices and expressed in the landscape as the preeminence of the utilitarian over the ornamental.

The 1770s landscape of the Carroll family was transformed under the Redemptorists from a formal terraced garden to a working farm. The ornamental or aesthetic qualities were subsumed instantly by the needs of the Congregation. The *Chronicles* mark this shift in the opening sentence of the first volume, which records the transfer of the Fathers to *"Caroli Carroll domum hunc cum agris adjacentibus"* (this Charles Carroll house together with the adjacent fields). During the first months of occupation in April of 1853 the chronicler recorded:

> *Domus in quantum fieri potuit reparta est, Hortus in ordinem restitutus Religiosis convenientem. Fratres Servientes sicut et Novitii multi erant in laboribus rusticis obeundis, quum multae manus necessariae essent ad ordinem illum restituendum. Viae et Semitae in horto erant sternendae, herbae inutiles eradicandae quae utilia essent plantata, inter alia, arbores pomiferae, vites, etc.*
> (Redemptorists, *Chronicles*, April 1853)

> The house was repaired to the extent that it was possible. The garden was restored in a manner appropriate to the Religious. There were many Brothers and Novices who performed manual labor since many hands were necessary so that it might be restored to order. Roads and narrow paths in the garden had to be spread out, and useless plants had to be eradicated in order that useful ones might be planted, among others, fruit bearing trees, vines, etc.

In short, Carroll's landscape garden was viewed by the congregation as useful, arable land. Early photographs and maps depict the metamorphosis of the landscape (figure 11.4), including newly constructed barns for livestock (cows, horses, ducks, chickens) and fields for crops. In the late 1860s, a vineyard, an underground stone vault, and a wine press were added to the west end of the Carroll house to produce wine for the use of the congregation. Excavations on the lowest terrace revealed an underground outbuilding, probably a springhouse, built in the latter part of the nineteenth century. Where there once stood a large framed addition with classical porticos and columned porch, excavations uncovered the foundations of a greenhouse used, most likely, to hang grapes for wine making and to start bedding plants for the Redemptorists' kitchen gardens.

Figure 11.4. Ca. 1892 photograph showing the Redemptorists' transformation of the Carroll garden. Courtesy of the St. Mary's Parish Archives.

The transformation of the landscape was echoed in architectural changes as well. In both cases the ideology of poverty was constructed both in the rituals enacted in the spaces and in the fabric of the buildings and grounds themselves. Perhaps the most literal example is an entry in the 1910 *Chronicles:* "When the whitewash from the walls of the top floor in the old house was removed an old inscription was brought to light above the door into the room above the common room. The inscription was thus: *Haec est Domus Dei at Porta Coeli* [This is the house of God and the gate of heaven]" (Redemptorists, *Chronicles,* 31 December 1910).[6]

In 1903 the Reverend Joseph Wissel, among the first priests to arrive, recalled their initial impressions:

> It was on Wednesday in Easter-week . . . that the steamboat . . . brought . . . fifteen students of the Redemptorist Order and three or four lay-brothers, led by a young Father. . . . As they approached the ancient city of Annapolis, a brick building of venerable appearance was pointed out to them, and they were told it was their future home. After landing, they . . . entered the old Carroll Mansion, where they were welcomed by their Superior. The door closed behind them—and the venerable building became at that hour a Monastic Institution. (As quoted in Anonymous 1928:67)

The metamorphosis into a "Monastic Institution," so instantaneous in the account above, was a physical as well as ideological transformation. Architectural analysis of the house by James Wollen and the Carroll house volunteers has revealed evidence of some of these early changes to the house.[7] Fireplaces were bricked in to provide more efficient heating. The kitchen fireplace in the lowest floor, which was excavated during the summer of 1991 (Logan et al. 1992), was converted into an enormous oven listed on the 1885 Sanborn Insurance Company map as a bread oven. More substantial structural changes included a three-story, sixteen-room addition built on the west end of the house and a massive rectory built onto the north side of the house. Much of the architectural ornamentation, like the marble mantle pieces, was stripped and the elaborate plaster work of the public rooms chopped through to create niches for altars and closets. In each instance, the changes made to the physical environment of the community were dictated by their vow of poverty, and the austere landscape they came to inhabit, in turn, reinforced the life of material denial they had chosen.

Public/Private

The discussion of both aspects in the formation of the congregation's identity—community and poverty—has dealt with the internal dynamics and organization of the group. This final section considers the nineteenth-century Redemptorist community within its larger setting of the town of Annapolis. Almost everything about the Redemptorists was designed to distance them from the secular world. They were founded to be a "house of God": to serve the people yet not be of the people. They removed themselves quite explicitly from the social setting around them by rejecting conjugal relations and adopting the congregation as their family. Not only were the Redemptorists of the Annapolis house placed in a liminal role by their constitution and mission, in the middle of the nineteenth century they were also one of the few Catholic establishments in the midst of a Protestant stronghold. The contradiction between this fundamentally private identity and their very public property—public in the sense that it was highly visible literally and historically—was mediated in the changes in the landscape and the ritual enactment of that space.

One of the most dramatic physical expressions of the resolution of the contradiction between the Carroll public persona and the Redemptorists' closed community was the visual masking of the Carroll house itself. In 1857, a new church was built between the Carroll house and Duke of Gloucester Street. Barns were raised in front of the house, and trees were planted along the terraces, profoundly altering the vistas from the garden and essentially screening the house from public view. Whereas Carroll's garden framed and accentuated the house, the Redemptorists built a row of boathouses along the waterfront. The addition of a massive rectory next to the church completely obscured the Carroll house from the street when it was finished in 1862 (figure 11.5). The result was that, within twenty years of the Redemptorists' arrival, a prominent historical landmark was made invisible to the town. The symbol of Carroll's patriotism, prosperity, and prominence had been hidden, and in its place stood a productive farmyard and a building of institutional scale and proportion unlike any then in Annapolis.

The veiling of the landscape was not simply an externally oriented mask of the ostentation of the house, however. The cloaked grounds shielded the Redemptorists from the outside world. The property was surrounded by walls that served as physical and symbolic barriers to those within and without. For the new students within, the walls defined the boundaries of the community. To cross them without authorization was to leave the group, as the 1886 chronicler records: "Novice Fr. Spengler jumped the fence early this Sunday morning" (Redemptorists, *Chronicles,* 12 August 1886). The walls were also a barrier to the outside

Figure 11.5. Taken from across Duke of Gloucester Street, this ca. 1876 view of the Redemptorist rectory shows how completely the Carroll house and gardens were screened from view. Courtesy of the St. Mary's Parish Archives.

world. A small fire in the Carroll house elicited the following report: "The news caused some excitement. A large number of people assembled in front of the church but few gained access to the grounds" (Redemptorists, *Chronicles,* 8 December 1907). The isolation of the community was not simply a product of the Redemptorist vows, however. During the first decades of their residence in Annapolis there was a marked hostility toward Catholics in the town, much of which may be attributed to the "Know-nothings." These members of a secret society, so named for their response to questions about their beliefs, eventually organized into the "American party" and achieved success in local elections promoting anti-Catholic and xenophobic platforms. At St. Mary's, several incidents revealed a distrust of the priests and suspicions about their religious practices. For instance, an anonymous letter accused the Redemptorists of holding hostages, burying bodies in the garden, and placing statues over their graves (Borgmann 1904:23). The social distance between the congregation and the town was reflected in and reified by the landscape. The walls that blocked the gazes of the townspeople and confined the residents within manifested and reinforced the boundaries of self and other between the congregation and the world beyond.

The changes to the landscape during the Redemptorists' first forty years on the property reveal a complete transformation. With the exception of the basic topography of slopes and falls, Carroll's ornamental, ordered garden had been replaced by a productive, working farm. Self-sufficient, communal labor had replaced the wealth display of profit made from the exploitation of workers and slaves. Dressed in their uniform habits, the novices and brothers grew the vegetables they ate, picked the grapes for the wine they drank, and collected eggs from the chickens for daily meals. In 1898 the chronicler even records, "Our candidates are busily engaged in digging a trench for the sewer pipes . . ." (Redemptorists, *Chronicles,* 14 March 1898). During some renovations, the chronicler writes of an old road leading to the boathouse that was "built, I believe, by the novices, and it recalls many old memories, since they uprooted many weeds during the novitiate" (Redemptorists, *Chronicles,* 13 April 1911). Whether in the garden or in a pipe trench, the Redemptorists' labor and sweat was as integral a part of their training as prayer and daily mass. The ritual communal performances and the settings in which they were played out reinforced their identity and resolved in part the contradictions posed by their chosen vocation. In contrast to Carroll's symbolic source of agrarian-based wealth that masked the true source of his profit making (Kryder-Reid 1991a, 1991b, 1994a), the Redemptorist landscape was one of utility, and what it produced was not simply caloric intake, but obedient novices committed to a life of service as well as material and sexual denial. The Carroll landscape presented the illusion of the natural legislator; the Redemptorists constructed one of a homogeneous, devout, and dutiful congregation. Both landscapes were constructions and reifications of their owners' identities, but whereas Carroll's garden legitimated his wealth, the Redemptorists' landscape was a consecration of their poverty and vows.

THE REDEMPTORISTS: THE TWENTIETH CENTURY

The turn of the century brought profound changes to the Redemptorist Congregation, many of which were in direct opposition to the central vows of the community. The congregation was becoming more involved in the "outside" world, their material resources were increasing, and individuals within the community were developing more specialized ministries. This change may be attributed to a number of factors. St. Mary's School was founded in 1867, bringing with it increased interaction with townspeople. The financial base of both the congregation and the parish was increasingly secure, enabling more participation in the local market economy. In addition, the priests' involvement in fund raising and other economic concerns appears to have commanded a larger portion of their administrative efforts. Organized fund-raisers included parish bazaars, theater productions, and an endless array of parish suppers, dances, and fairs. Outside workers were hired for major repairs and improvements to the physical plant such as the introduction of steam heat and electricity. Relations with the town improved; Know-nothingism had been eclipsed by the Civil War, and the Redemptorists' ministry to Catholics enrolled in the Naval Academy increased their visibility and interactions. The Redemptorist Congregation and the St. Mary's Parish were growing both in numbers and resources.

If the Redemptorist nineteenth-century landscape was a closed, internally focused space reinforcing the vows of poverty and communal life, one would expect changes in the congregation such as increasing wealth, the closing of the novitiate, more autonomy for priests, and expansion in the parochial and external ministries to be reflected in changes in the landscape. Particularly after the novitiate left in 1907, the congregation's primary emphasis was no longer on the training of candidates. The landscape, therefore, shifted from being solely an internally disciplining force to being an externally directed construction of the Redemptorists' communal identity as well. At least one of the priests was self-consciously aware of the changes from the formerly austere environment: "The history of medieval monasticism gives detailed accounts of the architecture of the entire plant—the church, the monastery, cloister, etc. The barns, wine cellars, etc. etc. etc. As time with the developments of science bringing in its train varied improvements rendered facilities not incongruous with the spirit of asceticism, Annapolis also gradually abandoned primitive and so called antiquated methods and introduced up-to-date practices" (Redemptorists, *Chronicles,* 10 March 1923).

During the first decade of the twentieth century, a planting program, paths, an arbor, and statuary restored the garden to a recreational and ornamental space (figure 11.6). The vineyard was torn up, and the greenhouse and winery, to the east and west of the house respectively, were demolished. In 1910 the chronicler writes: "Even the gardens have put on a new appearance. Instead of the old straight formal walks, there is now a continuous stretch of lawn, through which winds a pretty serpentine gravel path beginning at the step of the Fathers' Common Room and ending at the old [house?] road which leads down to the water" (Redemptorists, *Chronicles,* 15 March 1910). Described as "long an eye-sore in the garden," a second greenhouse next to the church that had been built with the labor of the candidates was demolished (Redemptorists, *Chronicles,* 27 June 1928). Rather than serving as a training ground for novitiates, the landscape became an ornamental surrounding for the Redemptorists' home and a showpiece for honored guests. During the visit of the Most Reverend General, the chronicler writes: "At this hour he . . . repaired to the garden. Three beautiful trees were lying there ready to be planted by our august guests. Father General chose a beautiful, well-branched tulip tree, as a living reminder to perpetuate the memory of the Visit. Father Hedel planted a silver maple and Father Foure an elm" (Redemptorists, *Chronicles,* 10 October 1910). After a visit from another order, the chronicler reports, "4 Fathers from Sacred Heart motored to St. Mary's . . . and returned home full of admiration on account of the extensive and beautiful improvement" (Redemptorists, *Chronicles,* 7 October 1925).

Figure 11.6. View of the "Old Carroll House" from the east with recent landscaping improvements, ca. 1920–25. Courtesy of the St. Mary's Parish Archives.

The beautification of the grounds was matched by improvements around the house that also reflected the outward focus of the congregation. "To render the entrance from Gloucester Street more respectable as well as more solid and suitable for the transportation of all sorts of goods, the same concrete and vitrified pavement was wisely procured by Father Rector. It forms a united whole and presents a good appearance conjointly with the main street with which it connects" (Redemptorists, *Chronicles,* 26 October 1901). The *Chronicles* report that in 1911, as part of the beautification project, "One of our working [*sic*] is putting holes in the wall along Gloucester St. between the Church and the school for the purpose of covering this wall with greens" (22 March 1911). The resulting effect was that the wall, once a barrier, was given the appearance of a decorative hedge. The entire "beautification" project not only reflects the construction of a public as well as private identity, but it also presents the identity of the congregation's public mission rather than private vows. In contrast to its earlier disciplining force of poverty, service, and obedience, the garden now served to communicate and construct the Redemptorists' identity as competent leaders of a prosperous school and parish.

Another aspect of the landscape change was the physical opening of the property for a variety of activities to the people of the parish and the community. The grounds were made available for public bazaars in the school, concerts in the church, and recreation days for visiting religious groups. In addition to the boating and swimming facilities on the grounds, boat rides became a favorite pastime after the rector purchased a motorized launch. A produce farm outside of town (leased and finally purchased in 1889) became a popular picnic spot. The garden even became a money-making proposition. The *Chronicles* describe one such fund-raising lawn fete:

The green-house nearest the church was used as a kitchen.... There were four supper tables set on the path leading over to the school yard. The lawn between that and the Mortuary Chapel was given up to the small ice-cream tables. Across the road and near the upper hedge was "Rebecca's Well" where grape juice punch was served.... Next to that, but nearer the Mortuary Chapel just at the turn of the wagon road was the Fish Pond. The orchestra was on the porch of the "old house."... Everyone said that our grounds were the most ideal in the city for a Lawn Fete.

(Redemptorists, Chronicles, 6 August 1913)

Part of this construction of the community's public identity is revealed in an increasing awareness of the history of the Carroll property and, with it, a claim to a piece of Annapolis history. Frequent reference is made in the *Chronicles* to the "Carroll Mansion," rather than simply to the "house" or the "old house." An entry in 1922 notes that "[r]epairs were begun on the interior of the so called 'Old House of Carroll Fame'" (Redemptorists, *Chronicles,* 13 March 1922). Numerous visitors requested tours of the home of the "Last Living Signer": "About 5 P.M., four prominent members of the Legislature ... came to the Rectory and asked to be shown about the grounds. Rev. F. Bonia accommodated them. After showing them the Old House and the grounds, he brought them to the church and explained to them, for they were all Protestants, the meaning of the Stations, Confessionals, etc." (Redemptorists, *Chronicles,* 13 March 1901). During a "Colonial Day" celebration, a somewhat facetious chronicler records: "About 300 people visited the Carroll gardens to view the old Carroll Manor which was hermetically sealed. Only a few favored gentlemen were surreptitiously smuggled inside for a glimpse of the famous mansion" (Redemptorists, *Chronicles,* 15 May 1928). The chronicler notes this change in the Redemptorists' attitude toward the Carroll house in 1923. Referring to the house, he writes, "This venerable building dating back to the very first quarter of the 18th century is gradually losing (at least interiorly) its primitive appearance ..." (Redemptorists, *Chronicles,* 10 March 1923).

Perhaps the most dramatic change in the landscape was in its segmentation and specialization. Now that it was no longer the training ground for the novitiate, the farmyard was no longer needed for communal labor projects. Instead, members of the community specialized in particular aspects of ministry; some did "missions," much like revivals, throughout the mid-Atlantic, others tended to the Annapolis parish, some worked primarily with the St. Mary's School, and still others occupied themselves with the African-American members of the parish. As the Redemptorists' understanding of their ministry changed, the landscape reflected and reified their community.

The grounds became more accessible to the public, but they also were increasingly segmented by function. The southwest waterfront was graded to serve as a small farmyard for cows, ducks, chickens, and a horse. To the west of the house and church, school buildings, including a separate "Colored" school for African Americans, occupied most of the lots. The space to the south of the church was landscaped with lawns and winding walks, while a wooden "mortuary chapel" was built for the transfer of Redemptorist burials from the church undercroft. The brothers continued to work primarily on the care of the animals and the upkeep of the house and garden, while the priests did the work of "ordained ministers."

In the midst of all this expansion, diversification, and segmentation, the site of the earlier Carroll garden continued to be the preserve of the priests, and in this space their identity was powerfully enacted and reenacted in the landscape. In this instance, the construction of self was through the sanctification of the landscape; that is, through the transformation of the ornamental space into an extension of the church itself. This process of the sanctification of the landscape was a gradual one of reification; perceptions and physical changes mutually reinforced each other. The physical changes included the construction of a mortuary chapel in which priests and brothers were buried, the placement of religious statuary in the garden, and, in 1948, moving the Redemptorist cemetery into the garden. These physical manifestations were enacted in rituals, both full parish liturgies and private community worship. On Rogation Day in 1910 "the community went in procession through the gardens, chanting the litanies, and asking God's blessing on the fruit of the field. The Procession was followed by High Mass in Church" (Redemptorists, *Chronicles,* 2 May 1910). The annual Corpus Christi Procession followed a standard route through the garden in which the structures, particularly the veranda on the west end of the Carroll house and the arbor on the fifth terrace, became not just landmarks, but stations of the liturgy:

> The whole parish took part. . . . The Procession passed from the Church through the carriage road to the porch of the 'Old House' where the first Benediction was given. Then the people passed along to the summer house down to the lower path while the altar boys went through the arbor to the altar erected in the middle facing the creek. Here the second Benediction was given. Immediately after this Benediction the procession passed through the arbor out through the kitchen gate, up the street and into the Church where the third and last Benediction was given. A large number of men, women, and children took part. . . . (Redemptorists, *Chronicles,* 6 June 1912)

The following year is described in even more detail:

> As the procession moved along hymns were sung. After leaving the Church we entered the property by the wagon road and went to the porch of the Carroll Manor where the first Benediction was given from a pretty altar erected there. Then we passed along the Carroll Manor to the summerhouse, here the people turned down the cement walk to the lower gravel path along the Spa and up the grass mound at the top of which another beautiful altar had been erected facing the Creek with the large box wood as a background. The torch bearers, flower girls and clergy, instead of walking down the cement walk, went directly to the altar and the second Benediction was given while the faithful knelt in the paths stretching from the Old Carroll House to the altar. After this we passed around the circular cement walk to the large gate near the kitchen, and up the street to the main door of the Church which we entered just as it began to grow dark. (Redemptorists, *Chronicles,* 27 May 1913)

The garden also became symbolically charged through the Redemptorist community's meditations and private worship. For example, the *Chronicles* note during the summer of 1916 that the Rosary was held in the garden on account of the heat. Perhaps the most visible sign of the sacred connotation of the garden was the excavation of a communion chalice, paten, and crucifix figurines that had been buried there, according to custom, after they were no longer suitable for use. While the particular objects unearthed had been buried relatively recently, the practice was a long-standing one. The use of the garden for church-related activities and the private meditations of the resident fathers reinforced the identity of the members of the community, now so disparate in their ministries. The ritual of the liturgy brought together brother and priest alike in the presence of their buried *confreres* and on the landscape of their ancestors. Together, in the formal ritual of Catholic liturgies and in the secular rituals of daily life, the fertile ground continued to be as powerful a metaphor as it had been throughout the Redemptorists' tenure. Father Seelos, rector of the Annapolis House in 1857, wrote to his sister:

> Our Novitiate is truly one of the most beautiful places that can be imagined not only on account of the situation of the garden that descends in terraces to the Bay, but especially on account of the piety of the good young novices, who live united in angelic innocence, preparing themselves for their sublime vocation. It appears as if God would represent exteriorly the virtues of these pious people, for in the fruitfulness of the garden, the lilies are especially present in such grandeur and luxuriance, as I have never seen. . . . (Quoted in Zimmer 1887)

Similarly, in a sermon during the 1903 celebration of the Golden Jubilee of the Redemptorist community in Annapolis, the Reverend Joseph Wissel said, "[T]he most precious fruit produced by this part of the Lord's vineyard, is that which grows only on the best cultivated soil. I mean the vocation to the religious life and to the exalted dignity of the priesthood" (quoted in Borgmann 1904:207). As in Carroll's time, the garden served as a theater, but for the Redemptorists it was a private performance and the script shaped not only the action of the performers, but the meaning of the theater itself.

THE MEANINGS OF LANDSCAPE

> Yes. Space is fundamental in any form of communal life; space is fundamental in any exercise of power.
>
> (Foucault 1984:252)

This essay began by asking how our actions and interactions with our surroundings shape who we are. For the Redemptorists, the landscape was not merely a product of their needs and beliefs; it was a material force in the creation of their communal identity. What had been in the eighteenth century a segregated space, an expression of the reason and rationale of an elite gentleman, became in the nineteenth century an expression of a community whose world was defined by faith and whose students were trained through labor. That community's work then changed, and as its identity became more public, its members' private preserve became sacred. Through these changes and the rituals that enacted them, the landscape has continued to be an expression of and active agent in the Redemptorists' changing identity. The rituals coalesced the labor, the landscape, and the ideology into the very actions by which these men became Redemptorists.

Throughout the twentieth century the physical boundaries of the garden shifted, but the remaining garden area, now much closer to the original 1770s configuration, remains the private reserve of the Redemptorists (figure 11.7). A school recreation field has replaced the mortuary chapel, and the demand for parking spaces has required the paving of most of the area to the west of the Carroll house. While the rest of the Redemptorists' property has become the open grounds of the school and parish, the area around the house that had been Carroll's original garden is marked as the "Fathers' area." In 1962, the *Chronicles* record: "A new fence (heavy wire) being installed around property to protect the privacy of Fathers' area and also the cemetery. Too many outsiders have been using the property for strolling and parking cars. Fence will extend from Carroll House across back of playing field and down the entrance on Shipwright St. Also the stone wall will have a fence on top of it. The bank of the creek, a favorite spot of trespassers, will be fenced off on the bridge end. Good idea altogether" (Redemptorists, *Chronicles,* 10 May 1962). Today those barriers, in the form of fences, "no trespassing" signs, and guard dogs, continue to guard the sanctuary. But the boundaries of this religious community and its historical legacy are constantly being negotiated.

As it has been throughout the site's history, the future of the St. Mary's landscape is a question of the construction of selves, and it is a question of power. Charles Carroll determined the form of the eighteenth-century landscape; in the Redemptorists' times, the rector has dictated the changes to the land. In each case, those in control have molded the landscape according to their vision of themselves and how they wished to be perceived. Now the actors on the stage include the Redemptorists, a group of highly invested volunteers, a foundation for the restoration and management of the house, a Historic District Commission with a mandate to control standards but a jurisdiction limited to what is visible from a public right-of-way, and an archaeological project called Archaeology in Annapolis.

The meaning of the landscape continues to change as the identities of its occupants and viewers transform it and are transformed by it. The role of landscape archaeology at the site has been, in part, to identify the physical changes on the property through time, but it also has the potential to interpret those changes, to articulate the significance of the landscape in the past, and to make explicit the relations of power that have determined and continue to determine the shape of the land.

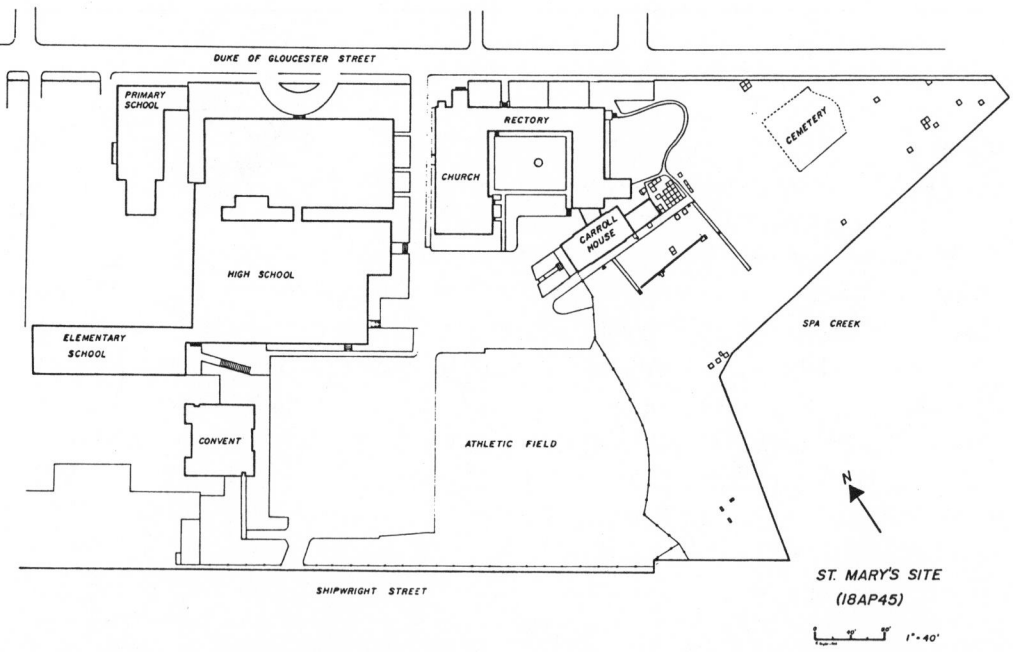

Figure 11.7. Map of the St. Mary's site in 1990 showing changes in the Redemptorist landscape. Archaeological units, excavated from 1987 to 1990 by Archaeology in Annapolis, are also shown.

NOTES

1. The *Chronicles* are housed at the Redemptorists' headquarters in Brooklyn, New York. The *Chronicles* are organized by house and province. The Annapolis House volumes cover the years from 1853 to the present. I wish to thank the archivist, Father Rush, for his generous assistance with the collection. I also wish to thank the Trustees of Harvard University for supporting much of this research with a Dumbarton Oaks Junior Fellowship, and to thank my colleagues of Archaeology in Annapolis, and particularly Mark Leone for his guidance.

2. *"Ipsi curam Catholicorum huius civitas eiusque vicinitas susciperant"* (Redemptorists, *Chronicles,* introduction).

3. For an analysis of how gender distinctions were maintained, despite this egalitarian ideal, see Kryder-Reid 1994b. Some of the ideas developed in this chapter were outlined in an earlier overview of the St. Mary's landscape (Kryder-Reid 1994a).

4. In 1853 the St. Mary's parish rolls list only thirteen members (Borgmann 1904:20–21), while St. Anne's, the town's most prominent Protestant Church, lists 217 communicants in 1857 (Paynter 1980:48).

5. For a detailed description and interpretation of the Carroll garden, constructed during the 1770s, see Kryder-Reid 1991a, 1991b, 1994a; Leone and Shackel 1987, 1990; and Leone et al. 1989.

6. These words came to light again eighty years later when plaster was removed during the restoration of the house interior (Robert Worden 1990, personal communication).

7. The Carroll house interior has undergone extensive restoration. A dedicated group of volunteers for the Carroll House Foundation, most notably Robert Worden and Tony Lindauer, have given generously of their time for the study and preservation of this structure.

REFERENCES

Anonymous
1928   *St. Mary's Diamond Jubilee, 1853–1928.* Privately printed, Annapolis, Maryland.

Borgmann, Henry
1904   *History of the Redemptorists at Annapolis, Maryland from 1853 to 1903.* College Press, Ilchester, Maryland.

Durkheim, Émile
1915   *The Elementary Forms of Religious Life.* 1912. Originally published as *Les Formes Élémentaires de la Vie Religieuse, le Système Totémique en Australie,* F. Alcon, Paris. Allen and Unwin, London.

Elder, William Voss, III
1975   The Carroll House in Annapolis and Doughoregan Manor. In *"Anywhere So Long As There Be Freedom": Charles Carroll of Carrollton, His Family and His Maryland,* exhibition and catalogue organized by Ann C. Van Devanter, pp. 59–81. Baltimore Museum of Art, Baltimore.

Foucault, Michel
1984   *The Foucault Reader,* edited by Paul Rabinow. Pantheon Books, New York.

Frazer, James George
1922   *The Golden Bough.* Macmillan Co., New York.

Geertz, Clifford
1973   Ritual and Social Change: A Javanese Example. In *The Interpretation of Cultures,* pp. 142–69. Basic Books, New York.

Kryder-Reid, Elizabeth
1991a   Landscape and Luxury: The Garden of Charles Carroll of Carrollton. Paper presented at the annual meeting of the Society for Historical Archaeology, Richmond, Virginia.

1991b   Landscape as Myth: The Contextual Archaeology of an Annapolis Landscape. Ph.D. diss., Department of Anthropology, Brown University. University Microfilms, Ann Arbor.

1994a   "As Is the Gardener, So Is the Garden": The Archaeology of Landscape as Myth. In *Historical Archaeology of the Chesapeake,* edited by Paul A. Shackel and Barbara J. Little, pp. 131–48. Smithsonian Institution Press, Washington, D.C.

1994b   "With Manly Courage": Reading the Construction of Gender in a Nineteenth-Century Religious Community. In *Those of Little Note: Gender, Race, and Class in Historical Archaeology,* edited by Elizabeth M. Scott, pp. 97–114. University of Arizona Press, Tucson.

Leach, Edmund

1968   Ritual. In *International Encyclopedia of the Social Sciences,* pp. 520–26. Macmillan Co., New York.

Leone, Mark P., Elizabeth Kryder-Reid, Julie H. Ernstein, and Paul A. Shackel

1989   Power Gardens of Annapolis. *Archaeology* 42(2):35–39, 74–75.

Leone, Mark P., and Paul A. Shackel

1987   Forks, Clocks and Power. In *Mirror and Metaphor: Material and Social Constructions of Reality,* edited by Daniel W. Ingersoll Jr. and Gordon Bronitsky, pp. 46–61. University Press of America, Lanham, Maryland.

1990   Plane and Solid Geometry in Colonial Gardens in Annapolis, Maryland. In *Earth Patterns: Essays in Landscape Archaeology,* edited by William M. Kelso and Rachel Most, pp. 153–67. University Press of Virginia, Charlottesville.

Levi-Strauss, Claude

1966   *The Savage Mind.* University of Chicago Press, Chicago.

Logan, George C., Thomas W. Bodor, Lynn D. Jones, and Marian C. Creveling

1992   1991 Archaeological Excavations at the Charles Carroll House in Annapolis, Maryland (18AP45). Report on file, Historic Annapolis Foundation and Charles Carroll House, Annapolis, Maryland.

Malinowski, Bronislaw

1948   *Magic, Science and Religion.* Beacon Press, Boston.

Paynter, William K.

1980   *St. Anne's Annapolis: History and Times.* St. Anne's Parish, Annapolis, Maryland.

Radcliffe-Brown, A. R.

1952   *Structure and Function in Primitive Society.* Free Press, Glencoe, Illinois.

Redemptorists

1853–1962   *Chronicles.* Bound manuscripts on file, Redemptorist Archives, Provincial Headquarters, Brooklyn, New York.

1939   *The Constitution and Rules of the Congregation of Priests Under the Title of the Most Holy Redeemer.* Translated from the Latin and published with the authority of The Most Reverend Father Patrick Murray. St. Mary's Clapham, London.

Robertson-Smith, William

1894   *Lectures in the Religion of the Semites.* A. & C. Black, London.

Tylor, Edward B.

1871   *Primitive Culture: Researches into the Development of Mythology, Philosophy, Religion, Art, and Custom.* Two volumes. J. Murray, London.

Visitatio Canonica

1862–94   *Statuta Visitationis Canaicae.* Reports for the House of Studies at Annapolis. On file in the Saint Mary's Parish Archives, Annapolis, Maryland.

Worden, Robert

n.d.   Carroll House History. Ms. on file, Carroll House Foundation, Annapolis, Maryland.

Zimmer, Peter

1887   *Life and Labors of Rev. Francis Xavier Seelos of the Congregation of the Most Holy Redeemer.* Translated from the German, *Leben und Wirten des Hochwürdigen P. Franz Xaxer Seelos aus der Congregation des Allerheil Erlössers.* Benzinger Brothers, New York. On file at the Redemptorist Archives, Brooklyn, New York.

12

"The Transient Nature of All Things Sublunary": Romanticism, History, and Ruins in Nineteenth-Century Southern Maryland

Julia A. King

For landscape archaeologists, a basic assumption is that landscapes are the setting for the interaction of people with the natural world and with one another. A second assumption is that landscapes are always changing, and from this, it follows that earlier landscapes often are visibly embedded in the contemporary landscape. In many ways, then, landscapes provide the setting in which most people interact not only with nature and with other people, but also with their past.

In the United States today, remnants of earlier landscapes can have considerable importance. These fragments are often tucked among a confusing and increasingly alien landscape. Earlier landscapes can provide identity and reinforce "traditional social order[s]" (Stilgoe 1982:3); it is no wonder that Americans seek to preserve these landscapes through the controls offered by zoning ordinances.

Earlier landscapes were also evident in the past. However, few archaeological studies in America have addressed the importance of past landscapes to the people archaeologists study. This is partially due to both the nature of the data base and the methods used to study that data base. Deciphering and reconstructing the chronological layers of a "frozen" landscape can be difficult if not impossible in many cases.

This chapter examines how one past group perceived the overlap of landscapes and incorporated the earlier landscape into its system of meaning. It focuses on the rural oligarchy in nineteenth-century southern Maryland and how that group used remnants of earlier landscapes. Architectural ruins dotted both the southern Maryland and the early American landscape during this period, but their significance has not been previously addressed. Archaeological and documentary research suggest that, although many architectural ruins could be found in the early-nineteenth-century southern Maryland landscape, some of these features cannot be explained simply by economics. Instead, certain ruins were maintained because they served as a visible link with the southern Maryland past. This study identifies three such ruins in southern Maryland. While this is an admittedly small sample, this research nonetheless demonstrates the symbolic significance of at least some architectural ruins and the need for further study of these features.

THE USE OF HISTORY IN NINETEENTH-CENTURY AMERICA

History as an interpretive process is much more than an explanation of a series of historically known facts or events.[1] The interpretation of history can be seen as a reflection of contemporary social structures and values. While the search for "objectivity" remains strong in the historical profession, "historians' attitudes . . . have always been closely tied to changing social, political, cultural, and professional contexts" (Novick 1988:628, chapters 13–16). In modern social science, critical theory and its various forms have been used to underscore the significance of contemporary thinking and social structures to the interpretation of the past. As a result, an increasing amount of history has been produced that challenges not only the subject matter of those who study the past, but the nature of the interpretive process itself (cf. Gero and Conkey 1991; Leone 1981; Leone, Potter, and Shackel 1987).

The interpretation and use of history is not restricted to professionals. All people regularly make use of the past to place their own actions and those of others into a recognizable and sensible context. Two recent studies suggest the importance of interpretations of this type to contemporary community life. T. H. Breen, hired to undertake an ostensibly professional and "real" historical study of the Mulford Farmstead in East Hampton, New York, found that the East Hampton past is constructed and reconstructed by residents to further various agendas (Breen 1989). Similarly, Anne Yentsch (1988) has examined why some houses and their associated families are remembered by local communities and others, of comparable age, are not.

This awareness of the impact of the present on the study of the past is important for analyzing how past societies interpreted history at any given period. During the first half of the nineteenth century, Americans were both repulsed and intrigued by the concept of an American past. On the one hand, the United States was a new sovereign nation: innocent, fresh, and unspoiled by the corruptions of history. The focus of the country was clearly "future-oriented"; history was an anchor of European nations (Commager 1967; Lowenthal 1976). Conversely, nineteenth-century Americans emphasized a past that virtually eulogized colonial and Revolutionary events (Van Tassel 1960). "Nothing in the history of American nationalism is more impressive than the speed and lavishness with which Americans provided themselves with a usable past," created largely through literature (Commager 1967:13–25). American history was considered useful for teaching citizens "their duties . . . and their obligations as patriots, obedience to law and acceptance of the existing social system" (Van Tassel 1960:91).

The ideas of the Romantics also influenced the development of a national history. Romanticism demanded historical associations, not just in Europe, but in America as well. Considered the triumph of "imagination over reason," romanticism placed an increased emphasis on the sentimentality of history over the order of the natural sciences (cf. Early 1965; Soby and

Miller 1979:8). In the Romantic period, archaeology, antiquarianism, and a heightened awareness of the past entered a new phase of development. The Romantics viewed history as progressive, almost goal-directed, and as the province of an entire people, not just a few great men. Both of these ideas were particularly attractive to Americans, and the historians known as the Romantic Nationalists articulated these ideas in the context of the national past (Van Tassel 1960).

251

The
Transient
Nature
of All
Things
Sublunary

In nineteenth-century Europe, one manifestation of the lessons of history was to be found in the ruins that abounded in the landscape. In America, ruins on the scale of those in Europe did not exist, and therefore little attention has been directed to the study of these features (cf. Ziff 1991:33). Instead, it has been suggested that "the landforms of the . . . West became ruin metaphors" (Lowenthal 1985:114). After all, wilderness had been a "basic ingredient of American civilization" since the beginning (Nash 1973:xv). According to nineteenth-century ideas, much of American history had consisted of the transformation of the wilderness into settled communities, and a good deal of wilderness remained to be tamed. Wilderness imagery could be picturesque, sublime, and horrifying, all themes associated with the Romantics.

Without a doubt, wilderness was an important symbol of American nationalism in the nineteenth century. However, not all landscapes in America were wilderness, and many had been settled for nearly two centuries. Places such as Mount Vernon, Plymouth Rock, and Independence Hall were also important symbols of American nationalism (Baker 1992; Commager 1967:14). Further, while ruins on the scale of those found in Europe were not found in America, a growing body of evidence suggests that architectural ruins did exist in the American landscape and that some of these ruins conveyed certain messages to the community.

ARCHITECTURAL RUINS
IN THE NINETEENTH-CENTURY LANDSCAPE

Inspired by Romantic and Gothic ideas, architectural ruins were an important element in eighteenth-century and early-nineteenth-century European landscapes. The decay embodied in ruins was not just aesthetic; decay evoked sadness, fear, and melancholy reflection. Ruins provided tangible evidence of the past and of the lessons of the past (Lowenthal 1985:173). This obsession with decay, and especially with the decay of architecture, is known as the "cult of the ruin" (cf. Lowenthal 1985; Watkin 1982).

William Gilpin, an eighteenth-century English landscape architect, considered a ruin to be "a sacred thing, [with] a sort of melancholy pleasure" (Watkin 1982:64; see also Nichols and Griswold 1978:85). Thomas Whately devoted a complete section to the importance of ruins in *Observations on Modern Gardening* (1770). Great efforts were made to incorporate ruins into English landscapes of the eighteenth century. For example, the Romantic garden at Studley Royal in North Yorkshire was designed to include striking and picturesque vistas of the eleventh-century Fountains Abbey ruin, located on neighboring land (The National Trust 1988:38–47; Watkin 1982:46). The ruins of Rievaulx Abbey, also in North Yorkshire, were incorporated into the garden landscape of Thomas Duncombe's estate (Watkin 1982:47).

So extensive was this "cult of the ruin" that many English landowners created sham ruins on their properties (Watkin 1982:45, 50–51). Perhaps the earliest sham ruin built was Alfred's Hall, constructed by Alexander Pope in the early eighteenth century (Brownell 1978:272). Others purchased architectural ruins and moved them to their estates (Watkin

1982:48). In a few cases, Roman ruins were acquired from overseas and reassembled in the English garden. The Temple of Augustus, constructed of fragments acquired from the Roman city of Lepcis Magna in North Africa, is an excellent example of this (Watkin 1982:63).

Romantic influences also spread to the newly formed United States. Unlike the countries of Europe, however, Americans had no obvious glorious past, despite some efforts to create a mythical Indian moundbuilder race (cf. Squier and Davis 1848). Americans turned to ancient Rome and Greece for both political and architectural inspiration; for example, the design of the state capitol building in Richmond, Virginia, was directly inspired by Thomas Jefferson's travels in Europe (Early 1965).

The dramatic architectural ruins found in Europe did not exist in the United States, and ruins have therefore not been considered especially significant in nineteenth-century American landscapes (cf. Ziff 1991). Studies of the use of "ancient" architecture have focused almost completely on Roman and Greek influences in the design of nineteenth-century American public architecture (cf. Early 1965). A "cult of the ruin" never developed in America, and ruins did not figure extensively into landscape design. Thomas Jefferson had no use for ruins in his garden at Monticello, and, later, Andrew Jackson Downing rarely, if ever, mentioned ruins.

However, architectural ruins did exist in the nineteenth-century American landscape, and some of these ruins appear to have been assigned special meanings. Charles Fraser, an important early American artist living in Charleston, rendered the "Ruins of the Church in Prince William's Parish," South Carolina, at least five times in the late eighteenth century. Sketch No. 3, which dates from 1796, shows the church windows with pointed Gothic-like arches that were not found in the actual church (figure 12.1) (Severens and Wyrich 1983:84).

Figure 12.1. "Ruins of the Church in Prince William's Parish, Sketch No. 3," dated 1796, by Charles Fraser. Courtesy of The Charleston Museum, Charleston, South Carolina.

253
The
Transient
Nature
of All
Things
Sublunary

Benson Lossing, a well-known nineteenth-century American historian, chronicled the events of the American Revolution using illustrations of significant Revolutionary sites. Ruins are frequently presented among the hundreds of sketches found in the book. One of these ruins, the seventeenth-century church tower at Jamestown (figure 12.2), inspired Lossing to recount that he "sat within the shadow of the old church tower, which stands like a sentinel watching the city of the dead at its feet. . . . This crumbling pile, surrounded by shrubbery, brambles, and tangled vines; and the old church-yard wall . . . enclosing a few monuments, half buried in earth or covered with a pall of ivy and long grass, are all the tangible records that remain of the first planting of an English colony in America" (Lossing [1855] 1970:241). Lossing finally exclaims, "[T]his irrepressible reverence and tender affection with which I look at this broken steeple. . . . Is it that my soul, by a secret, subtile process, invests the moldering ruins with her own powers" (1970:241).

These examples suggest the symbolic importance placed on architectural ruins in some nineteenth-century American landscapes. A closer examination of several sites in southern Maryland will serve to amplify these points. These sites are all located in St. Mary's County, the first area of the state to be colonized by Europeans.

RUINS AT JAMESTOWN.[1]

Figure 12.2. "Ruins at Jamestown," 1855, illustrated in Benson Lossing's The Pictorial Field Book of the Revolution, 1775–1783 (Lossing [1855] 1970:241).

Background

St. Mary's County, located in southern Maryland, is a peninsula of land bounded by the Potomac and Patuxent Rivers and the Chesapeake Bay (figure 12.3). This region of Maryland was first occupied by English colonists in 1634, and settlement quickly spread along the creeks of the Potomac and Patuxent. Maryland was founded as a proprietary colony, its sole proprietor being Cecil Calvert, a Catholic and the second Baron of Baltimore. In order to attract the investors needed to underwrite the cost of colonization, Calvert offered large tracts of land, along with manorial privileges, to those settlers transporting five or more adults to the colony (Stone 1987a:5).

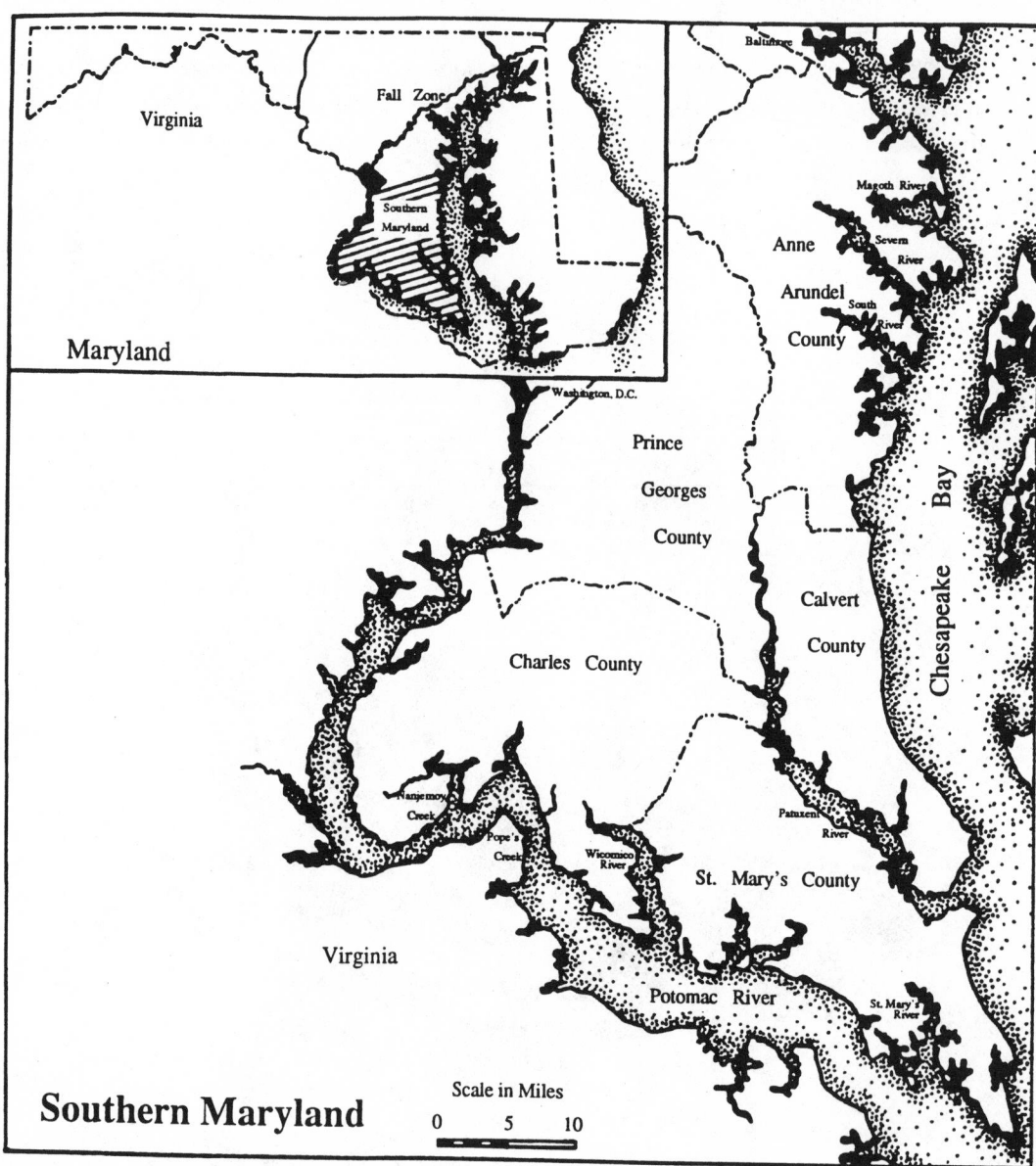

Figure 12.3. Location of the Southern Maryland region.

A number of manors were granted and many occupied. Most (but not all) of these were in St. Mary's County, with names like Cornwaleys' Cross, Snow Hill, and St. Inigoes. Overall, however, the manorial system met with only limited success, and after 1645 "a vigorous class of middling planters" dominated the economic and social scene in St. Mary's (Stone 1987a:76). From this group of middling planters emerged some of the most influential colonists in early Maryland.

255

The
Transient
Nature
of All
Things
Sublunary

Here in Maryland, as in the rest of the Chesapeake Tidewater region, a plantation economy prevailed from the earliest years of settlement. Tobacco was the staple crop raised on most colonial Chesapeake plantations through the late eighteenth century, and it continued to underpin the southern Maryland economy well into the nineteenth century. In St. Mary's County, the tobacco economy and the social structure that developed in the nineteenth century have been the focus of considerable historical research (e.g., King 1994; Marks 1979; Ridgway 1979).

Virtually no economic diversification existed in St. Mary's, and almost all people were tied to the production of tobacco. By 1800, the tobacco economy was restricting growth and development in St. Mary's. Land and labor costs were too high to justify investment, and few people had the resources to invest. Fully one-half of the population consisted of African-American slaves, people with few legal or economic rights. Of the remaining free population, only one-third of the male heads of households owned land; the remainder farmed as tenants (Marks 1979).

By the nineteenth century, southern Maryland was controlled politically and economically by an oligarchic class that sustained its power primarily through marriage and inheritance (Ridgway 1979). Members of this oligarchy controlled the most productive land, the majority of the labor supply, access to the region's waterways, and local politics. In the absence of a diversified economy, the oligarchic elite faced little challenge, ruling throughout this period as "a seamless web" (Ridgway 1979:20).

The poverty of nineteenth-century southern Maryland was often noted by travelers to the region. "Nothing can present to the . . . eye a more dreary and miserable aspect, than the condition of most parts of the lower counties on the western shore of Maryland" (*American Farmer* 1819). A correspondent to the Baltimore-based *American Farmer* (1844) described "desolate" landscapes resulting from the system of shifting agriculture used not only in southern Maryland but in Virginia. In 1829, Frances Trollope sarcastically described the pretensions of farmers in this region of Maryland, "[living] with as few of the refinements, and . . . as few of the comforts . . . as the very poorest English peasant" (Smalley 1949:241).

Despite the harsh economic reality of the present and the uncertainty of the future, southern Marylanders had an impressive past. The colony's first capital was at St. Mary's City from 1634 until 1695. In that small village in 1649, the Maryland Assembly passed "An Act Concerning Religion" (Archives 1:244–47). For more than forty years, this law guaranteed the toleration of different, albeit Christian, religions in Maryland. This law was designed to encourage settlement in a colony predominantly controlled by Catholics. Nonetheless, in an era of revolutionary ideas about religion, the action of the Maryland Assembly was of great significance in the context of western European history. More important, for nineteenth-century Marylanders, this 1649 law preceded—even foreshadowed—the freedom of religion outlined in the newly adopted United States Constitution.

Religious toleration was not all that the southern Maryland past offered. Deeply rooted American ideologies traceable to the nineteenth century celebrate the transformation of the American wilderness in the colonial period. Maryland's earliest settlers transformed what to European populations was a virtual wilderness, and colonization was often romanticized in literature and in art of the late eighteenth and nineteenth centuries (cf. Stilgoe 1982).

In literature, the events of early colonial Maryland history were romanticized in John Pendleton Kennedy's *Rob of the Bowl: A Legend of St. Inigoes* ([1854] 1965). Kennedy, a writer and statesman from Baltimore, had spent a great deal of time studying seventeenth-century documents and walking the abandoned town lands of St. Mary's City. Of the colonial period in Maryland, he wrote: "And a brave story it is of hardy adventure, and manly love of freedom! . . . the bold cavalier . . . the deep unconquerable faith of religion, and the impassioned instincts of the Anglo-Saxon devotion to liberty . . ." (Kennedy [1854] 1965:36).

Such romantic description of early Maryland was not restricted to novelists. Emily Regina Jones, living at nearby Cross Manor in St. Inigoes, recorded in her journal, "it is strange, but it is true, that bosomed in these hills is the only spot where an Anglo-Saxon city once stood . . ." (Rea and Rea 1982:6). The General Assembly of Maryland also recognized the significance of St. Mary's City to nineteenth-century Marylanders. In 1840, the assembly authorized a lottery for the purpose of raising funds "to establish a female seminary in St. Mary's County, on the Site of the Ancient City of Saint Mary's." The law was enacted partly because "a large and respectable portion of the people of Maryland have long entertained a desire to commemorate . . . the site on which stood the City of St. Mary's, the ancient capital of the State the sad remains of which cannot but recall to mind the transient nature of all things sublunary. . . ." How fitting, then, to establish a female seminary so "that those . . . destined to become the mothers of future generations . . . [may be inspired by] affection and attachment for our native State . . ." (quoted in Fausz 1990:31).

RUINS IN THE LANDSCAPE: EXAMPLES FROM ST. MARY'S COUNTY

Archaeological and documentary research has revealed that many buildings were to be found in a ruined condition in nineteenth-century St. Mary's County. Many of the real estate valuations of the Orphan's Court, for example, list abandoned or derelict buildings found on a deceased parent's farm. Although these buildings usually had no monetary value, they were nonetheless recorded to protect the interests of both the orphans and their guardians. The meaning some of these buildings had for the appraisers was clear: in one case, a frame dwelling was described as "unfit to be repaired and perfectly unfit for any white person to live in" (Valuations of the Orphan's Court 1858:262–63). Another dwelling, one of the few houses constructed of brick, was simply "unfit for use" (Valuations of the Orphan's Court 1841:8).

Almost certainly, these buildings and others like them had been abandoned and left to decay because the alternatives—repair or demolition—were too costly or time consuming. Further, the price of nails had decreased considerably in the nineteenth century with the advent of machine-cut nails, making the recycling of nails unnecessary (Lorena Walsh 1990, personal communication). A few of these derelict structures were reused as barns for storage or for housing livestock. The abandoned dwellings of landowners do not appear, however, to have been generally reused as shelter for tenants or for slaves. This suggests that the architectural spaces occupied by individuals of different groups were fairly rigidly defined in nineteenth-century southern Maryland.

Other architectural ruins existed that cannot be explained with reference to the cost of repair or of demolition. At least three ruins appear to have served as reminders of the past and possibly served important roles in the network of social relationships: the abandoned shell of the seventeenth-century statehouse, the ruins of Lord Baltimore's Mattapany House, and a ruin in the house yard of Susquehanna, the Carroll family property. These ruins provided a past firmly grounded in the landscape, visible on a daily basis to certain members of the plantation community. The ruins not only reminded the plantation owners and their families of the role played by their ancestors in the formation of the state and the nation, but they may have also subtly reinforced and justified a way of life that was failing both economically and socially for more than three-quarters of the population.

The statehouse and Mattapany are examined using documentary evidence. The Susquehanna ruin was discovered through archaeology and is analyzed using both documentary and archaeological data.

The Seventeenth-Century Statehouse

In 1632, Charles I granted Cecil Calvert, second Lord Baltimore, a charter for the Maryland colony. In 1634, Lord Baltimore's colony was established with permanent settlement at St. Mary's City. Located near the Potomac River in southern Maryland, St. Mary's City was the capital of Maryland until 1695, when the capital was moved to Annapolis. St. Mary's primarily served a political role as the colonial capital, and during the earliest years of settlement most of these political functions were conducted in private homes and in ordinaries.

In 1676, the colonial assembly undertook construction of a magnificent statehouse located on a high bluff in St. Mary's City, overlooking the entrance to the village's harbor (figure 12.4). A full two stories in height, the State House was one of a few buildings in Maryland constructed almost entirely of brick. While most of the town buildings decayed and disappeared when the capital was moved to Annapolis, the statehouse remained standing. Throughout the eighteenth century, it served as a meeting place for William and Mary Parish even as it began to deteriorate. Around 1830, the parish built a new church, using bricks salvaged from the walls of the statehouse. The foundation and lower walls of the statehouse were left intact, however, and hence its "footprint" survived above ground.

A number of nineteenth-century historical references to the statehouse and to St. Mary's City survive, revealing how people viewed and drew meaning from the ruins. John Pendleton Kennedy, mentioned earlier, visited St. Mary's City in the 1830s to collect ideas about the colonial capital. Kennedy described "the mouldering and shapeless ruin of the ancient State House . . . the wreck of this early monument of the founders of Maryland. . . . [These ruins] remind us of the launching of the bark, the struggle with the unfamiliar wave, the array of the wonder-stricken savage" (Kennedy [1854] 1965:36).

Emily Regina Jones lived less than one mile by boat from St. Mary's City, at Cross Manor. On her visits to the grounds of the ancient capitol, Jones observed "that sacred heirloom of our ancestors is a shattered pile of bricks and mortar, overrun with weeds and vines, like Caesar's robe, covering the ingratitude of his fall" (Rea and Rea 1982:7). Nearby was the

Figure 12.4. Reconstructed statehouse of 1676, Historic St. Mary's City. The original building is believed to have been similar in shape and size to this early-twentieth-century reconstruction. Courtesy of the Historic St. Mary's City Commission.

"Governor's vault," the key to which was "thrown into the river, that its reverend inmates might repose forever under the soil they had won from the wilderness" (Rea and Rea 1982:8).

In 1839, the General Assembly moved to establish St. Mary's Female Seminary (now St. Mary's College of Maryland) in celebration of the bicentennial of the founding of Maryland. That law, passed 4 March 1840, referred to "the ancient capital of the State . . . that nothing now remains but a few mouldering bricks to point out to the antiquarian the spot where Civilization and Christianity were first introduced into our State" (quoted in Fausz 1990:31).

The statehouse was used for a time as a church—in fact, it was used for a longer time as a church than as a statehouse. Yet, these contemporary accounts and descriptions suggest that its primary significance for nineteenth-century visitors was its former role as the statehouse, its present (nineteenth-century) condition as a ruin, and the role of the ruin in developing a mythology of Maryland's past.

Mattapany, Home of the Third Lord Baltimore

Mattapany was the Maryland plantation of Charles Calvert, third Baron of Baltimore, from 1666 until 1684. During this time, the Provincial Council and Court often met at Mattapany, and a magazine was maintained there as early as 1673. After Baltimore returned permanently to England in 1684, the council continued to meet at Mattapany until 1689, when the house and magazine were seized in the Protestant uprising of that year. The Protestant dissidents used the property as their headquarters and as a prison for colonists loyal to Lord Baltimore. Ultimately, these events and a series of others in England led to the collapse of proprietary rule in Maryland (Carr and Jordan 1974; Chaney and King 1992).

Lord Baltimore's dwelling at Mattapany appears to have been well built. In 1671, John Ogilby described it as "a fair house of Brick and Timber, with all Out-houses, and other offices thereto belonging . . ." (Ogilby 1671:189). Archaeological investigations conducted at Mattapany indicate that the site was abandoned by 1740 (Chaney and King 1992; Pogue 1987). The ruins of Mattapany, however, were visible well into the late nineteenth century.

The plantation remained in the possession of Baltimore's wife's family until about 1840. After that time, it was sold to the Thomas family, also from St. Mary's County. In 1873, the Thomases commissioned County Surveyor George B. Dent to plat a subdivision of the large Mattapany farm (figure 12.5). This plat depicts the property's boundaries, major structures, and important landmarks. One of these landmarks was the ruins of Lord Baltimore's seventeenth-century dwelling. Subsequent archaeological testing has demonstrated the accuracy of the plat in depicting the site, suggesting that the ruins were indeed visible.

259

The
Transient
Nature
of All
Things
Sublunary

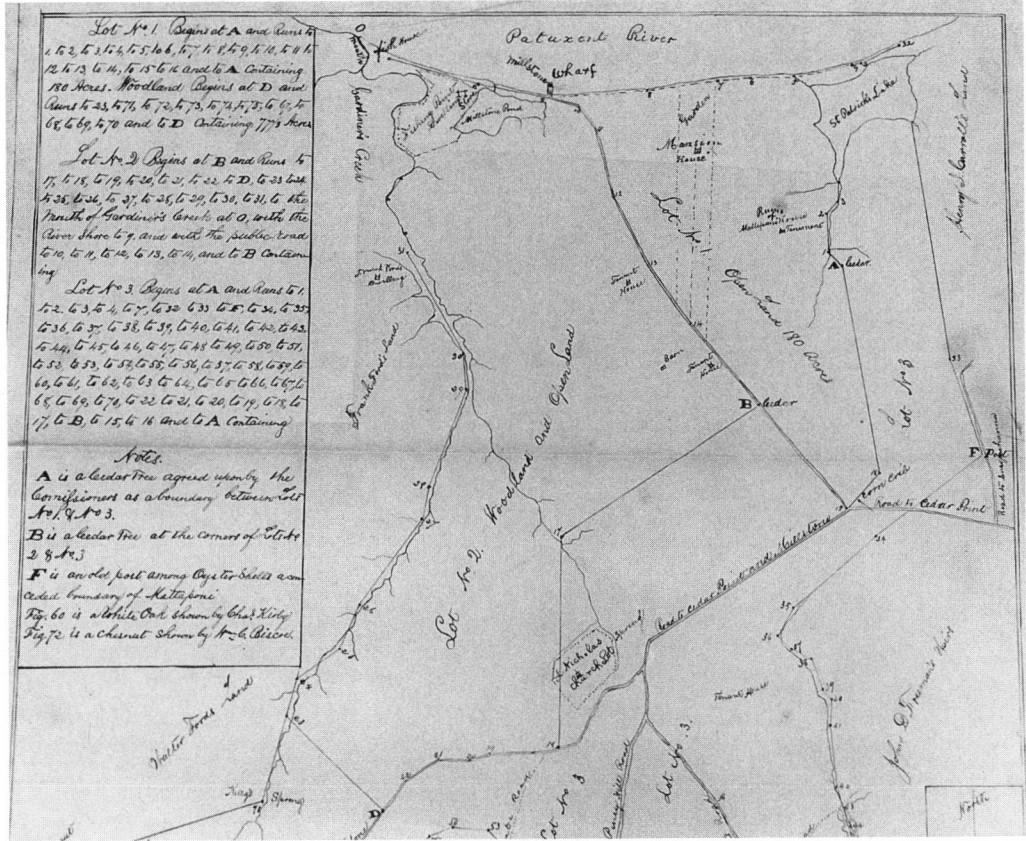

Figure 12.5. Subdivision of Mattapany farm as platted by George Dent in 1873; note the ruins east of the mansion house, identified here as "Ruins of Mattaponi House." Office of Land Records, Decree Record, Liber JFF, Folio 347–57, St. Mary's County Courthouse.

The inclusion of this site on the plat is significant for a number of reasons. First, the surveyor recognized the ruin, knew its identity, and took the time to include it on the plat of subdivision. Other buildings known to have been present in 1873, primarily through archaeological evidence, are not shown. Second, Lord Baltimore's dwelling was abandoned ca. 1740, and the ruin had therefore survived for approximately 170 years. The owners of Mattapany in the eighteenth and nineteenth centuries had the resources to remove the ruin, but apparently chose not to do so. Finally, the ruin and knowledge of its location had vanished from local memory by the early twentieth century, suggesting that the meaning attached to this spot had changed by that time.

"Bricks and Other Signs of Ruin" at Susquehanna

The ruin at Susquehanna was discovered as a result of an archaeological investigation undertaken by the author for the Henry Ford Museum (King 1989). Susquehanna was a large farm located on the Patuxent River in the eighteenth and nineteenth centuries; the plantation comprised approximately seven hundred acres of some of the most fertile soils in southern Maryland. The surviving early-nineteenth-century principal dwelling at the farm was moved to the Henry Ford Museum in 1942, and the former site of the extant dwelling is well known. Archaeological investigations at that site revealed evidence of an architectural ruin incorporated within the formal landscape design of the Susquehanna yard.

Like most valuable landholdings in southern Maryland, Susquehanna had been in the same family since the late seventeenth century (Walsh 1981). Sometime prior to 1684, the land was acquired by Christopher Rousby, an attorney and tax collector for the king. Rousby almost certainly resided on the Susquehanna property. Significantly, the property shares its western boundary with Lord Baltimore's Mattapany.

Rousby, who was a Protestant, was in open political conflict with Lord Baltimore by the late 1670s; by 1681, Baltimore was seeking Rousby's removal as tax collector. Baltimore was apparently unsuccessful, as Rousby held onto his position until 1684. In that year, Rousby was fatally stabbed on board the *Quaker* by George Talbot, an agent of Baltimore's and possibly his cousin. Rousby was buried at Susquehanna in a grave marked with an elaborately carved table stone (figure 12.6). Baltimore subsequently returned to England in that year, where his position as proprietor was becoming increasingly shaky.

Rousby's nephew ultimately inherited the property, and this family became one of the wealthiest in St. Mary's County. Only the name changed when, at one point, the remaining heir was an unmarried daughter. The Rousby and, subsequently, the Carroll families maintained one of the largest slave-labor forces in the region. Through a web of calculated marriages and other types of social alliances, this family managed to control some of the best land, labor, and water access in southern Maryland for more than six generations.

The surviving house, which is now in Dearborn, was constructed sometime between 1825 and 1840 (figure 12.7) (Heikkenen 1988; King 1989). By nineteenth-century standards, this frame dwelling was one of the largest houses in St. Mary's County, consisting of nine hundred square feet on the ground floor. At least two other dwellings, built and occupied by members of the Carroll and Rousby family, are known to have existed on the Susquehanna farm prior to this date.

Figure 12.6. Carved table stone found at a site believed to be the Christopher Rousby grave. Courtesy of the Henry Ford Museum & Greenfield Village, Dearborn, Michigan.

261
The
Transient
Nature
of All
Things
Sublunary

Figure 12.7. Surviving early-nineteenth-century Susquehanna dwelling as it appeared in Maryland in 1941. The house has since been reassembled at Greenfield Village. Courtesy of the Henry Ford Museum & Greenfield Village, Dearborn, Michigan.

The ruin at Susquehanna is one of these earlier dwellings. The 1798 Federal Direct Tax Assessment describes a frame house at Susquehanna, measuring 28 by 32 feet, "in bad repair." This house was probably built about 1770–75 by Captain Henry Carroll and his wife, Araminta Thompson Carroll. Carroll, a cousin of the well-known Charles Carroll of Carrollton, was a planter and a merchant. He had married Araminta Rousby Thompson by 1767, and he established a large farm on the property Araminta had inherited from her grandfather, John Rousby. When Carroll died in late 1775, he was one of the wealthiest farmers in St. Mary's County, due in no small part to his marriage into a well-connected southern Maryland family.

Araminta soon remarried, this time to George Biscoe, a fairly prosperous farmer from St. Mary's County. Araminta and George continued to reside at Susquehanna, together with Araminta's six children from her first marriage. However, few, if any, resources appear to have been invested in the upkeep of the Susquehanna house. Described in 1798 as "in bad repair," the condition of the house may have deteriorated even further by 1813, when the Biscoe family moved to Prince George's County. The dwelling may have been uninhabited and in an advanced state of deterioration by 1824, since it is not shown on a U.S. Army Engineer's topographic map of that date. The Susquehanna barns, located 400 feet west of the dwelling, are depicted on that map (figure 12.8). A detailed study of this map indicates that it would have been very unusual for the army surveyors to have included the agricultural outbuildings on the map and not the principal dwelling, unless the principal dwelling was no longer habitable.

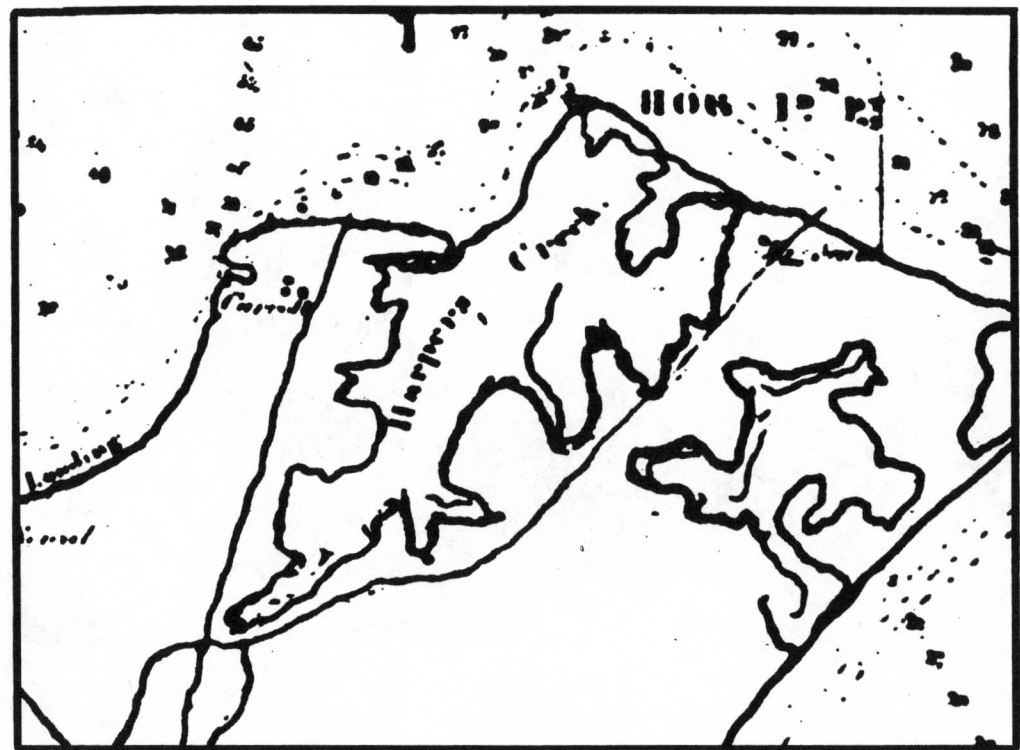

Figure 12.8. 1824 U.S. Army Engineer's map showing buildings at Susquehanna, here called "Carroll" (upper left).

263
The
Transient
Nature
of All
Things
Sublunary

After the Biscoes moved to Prince George's County, the exact sequence of ownership for the Susquehanna tract becomes unclear. No deeds survive, and tax records suggest that the property was shuffled among the children of Araminta and Henry Carroll. What is clear is that the property remained in the Carroll family, although one son nearly lost the farm at a sheriff's sale.

In the 1840s, Henry J. Carroll, a grandson of Araminta and Henry, gained possession of the farm, probably through inheritance. The younger Henry may be the builder of the dwelling now in Dearborn, and he managed one of the most valuable farms in all of St. Mary's County in the mid-nineteenth century. When he married Lucretia Leeds Briscoe, Carroll aligned himself with another prominent St. Mary's family. Briscoe died in childbirth, within a year of the marriage, and Carroll then married Elizabeth Pyle from neighboring Charles County. The Carroll family resided at Susquehanna until 1894, when the farm was finally sold to pay debts. More than two centuries of land ownership by the same family came to a close (King 1989; Walsh 1981).

During Henry Carroll's tenure in the mid-nineteenth century, the farm community at Susquehanna comprised the Carroll family (including four children), forty slaves, and an unknown number of tenant farmers. Archaeological and historical data indicate that Susquehanna was a productive farm and that Henry Carroll was one of a few successful farmers in an otherwise deteriorating economy. While Susquehanna was typical of the farms of the oligarchic elite class, it was not typical of the majority of farms in St. Mary's County. Carroll appears to have paid close attention to farm management, preserving the rich topsoils and woodlands on his farm. Research has also shown that the Susquehanna community was physically organized in a manner that reinforced rigid class distinctions among its members (King 1994).

The archaeological investigations that located the earlier dwelling at Susquehanna were designed to recover evidence on the organization and use of the nineteenth-century dwelling yard (King 1989). Shovel test units were systematically spaced at ten-foot intervals over an area measuring 100 by 160 feet. The fill from each shovel test unit was dry-screened through quarter-inch mesh, and all cultural materials were collected. Three domestic outbuildings, a number of fence lines, refuse disposal patterns, and other types of yard use from the late eighteenth century through the mid-twentieth century were identified in the Susquehanna yard. One of these features appears to be the remnants of the dwelling described in the 1798 Tax Assessment.

Limited testing in the yard immediately east of the early-nineteenth-century dwelling revealed the brick foundations and cellar of an earlier structure. This building measured approximately 25 to 30 feet by 30 to 35 feet and was found less than ten feet from the site of the surviving dwelling. Both buildings clearly shared the same alignment (figure 12.9). The size of the brick foundation, a small but significant assemblage of eighteenth-century artifacts, and the documentary evidence, including the 1798 Tax Assessment, strongly support the interpretation of this foundation as the dwelling of Araminta and Henry Carroll.

The cellar fill of this earlier building contained numerous pieces of both wire nail fragments and clear bottle glass, indicating that the cellar was not filled until the late nineteenth century. This finding was unexpected in the context of the historical and cartographic research, which suggested that the house was abandoned and derelict by 1824. No attachment or any other passage between this eighteenth-century building and the nineteenth-century

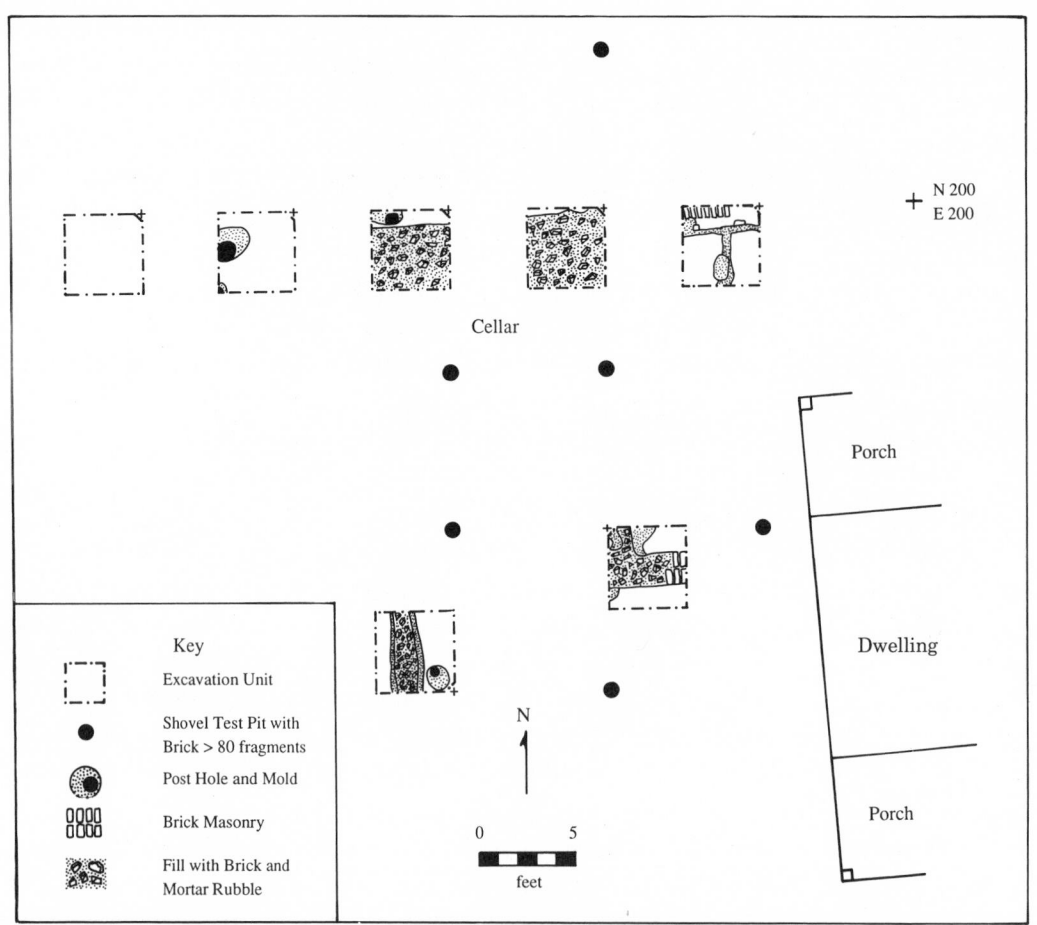

Cellar

+ N 200
E 200

Porch

Dwelling

Porch

Key

Excavation Unit

Shovel Test Pit with
Brick > 80 fragments

Post Hole and Mold

Brick Masonry

Fill with Brick and
Mortar Rubble

N

0   5

feet

Figure 12.9. Archaeological plan of the Carroll dwelling listed in the 1798 Federal Direct Tax Assessment. The ruins of this dwelling were incorporated into the formal landscape of the nineteenth-century Susquehanna yard.

Susquehanna dwelling exists, and the one is not an addition of the other (Ridout 1989; J. Richard Rivoire 1992, personal communication). Nonetheless, the presence of these later materials in the cellar fill indicates that at least some portion of the earlier dwelling survived in the yard well into the late nineteenth century.

The distribution of iron nails at the site suggests, however, that the framed portion of the earlier dwelling had been removed, leaving, at most, a ruinous foundation, cellar, and chimneys. By the early nineteenth century, the cost of nails had declined significantly with the advent of machine-cut nails. Nails were no longer so expensive that they had to be salvaged and reused from decayed buildings (Lorena Walsh 1990, personal communication). If the earlier Susquehanna house was simply abandoned in place, concentrations of nails, particularly wrought nails, would be expected in the archaeological deposits associated with the foundation. In fact, not one positively identified wrought nail was recovered from the vicinity of the earlier house, although concentrations of wrought nails occurred elsewhere in the yard (figure 12.10). This evidence suggests that the framed portion of the house was removed from its foundation in the early nineteenth century.

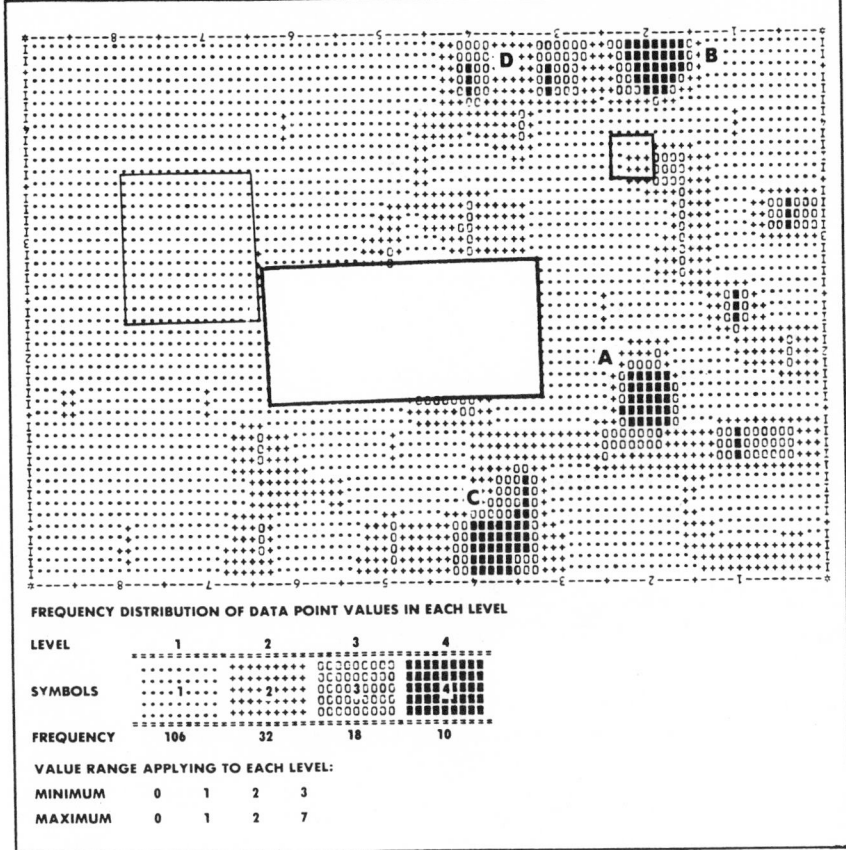

265

The
Transient
Nature
of All
Things
Sublunary

Figure 12.10. Distribution of wrought nails at Susquehanna. Note the lack of concentration over the ruin, which appears to the left of the dwelling (center). The dairy appears in the upper right corner.

A small but important historical reference corroborates these findings. During an interview conducted in 1947 by the staff of the *Maryland Historical Magazine,* Mrs. Fanny Combs Gough recalled visits to Susquehanna farm in the late nineteenth century. She remembered the site of the earlier dwelling, because "nearby . . . bricks and other signs of ruin were still to be seen" (*Maryland Historical Magazine* 1947:120). Mrs. Gough also learned from the Carroll family that this ruin was associated with an earlier house.

Documentary evidence further suggests that the ruin of this earlier dwelling may have been purposely maintained and therefore of symbolic value. An impressively detailed and accurate 1848 U.S. Coast and Geodetic Survey map depicts the ca. 1840 Susquehanna farmhouse within an unusual elliptical fence (figure 12.11) (King 1989; Stone 1987b). Trees appear to have been carefully planted along the perimeter of this fence.

Virtually no nineteenth-century domestic refuse was found in the yard containing the ruin, although pottery, bone, and shell were recovered in large amounts in the yard adjacent to the dwelling's kitchen (figure 12.12). Further, the ruin is located off the end of the dwelling containing the parlor, which served as a formal room in the early nineteenth-century. The dwelling's kitchen and associated outbuildings are located at the end opposite the ruin (figure 12.13). The central placement of dwelling and ruin within the elliptical yard, the location of the ruin adjacent to the nineteenth-century dwelling's formal parlor, and the general cleanliness of the yard in this area all strongly suggest the ruin was part of a conscious formal design by Henry Carroll.

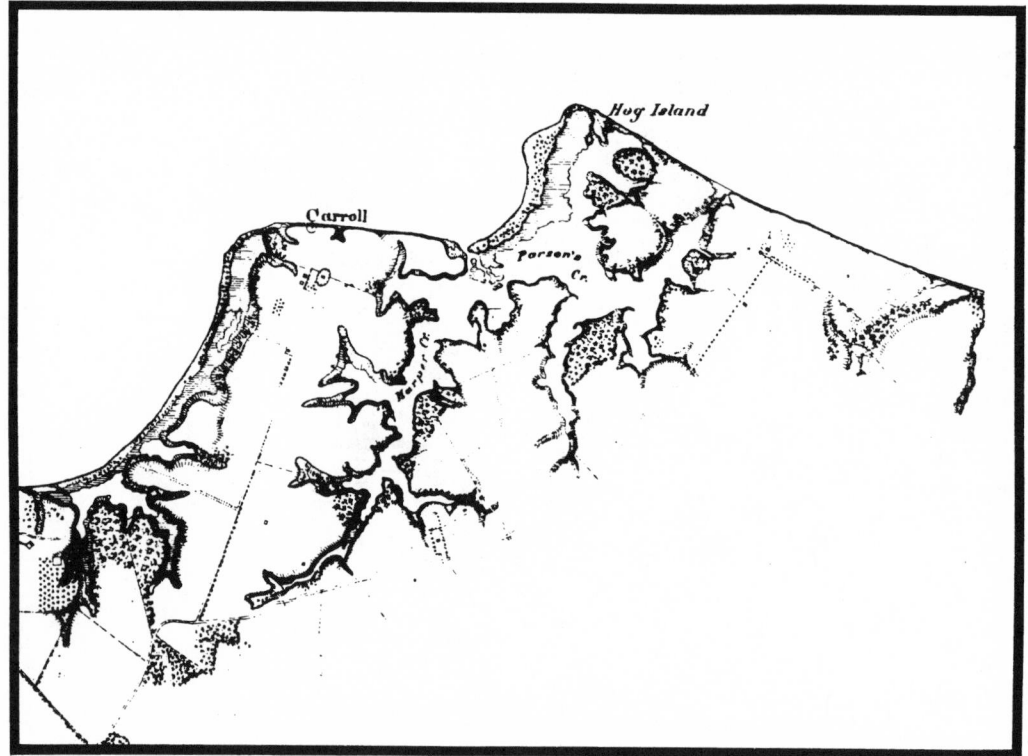

*Figure 12.11.
1848 U.S.
Coast and
Geodetic Survey
map showing
Susquehanna.
Note the elliptical
fence surrounding
the principal
dwelling.*

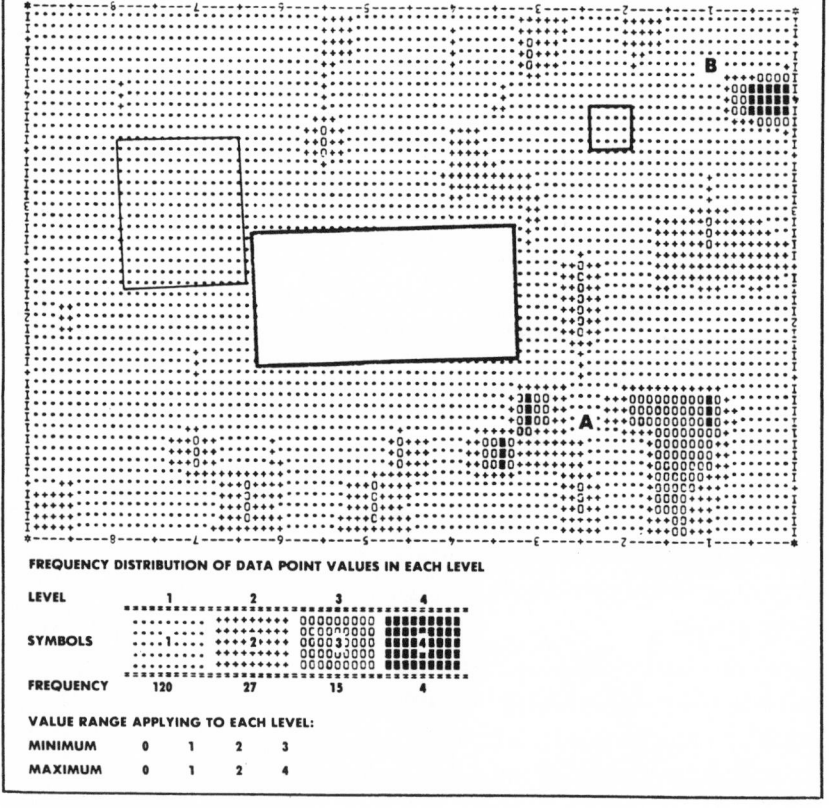

*Figure 12.12.
Distribution of
positively
identified
nineteenth-
century domestic
refuse at
Susquehanna.
Note that the
concentrations
occur in the right
(service) yard,
opposite the ruin.*

DAIRY

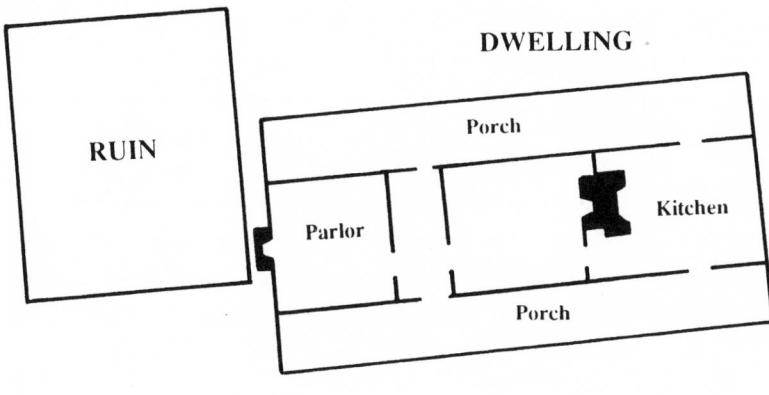

DWELLING

RUIN

Porch

Parlor

Kitchen

Porch

OUTBUILDING

SUSQUEHANNA

0   10

N   FEET

Figure 12.13. Relationship of the ruin to rooms within the nineteenth-century dwelling and outbuildings at Susquehanna.

Like his neighbors at Mattapany, Henry Carroll surely had the resources to remove and bury the ruin at Susquehanna. When the Carroll family sold the farm in 1894 to the first of a series of absentee landlords, the tenants immediately dismantled the ruin and converted that portion of the yard into an agricultural field. The salvaged bricks were reused in the construction of nearby barn foundations (King 1989).

In the mid-nineteenth century, Susquehanna was a well-managed farm, with good soil preservation practices and very little erosion. The plantation layout was structured to maximize efficiency while observing strict roles of social interaction among the more than seventy people living at Susquehanna. In this context, the ruin of the earlier dwelling was not some unkempt loose end, but an important element in a highly controlled landscape. The question that is raised by these findings is the role of these ruins in the social landscape of southern Maryland. Why were the ruins at Mattapany and Susquehanna allowed to remain? What significance did these features have for the members of this oligarchic society?

In eighteenth- and nineteenth-century Europe, ruin and decay were important and frequent components of the landscape. Images of ruin and decay often appeared in poetry, literature, and painting. The importance of ruins in Europe has been well documented, and the "cult of the ruin" has been a topic of scholarly study by professionals from widely varying backgrounds. Ruins such as those found in Europe did not exist in the United States, either in scale or in frequency. However, the provocative studies of ruins in European landscapes may provide a starting point for interpreting ruins in the nineteenth-century American landscape.

While a systematic survey of ruins in the nineteenth-century American landscape remains to be undertaken, the ruins described in this chapter, in southern Maryland as well as in Charleston and Jamestown, suggest that these features are most likely to be found in the areas of the United States that were first occupied by Europeans. In the case of mid-nineteenth-century southern Maryland, the region had been settled for nearly two centuries and was no longer the "wilderness" that characterized much of the rest of the United States at that time.

In a study of the use of ruins in the English landscape, specifically in poetry, Anne Janowitz argues that the eighteenth-century ruin and the figure of decay were "image[s] used to authorize England's autonomy as a world power" (Janowitz 1990:2). According to Janowitz, ruins suggested the "authority of antiquity" and were used to bind culture to nature. The result was the "naturalizing" of the nation, which "subsume[d] cultural and class differences into a conflated representation of Britain as nature's inevitable product" (Janowitz 1990:4).

In the mid-nineteenth century, southern Maryland was controlled by a rural oligarchy that maintained its economic and social power through marriage and inheritance. This oligarchy formed a very small proportion of the population, and in St. Mary's County as many as three-quarters of the inhabitants were experiencing serious downward economic mobility. The region's dependence on tobacco, with only limited cultivation of grain, and on an enslaved labor force fostered an unproductive situation for most inhabitants of the region. The poverty of the region was evident in its landscape and was often mentioned in travelers' accounts and in correspondence of the period.

Almost certainly, members of southern Maryland's oligarchic elite, men like Henry Carroll, read these accounts in agrarian journals. Yet, no rebuttals or defensive essays appear to have been offered in response, and little effort was made to shift from the cultivation of tobacco. Only when the price of tobacco plummeted below two dollars a pound did southern Maryland farmers consider abandoning tobacco, and only those who could afford the investment in grain cultivation actually made the shift to diversification. However, the price of tobacco rose again after a brief period, and tobacco and slaves remained entrenched in the southern Maryland economy.

Under criticism, facing an uncertain future, members of the oligarchic elite may have looked to the past for justification of their fading social and economic order. St. Mary's County was the site of the first capital and early settlements of Maryland, and nearly all the members of the nineteenth-century landed gentry could trace their genealogical roots to the seventeenth century. In the nineteenth-century view, these early settlers had encountered a virtual wilderness and transformed it into settled plantations and farms. Many of these plantations and farms remained, undivided, in the hands of descendants of these early colonists.

269
The
Transient
Nature
of All
Things
Sublunary

Contemporary literature, journal accounts, and even laws of the Maryland Assembly testify to the significance of the past to nineteenth-century St. Mary's County. This impressive past encompassed all the symbols of the national mythology—the taming of the wilderness and the founding of the nation.

Several meanings may then be suggested for the ruins described in this chapter. Foremost, the ruins, their settings, and nineteenth-century descriptions indicate that these remnants of earlier days gave a tangible quality to the abstract concept of the past. The presence of the ruins in the landscape and the past that they represented, in nineteenth-century terms, may then have given a certain legitimacy to an economic and social system that was not succeeding for the majority of the population and was under attack from without. The ruins embedded in the landscape, part cultural, part natural, may have served to justify a system that, through inheritance, kept land ownership out of reach for most people.

Conversely, the three ruins examined in this chapter have important differences. The Mattapany and Susquehanna ruins are the remains of buildings that were private dwellings. The statehouse ruin represents a public government building. In the early nineteenth century, the statehouse was owned by William and Mary Parish, which would have been less likely to maintain an interest in using ruins to justify a particular economic and social situation. However, all three sites played significant roles in major seventeenth-century events, particularly in the struggles between Catholic Lord Baltimore and certain Protestant colonists. Perhaps, then, the theme underlying and binding these ruins, in terms of the history of St. Mary's County, is the tension between Catholicism and Protestantism.[2] The statehouse and Lord Baltimore's Mattapany—symbols of Baltimore's Catholic government—were both seized by Protestant rebels in the late seventeenth century. Further, Susquehanna was the seventeenth-century plantation of a Protestant agent of the king murdered by a relative of Baltimore. And Susquehanna and Mattapany share a common boundary.

To date, only three ruins have been investigated in detail. Much more work, beginning with the systematic survey of ruins in the nineteenth century, remains to be done. With future research, inferences about the meaning of ruins may be possible. The present project has indicated that ruins did exist in the nineteenth-century landscape and, more significantly, that some ruins may have served important symbolic roles for the communities in which they were found. These ruins were not prolific in the young, future-oriented United States, and they appear to have been restricted to areas of early settlement. Nonetheless, ruin, decay, and the concept of the past were not foreign to nineteenth-century Americans and may have served as reminders of a remarkable past. Not surprisingly, the presence of ruins in the nineteenth-century landscape suggests that these features had the power to evoke, as they do today, the symbolic imagery of the past and the "transient nature of all things sublunary."

ACKNOWLEDGMENTS

I am indebted to the Edison Institute of the Henry Ford Museum for funding the archaeological research at Susquehanna. The Patuxent River Naval Air Station generously provided laboratory and storage space for the project. The Maryland Historical Trust/Jefferson Patterson Park and Museum provided administrative oversight for the project. St. Mary's College of Maryland provided access to its VAX/VMS computer facility.

Ed Chaney, Julie Ernstein, Elizabeth Kryder-Reid, Mark Leone, Jessica Neuwirth, and J. Richard Rivoire have all been extremely helpful to me as I developed these ideas. Karen Bescherer Metheny and Rebecca Yamin did an excellent job of making a cumbersome paper readable. Anne Yentsch and Christa Wilmanns-Wells deserve a special acknowledgment of my appreciation. Both Anne and Christa provided a detailed review of the paper, and I hope they both feel that a much stronger chapter was the result. Finally, my friend and colleague Andrea Hammer showed me the importance of a truly interdisciplinary approach to landscape study, in which not just techniques but ideas from other disciplines are shared.

NOTES

1. History is here used in a broad sense and includes any attempt in any discipline to study an event or process that occurred in the past. Archaeology, generally considered anthropology, is easily included in this definition.
2. I am indebted to Anne Yentsch for her insight on this topic.

REFERENCES

American Farmer
1819   A View of the Agricultural Condition of the Lower Counties of Maryland. *American Farmer* 1:98–99.
1844   *American Farmer* 6:250.
Archives
1637/8–64   Proceedings and Acts of the Assembly. Maryland Historical Society, Baltimore.
Baker, James W.
1992   Haunted by the Pilgrims. In *The Art and Mystery of Historical Archaeology: Essays in Honor of James Deetz,* edited by Anne Elizabeth Yentsch and Mary C. Beaudry, pp. 343–58. CRC Press, Boca Raton, Florida.
Breen, T. H.
1989   *Imagining the Past: East Hampton Histories.* Addison-Wesley Publishing Co., Inc., New York.
Brownell, Morris R.
1978   *Alexander Pope and the Arts of Georgian England.* Clarendon Press, Oxford.
Carr, Lois Green, and David Jordan
1974   *Maryland's Revolution of Government, 1689–1692.* Cornell University Press, Ithaca, New York.
Chaney, Edward E., and Julia A. King
1992   His Lordship's Manor: An Archaeological Survey of Mattapany. Jefferson Patterson Park and Museum, St. Leonard, Maryland.
Commager, Henry Steele
1967   *The Search for a Usable Past and Other Essays in Historiography.* Alfred A. Knopf, New York.
Early, James
1965   *Romanticism and American Architecture.* A. S. Barnes, New York.
Fausz, J. Frederick
1990   *Monument School of the People: A Sesquicentennial History of St. Mary's College of Maryland, 1840–1990.* St. Mary's College of Maryland, St. Mary's City.
Gero, Joan M., and Margaret W. Conkey, editors
1991   *Engendering Archaeology: Women and Prehistory.* Basil Blackwell, Inc., Cambridge, Massachusetts.
Heikkenen, Herman J.
1988   Report on the Dendrochronology of Susquehanna. Ms. on file, Henry Ford Museum, Dearborn, Michigan.

271
The
Transient
Nature
of All
Things
Sublunary

Janowitz, Anne
1990   *England's Ruins: Poetic Purpose and the National Landscape.* Basil Blackwell, Inc., Cambridge, Massachusetts.

Kennedy, John Pendleton
1965   *Rob of the Bowl: A Legend of St. Inigoes.* 1854. Reprint. Edited by William S. Osborne. College and University Press, New Haven, Connecticut.

King, Julia A.
1989   Archaeological Investigations at Susquehanna: A 19th Century Farm Complex Aboard the Patuxent River Naval Air Station, St. Mary's County, Maryland. Jefferson Patterson Park and Museum, St. Leonard, Maryland.
1994   Rural Landscape in the Mid-Nineteenth-Century Chesapeake. In *Historical Archaeology of the Chesapeake,* edited by Paul A. Shackel and Barbara J. Little, pp. 283–99. Smithsonian Institution Press, Washington, D.C.

Leone, Mark P.
1981   Archaeology's Relationship to the Present and the Past. In *Modern Material Culture: The Archaeology of Us,* edited by Richard A. Gould and Michael B. Schiffer, pp. 5–14. Academic Press, New York.

Leone, Mark P., Parker B. Potter Jr., and Paul A. Shackel
1987   Toward A Critical Archaeology. *Current Anthropology* 28(3):283–302.

Lossing, Benson
1970   *The Pictorial Field Book of the Revolution, 1775–1783.* 1855. Reprint. Benchmark Publishing Corporation, Glendale, New York.

Lowenthal, David
1976   The Place of the Past in the American Landscape. In *Geographies of the Mind: Essays in Historical Geosophy in Honor of John Kirtland Wright,* edited by David Lowenthal and Martyn J. Bowden, pp. 89–117. Oxford University Press, New York.
1985   *The Past is a Foreign Country.* Cambridge University Press, Cambridge.

Marks, Bayly E.
1979   Economy and Society in a Staple Plantation, St. Mary's County, Maryland. Ph.D. diss., Department of History, University of Maryland.

Maryland Historical Magazine
1947   Susquehanna, A Maryland House in Michigan. *Maryland Historical Magazine:*115–23.

Nash, Roderick
1973   *Wilderness and the American Mind.* Revised Edition. Yale University Press, New Haven.

National Trust (U.K.)
1988   *Fountains Abbey and Studley Royal.* Lecturis bv, the Netherlands.

Nichols, Frederick D., and Ralph E. Griswold
1978   *Thomas Jefferson, Landscape Architect.* University Press of Virginia, Charlottesville.

Novick, Peter
1988   *That Noble Dream: The "Objectivity Question" and the American Historical Profession.* Cambridge University Press, New York.

Ogilby, John
1671   *America: Being the Latest and Most Accurate Description of the New World.* London.

Pogue, Dennis J.
1987   Seventeenth-Century Proprietary Rule and Rebellion: Archeology at Charles Calvert's Mattapany-Sewall. *Maryland Archeology* 23(1):1–37.

Rea, Eugene, and Jean G. Rea, editors
1982   *The City of St. Maries, Maryland: A Story and Personal Recollections.* The Press of William Nuthead, St. Mary's City, Maryland.

Ridgway, Whitman H.
1979   *Community Leadership in Maryland, 1790–1840.* University of North Carolina Press, Chapel Hill.

Ridout, Orlando, V

1989   Notes on the Architecture of Susquehanna. In *Archaeological Investigations at Susquehanna: A 19th Century Farm Complex Aboard Patuxent River Naval Air Station, St. Mary's County, Maryland,* by Julia A. King, pp. 101–7. Jefferson Patterson Park and Museum, St. Leonard, Maryland.

Severens, Martha R., and Charles L. Wyrich Jr.

1983   *Charles Fraser of Charleston: Essays on the Man, His Art and His Times.* Charleston Art Association, Charleston, South Carolina.

Smalley, Donald, editor

1949   *Domestic Manners of the Americans,* by Frances Trollope. Alfred A. Knopf, New York.

Soby, James Thrall, and Dorothy C. Miller

1969   *Romantic Painting in America.* Museum of Modern Art, New York.

Squier, Ephraim G., and Edwin H. Davis

1848   *Ancient Monuments of the Mississippi Valley.* Smithsonian Institution Press, Washington, D.C.

Stilgoe, John R.

1982   *Common Landscape of America, 1580 to 1845.* Yale University Press, New Haven.

Stone, Garry W.

1987a   Manorial Maryland. *Maryland Historical Magazine* 82(1):3–36.

1987b   Letter to Peter Cousins, 13 January 1987. On file, Jefferson Patterson Park and Museum, St. Leonard, Maryland.

Valuations of the Orphan's Court

1841   Valuation for Joshua Estep. Liber GC 1, folio 8. On file, Office of the Register of Wills, St. Mary's County Courthouse, Leonardtown, Maryland.

1858   Valuation for Emily Joy, James Ignatius Joy and Margaret Joy. Liber GC 1, folio 262–63. On file, Office of the Register of Wills, St. Mary's County Courthouse, Leonardtown, Maryland.

Van Tassel, David D.

1960   *Recording America's Past: An Interpretation of the Development of Historical Studies in America, 1607–1884.* University of Chicago Press, Chicago.

Walsh, Lorena

1981   Documentary Research on Susquehanna Point Property, St. Mary's County, Maryland. Prepared for the Henry Ford Museum. Ms. on file, Jefferson Patterson Park and Museum, St. Leonard, Maryland.

Watkin, David

1982   *The English Vision: The Picturesque in Architecture, Landscape and Garden Design.* Harper and Row, New York.

Whately, Thomas

1770   *Observations on Modern Gardening.* London.

Yentsch, Anne

1988   Legends, Houses, Families, and Myths: Relationships Between Material Culture and American Ideology. In *Documentary Archaeology in the New World,* edited by Mary C. Beaudry, pp. 5–19. Cambridge University Press, Cambridge.

Ziff, Larzer

1991   *Writing in the New Nation: Prose, Print, and Politics in the Early United States.* Yale University Press, New Haven.

Selected References

Agnew, John A., and James S. Duncan, editors
1989   *The Power of Place.* Unwin Hyman, Winchester, Massachusetts.

Aston, Michael
1985   *Interpreting the Landscape.* B. T. Batsford, London.

Beaudry, Mary C.
1986   The Archaeology of Historical Land Use in Massachusetts. *Historical Archaeology* 20(2):38–46.
1989   The Lowell Boott Mills Complex and Its Housing: Material Expressions of Corporate Ideology. *Historical Archaeology* 23(1):19–32.
1993   Public Aesthetics Versus Personal Experience: Worker Health and Well-Being in 19th-Century Lowell, Massachusetts. *Historical Archaeology* 27(3):90–105.

Bender, Barbara, editor
1993   *Landscape: Politics and Perspectives.* Berg Publishers, Providence, Rhode Island.

Birks, Hilary, H. J. B. Birks, Peter Kalund, and Dagfinn Moe, editors
1988   *The Cultural Landscape: Past, Present and Future.* Cambridge University Press, Cambridge.

Breen, T. H.
1989   *Imagining the Past: East Hampton Histories.* Addison-Wesley Publishing Co., Inc., New York.

Cosgrove, Denis E.
1984   *Social Formation and Symbolic Landscape.* Barnes and Noble Books, Totowa, New Jersey.

Cronon, William
1983   *Changes in the Land: Indians, Colonists, and the Ecology of New England.* Hill and Wang, New York.

Crumley, Carole L., and William H. Marquardt, editors
1987   *Regional Dynamics: Burgundian Landscapes in Historical Perspective.* Academic Press, San Diego.

Deetz, James

1990   Prologue: Landscapes as Cultural Statements. In *Earth Patterns: Essays in Landscape Archaeology,* edited by William M. Kelso and Rachel Most, pp. 1–4. University Press of Virginia, Charlottesville.

Fee, Jeffrey M.

1993   Idaho's Chinese Mountain Gardens. In *Hidden Heritage: Historical Archaeology of the Overseas Chinese,* edited by Priscilla Wegars, pp. 65–96. Baywood Publishing Company, Amityville, New York.

Garrison, J. Ritchie

1991   *Landscape and Material Life in Franklin County, Massachusetts, 1770–1860.* University of Tennessee Press, Knoxville.

Hall, Martin

1991   High and Low in the Townscapes of Dutch South America and South Africa: The Dialectics of Material Culture. *Social Dynamics* 17(2):41–75.

1992   Small Things and the Mobile, Conflictual Fusion of Power, Fear, and Desire. In *The Art and Mystery of Historical Archaeology: Essays in Honor of James Deetz,* edited by Anne Elizabeth Yentsch and Mary C. Beaudry, pp. 373–99. CRC Press, Boca Raton, Florida.

Harrington, Faith

1989   The Emergent Elite in Early 18th Century Portsmouth Society: The Archaeology of the Joseph Sherburne Houselot. *Historical Archaeology* 23(1):2–18.

Herman, Bernard L.

1987   *Architecture and Rural Life in Central Delaware, 1700–1900.* University of Tennessee Press, Knoxville.

Hodder, Ian

1986   *Reading the Past: Current Approaches to Interpretation in Archaeology.* Cambridge University Press, Cambridge.

1991   Interpretive Archaeology and Its Role. *American Antiquity* 56(1):7–18.

Isaac, Rhys

1982   *The Transformation of Virginia, 1740–1790.* Institute of Early American History and Culture, University of North Carolina Press, Chapel Hill.

Jackson, John Brinckerhoff

1984   *Discovering the Vernacular Landscape.* Yale University Press, New Haven.

Kelso, Gerald K.

1993a   Pollen-Record Formation Processes, Interdisciplinary Archaeology, and Land Use by Mill Workers and Managers: The Boott Mills Corporation, Lowell, Massachusetts, 1836–1942. *Historical Archaeology* 27(1):70–94.

1993b   The Kirk Street Agents' House, Lowell, Massachusetts: Interdisciplinary Analysis of the Historic Landscape. *Landscape Journal* 12(2):143–55.

Kelso, Gerald K., and Mary C. Beaudry

1990   Pollen Analysis and Urban Land Use: The Environs of Scottow's Dock in 17th-, 18th-, and Early 19th-Century Boston. *Historical Archaeology* 24(1):61–81.

Kelso, William M.

1984   Landscape Archaeology: A Key to Virginia's Cultivated Past. In *British and American Gardens in the Eighteenth Century,* edited by Robert P. Maccubbin and Peter Martin, pp. 159–69. The Colonial Williamsburg Foundation, Williamsburg, Virginia.

Kelso, William M., and Rachel Most, editors

1990   *Earth Patterns: Essays in Landscape Archaeology.* University Press of Virginia, Charlottesville.

King, Julia A.

1994   Rural Landscape in the Mid-Nineteenth-Century Chesapeake. In *Historical Archaeology of the Chesapeake,* edited by Paul A. Shackel and Barbara J. Little, pp. 283–99. Smithsonian Institution Press, Washington, D.C.

Kryder-Reid, Elizabeth
1994 "As Is the Gardener, So Is the Garden": The Archaeology of Landscape as Myth. In *Historical Archaeology of the Chesapeake,* edited by Paul A. Shackel and Barbara J. Little, pp. 131–48. Smithsonian Institution Press, Washington, D.C.

Kryder-Reid, Elizabeth, and D. Fairchild Ruggles, editors
1994 Site and Sight in the Garden. *Journal of Garden History* 14(1).

Leone, Mark P.
1984 Interpreting Ideology in Historical Archaeology: Using The Rules of Perspective in the William Paca Garden in Annapolis, Maryland. In *Ideology, Power and Prehistory,* edited by Daniel Miller and Christopher Tilley, pp. 25–36. Cambridge University Press, Cambridge.
1987 Rule by Ostentation: The Relationship Between Space and Sight in Eighteenth-Century American Landscape Architecture in the Chesapeake Region of Maryland. In *Method and Theory for Activity Area Research: An Ethnoarchaeological Approach,* edited by Susan Kent, pp. 604–33. Columbia University Press, New York.
1988 The Relationship Between Archaeological Data and the Documentary Record: 18th Century Gardens in Annapolis, Maryland. *Historical Archaeology* 22(1):29–35.

Lewis, Peirce E.
1979 Axioms for Reading the Landscape: Some Guides to the American Scene. In *The Interpretation of Ordinary Landscapes: Geographical Essays,* edited by D. W. Meinig, pp. 11–32. Oxford University Press, New York.
1983 Learning from Looking: Geographic and Other Writing about the American Cultural Landscape. *American Quarterly* 35(3):242–61.

Lowenthal, David
1985 *The Past Is a Foreign Country.* Cambridge University Press, Cambridge.

Luccketti, Nicholas
1990 Archaeological Excavations at Bacon's Castle, Surry County, Virginia. In *Earth Patterns: Essays in Landscape Archaeology,* edited by William M. Kelso and Rachel Most, pp. 23–42. University Press of Virginia, Charlottesville.

Meinig, D. W., editor
1979 *The Interpretation of Ordinary Landscapes: Geographical Essays.* Oxford University Press, New York.

Miller, Naomi F.
1989b What Mean These Seeds: A Comparative Approach to Archaeological Seed Analysis. *Historical Archaeology* 23(2):50–59.

Miller, Naomi F., and Kathryn L. Gleason, editors
1994 *The Archaeology of Garden and Field.* University of Pennsylvania Press, Philadelphia.

Mrozowski, Stephen A.
1987 Exploring New England's Evolving Urban Landscape. In Living in Cities: Current Research in Urban Archaeology, edited by Edward Staski. *Special Publication Series* No. 5:1–9. Society for Historical Archaeology.

Paca-Steele, Barbara, and St. Clair Wright
1987 The Mathematics of an Eighteenth-Century Wilderness Garden. *Journal of Garden History* 6(4):299–320.

Pearsall, Deborah M.
1989 *Paleoethnobotany: A Handbook of Procedures.* Academic Press, San Diego.

Piperno, Dolores R.
1988 *Phytolith Analysis: An Archaeological and Geological Perspective.* Academic Press, San Diego.

Praetzellis, Adrian, and Mary Praetzellis
1989 "Utility and Beauty Should Be One": The Landscape of Jack London's Ranch of Good Intentions. *Historical Archaeology* 23(1):33–44.

Pulsipher, Lydia Mihelic

1994   The Landscapes and Ideational Roles of Caribbean Slave Gardens. In *The Archaeology of Garden and Field,* edited by Naomi F. Miller and Kathryn L. Gleason, pp. 202–21. University of Pennsylvania Press, Philadelphia.

Rodman, Margaret C.

1992   Empowering Place: Multilocality and Multivocality. *American Anthropologist* 94(3):640–56.

Rubertone, Patricia

1989   Landscape as Artifact: Comments on "The Archaeological Use of Landscape Treatment in Social, Economic and Ideological Analysis." *Historical Archaeology* 23(1):50–54.

Samuels, Marwyn S.

1979   The Biography of Landscape: Cause and Culpability. In *The Interpretation of Ordinary Landscapes: Geographical Essays,* edited by D. W. Meinig, pp. 51–88. Oxford University Press, New York.

Sauer, Carl O.

1963   The Morphology of Landscape. In *Land and Life: A Selection From the Writings of Carl O. Sauer,* edited by John Leighly, pp. 315–50. University of California Press, Berkeley.

Stilgoe, John R.

1982   *Common Landscape of America, 1580 to 1845.* Yale University Press, New Haven.

1988   *Borderland: Origins of the American Suburb, 1820–1939.* Yale University Press, New Haven.

Tilley, Christopher

1991   *Material Culture and Text: The Art of Ambiguity.* Routledge, New York.

Trigger, Bruce G.

1991   Distinguished Lecture in Archeology: Constraint and Freedom—A New Synthesis for Archeological Explanation. *American Anthropologist* 93(3):551–69.

Tuan, Yi-Fu

1977   *Space and Place: The Perspective of Experience.* University of Minnesota Press, Minneapolis.

Upton, Dell

1990   Imagining the Early Virginia Landscape. In *Earth Patterns: Essays in Landscape Archaeology,* edited by William M. Kelso and Rachel Most, pp. 71–86. University Press of Virginia, Charlottesville.

1992   The City as Material Culture. In *The Art and Mystery of Historical Archaeology: Essays in Honor of James Deetz,* edited by Anne Elizabeth Yentsch and Mary C. Beaudry, pp. 51–74. CRC Press, Boca Raton, Florida.

Wagstaff, J. M., editor

1987   *Landscape and Culture: Geographical and Archaeological Perspectives.* Basil Blackwell, New York.

Weber, Carmen A., Elizabeth Anderson Comer, Louise E. Akerson, and Gary Norman

1990   Mount Clare: An Interdisciplinary Approach to the Restoration of a Georgian Landscape. In *Earth Patterns: Essays in Landscape Archaeology,* edited by William M. Kelso and Rachel Most, pp. 135–52. University Press of Virginia, Charlottesville.

Westmacott, Richard

1992   *African-American Gardens and Yards in the Rural South.* University of Tennessee Press, Knoxville.

Wood, Denis, with John Fels

1992   *The Power of Maps.* The Guilford Press, New York.

Wood, Joseph

1984   Elaboration of a Settlement System: The New England Village in the Federal Period. *Journal of Historical Geography* 10(4):331–56.

Yentsch, Anne

1988   Legends, Houses, Families, and Myths: Relationships Between Material Culture and American Ideology. In *Documentary Archaeology in the New World,* edited by Mary C. Beaudry, pp. 5–19. Cambridge University Press, Cambridge.

1990a   Historic Morven: The Archaeological Reappearance of an 18th Century Princeton Garden. *Expedition* 32(2):14–23.

1990b   The Calvert Orangery in Annapolis, Maryland: A Horticultural Symbol of Power and Prestige in an Early Eighteenth-Century Community. In *Earth Patterns: Essays in Landscape Archaeology,* edited by William M. Kelso and Rachel Most, pp. 169–87. University Press of Virginia, Charlottesville.

Yentsch, Anne, Naomi F. Miller, Barbara Paca, and Dolores Piperno

1987   Archaeologically Defining the Earlier Garden Landscapes at Morven: Preliminary Results. *Northeast Historical Archaeology* 16:1–29.

Contributors

Mary C. Beaudry is Associate Professor of Archaeology and Anthropology at Boston University. She has served as President of the Society for Historical Archaeology (1989) and has been the editor of *Northeast Historical Archaeology,* the journal of the Council for Northeast Historical Archaeology, since 1986. Her publications include *Documentary Archaeology in the New World* (1988); with Anne Yentsch, *The Art and Mystery of Historical Archaeology: Essays in Honor of James Deetz* (1992); and with Steven A. Mrozowski and Grace H. Zeising, *Living on the Boott: Historical Archaeology at the Boott Mills Boardinghouses in Lowell, Massachusetts* (1996). Dr. Beaudry received her Ph.D. in anthropology from Brown University in 1980.

Sarah T. Bridges is the Cultural Heritage Program Lead for the Eastern States Regional Office of the Bureau of Land Management, U.S. Department of the Interior, in Springfield, Virginia. She holds graduate degrees from New York University in anthropology, with a specialty in archaeology, and history, with a specialty in American colonial history. Ms. Bridges has worked in public service archaeology and historic preservation within federal and state government for over twenty years. Her research interests include urban and maritime historical archaeology in the eastern United States. Currently she is involved in the analysis of historical documents created by the first federal surveyors to describe and map the public lands of the United States, beginning in 1785 in Ohio.

LU ANN DE CUNZO is Assistant Professor of Anthropology at the University of Delaware. She received her B.A. in anthropology from the College of William and Mary and her M.A. and Ph.D. in American civilization from the University of Pennsylvania. Her work focuses on the historical anthropological study of American culture, emphasizing archaeological perspectives on material culture as cultural expression. Her research interests include industrialization, urbanization, agriculture and rural life, gender, religion, and reform in the mid-Atlantic region.

CONRAD M. GOODWIN is Historical Archaeologist and Principal Investigator for the International Archaeological Research Institute, Inc., Honolulu, Hawaii. He also holds an appointment as Research Assistant Professor in the Department of Anthropology, University of Tennessee. Dr. Goodwin earned a Ph.D. in archaeology from Boston University in 1987. His research interests include the history and culture of North America, the circum-Caribbean, the Pacific, and their Old World precursors, with a focus on cultural and ecological adaptation, agricultural systems, landscape analysis, urbanization processes, cultural resource planning and management, and the concept, development, and implementation of public interpretation programs for historical sites and museums.

BERNARD L. HERMAN is Associate Professor of Art History, History, and Urban Affairs and Public Policy at the University of Delaware. He is also the Associate Director of the Center for Historic Architecture and Engineering at the University. Dr. Herman's research has focused on vernacular architecture and material culture studies and, most recently, the material culture of the trans-Atlantic world. He has published several books and articles in this field, including *The Stolen House* (1992) and *Architecture and Rural Life in Central Delaware, 1700–1900* (1987), for which he received the Abbott Lowell Cummings award. Dr. Herman received his Ph.D. from the University of Pennsylvania.

J. EDWARD HOOD is the Research Historian for Architecture and Material Life at Old Sturbridge Village in Massachusetts. He is currently directing an archaeological investigation of African-American and Native American communities of nineteenth-century Worcester County, Massachusetts. Mr. Hood received his M.A. in anthropology from the University of Massachusetts at Amherst, where he studied the development of the colonial English settlement pattern in the Connecticut River Valley.

JULIA A. KING is currently head of the research program at the Jefferson Patterson Park and Museum, an agency of the Maryland Historical Trust, and an Adjunct Assistant Professor of Anthropology at St. Mary's College of Maryland. She holds graduate degrees from the Florida State University and the University of Pennsylvania. She is the author of numerous publications on Chesapeake archaeology and landscape studies. Dr. King was awarded a Dumbarton Oaks Fellowship for Studies in Landscape Architecture in 1994.

JUDSON KRATZER, who recently earned a master's degree from Armstrong State College, works as an archaeologist for the Public History Program at Armstrong State. His work for the past decade has focused on issues surrounding the recovery and interpretation of historical landscapes, with emphasis on the interpretation of historic properties in the mid-Atlantic region. Mr. Kratzer recently served as an intern at Andalusia, home of Nicholas Biddle, located outside of Philadelphia, where he excavated a nineteenth-century greenhouse used for grape production. He is co-author, with Anne Yentsch, of a recent article in *The Archaeology of Garden and Field* (1994) on the excavation of eighteenth-century gardens.

ELIZABETH KRYDER-REID is a Research Associate at the Center for Advanced Study in the Visual Arts, National Gallery of Art. She has published several articles on landscape archaeology in the Chesapeake region. More recently her studies have centered on an examination of California mission landscapes. From 1989 to 1990 she held a Junior Fellowship for Studies in Landscape Architecture at Dumbarton Oaks. She received her Ph.D. in anthropology from Brown University in 1991.

MICHAEL J. LEWIS is the author of *The Politics of the German Gothic Revival* (1993) and has collaborated with George E. Thomas on the publication of two recent architectural studies, including one on the noted architect Frank Furness. He received his Ph.D. from the University of Pennsylvania in 1989. His research interests include German architecture and Utopian and communal societies in America. He is currently an Assistant Professor of Art at Williams College.

SARA F. MASCIA earned her Ph.D. in archaeology at Boston University in 1995. She was Project Archaeologist for the historical archaeology program at the Spencer-Pierce-Little house in Newbury, Massachusetts, from 1986 to 1994. For the past ten years, her work has centered on farm sites in New England and the Northeast, with a particular focus on the nineteenth-century agricultural landscape and the transition from rental tenancy to ownership. She is currently a Project Archaeologist for Historical Perspectives, Inc.

LARRY MCKEE is Staff Archaeologist at the Hermitage in Tennessee. He also holds an appointment as Adjunct Assistant Professor of Anthropology at Vanderbilt University. Dr. McKee received his Ph.D. in anthropology from the University of California at Berkeley in 1988. He has written several articles on plantation archaeology, which is his primary research interest. Presently he is working on a book describing the archaeological investigations of slave life at the Hermitage.

KAREN BESCHERER METHENY is presently completing a Ph.D. in archaeology at Boston University, where she was a Teaching Fellow from 1991 to 1994. Her dissertation research examines a late-nineteenth–early-twentieth-century coal company town in western Pennsylvania. She received her B.A. and M.A. in anthropology and historical archaeology from the College of

William and Mary. She has participated in several landscape projects in the mid-Atlantic region, including the Morven Landscape Archaeology Project, where she worked as Laboratory Director from 1988 to 1990. Her research interests also include industrial archaeology, historical anthropology, historical ethnography, and oral history.

THERESE O'MALLEY is the Associate Dean at the Center for Advanced Study in the Visual Arts, National Gallery of Art, and is currently on the Senior Fellows Committee in Landscape Architecture at Dumbarton Oaks. She received her Ph.D. from the University of Pennsylvania, where she wrote a dissertation entitled "Art and Science in American Landscape Architecture: The National Mall, Washington, D.C., 1791–1851." She is a specialist in the history of eighteenth- and nineteenth-century American landscape design.

DENNIS J. POGUE is the Director of Restoration for the Mount Vernon Ladies' Association and oversees restoration activities, archaeological research, and the implementation of historic restorations and reconstructions at the site. Mr. Pogue previously served as Chief Archaeologist at Mount Vernon from 1987 to 1994. He earned an M.A. in American studies from the George Washington University in 1981 and is currently completing his doctorate in anthropology at the American University. His research has focused on plantation archaeology, African-American archaeology, and the development of Anglo-American culture and society in the Chesapeake.

GEORGE E. THOMAS is a Lecturer in Urban Studies and Historic Preservation at the University of Pennsylvania and has been a private consultant since 1973. He is co-author of *Frank Furness: The Complete Works* (1991) and *The Architecture of Frank Furness* (1973). Dr. Thomas received his doctorate in the history of art at the University of Pennsylvania in 1975.

CARMEN A. WEBER is currently Senior Archaeologist for the Cultural Resource Services division of Dames & Moore, an international consulting firm. She received her B.A. and M.A. degrees in anthropology from Ohio State University and completed graduate courses in public history at Temple University. Ms. Weber is former Research Director for the Baltimore Center for Urban Archaeology (1983–86) and was the City Archaeologist for Philadelphia from 1986 to 1990. Her interests include urban and industrial archaeology, landscape archaeology, gender studies, and the public interpretation of historical archaeology.

CHRISTA WILMANNS-WELLS teaches American cultural landscape courses in the Graduate Group in Historic Preservation and graduate courses in material culture for the American civilization program at the University of Pennsylvania. She received her M.A. and Ph.D. degrees in American civilization at the University of Pennsylvania. Dr. Wilmanns-Wells is particularly interested in historical perceptions and uses of plants and landscapes, as well as landscape design, by various ethnic groups, with a focus on gender, class, religion, and cultural heritage. She also holds competencies in the history of botanical medicine, modern languages, and seventeenth- and eighteenth-century literature.

REBECCA YAMIN is a Principal Archaeologist and Project Manager with John Milner Associates in Philadelphia. She is currently directing the analysis of material recovered on the site of a new federal courthouse in lower Manhattan, once part of the infamous Five Points, which was characterized in the nineteenth century as New York City's worst slum. Dr. Yamin received her Ph.D. in anthropology from New York University in 1988 and subsequently joined the Morven Landscape Archaeology Project in Princeton, New Jersey, where she developed an interpretive program for the site. Her dissertation focused on local trade in pre-Revolutionary New Jersey.

ANNE ELIZABETH YENTSCH is an Associate Professor of Historical Archaeology in the Public History Program at Armstrong State College, Savannah, Georgia. She is an active scholar whose latest book, *A Chesapeake Family and Their Slaves: A Study in Historical Archaeology,* was published in 1994. Dr. Yentsch has directed landscape archaeology projects at more than a dozen sites in the United States and has published numerous articles in books and journals on her research in this area. She received her Ph.D. in anthropology from Brown University in 1980. In 1991 Dr. Yentsch was a recipient of the first annual James Marston Fitch Award for innovative research and creative design in the field of historic preservation.

MARTHA A. ZIERDEN is Curator of Historical Archaeology at The Charleston Museum, a position she has held since 1981. Her work at the museum involves archaeological research, interpretation, exhibition, and curation. Ms. Zierden received her M.A. in anthropology from the Florida State University in 1981. Her research has focused on urban studies, landscape archaeology, and African-American studies.

Index

above-sea-level measurements, 19, 25, 28
accommodation, 194, 203–7, 223–24; *see also*
    urban site formation processes
aerial photography, 154
agricultural census, 180
agricultural journals, 151–52, 165, 183, 255
"agricultural ladder," 148–49, 154, 155, 167;
    transition from tenant to owner, 147, 148–
    49, 151, 152, 154, 155–56, 163, 164–70
agricultural landscapes, 124–39, 147–70, 175–
    91, 255–69; domestic compound, 148, 155,
    160, 166–69, 170; domestic reform move-
    ment, 151–52, 185; effects of suburbaniza-
    tion, 176, 177, 182; effects of transportation
    systems, 175, 180–82, 186; enclosure, 124–
    33, 150, 194, 207–11, 213, 221; English,
    124, 125–33, 134; field systems, 125–33,
    134, 136–39, 154, 167; market gardening,
    163, 175, 182; mixed commercial, 163;
    New England, 136–39, 147–70; plantation
    landscapes, 52–53, 55, 60–65, 71–77, 81,
    86, 87, 151, 153, 205, 221, 255, 256, 258–
    69; suburban farms, 175–76, 177, 180, 182–
    83, 185, 190; tenancy, 147–49, 151–53,
    154, 170; *see also* land tenure systems
Aiken-Rhett house, Charleston, S.C., 196, 197,
    203, 208, 212, 218–20
Annapolis, Md., xxx, 66, 75; Charles Carroll
    garden, 232, 234–35, 237, 239, 240, 243,
    245, 246; Redemptorist garden, 228–46
Ansonborough/Society Street sites, Charleston,
    S.C., 200, 213
anthropological theory, xiv–xvii, 104, 123, 228–
    29, 230–31, 232; cognitive models, xxix, 4,
    104; contextual approaches, xiii–xvii, xxvi,
    4, 6, 22, 23, 148, 180, 231; discourse analy-
    sis, xvi, xvii, xxx, xxxi; emic models, xxix,
    6, 23, 28; hermeneutics, xiv, xv, xxvii;
    Marxism, xxvi, 123; post-processualism,
    xiv; symbolic, xxiv–xxv, xxvii, xxix, xxxv,
    4, 104, 228–29, 230–31, 232
aprons, 17, 20

archaeobotany, xiv, xxiv–xxv, 4, 10–11, 16, 25, 65, 98, 103, 155, 165–66, 167, 200, 202, 228

archaeological method. *See* landscape archaeology: method

archaeological sites: Aiken-Rhett house, Charleston, S.C., 196, 197, 203, 208, 212, 218–20; Ansonborough/Society Street sites, Charleston, S.C., 200, 213; Bacon's Castle, Surry County, Va., 56, 75–76; Belvoir, Va., 56; Miles Brewton house, Charleston, S.C., 196, 197, 202, 203, 207–8, 211–12, 220, 221; Charles Carroll garden, Annapolis, Md., 232, 234–35, 237, 239, 240, 243, 245, 246; William Gibbes house, Charleston, S.C., 196, 197, 212, 220; Hamlin farm, N.J., 153; Henry A. Hopper farm, Fairlawn, N.J., 175–91; Joseph Manigault house, Charleston, S.C., 196, 197; Mattapany, Md., 257, 258–60, 269; Monticello, Va., 64; Morven, Princeton, N.J., 6–29; Mount Clare, Md., 37, 39–41; Mount Vernon, Va., 52–67; Rachel's Garden, the Hermitage, Tenn., 70–87; Father George Rapp's garden, Economy, Pa., 91–113; Redemptorist garden, Annapolis, Md., 228–46; John Rutledge house, Charleston, S.C., 196, 197, 202, 212, 213, 221; Spencer-Pierce-Little farm, Newbury, Ma., 164–70; Stenton, Philadelphia, Pa., 43, 45; Susquehanna, Md., 257, 260–67, 269; Vergelegen, South Africa, xxxi

archaeomagnetic dating, 80

architectural analysis, 22, 23, 29n. 6, 34, 36, 39–42, 193, 194, 203, 204–5, 207, 209, 213–16, 218–20, 221–22, 238

architectural elements in gardens. *See* garden features

architectural infill, 194, 207, 213–20, 222, 223–24; *see also* urban site formation processes

architectural ruins. *See* ruins

areal excavation, 17–18, 20, 23–25, 28, 98, 104

artifact distribution maps, 155, 169, 264–66

backlot development, 198, 205–9, 213–20, 222; *see also* urban site formation processes

Bacon's Castle, Surry County, Va., 56, 75–76

Bartram, John, 36, 49

Belvoir, Va., 56

biblical imagery, 105, 106–9, 111

bilateral symmetry, 22, 57; *see also* geometry

block excavation. *See* areal excavation

borderlands, 175–76, 180, 185–86, 188, 190; *see also* suburbanization

borders, red shale, 17, 20

boundary divisions, 154; *see also* enclosure

Branscombe, England, 130, 131–32

Brewton house, Charleston, S.C., 196, 197, 202, 203, 207–8, 211–12, 220, 221

Carroll, Margaret Tilghman, 32, 34, 35–39, 42–43, 59; correspondence with George Washington, 36, 42, 59

Carroll garden, Annapolis, Md., 232, 234–35, 237, 239, 240, 243, 245, 246; *see also* Redemptorists

Charleston, S.C., 193–224; Aiken-Rhett house, 196, 197, 203, 208, 212, 218–20, 221; Ansonborough/Society Street sites, 200, 213; Miles Brewton house, 196, 197, 202, 203, 207–8, 211–12, 220, 221; William Gibbes house, 196, 197, 212, 220; Joseph Manigault house, 196, 197; John Rutledge house, 196, 197, 202, 212, 213, 221

Charleston townhouses, 195, 196–200, 203–22; double houses, 196–98, 204, 207–8, 211–13, 218–21; single houses, 198, 200, 204–7, 208–9, 213–18, 221–22

class relations, xxx–xxxi, 65–66, 121–39, 178–79, 185–86, 200, 257, 268–69; *see also* ideology; symbols

classical imagery, 252

classical influence in garden design, 108

cold frames, 84

colonization models, English, 136, 200–202

communal ideology, 92, 105, 110, 112, 233–35, 238, 240, 241, 243, 245

communal societies, 92, 105

compliance archaeology, 176, 195

conversion, 193, 194, 200–203, 223–24; *see also* urban site formation processes

"cult of the ruin," 251–52, 268

cultural geography, xv–xvi, 122

cultural landscape, 4, 17, 102, 111, 133–34, 136, 138–39; definition of, 3, 121–25

Deerfield, Ma., 135–38

deforestation, 194, 202

distribution maps, 155, 169, 264–66

ditches, 62–64, 65

documentary analysis, 8–10, 32–33, 46, 97–101, 154, 164–65, 193–94, 229

—life history approach, 154

—primary sources, 99, 105, 154; account books, 74, 137, 164, 165; agricultural census, 180; agricultural journals, 151–52, 165, 183, 255; colonial records, 256, 258; county records, 130–31, 158–62, 256; diaries, 36, 43–45, 47, 64, 159–60; garden manuals, 33, 34, 39, 41, 42, 53, 57–59, 62, 64, 75, 105, 110, 185, 251; maps, 135, 180–83, 200–202, 262–63, 265–66; military maps, 9; obituaries, 169, 190; personal letters, papers, and general correspondence, 8, 9, 10, 34–36, 42, 49, 59, 62–64, 74, 78–79, 81, 103, 105, 163–65; pictorial evidence, 46, 97, 101, 108, 164, 183–85, 252–53; plant lists, xxxv, 102, 112; plats, 193, 199, 201, 204–7, 209–10, 213–17, 259; probate inventories, 159, 193; property deeds, 159, 160, 162, 180; property maps and surveys, 10, 12, 101–2, 160–61, 166–69, 201; religious writings and chronicles, 109–10, 113, 229, 231, 233–46; tax records, 131–32, 262, 263; town records, 137–38; travelers' accounts, 35, 57, 77, 78, 81–82, 99–101, 105, 112, 159–60, 255, 259; Valuations of the Orphan's Court, 256; wills, 159

—secondary sources, 46, 131, 154, 165, 179, 253, 256, 257–58

—women in the documentary record, 32–33

documentation of existing landscapes, 10–11, 19, 25, 97, 154–55, 165, 167

domestic compound, 148, 155, 160, 166–69, 170

domestic reform movement, 151–52, 185

Downing, Andrew Jackson, 185, 186, 252

economic scaling, 155, 189–90

Economy, Pa., 91–93, 96, 97, 99, 100, 101, 109, 110–11

eighteenth-century gardens, xxvii–xxix, xxx–xxxii, xxxviii, 4, 6–29, 32, 33–34, 52–67, 75, 111, 121, 211–13, 216, 232, 234–35, 237, 239–40, 243, 245–46, 251–52

Einsiedeley, 110–11, 112; see also hermitages

emic models, xxix, 6, 23, 28

enclosure, 124–33, 150, 194, 207–11, 213, 221; effects of, 128; resistance to, 129, 132–33

English gardens and landscapes, xxviii, 8–9, 33–34, 106, 124, 125–33, 134, 136, 138, 139, 251–52, 268; influence of English landscape design, 8–9, 52–53, 57, 65–66, 75; Open Fields region, 125–29; Woodlands region, 126–27, 129–33

environmental constraints on settlement, 194

ethnobotany, 4, 25, 98

European gardens and landscapes, 251, 268; influence of European landscape design, 105, 107–8, 111

excavation strategies, 4, 6, 23–29, 60; areal excavation, 17–18, 20, 23–25, 28, 98, 104; evaluation of, 16–17, 23–29; exploratory, 10, 13–16, 23, 25, 28; hand-excavated test units, 13, 15, 16, 23, 25, 60, 104; horizontal exposure, 17–18, 20, 23–25, 28; sampling strategies, 16–17; stripping, xxxii, 60–61; subsurface testing, 10, 13, 16, 60, 97, 103, 263; systematic sampling, 13, 16, 23, 263; trenching, 13–15, 16, 23–25, 28, 98, 103

farm tenancy. See tenancy

faunal analysis, 166, 200, 203, 211, 221

fence lines, 26, 60, 61–62, 64–65, 71, 72, 73, 79–81, 82, 83–84, 86, 208; see also enclosure

field patterns, 154, 167

field systems, 125–33, 134, 136–39, 154, 167

field techniques. See excavation strategies

fill episodes, 13, 15, 18, 19, 21–22, 25, 29

flotation, 10, 98; see also macrobotanical remains

focus of archaeological features and surfaces, 8, 18, 19, 28

formal gardens and landscapes, xxviii, xxxiii, 3–4, 9, 26, 53, 56, 57, 60, 66, 70–73, 75–77, 121–22, 123, 212, 213, 237; influence of formal design, 111

fountains, 98, 99, 100–101, 106, 107

fruit gardens, 53, 60–65, 66; see also orchards

garden archaeology, xvi, xxiii, 3–5

garden clubs, 32

garden features: aprons, 17, 20; borders, 17, 20; as diagnostic artifacts, 20; ditches, 62–64, 65; embellishments, 20; fence lines, 26, 60, 61–62, 64–65, 71, 72, 73, 79–81, 82, 83–84, 86, 208; fountains, 98, 99, 100–101, 106, 107; fruit gardens, 53, 60–65, 66; grottos, 8, 94; ha-has, 57, 60; hermitages, 94, 98, 99, 100, 101, 104, 110–11, 112; labyrinth, 111; live fence, 62–63; mounds, 22, 94, 98, 100, 101, 102–3, 106, 111, 228; orchards, 64, 92, 94, 99, 100; parterres, 9, 19, 26, 56, 57, 60; paths and walks, 10, 13, 15, 16, 19–20, 22, 26, 57, 71, 72, 73, 77, 81, 82, 83, 86, 94, 98, 101, 103–4, 108, 241; patterning in, 19–20; pavilions, 94, 100–101, 108, 228, 234; planting beds, 15, 18, 19, 26, 56, 65, 71–73, 77, 79, 81, 84, 87, 98, 101, 103, 104, 211–12, 228; planting holes, 17, 19, 26, 60, 64–65, 98, 103, 104; ramps, 228, 235; root holes, 60, 64, 103, 228; ruins, 249–69; statuary, 94, 99, 100–101, 107, 108, 109, 228, 235, 240, 244; temples, 100, 101, 228; terraces, 7, 13, 15, 19, 21, 26, 235, 239, 244; tombs, xxxiii, 72, 78–79, 82, 244–45, 246; tree holes, 15, 19; vineyards, 92, 94, 98, 99, 100, 101, 102–3, 106, 111, 113, 234, 236, 237, 241; wildernesses, 57, 98, 99, 101, 104, 110–11; yard surfaces, 13, 15

garden manuals, 33, 34, 39, 41, 42, 53, 57–59, 62, 64, 75, 105, 110, 185, 251

garden reconstruction, 4, 5, 71, 96, 102, 113

garden restoration, 4, 70–71, 73, 83–84, 86–87, 96, 97, 98

gardens, popular interest in, xxv, 3–5

gender roles: eighteenth-century gardening, 8, 32–34, 35–37, 39, 42–43, 45–46, 49; historical role of women in gardening, 32–34; influence of English women in garden design, 33–34; nineteenth-century gardening, 77–78

gender studies in landscape archaeology, xvi, xvii, 32–33, 49

gentlemen farmers, 183–84

geometry, use in garden and landscape design, xxix, xxx, 22–23, 26, 29n. 5, 53, 56–57, 60, 94, 112, 235; geometric relationship between house and garden, 9, 22–23, 29n. 6

geophysical survey, 4, 10, 13, 19

Georgian mindset, 200

Georgian order, 6, 22, 39, 52, 77, 112, 160, 198, 205

Georgian symmetry, 22, 57

Gibbes house, Charleston, S.C., 196, 197, 212, 220

greenhouses, 32, 33, 34–36, 37, 39–43, 45–49, 59, 60, 66, 75, 100, 237, 241, 243; construction techniques, 34, 36, 39–42; heating systems, 34, 36, 39, 41; symbolism of, 35, 37, 43, 46, 49, 59, 75; *see also* orangeries

grid systems, 6, 22–23, 28, 98

grottos, 8, 94; *see also* hermitages

ground-penetrating radar, 13

ha-has, 57, 60

Hamlin farm, N.J., 153

Harmony, Pa., 92, 99, 105, 110, 111

Harmony Society, 91–113

the Hermitage, Tenn., 70–87

hermitages, 94, 98, 99, 100, 101, 104, 110–11, 112

Hopper farm, Fairlawn, N.J., 175–91

horizontal planes, 18–19

horticultural exchange: information, 36, 42, 49, 53, 59, 101, 105; plants and seeds, 36, 99

horticultural experimentation, 53, 59, 60, 77

identity, construction through landscape, 5, 228–31, 232–36, 238–44, 245–46

ideology, 4, 104; class relations, xxx–xxxi, 65–66, 75–77, 124–25, 134, 136, 138–39, 239, 240, 257, 268–69; contemporary, xv, 86–87; Georgian mindset, 200; national, 3, 73–74, 83, 84–85, 239–40, 250–53, 256, 257–58, 268–69; political, xxx–xxxi, 34, 65–66, 75–77, 124–25, 134, 136, 138–39, 239–40, 257; religious, 92, 104–13, 231–40, 245

intensification, 194, 207–20, 223–24; *see also* urban site formation processes

interdisciplinary approaches, 6, 7, 17, 25, 29, 96, 97–98, 113

interpretive approaches, xiii–xvii, xxiii–xxxviii, 4, 6, 22, 32–33, 49, 65–66, 70–71, 86–87, 96–99, 102, 104–13, 122–25, 139, 147–48, 154–56, 164–70, 175–76, 177–86, 190–91, 193–95, 223–24, 228–32, 245–56, 249–53, 268–69; *see also* anthropological theory

Jackson, Andrew, 70–87
Jackson, Rachel, 70–87
Jamestown church tower, Va., 253, 268
Jefferson, Thomas, 81, 252

kinship networks, 37–38, 42–43, 47–49, 260,
    262–63
kitchen gardens, 33, 75–77, 81, 84, 86, 237; *see
    also* vegetable gardens

Ladies' Hermitage Association, 70–71, 73–74,
    83–84, 86–87
land clearance, 194, 202
land tenure systems: England, 128, 129, 130–32;
    U.S., 148–51, 152–53; New England, 147,
    150, 151, 152–53; southern U.S., 151, 153
land-use patterns, 127–33, 134–39, 154–55,
    166–69, 175, 182, 186, 190, 234–37, 241–45
landscape archaeology
—direction of, xvi–xvii, xxxvii, 4
—growth of, xxvi, xxvii–xxix
—method, 4, 6–29, 53, 97–98, 147–48, 153,
    154–56, 164–67, 169, 193–94, 200, 263–
    64; analytical tools, 6, 8, 18–21, 23, 26, 28;
    archaeobotany, xiv, xxiv–xxv, 4, 10–11, 16,
    25, 65, 98, 103, 155, 165–66, 167, 200, 202,
    228; ethnobotany, 4, 25, 98; evaluation of,
    16–17, 23–29; excavation strategies, 4, 6, 10,
    13–18, 20, 23–29, 60–61, 97–98, 103, 104,
    263; grid systems, 6, 22–23, 28, 98; interac-
    tive approach, 6, 17, 25–26, 28; interdisci-
    plinary approach, 6, 7, 17, 25, 29, 96, 97–98,
    113; multidisciplinary approach, xiv, xvi,
    xvii, xxvii–xxviii, 4, 7, 17, 96, 193; predic-
    tive framework for testing, xxix, 6, 15, 16,
    22–23, 28; remote sensing techniques, 4,
    10, 13, 16, 19, 28, 29n. 3, 154; research de-
    sign, 6, 8, 13, 96, 154–56, 164, 193; scales
    of analysis, xvi–xvii, 8, 16–17, 25, 164, 176,
    190–91, 193–94, 223–24; spatial analysis,
    xv–xvi, 8, 60–65, 98, 103, 147–48, 153,
    155, 166–69, 190, 193, 194, 200–209, 212–
    23, 228–29, 234–35, 237, 243–44; strati-
    graphic analysis, 4, 6, 8, 18, 60–61, 103;
    topographic survey, 19, 26, 97, 154, 165;
    vegetation survey, 10, 25, 97, 154, 155, 167
—theory. *See* anthropological theory

landscape preservation, 3–4, 67, 70–71, 73, 83–
    84, 86–87, 96, 97, 249
landscape transformations, 7, 21–22, 52, 56–57,
    81–82, 122–23, 125, 128–33, 134–36, 147–
    48, 153, 154–56, 164–69, 180, 186, 193–
    94, 200–202, 207, 220, 229, 234–35, 237,
    239–40, 241–44, 268–69; sanctification of
    landscape, 244; traditionalizing effect of
    landscape, 10, 86, 124, 128, 130, 138–39
landscaping materials: as diagnostic artifacts, 20;
    bark, 103; clay, 103–4, 108; cobbles, 17;
    fieldstone, 10, 13, 15, 16, 19, 20, 22, 29n.
    2; gravel, 10, 13, 20, 22; limestone, 20; pat-
    terning in, 19–20; red shale, 17, 20
Latrobe, Benjamin Henry, 57, 60, 100
Little, Edward H., 148, 149, 162–63, 164–70
live fences, 62–63
living history museums, 4
Logan, Deborah Norris, 33, 43, 45, 47, 49

macrobotanical remains, 10, 65, 155, 166, 200,
    202, 228
macro-landscape, 176, 190–91
magnetometer survey, 13
Manigault house, Charleston, S.C., 196, 197
market gardening, 163, 175, 182
Mattapany, St. Mary's County, Md., 257, 258–
    60, 269
medieval garden design, influence of, 106
metaphors, use in garden design, 104, 106–13, 245
methodology. *See* landscape archaeology:
    method
micro-landscape, 176, 191
middle Connecticut River Valley, 136–39
millenarianism, influence of, 92–93, 105–6, 109,
    110–13; *see also* ideology
millennialist societies, 92–93, 105–6, 109
modern gardens, documentation of, 97, 154–55;
    topographic survey 19, 26, 97, 154, 165;
    tree coring, 4, 10–11, 155, 165, 167; veg-
    etation survey, 10–11, 25, 97, 154, 155, 167
Monticello, Va., 252; landscape archaeology con-
    ference, xxviii; orchard, 64
Morven, Princeton, N.J., 6–29
mounds, 22, 94, 98, 100, 101, 102–3, 106, 111, 228
Mount Airy, Va., orangery, 42
Mount Clare, Md., 32, 33–43, 46

Mount Clare (cont.)
—orangery, 34–36, 39–42, 43; similarity to Wye House orangery, 39, 41–42
—orchard, 64
Mount Vernon, Va., 36, 52–67, 74–75, 81, 251
—greenhouse, 36, 42, 59, 60, 66; association with Mount Clare orangery, 36, 42, 59
—influence on Andrew Jackson, 74–75
Mount Vernon Ladies' Association, 67
multidisciplinary approach, xiv, xvi, xvii, xxvii–xxviii, 4, 7, 17, 96, 193
multilocality, xvi–xvii
multivocality, xvi–xvii, xxv, xxx, 125
mythic history xv, xxvi, xxxvi, 3, 8, 12, 104, 177, 179, 243, 251, 252, 256, 257–58, 268–69

national mythology, 250–51, 253, 256, 257–58, 268–69
Native American landscapes, 122, 123, 133–34
naturalistic landscape design, 56–60, 111, 112, 121–22
New England landscapes, 122, 123, 125, 133–39, 147–70; settlement patterns, 134–39; town system, 150
New Harmony, Ind., 92, 99, 105, 110, 111
nineteenth-century gardens and landscapes, xxxviiin. 3, 10, 17, 21–22, 70–87, 91–113, 205–7, 209–11, 213–24, 234–36, 237, 239, 240, 246
nucleated villages, 125, 128, 134–39

Old Economy Village, Pa., 91, 93, 101, 113
opal phytoliths. *See* phytoliths
Open Fields region, England, 125–29, 130, 132–33, 134
oral history, 10, 176, 178–79, 180, 186, 190–91, 265
oral traditions, xxvi, xxxvi, 8, 10, 12, 82, 177
orangeries, 33, 35–36, 37, 39–42, 43, 49, 75; association with women, 36, 37, 39, 42–43; symbolism of, 35, 37, 43, 49, 75; *see also* greenhouses
orchards, 64, 92, 94, 99, 100; *see also* fruit gardens
original topsoil, as a marker, 20–21, 29n. 4
ornamental landscapes, xxviii, xxix, xxx, xxxi, 7, 22, 26, 52, 235, 240, 241

palynology. *See* pollen analysis
parterres, 9, 19, 26, 56, 57, 60

paths, 10, 71, 72, 73, 77, 81, 82, 83, 86, 94, 98, 101, 103–4, 108, 241
pavilions, 94, 100–101, 108, 228, 234
perspective, use of, xxix, xxx, 7, 19, 57, 239
Philadelphia gardens, 33, 43, 45–49, 50nn. 1–2; greenhouses, 43, 45–49, 50nn. 1–2
phytolith analysis, 4, 25, 65, 98, 103, 155
piazzas, 17, 204, 207, 208, 214, 221
picturesque landscape design, 56–60, 111
planned communities, 178, 179, 182, 186, 191; *see also* suburbanization
plant census. *See* vegetation survey
plantation archaeology, 153
plantation landscapes, 52–53, 55, 60–65, 71–77, 81, 86, 87, 151, 153, 205, 221, 255, 256, 258–69; urban plantations, 203, 205, 213, 218, 222
planting beds, 15, 18, 19, 26, 56, 65, 71–73, 77, 79, 81, 84, 87, 98, 101, 104, 211–12, 228; drainage of, 18, 103, 211–12
planting holes, 17, 19, 26, 60, 64–65, 98, 103, 104
plants, symbolic meaning of, xxiv–xxv, xxxv, 43, 99, 106, 108, 113, 228
political symbolism. *See* ideology; symbols
pollen analysis, 4, 25, 65, 155, 166, 200, 202
Pope, Alexander, 8–9, 251
postbellum tenant plantations, 151, 153
post-medieval land-use practices, 125–33, 134
predictive framework for testing, xxix, 6, 15, 16, 22–23, 28
prehistoric landscape analysis, xiv, xxiv
preservation efforts, xvi, xxiii, xxix, 3–4, 67, 70–71, 73, 83–84, 86–87, 96, 97
preservation organizations, 67, 70–71, 73–74, 83–84
progressive farm movement, 151–52, 163, 165, 166
public interpretation, 9, 70, 71, 73, 86–87, 97, 99, 163

quadripartite garden design, 64, 71–72, 81, 93, 94, 99, 101, 106, 112
Quaker elite, Philadelphia, 47–49

Rachel's Garden, the Hermitage, Tenn., 70–87
ramps, 228, 235
Rapp, Frederick, 99, 100–101, 103, 108, 111
Rapp, George, 91–113; garden at Economy, 91–113; religious ideology/world view, 92–93, 104–13

Redemptorists, 228–46; construction of identity through landscape, 228–36, 238–44, 245–46; relationship with town of Annapolis, 231, 232, 238–46; ritual use of landscape, 229, 230–32, 234–36, 238, 240, 244–45; transformation of Charles Carroll garden, 229, 234–35, 237, 239–40

refuse disposal, 103, 147–48, 155, 166, 168, 169, 194, 211–13, 219, 220–21, 222, 265; *see also* urban site formation processes

regulation, 193, 194, 219, 220–22, 223–24; *see also* urban site formation processes

religious ideology. *See* ideology

remote sensing techniques, 4, 10, 13, 16, 19, 28, 154; limitations of 13, 16, 29n. 3

Renaissance garden design, xxix, 57, 106

rental tenancy, 147, 149, 151, 152, 153; in New England, 147, 152, 153, 164, 170; methodology for study of, 147–48, 154–56

research design, 6, 8, 13, 96, 154–56, 164, 193

restoration. *See* garden restoration

ritual in landscape, 104, 109–10, 112, 229, 230–31, 232, 234–36, 238, 240, 244–45

romantic imagery, 250–53, 256, 257–58, 268–69; in ruins, 251–53, 257–58, 268–69

root casts, 4

root holes, 60, 64, 103, 228

ruins, xxxvi, 249–69; in Europe, 251–52, 268; in southern Maryland, 249–50, 253–69; in U.S., xxxvi–xxxvii, 249–50, 252–53, 256–69; symbolism of, xxxvi, 250–53, 265, 269

rural reform movement, 151–52, 185

Rutledge house, Charleston, S.C., 196, 197, 202, 212, 213, 221

sanitation, 193, 194, 211–13, 219–22; drain systems, 219–20, 222; paved yards, 211, 212, 213, 219, 221, 222; sewage systems, 222; *see also* refuse disposal; urban site formation processes

scales of analysis, xvi–xvii, 8, 16–17, 25, 164, 176, 190–91, 193–94, 223–24; farmstead, 164; homelot, 164; intrasite/intersite, xxvii, 223; macro-landscape, 176, 190–91; micro-landscape, 176, 191; urban landscape, 193–94

scientific approaches. *See* landscape sciences

seeds, xxiv, 10, 65, 155, 166, 228; *see also* flotation; macrobotanical remains

segmentation/specialization, 193–94, 220–22, 243; *see also* urban site formation processes

settlement patterns, 124, 125–29, 134–39, 182, 186, 254

seventeenth-century gardens, xxviii, xxxi, 56, 75–76, 106

site formation processes, 154; *see also* urban site formation processes

slave quarters, 198, 205, 207, 208, 213, 216, 218, 219, 220

social relations in landscape, 121–25, 128–39; *see also* class relations; ideology; symbols

soil enrichment, 64, 103, 211

soil resistivity studies, 13

soils analysis, 4, 167

spatial analysis, xv–xvi, 8, 60–65, 98, 103, 147–48, 153, 155, 166–69, 190, 193–94, 200–209, 212–23, 228–29, 234–37, 243–44

Spencer-Pierce-Little farm, Newbury, Mass., 148, 149, 156–70

Sprigettsbury, Pa., 45, 46–47, 50nn. 1–2

St. Mary's County, Md., 253–69; Mattapany, 257, 258–60, 269; St. Mary's City, 255–56, 257–58; statehouse at St. Mary's City, 257–58, 269; Susquehanna, 257, 260–67, 269

statehouse at St. Mary's City, Md., 257–58, 269

statuary, 100, 228, 240; "Harmony," 94, 99, 100–101, 107, 108, 109; religious, 235, 244

status, indicators of: artifacts, 147, 153, 155–56, 177, 188, 189–90; ceramics, 155, 189–90; farms, improvements to, 147–48, 153, 155–56, 169, 170; gardens, xxviii–xxix, xxx–xxxi, 52–53, 65–66, 75–76, 77, 112; greenhouses/orangeries, 35, 37, 46, 59

Stenton, Philadelphia, Pa., 43, 45

Stockton gardens, Princeton, N.J. *See* Morven

stratigraphic analysis, 4, 6, 8, 18, 60–61, 103

suburban farms, 175–76, 177, 180, 182–83, 185, 190

suburbanization, 175, 176, 180, 182, 186; borderlands, 175–76, 180, 185–86, 188, 190; effects on landscape, 176, 177, 182; planned communities, 178, 179, 182, 186, 191; transportation systems, 175, 180–82, 186

suburbs, 175–76, 182, 185–86, 190; eighteenth-century, 200, 201

Susquehanna, St. Mary's County, Md., 257, 260–67, 269

symbolic approaches. *See* anthropological theory

symbols, xiii, xv, xxiv–xxvii, xxx–xxxvi, 4, 96, 104, 134, 139, 159, 193, 228–29, 230–31, 232, 269; American nationalism, 251–53, 269; architectural ruins as, xxxvi, 250–53, 265, 269; class-based, xxviii–xxix, xxx–xxxi, 59, 65–66, 75, 76, 112, 124–25, 136, 139, 179, 239–40, 269; farms as, 153, 169, 190; garden features as, 20, 111; gardens as, xxx–xxxi, xxxiii, xxxv, 5, 78–79, 86, 96, 105, 109–10, 113, 239–40, 244; gender-based, 37, 43, 49; greenhouses as, 46, 49, 59, 75; hedges as, 124, 129, 132–33; houses as, xxvi, xxviii, 6, 67, 177, 239; orangeries as, 35, 37, 43, 49, 75; plants as, xxiv–xxv, xxxv, 43, 99, 106, 108, 113, 228; political, xxx, xxxi, 6, 34, 65–66, 124–25, 200, 239, 269; religious, 105–10, 244, 269; resistance to, xxxi, 124–25, 129, 132–33; status, xxviii, xxxi, 35, 65–66, 75–76, 112, 153

symmetry in garden design, xxviii, xxix, 22–23, 26, 29n. 5, 56–57, 60, 94, 112

systems of measurement: archaeological, 23; eighteenth-century, 23

temples, 100, 101, 228

tenancy, agricultural, 128–29, 130–32, 133, 138, 147, 148–49, 151–53, 154, 170; archaeological approach to, 147–48, 153, 154–56; historical studies in New England, 152–53

terrace falls, 15, 19, 26, 29n. 4, 228, 240

terraced gardens, xxviii, xxix, 9, 19, 22, 26, 56, 232, 234, 237

terraces, 7, 13, 15, 19, 21, 26, 235, 239, 244

theoretical approaches. *See* anthropological theory

tombs, xxxiii, 72, 78–79, 82, 244–45, 246

topographic survey, 19, 26, 97, 154, 165; base map, 97

town plans, 150; *see also* nucleated villages; planned communities

transportation systems, effects on landscape, 175, 180–82, 186

tree coring, 4, 10–11, 155, 165, 167

tree holes, 15, 19

trenching, 13–15, 16, 23–25, 28, 98, 103

Twickenham, England, 8–9

twig and turf, 159

urban archaeology, 193

urban grids, 200–202

urban landscapes, 193–224; gardens, 205, 207, 209, 211–12, 213, 214

urban plantations, 203, 205, 213, 218, 222

urban site formation processes, 193–224; accommodation, 194, 203–7, 223–24; architectural infill, 194, 207, 213–20, 222, 223–24; conversion, 193, 194, 200–203, 223–24; intensification, 194, 207–20, 223–24

vegetable gardens, 92, 94, 104, 236; *see also* kitchen gardens

vegetation patterns, 154, 167

vegetation survey, 10, 25, 97, 154, 155, 167

Vergelegen, South Africa, xxxi

"Vineyard Enclosure," Mount Vernon, Va., 53, 60–65, 66

vineyard mount, in Father Rapp's garden: construction and appearance of, 94, 98, 100, 101, 102–3, 106; symbolism of, 106, 111

vineyards, 92, 94, 98, 99, 100, 101, 102–3, 106, 111, 113, 234, 236, 237, 241

visibility of buried features and surfaces, 8, 18, 19, 28

walks, 10, 13, 15, 16, 19–20, 22, 26, 57, 241; *see also* paths

Washington, George, 52–67; correspondence with Margaret Tilghman Carroll, 36, 42, 59

wilderness imagery, 3, 5, 105, 107, 109, 110, 111, 122, 251, 253, 257–58, 268–69

wildernesses, 57, 98, 99, 101, 104, 110–11

women, garden interests of, 8, 32–37, 39, 42–43, 45–46, 77–78; role in garden design and operation, 32, 33–34, 36; *see also* gender roles; gender studies

Woodlands region, England, 126–27, 129–33

workyards, 17, 196, 205, 211–13, 219, 220–21, 222; *see also* backlot development

Wye House orangery, Md., 37, 39, 41–42, 43; similarities to Mt. Clare orangery, 39, 41–42

yard surfaces, 13, 15